D1565650

Every Breath You Take

Every Breath You Take

Stalking Narratives
and the Law

Orit Kamir

Ann Arbor

THE UNIVERSITY OF MICHIGAN PRESS

2004   2003   2002   2001   4   3   2   1

A CIP catalog record for this book is available from the British Library.

Library of Congress Cataloging-in-Publication Data

Kamir, Orit, 1961–
    Every breath you take : stalking narratives and the law / Orit
Kamir.
        p.   cm.
    Includes bibliographical references and index.
    ISBN 0-472-11089-6 (alk. paper)
        1. Stalking—United States.   I. Title.
    HV6594.2 .K36   2001
    364.15—dc21   00-009896

To my family,
Holocaust victims and survivors, living and dead

The Gliklichs, Frims, Kanners, Kachkas
and many others

Contents

Acknowledgments

In one form or another, this book has been with me throughout the past decade. Friends, family, teachers, and colleagues offered precious assistance and support. Without them, this book would never have happened. It is a great pleasure to thank them wholeheartedly, and in particular Ibrahim Abu-Libdeh, Peter Bauland, Rachel Elior, Rebecca Johnson, Dan, Yvonne, and Steve Kaplan, Catharine MacKinnon, Jim McHenry, Roberta Nerison-Low, Adela Pinch, Yoram Shachar, Joseph Weiler, and Robin West.

James Boyd White and Bill Miller's trust and guidance were invaluable.

I am deeply grateful to Ami Dar, Joyce Frim, Barbara Garavaglia, Adam Harmon, Nita Schechet, Marc Spindelman, Maryse Brouwers, and Rona May-Ron for conversation and vital assistance in research and editing.

Warm thanks to the University of Michigan Law School and Dean Jeff Lehman for generous hospitality and support, and to the University of Michigan Press, and LeAnn Fields in particular, for believing in the project.

Special thanks go to my parents Shulamit and Amior, my sister Anat, and Pitzi, who were always there with me and for me.

Orit Kamir
Jerusalem
2000

Introduction

Legal Perspectives

In 1990 the State of California enacted the first "antistalking" law in the United States. This law, as it was then formulated, prohibited a course of conduct that included a credible threat, a willful and malicious intention to place a target under reasonable fear for her or his bodily safety, and the actual arousal of such reasonable fear. Over the following three years, every state, as well as the federal government, followed suit, establishing "stalking" as a legal term and a legal issue.[1]

This dramatic creation of stalking as a legal category invites inquiry into not only its legal but also its metalegal implications. That is, it poses a set of theoretical questions that are inseparable from the (meta)legal treatment of any issue. What is the harm and/or damage caused by stalking to its targets, to a society, and to that society's fundamental principles? Which of society's protected values are affected by stalking, how, and to what extent? Why and in what terms are such effects significant enough to justify legal action? In order to better confront these (meta)legal aspects, it is necessary to pose questions of a more cultural nature. Why do targets respond to stalking the way they do? How do they experience stalking? What is behind society's response? What is the cultural background against which stalking is perceived as damaging and/or harmful? How has stalking come to mean what it does? What are the ideological assumptions underlying our conception of stalking? In other words: what, in the broad, cultural sense, *is* stalking? Answering these questions is essential for a theoretical assessment and critical analysis of the legal treatment of stalking. Only then may we approach issues such as the justification of antistalking laws. Do they address the relevant elements of stalking, that is, those that pose a substantial threat to rightly protected social values? Do they define stalking accurately? Are they structured in the best possible way to address the threat posed by stalking? Is their scope appropriate?

This is the multilayered set of questions this book seeks to explore; in this respect, its framework and motivation are (meta)legal.

However, stalking is not a uniquely legal issue. As a human behavior and a social phenomenon, it may be an object of inquiry in various human

1. Different states have defined stalking differently, and the state of California has changed its definition several times. For further discussion of the legal definitions of stalking see chapters 8 and 9. For a different, culturally oriented definition of stalking, see the last section of this chapter.

sciences. Stalking may interest psychologists, sociologists, criminologists, and psychiatrists. But the aspects of the issue that concern social scientists are distinct from the (meta)legal issues presented above. For example, from the psychiatric and psychological perspectives, the relevant questions regarding stalking may include the following: Who are the individuals who engage in this conduct? What is the makeup of their personalities? Why do they engage in stalking? How does the pattern of their behavior reflect personality difficulties? How do they choose their victims? What are the types of stalking behaviors, and how do they correspond with types of characters? How can stalkers be cured? How do victims of stalking respond to it? How can *they* be helped? These and related questions are at the heart of fifteen scholarly articles that have recently been published in Reid Meloy's *The Psychology of Stalking: Clinical and Forensic Perspectives.*

The two sets of questions described above are closely connected; it is almost impossible to treat one without touching on the other. Yet they are, and should be, distinct. As fascinating as the demographic and psychiatric makeup of stalkers may be, it is not, nor should be, at the center of a critical legal discussion. While the social sciences may conceptualize the stalker's conscious and unconscious motives and goals, the legal and metalegal perspective must focus on society's protected values, on the nature of the threat posed by stalking to these values, and on the normative justification for legal intervention. This is why this book does not attempt to reveal "the stalker," but rather to understand the social construction of the threat posed by stalking to individuals and to the social order. When touching upon stalkers and their targets, my discussion does not aim to define human categories or deficiencies, but merely to better understand the social phenomenon as it is conceived and constructed within the relevant culture.[2]

The Cultural Legacy

The legal treatment of stalking is new. But stalking as a concept and the fear of stalking as a perceived personal and social harm have been with us for many centuries, interwoven with some of our culture's stories, its fictional characters and literary images. The fear of stalking, on both the personal and the collective level, has been expressed through and developed by powerful literary images; it is inseparable from stories told of mythological characters, legendary entities, literary protagonists, and film personae. Such stories express the fear of stalking as molded within culture, while furnishing it

---

2. So far, much of the legal, professional discussion of stalking has addressed the "psychological" set of questions, rather than the legal one. Other writers analyze the existing positive law, particularly its constitutionality. Not enough attention has so far been given to the fundamental (meta)legal questions presented above. For further discussion of this point see chapter 8.

with details and perpetuating it in our collective memory as well as in our individual psyches. In other words: the fear of stalking within our culture is a product of an ongoing interaction between fears and the stories told about them. In my attempt to identify the components of stalking and its effects, I turn to several cultural discourses, examining the stories and characters that have manifested and created our fear of stalking. These discussions offer a cultural analysis of stalking.

The antistalking legislation of the 1990s regenerated in legal form an ancient fear freighted with a cultural legacy of perceptions and connotations that began to accumulate within Western culture perhaps as early as five thousand years ago. When integrated into our contemporary legal system, the fear of stalking carried with it faint echoes and images of worlds haunted by supernatural creatures, cosmic quests, and tragic fates. Making their acquaintance enables us to better understand how we, as lawyers, judges, stalkers, targets, and potential jurors, feel and think when we encounter stalking. Exploring its cultural origins helps us determine which parts of this rich cultural heritage we wish to maintain, for what reasons, and in what forms.

In my exploration of stalking, I recognize that earlier concepts, images, and symbolic meanings, with which we may not be consciously familiar, influence the stories we tell ourselves. Historical developments and changing discourses can reshape or transform images and stories to the extent that current users may be completely unaware of former incarnations of figures of speech, legends, and ideological assumptions. We may have collectively forgotten, suppressed, or reinterpreted earlier contexts and symbolic systems within which the precursors of our modern ideas grew and flourished. Nevertheless, though disguised and cloaked in layers of later meanings, old stories, images, and concepts are very much alive and may manifest themselves in our dreams, myths, religions, languages, movies, social sciences, and legal discourse. Like ghosts, they haunt our lives and alter our behavior.

Fundamental Concepts of Male and Female Stalking

The cultural analysis of stalking stories reveals fundamental differences between stalking by males and stalking by females, as each corresponds to distinct emotional experiences, narratives, and social constructions.

The pursuit of stalking (stories) has led me centuries and millennia back to Mesopotamia, the "Cradle of Western Civilization" and to its mythological night-stalking female demon, Lilit ("owl").[3] I suggest that Lilit embodied the demonized, powerful aspects of the almighty ancient Great Goddess Inanna, after the Goddess was replaced by a younger generation of male

3. The demon's English name is *Lilith*. I chose to use *Lilit*, which is the transliteration of the Hebrew name.

Gods. In their narration of Lilit's nocturnal forays, formulating the notion, image, and story of female stalking, the Sumerians expressed a patriarchal fear (laden with guilt and desire): that of a vilified, prepatriarchal feminine entity, who returns repeatedly to haunt them. Patriarchal fear of female stalking and Lilit's story subsequently merged. In later Jewish mythology, the female night stalker Lilit became Adam's sister and first wife (prior to the creation of Eve), who flew away from the Garden of Eden refusing to comply with Adam's attempt to establish his dominance. In Adam's sons' story of Lilit, fear of female stalking took on additional association with a strong, independent, sexual, long-lost mirror-image "sister," greatly loved and feared, much desired and hated. A detailed analysis of the exact elements of Lilit's story testifies to, and enables us to construct, the fear of female stalking as it may have been felt and perceived by the authors and audiences of the story, that is, by individuals as well as by the patriarchal social order. Moreover, throughout the ages and territories of Western civilization, Lilit's image has taken on many names and faces. (Glenn Close's character in the film *Fatal Attraction* is one conspicuous, contemporary example.) Tracing the development of Lilit's archetypal character and stalking story exposes the source and politics of the fear surrounding female stalking. It also sheds light on modern legal perceptions of the personal and social harm caused by stalking.

The journey into the history of stalking stories also led me to stories of archetypal male stalkers, that is, to the cultural manifestations and constructions of our fear of male stalking. In cultural narratives, male stalking is experienced as a lurking, watchful, controlling, supernatural threat. The corresponding fear is of an ever-present, omnipotent, overpowering, and "objectifying" entity. It is the fear of being ever supervised, judged, and condemned. The most illuminating metaphor of male stalking is God's watchful, ever-present, unseen eye, waiting to witness man's fall. The medieval overreaching Faust is a human version of the stalking Godly image; his insatiable quest for Knowledge is perceived as an attempt to penetrate and control. Satan is yet another "derivative" mythological male stalker, present at people's moments of weakness and failure, ever ready to seduce, report, and condemn. The legendary vampire is the most powerful image of male stalking. With his penetrating gaze, the nocturnal vampire stalks his human prey (women in particular), exposing and punishing the carnal and sinful. Like Lilit, Faust, Satan, and the vampire reappear throughout the ages, forming and perpetuating our fear of male stalking. (Frankenstein's creature, Dracula, and the monstrous serial killer Michael in the film *Halloween* are prominent examples.)

Comparison of male and female stalking in cultural narratives reveals their unique features. From the individual's perspective, male stalking is typically experienced as controlling, overpowering, oppressive, and ever-present. Female stalking is felt as repetitively returning, sexual, seducing, terrifying, and guilt inducing. The individual damage associated with male and female stalking is, therefore, distinctly different. The wider perspective of collective, social harm reveals an even more significant difference. Stories of female stalking have served the patriarchal social order as a disciplinary mechanism. Lilit's devilish image terrifies men, causing them to fear undomesticated, nonpatriarchal women, while demonstrating to women the horrible price of condemnation and isolation to be paid for choosing such a nontraditional feminine existence. Yet Lilit's character and story are also highly subversive and therefore dangerous to the ruling social order, because Lilit is not merely threatening, but also alluring and desirable. Like the carnival, stories of female stalking are a risky outlet for subversive undercurrents and a potentially dangerous component of the patriarchal social order. Like the carnival, such stories may be useful for the ruling classes if wisely controlled and manipulated in the service of their interests. The threat of male stalking, on the other hand, is a straightforward, highly efficient disciplinary mechanism of the patriarchal social order. Lacking the subversive qualities of female stalking, it effectively frightens men and women into social roles designed for them, subordinating them to the ruling ideology, ruling classes, and ruling deity.

This fundamental difference between concepts of male and female stalking may explain the different social functions they have been assigned throughout history. As this book illustrates, stories of male stalking have been regularly nourished and nurtured in the daily service of the social order. In dangerous times of social instability, the fear of female stalking, preserved in female stalking stories, was used to incite witch-hunts (moral panics), in which society united in pursuit of appropriate female scapegoats.

In mythology, folklore, literature, and film, women stalkers are at least as present and threatening as their male counterparts; Lilit, witches, prostitutes, and *Fatal Attraction*'s female protagonist are powerful female stalking characters. In reality, however, stalking seems to be a behavior predominantly perpetrated by men on women. This fact is an arresting reminder that stories do not necessarily reflect lived experiences, but can also express anxieties and dreads, constructing our perceptions of social realities. Such is also the close connection between stories of female stalking and periods of moral panic.

Stalking and Moral Panic

The sociological term *moral panic* refers to a period of public preoccupation with a social phenomenon that is irrationally perceived as exceptionally dangerous to the collective well-being. Such public preoccupation manifests collective insecurities. It labels and targets defined, unpopular groups and sometimes results in legislation or adoption of new social policies. Stanley

Cohen, first to develop the term, defined moral panic in the following manner:

> Societies appear to be subject, every now and then, to periods of moral panic. A condition, episode, person or group of persons emerges to become defined as a threat to societal values and interests; its nature is presented in a stylized and stereotypical fashion by the mass media; the moral barricades are manned by editors, bishops, politicians and other right-thinking people; socially accredited experts pronounce their diagnoses and solutions; ways of coping are evolved or (more often) resorted to; the condition then disappears, submerges or deteriorates and becomes more visible. Sometimes the panic passes over and is forgotten, except in folklore and collective memory; at other times it has more serious and long-lasting repercussions and might produce such changes as those in legal and social policy or even in the way the society conceives itself. (1980, 9)

A wider and more detailed definition is offered by Erich Goode and Nachman Ben-Yehuda:

> At times, societies are gripped by moral panics. During the moral panic, the behavior of some of the members of a society is thought to be so problematic to others, the evil they do, or are thought to do, is felt to be so wounding to the substance and fabric of the body social, that serious steps must be taken to control the behavior, punish the perpetrators, and repair the damage. The threat this evil presumably poses is felt to represent a crisis for the society: something must be done about it, and that something must be done now; if steps are not taken immediately, or soon, we will suffer even graver consequences. The sentiment generated or stirred up by this threat can be referred to as a kind of fever; it can be characterized by a heightened emotion, fear, dread, anxiety, hostility, and a strong feeling of righteousness. In a moral panic, a group or category engages in unacceptable, immoral behavior, presumably causes or is responsible for serious harmful consequences, and is therefore seen as a threat to the well-being, basic values, and interests of the society presumably threatened by them. These perpetrators or supposed perpetrators come to be regarded as the enemy—or an enemy—of society, "folk devils" (Cohen 1972), deviants, outsiders, legitimate and deserving targets of self-righteous anger, hostility, and punishment. (1994, 31)

Goode and Ben-Yehuda add that "it is almost axiomatic in the literature that moral panics arise in troubled times, during which a serious *threat* is sensed to the interests or values of the society as a whole or to segments of a society" (32).[4] Furthermore,

> when a society's moral boundaries are sharp, clear and secure, and the central norms and values are strongly held by nearly everyone, moral panics rarely grip its members—nor do they need to. However, when the moral boundaries are fuzzy and shifting and often seem to be contested, moral panics are far more likely to seize the members of a society. (52)

Cohen's (1972) research focuses on the preoccupation of the English public in the 1960s with a particular form of youth culture (the mods and rockers), which was perceived as deviant and dangerous. Goode and Ben-Yehuda (in 1994) explore what they define as the Renaissance witch craze, the LSD panic of the 1960s, the panic concerning satanic ritual abuse, the American drug panic of the 1980s, and the Israeli drug panic of May 1982. In each of these cases, they claim, there appears "a certain *disassociation* between protectionism and concern, that is, . . . concern and fear are not *strictly* a product of the magnitude of the threat, and therefore . . . the steps taken to protect the society from that threat may be somewhat misplaced" (20).

I have so far referred to stalking as a legal concept and as a set of stories that formulate and express individual and collective fears. I suggested that critical investigation of the legal concept of stalking can be assisted by exploring the details of the stories about stalking. I now suggest further that the (legally oriented) study of stalking stories is intertwined with the study of certain moral panics, which have been fueled by the stories and fears surrounding stalking.

In times of turmoil and insecurity, "when the moral boundaries are fuzzy and shifting," when collective frustration must find an outlet, stalking stories offer a structure for the public manifestations of anxiety and hostility that become moral panics. Such moral panics focus on social events that can be narrated as stalking stories and on characters who can be presented as archetypal stalkers. Images of fictional stalkers serve to create social categories of the deviant, the other, the enemy, and the folk devil who must be prevented from causing social harm.

As stories of both male and female stalking are deeply connected with the patriarchal social order, these stories are likely to evolve into moral panics when social turmoil affects the basis of patriarchy. Fictional male stalkers

---

4. Nevertheless, "there must be substantial or widespread agreement or consensus—that is, at least a certain minimal measure of consensus in the society as a whole or in designated segments of the society—that the threat is real, serious, and caused by the wrongdoing group members and their behavior" (Goode and Ben-Yehuda 1996, 34).

tend to strengthen the grip of the patriarchal social order; fictional female stalkers pose an inherent threat to patriarchy. It is the female stalking stories, therefore, that are likely to be used to fuel moral panics, legendary female stalkers skillfully constructed as models for human categories of "folk devils" targeted during these periods.

The most prominent example of a female-stalking moral panic is what Ben-Yehuda defines as the European witch craze, better known as the European witch-hunts. Lilit's stalking image was superimposed on women labeled "witches," who were promptly prosecuted and executed. The image of the witch served as a mediator between the mythological Lilit and real women. It facilitated the creation of a social category of women who were associated with the demonic, murderous, semen-stealing night stalker Lilit. In this respect, the witch craze was an enduring acting-out of Lilit's ancient stalking story.[5] Similarly, the Victorian treatment of streetwalkers was, from this perspective, analogous to that of witches by medieval and Renaissance society. The category "prostitute," much like "witch," served as a mediator between the archetypal night stalker Lilit and certain nineteenth-century lower-class women. Interestingly, the panic associated with Victorian prostitutes was accompanied by one incited by a mythologized male stalker, Jack the Ripper. The Ripper panic targeted lower-class immigrants and minorities, but above all it disciplined women, in particular those who desired to follow the model of the New Woman and forsake their roles as "angels in their houses" in favor of the public sphere. The panic regarding Jack's stalking image, lurking in the dark streets of London, served, above all else, to frighten rebellious women back to their traditional roles within the patriarchal social order.

Periods of moral panic often trigger the adoption of legal measures, in particular legislation. In both the cases of "witches" and prostitutes, new laws were enacted to better address the threat posed by these categories of stalking women. By using an interdisciplinary perspective, combining law, sociology, and literature, we can reveal the scope of sociocultural mechanisms—the storytelling, labeling, demonizing, and legislating—by which societies create, target, and discipline their scapegoats. Once these mechanisms are identified, they can be applied to analysis of contemporary social reality and positive law.

Stanley Cohen concludes his book on moral panics and folk devils with the following statement: "It is not enough to say that witches should not have been burnt or that in some other society or in another century they

5. Goode and Ben-Yehuda rightly note that a moral panic that "seems to have been sustained over a long period of time is almost certainly a conceptual grouping of a series of more or less discrete, more or less localized, more or less short-term panics." More specifically, "The Renaissance witch craze . . . was not active during the entire period of its 200 to 300 years of existence. It flared up at one time and place and subsided, burst forth later in another location and died down and so on" (1996, 39).

might not have been called witches; one has to explain why and how certain people get to the stake now" (1980, 204). This book examines stories of stalking and some of the moral panics they provoked over the course of history. It critically analyzes the contemporary treatment of stalking and stalkers in the context of the new legislation, and concludes that contemporary antistalking legislation is motivated by a stalking moral panic that has been developing in the United States over the last three decades.[6]

The analysis of contemporary popular culture suggests that, since the 1970s, stalking has been associated with deep insecurities regarding what is perceived as feminine empowerment, on the one hand, and failed, castrated manhood on the other. The fear of femininity triggered by feminist activism is manifested in popular fictional characterizations of obsessive female stalkers such as Alex, Glenn Close's character in *Fatal Attraction*. The failed military adventure in Vietnam, described by sociologists as a castrating "abortive rite of passage for an entire generation of American males" (Raphael 1988, 146–47), generated fictional male stalkers such as Robert De Niro's war veteran in the film *Taxi Driver*. Influenced by the real-life serial killer Son of Sam, these fictional male stalkers evolved into deranged, serial-killing monsters (think of *Halloween*'s Michael).

By portraying independent women, veterans, and social outcasts as obsessed, deranged, serial-killing stalkers, popular culture has created mediating images that facilitate the identification of members of certain social categories as stalkers. Furthermore, the mass media and professional literature have joined forces with popular culture in generating a contemporary stalking moral panic. The new antistalking legislation is a product of this moral panic. It was motivated by disproportional fear of deranged serial-killing stalkers and designed to punish, and preferably eliminate, distinct types of people who have become "folk devil" stalkers. Because of this origin, antistalking legislation cannot address the real problems of stalking in contemporary social reality.

Stalking seems to be a serious, prevalent problem in contemporary American society. Victims experience damage and loss, and their rights to privacy and autonomy are severely infringed. The popularity of film may amplify some people's fear of being stalked while provoking others to actively engage in stalking. Stalking may, therefore, be more widespread and more disturbing than in previous times. Consider the following eight testimonies of victims, some of which were formulated by the mass media:

> Being stalked is the stuff of nightmares, a favorite topic of scary movies such as *Fatal Attraction*. In real life, it's a mental game, a war of control, with sometimes deadly results. . . . "I think it's the way relationships are now and how volatile society is. The pressure on people in relationships

6. The first writer to analyze antistalking legislation (in Canada) as part of a moral panic is Rosemary Cairns Way (1994).

is incredible with the ways the family is breaking up. Everyone is under stress. . . . The majority of the victims feel there's no way out. The stalking will go on forever, and they'll never get their life back," Golubic [Marc Golubic, of the Exodus Group, a Houston company that provides personal protection and antistalking training] said. "A victim feels like a mouse in a maze in a cage. She gets tired. There's despair and hopelessness." (Lake 1995)

"The day his sentence ends, mine begins," Betty said. "I have no doubt he'll be right back on my doorstep." . . . "Hey, somebody is always watching you," a bank guard wrote to a teller he had been stalking. "Somebody is watching you in or out of the office, in or out of bed, in or out of the bathroom. . . . The road ahead for you is a real bitch. It's going to get more and more and more ugly!" (Corwin 1993)

What had begun as a relentless inconvenience became something more oppressive. . . . Hopewood says that the most upsetting part of the experience was his utter lack of control. (Gerrard 1994)

Let me first tell you a little about myself. I'm a single mother of a college-age daughter. I hold a corporate level position with a prominent company. Up until six months ago, I was excited about my job, about my future, about my life in general. I felt I had it together, and that all my hard work had finally paid off. I was in control. That was then, and this is now. Now my hands shake and I often feel as though my heart is pounding through my chest. I don't sleep without nightmares, and I can't seem to concentrate on anything. Adrenaline rushes are a routine part of my day. I feel as though my entire being has somehow been altered. My lifestyle is changed. My coping mechanisms have been challenged to the max. Relationships both working and personal have paid a heavy penalty. Anxiety remains at a peak level with only moments of relief. A phone call, a door slamming outside, a family member arriving home later than expected, all prove to cause the adrenaline to rush once more. My home has become a fortress, blinds pulled, doors double locked, and a high security alarm system in place, not to shut the world out, but to shut me in.[7]

I began to realize that I couldn't leave my home. In effect, I was a prisoner. I couldn't leave and subject my children and baby-sitters to this terror, so I stayed home. I felt as if I were being watched day as well as

7. This and the next four quotations are from testimony given in hearings before the Michigan Senate Judiciary Committee in May 1992. I have recordings of these hearings. I thank David Cahill for furnishing me with the tapes, and Rebecca Johnson for helping me in their transcription.

night. I even questioned things that I did: had I asked for this? Did I dress suggestively? Did I do anything? . . .

I lost my freedom for three years. I am still watchful and scared. I look out my window constantly at night, and I'm afraid he's outside my window when I go to bed.

I am living a never-ending nightmare. . . . As in rape, assault, kidnapping, and murder, they all go hand in hand, because it violates my privacy and body, as well as my mind. . . . We are prisoners in our own home. We have no freedom and no safety.

I have slept in fear. . . . He has spied on me from parking lots in the middle of the night when I get off work . . . and [will] call and call and call and call. . . . He wants to control me. He wants what he wants and damn what I want. . . . He wants to be the victim. He doesn't believe I am the victim . . . wanting me to understand what he's been through. . . . I don't have freedom from driving wherever I am around my small town without fearing that he's just going to pop out. It's a devastating situation . . . and in the past responses have been "Well, he's just in love."

He took something away from us that no other person could: he took away our freedom, and he took away our faith. . . . I just lost hope. . . . He's promised us that he won't leave us alone, and I believe him.

Judging by the statistical data that has just begun to accumulate, stalking seems to serve as a pattern of abuse, perpetrated by men on women they know. Its consequences seem to be significant. It may, therefore, justify legal intervention, including new legislation and enforcement policies. But legal intervention must attempt to see through the moral panic and define the harm of the lived social phenomenon, addressing the relevant legal and metalegal issues. The current legislation, motivated by moral panic rather than by reality, cannot live up to this task. Instead of identifying and determining the individual damage and social harm, legal discourse has been fascinated with analyses of stalkers' mental makeup and the psychological motivations for their conduct. Legal preoccupation with psychiatric issues invites stereotyping, labeling, and, probably, the demonizing of "deviants." I therefore suggest that stalking legislation be reassessed and reformulated to address the real social problem and not the moral panic surrounding it. It is difficult, at a time of an ensuing moral panic, to distinguish the "real" issue from its public perception; I believe a close reading of the relevant stories and their historical development may assist in confronting this necessary task.

Having established moral panic as one underlying theme of this work, I must register a substantial reservation regarding the term and its moral undertones. Goode and Ben-Yehuda mention Waddington's criticism:

"Conceptually, the notion of 'moral panic' lacks any criteria of proportionality, without which it is impossible to determine whether concern about any . . . problem is justified or not. . . . Perhaps . . . it is time to abandon such value-laden terminology" (Goode and Ben-Yehuda 1996, 42). Despite plausible replies to this criticism, the choice of words (*moral* and *panic*) does seem to be judgmental and moralizing. Worried by these concerns, I considered replacing *moral panic* with a more benign phrase. I have decided to remain within the boundaries of accepted professional terminology, but would urge the reader to keep in mind the value-laden implications of the term.

The Argument

The pursuit of stalking led me to unexpected times and places. I began in the ancient Near East, only to find myself in medieval Europe, in nineteenth-century England, and in the world of cinema. Articulating this voyage to earlier cultures as a book, I was faced with the dilemma of how to go about it. Plunging directly into the fascinating past, I risk losing the reader, who might not see the purpose of this excursion and where it is leading. Yet starting from the present and making my way back may result in imposing too many of our own assumptions on earlier stages of development, which would, of course, undermine the project. After much thought, I found myself convinced by the position taken by Mieke Bal in her reading of fatal love stories in the Hebrew Bible. "In the case of a developmental story, starting at the end means losing sight of the development. In the linear reading, the possibility that these features are self-evident is questioned by the very concept of development" (1987, 130).

I therefore decided to start at the beginning and move through the historical phases of the sociocultural development of stalking, as we know and understand it from a contemporary perspective. In this sense, this work offers a linear reading of stalking in Western culture. At the same time my reading is also cyclical and repetitive. Each of the following chapters focuses on a different historical period and on a different sociocultural phenomenon; but at the same time each discusses the fundamental narrative structures, plots, characters, and specific motifs of stalking that, by taking on new shapes and meanings at different times in different places, move from one phase to another. In this respect, the fundamental themes recur in every chapter. This is not meant to imply the existence of any mystical, metaphysical, or collective universal truths. It is merely another way of saying that within a given culture ideas never die, but only take on new forms.

Having chosen a linear format, I begin with a presentation of female stalking: the stories, fears, and images as they were formulated, mostly through mythology, in the ancient Sumerian and Hebrew cultures. Thus, chapter 2 explores the story of the night-stalking Lilit, demonized descendant of the ancient Great Goddess of antiquity, Inanna. It follows the development of Lilit's stalking story, analyzing the significance of particular elements associated with her, such as the moon, the gazing eye, and her close family ties with Adam, her brother, lover, and target. Two appendixes elaborate the methodological issue of approaching antiquity and the historical development of Lilit in Jewish culture. Chapter 3 offers a close reading of two occurrences of female-stalking moral panic. Looking at the medieval and Renaissance witch-hunts and at the hysterical public treatment of prostitutes in Victorian England, I suggest that both were outbursts of anxieties associated with and formulated through stories of female stalking. I show that the terms *witch* and *prostitute* facilitated the connection of specific groups of women with the archetypal stalker, Lilit.

Chapter 4 introduces male stalking, the stories and the related fears. I present four distinct male characters and their literary patterns of stalking: the all-seeing, overpowering God of the Hebrew Bible; the overreaching Faust, who attempts to know all; the lurking, spying, condemning Satan; and, above all, the nocturnal, undead, bloodsucking vampire of folklore. Two appendixes discuss relevant philosophical terminology and the vampire as a shadow image of the son God. Chapter 5 follows these characters, as well as Lilit, into nineteenth-century English literature. Concentrating on two highly influential works, Mary Shelley's *Frankenstein* and Bram Stoker's *Dracula*, I show how notions and definitions of stalking, originally created in popular genres such as mythology and folklore, were reformulated and reconceptualized by art. Working with familiar images, Shelley's story criticized modernity's scientific inhumanity while sympathizing with its tormented creation and victim, the monstrous stalker. Stoker's *Dracula*, on the other hand, used the same cultural materials to reestablish the male stalker as a modern, disciplining, patriarchal character. An appendix supplies Shelley's literary biography; another includes the first chapter of a popular nineteenth-century serial *Varney the Vampire*.

Chapters 6 to 9 study stalking in the twentieth century. Chapter 6 focuses on the construction of stalking in film during the first half of the century. I claim that film is experienced as simulated stalking, training viewers in voyeuristic stalking. At the same time, film subjects viewers to the intense experience of being stalked. Through those experiences, stalking becomes an important part of viewers' lives. The expectation and fear of stalking linger on when the audience leaves the theater. The idea of expressing their own emotions and needs through stalking becomes plausible.

Chapter 7 explores the contribution of popular film, professional literature, and mass media to the emergence of a stalking moral panic in the United States during the last quarter of the twentieth century. It analyzes the process by which the film industry, the mass media, mental health professionals, and social scientists formulated powerful contemporary stalking images. These images mediate between images of archetypal stalkers and real individuals.

Chapters 8 and 9 review the legal treatment of stalking since the first antistalking legislation in 1990. Chapter 8 depicts the growth of the new legislation, which reflected and augmented the developing moral panic. Chapter 9 offers an alternative legal perspective, distinguishing the real social problem of stalking from the moral panic surrounding it, and proposing appropriate legal responses. It suggests that a legal solution formulated from within a moral panic cannot effectively address the real problems posed by stalking. To meet the needs of social reality, the law must focus on the appropriate questions and formulate relevant means of addressing them. This final chapter also presents a draft of legislation that I believe both defines and treats stalking in a legally responsible manner.

Several other themes recur throughout this text. Constancy and change in symbolic imagery of stalking is a prominent theme. Other issues are the process of creating cultural archetypes, the relationships among images, archetypes, and narratives, and the transformations of stories and images by ever-changing social ideologies. The discussion explores mechanisms of mutual influences between fact and fiction, story and history, individual and community. It traces the evolution of gender imagery within patriarchy and compares its manifestations and consequences in different social discourses and in different historical settings. One fundamental theme, which connects all the others, is the ongoing dialogue among such cultural discourses as religion, the media, folklore and myth, literature, film, social sciences, and the law.

I have so far emphasized the diachronic aspects of this work. From a synchronic perspective, it can be said to examine and compare the story of stalking as it is told in the fields of Near Eastern studies, medieval studies, English literature, film theory, social sciences, and the law. Viewed in this manner, the professional literature I present is not merely secondary to the phenomena investigated, but an important primary source in its own right. Thus my frequent quoting of various opinions on many issues. The presentation of many voices allows for a conversation, within this text, among different scholars and between them and me.

The Story of Stalking

I started this introduction with a short definition of stalking as formulated in California's first antistalking law of 1990. I wish to conclude these opening remarks with a different portrayal of stalking. Reading stalking stories that have been created in our culture over many centuries, I encountered recurring themes and motifs that will gradually be encountered in this book.

Typically, in these accounts, at least one person, usually the stalker, believes that an extraordinary, fundamental (potential or materialized) bond exists between two people, usually the stalker and the target. Stalking ensues where such a perceived union is experienced as primary, eternal, and inevitable. Often, the stalker views the relationship with the other as preceding time and history; as stronger than nature, culture, and death itself (hence primordial stalking characters and frequent returns from death in stalking stories). The attachment springs from the very essence of the characters' beings: they are as inseparable as mother and son, brother and sister, lover and beloved, two halves of one whole. Their assumed symbiotic existence makes their separation unbearably painful. (Think of Jekyll and Hyde, whose separation literally means death.) Stalking stories often take the point of view (usually the stalker's) that sees a deep bond between stalker and target. Stalking is frequently an attempt to rescue a relationship from change or termination, which is experienced as insufferable. If the relationship has not been fulfilled, stalking may be an attempt to consummate it. It is always a desperate endeavor to force a relationship on another party, who seems to be indifferent, uncooperative, or trying to break away.

Stalking behavior often consists of the stalker's repetitive returns into the life and consciousness of the other party, returns that may be experienced by the target as the pursuer's perpetual presence in his or her life. The stalker may simply reappear in the other's presence, as a constant reminder of the stalker's existence and expectations, and sending the message that he or she, the stalker, will always be there. The stalker may follow the other person, becoming an ever present "shadow." The stalker may watch the other person and communicate his or her knowledge of (and therefore control over) the other's life. There may be nightly visits or attempts to impose on the target through metanatural means, such as magic, telepathy, or hypnosis. Whatever the particular manifestations, the behavior always invades the other person's privacy, disregards the other's will, and denies his or her right to self-determination. Stalking consists of recurring events that undermine the other person's control over his or her own time and space. (This is the symbolic meaning of magic, telepathy, and hypnosis.) The stalker's repeated returns to the other's life create a circular time frame that unites pursuer and prey in a closed, seemingly eternal cycle. This circular time (often symbolized by the moon) constantly imposes the (shadow of the) past on the victim's present and future and precludes a progression that would allow gradual movement away from the stalker.

From a slightly different perspective, stalking is about the tension between a perceived center and a perceived exterior; between an inside and an outside, a present and a past, strength and weakness. Stalking is a response to feeling left out in the past by the other person. It is the stalker's struggle to move (back) into the other person's life, which the stalker perceives as the inside, the present, the center of everything that is meaningful.

In a typical story, the stalker feels that he or she is seeking justice and/or aspiring to correct a wrong. The relationship with the victim must be established or saved at any cost. The stalker is typically motivated by a desire to gain the other party's acknowledgment, acceptance, respect, affection, or pardon. Some stalk to maintain or to achieve control over another party. Retaliation, revenge, and punishment are common drives that lead to stalking, as are jealousy, dependence, anger, and humiliation. Most often, several motives join forces, either sequentially or simultaneously. In stalking an individual, the stalker often also "communicates" with society at large. Stalking stories often involve extreme emotional investments and separations that are inherently stormy. Stalking is, therefore, usually embedded in such paradoxical, confusing, and contradictory passions as love and hate, jealousy and self-interest, attraction and repulsion, intimacy and fear, desire for acceptance and retaliatory hostility. Such emotions can be experienced concomitantly. Almost inevitably felt by the stalker, they are often shared by the victim. The latter may also experience guilt, longing, loneliness, failure, sorrow, anger, anxiety, entrapment, and fear. Stalking behavior is often so remote from the stalker's normal conduct that the victim or stalker may perceive the person who stalks as an unfamiliar double, dark shadow, or evil mirror reflection. (These images are widely used in stalking stories; think of a man who turns into a werewolf.)

A stalking story often reflects a perceived shift in the power relations between stalker and target. In other words, the perceived gain or loss of power in a relationship may lead a person to stalk. Paradoxically, loss *or* gain of perceived power can provoke this response. Either type of change may cause one party to feel stalked by the other and may lead him or her to stalk in return. This pattern elucidates several fundamental and closely connected points in stalking stories. The first is that stalking is very often mutual, in the sense that each party perceives him- or herself as the victim and may, in response, resort to stalking the other party. The second point exposes stalking's paradoxical nature: stalking behavior, as well as a person's perception that he or she is being stalked, may result from feelings of either gain or loss of power in a relationship. In this complex sense, stalking stories are never rational and are always highly subjective. Many such narratives suggest that the relevant faculty for understanding stalking is not so much reason as intuition. (In stalking films, animals are often the best judges of events.) The third and most pertinent point is that these stories are largely determined by the point of view from which they are told. Told or read from different perspectives, different behaviors may be viewed as stalking and different motivations may be revealed.

Stalking stories have been interpreted in many different fashions. Most interpretations stress one perspective and associated elements while ignoring other aspects. But the narratives themselves often convey at least two points of view, presenting elements that belong to different and sometimes contradictory perspectives. Such multiple perspectives are what make these stories so paradoxical, elusive, and uncanny. They also make them real, truthful, whole, and gripping. Stalking, like its stories, is messy, irrational life.

Stalking stories establish stalking as a transformative relationship. In addition to a shift in power relations between parties, stalking can also cause a shift in a person's sense of identity. Either party may experience a deep change in self-perception. The most common and obvious change is the victim's loss of a sense of freedom, individuality, and autonomy. Either party or both may also experience a change in their perceptions of time since, as noted earlier, stalking tends to replace a linear feeling of passing time with a cyclical one. Any discussion of stalking must take into account the possibility that the parties involved will change and will experience transformations in their perceptions of time and of their shared relationship. With this possibility in mind, we can view stalking as an assault on a person's self-perception. I stress this point because contemporary Western legal thought tends to assume atomic individuals and a linear time frame and to separate the former from the latter. Legal discourse perceives persons as stable separate entities, and human behaviors as taking place in linear time. Behaviors, in legal discourse, are commonly external to individuals, and individuals are unchanged by behaviors. These essentialist notions of individuality and time may obscure the nature of stalking, especially because the stalking story, like some of its central characters, is about transcending categories and distinctions. Conventional legal categories cannot recognize this transcendence and are, therefore, inevitably inaccurate in application.

Stalking episodes can occur between persons of the same sex. A stalking story can develop between father and son (think of Frankenstein and his creature), or between a man and his double or shadow self (consider Jekyll and his Hyde, or *Cape Fear*). Many stalking stories contain a homosocial aspect (directed either at an individual or at society at large), and often the stalker's target is not his or her immediate or only victim. But most typically, stalking involves a man and a woman, and it is on this pattern that I have focused. In this context, the stalking stories of the West (as all stories of that culture) have developed within a patriarchal framework. Although many of these narratives contain elements that can be read against the grain, most are structured in accordance with patriarchal images of masculinity and, especially, of femininity. Most such stories conform to one or more of the following structures: (1) a strong, sexually initiating, dangerous Lilit woman stalks a man, threatening him and his family; (2) a "Jack the Ripper"/serial-killer "shadow" male character stalks a sexual, evil woman because she "asked for it," "had it coming," and "brought it on herself"; or (3) a monstrous male stalks a weak, domestic, Eve-woman, who is saved only if she is revealed to be a Virgin Mary character. All three structures reflect and perpetuate stereotypically patriarchal images of women. Women are either good and weak (castrated), or strong, sexual, and evil (castrating). In this sense, at least, stalking stories as we know them are products of the ruling patriarchal culture and its basic images and values. Through their structures they perform a second rape (figuratively speaking) of their women characters (sometimes with much pornographic pleasure). This is an issue that legal discourse should study in order to avoid the stereotyping associated with stalking and to begin a genuinely legal analysis of it.

CHAPTER 2

The Archetypal Female Stalker, Lilit

The female of Samael [Lilit] is called "snake," "a wife of harlotry,"
"the end of all flesh," "the end of days." . . . She dresses herself in
finery like an abominable harlot and stands at the corners of streets
and highways in order to attract men. . . . [This is] the finery that she
uses to seduce mankind: her hair is long, red like a lily; her face is
white and pink; six pendants hang at her ears; her bed is made of
Egyptian flax; all the ornaments of the East encircle her neck; her
mouth is shaped like a tiny door, beautified with cosmetic; her tongue
is sharp like a sword; her words smooth as oil; her lips beautiful, red
as a lily, sweetened with all the sweetness in the world; she is dressed
in purple, and attired in thirty-nine items of finery.

This fool [who was seduced by her] turns aside after her, and
drinks from the cup of wine, and commits harlotry with her,
completely enamored of her. What does she do? She leaves him asleep
on the bed and ascends to the realms above, accuses him, obtains
authority, and descends. The fool wakes up, thinking to sport with
her as before, but she takes off her finery, and turns into a fierce
warrior, facing him in a garment of flaming fire, a vision of dread,
terrifying both body and soul, full of horrific eyes, a sharpened sword
in his hand with drops of poison suspended from it. He [the warrior]
kills the fool and throws him to Gehinnom.

(Zohar I, 148a–b)

Looking deep into the layers of Lilith mirrors, I see an ancient
Goddess, She who brought the gift of agriculture, transformed into a
demon; the image of woman as strong and independent degraded for
her strength—thus distorted into a temptress of men—even as they
admitted that she had chosen well between oppression and freedom.

(Stone 1984, 128)

Preview

Lilit is the dark, long-haired, night-flying she-devil. In legends and myths, this strong, sexual, supernatural woman is man's long-lost other-self, sister, and lover. She is also Western culture's ancient and enduring archetypal female stalker.[1] Dark and transparent as the night air, her gazing, bewitch-

---

1. In its traditional Jungian sense an archetype is a universal image that is embedded in the human psyche. My usage of Jungian terminology, such as *archetype, collective unconscious,* and *shadow image* is strictly metaphoric. In this work, archetypes are culturally created images.

ing "evil eye" is ever present. For millennia, she has been leaping from the shadows, snatching helpless babes from the arms of their mothers and initiating illicit sexual liaisons with their sleeping fathers. In our homes, in our streets, in our minds, and in our collective memories, she is ever ready to attack and take her pleasure. Under various names and in numerous disguises, her shadow reappears in our literature, our films, and our scientific discourses. We may have forgotten her ancient name, but never the idea of her, nor the thrilling sensation she inspires. Our paralyzing fear of her, inseparable from our unruly longing and desire for her, is what dreams and nightmares are made of.

Lilit's compelling, ever-gazing presence and her uncanny returns are what we experience and conceptualize as female stalking. Female stalking is, therefore, that to which we feel Lilit subjects us. The cultural notion of female stalking exhibits deeply rooted collective fears, longing, and guilt; these emotions are masterfully expressed, elaborated, and perpetuated through stalking stories and the image of the stalking protagonist, Lilit.

Lilit and her story, including the origins and the developments of her legendary character and of her archetypal role as the female stalker, illuminates our notion of female stalking and the emotions it both discloses and reinforces. My argument is that Lilit was initiated as Western culture's archetypal female stalker when the Great Goddess of antiquity was conquered and replaced by patriarchy's omnipotent male God. Creating a new world order, the patriarchal culture split the ancient Great Goddess in two: her life-giving, motherly traits were domesticated and remodeled into the character of Eve, while the Goddess's wisdom, sexuality, strength, and intimate connection with death and the dead were vilified and demonized, transforming her into the fearsome, stalking image of Lilit. The Hebrews established that this Lilit was Adam/Man's other-self sister as well as his first, lost love. In this process, the symbols that represented the Goddess's mighty powers, such as the eye, the moon, the snake, and the owl, were subsequently attributed to the shadowy Lilit and saddled with new cultural meanings. These symbols became allegorical manifestations of the evolving notion of female stalking.

Within patriarchy, Lilit's stalking has become a disciplinary social mechanism in the sense that it portrays the female stalker as a threatening devil. Nevertheless, Lilit's primordial image still provokes deep attraction and longing. These qualities make female stalking, and the archetypal female stalker, inherently subversive within the social order.

In order to flesh out the argument, let us turn to Mesopotamia, the cradle of Western culture and the birthplace of the Great Goddess, Eve, Lilit, and female stalking. I start with a brief introduction of the Great Goddess of ancient Mesopotamian culture, followed by a description of her gradual denigration at the hands of patriarchy. (For a discussion of the possibility and perils of approaching antiquity, as well as for background for the Great

Goddess, matriarchy, and such related issues as virginity, incest, and circular time, see appendix 2.1.) The chapter focuses on the reformulation of the Goddess and her symbols into the images of Eve and Lilit, while describing the cultural creation of Lilit, first in ancient Sumer and Babylon and then in Jewish culture.

The Great Goddess: Inanna/Ishtar/Anat

Once upon a time, many many moons ago, in a far and beautiful kingdom called Sumer, there lived an awesome Goddess, Inanna. The people of Sumer loved, feared, and worshipped her. Their poets composed many songs of praise in her honor:

> Proud Queen of the Earth Gods, Supreme Among the Heaven Gods,
> Loud Thundering Storm, you pour your rain over all the lands and all
>   the people.
> You make the Heavens tremble and the earth quake.
> Great Priestess, who can soothe your troubled heart?
> (Wolkstein and Kramer 1983, 95)

Sumerian painters and sculptors were inspired by her beautiful naked body, and they hailed her image, endowing it with magnificent snakelike hair, wings, and bird's feet. Images of her devoted owls and lions surrounded her statues.[2]

She, the splendid virgin Goddess, Queen of Heaven and Earth, also admired her own youth and loveliness:

> When she leaned against the apple tree, her vulva was wondrous to
>   behold.
> Rejoicing at her wondrous vulva, the young woman Inanna
>   applauded herself.
> (Kinsley 1989, 126)

Inanna was "identified with life in all its rambunctious, teeming, vigorous manifestations and bubblings" (138). And since she was Life, she was also Death, for the two were perceived as two aspects of one whole.

Inanna was powerful and uncontrollable. She transcended and combined all oppositions (Frymer-Kensky 1992, 29, 66). She was "the one who is joy" and "mistress of battle." She was, at once, very "feminine" and very

2. As Baring and Cashford point out, "Both the serpents and the wings springing from her shoulders show her descent from the Neolithic Bird and Snake Goddess" (175). For a picture of the Burney Relief, a splendid plaque of Inanna/Ishtar, see Baring and Cashford 1991, fig. 30.

"masculine." She was the "lady of myriad offices" (Kinsley 1989, 137); her titles as diverse as her adventures, roles, and features. "Prophetess of Deities," they called her, for she interpreted their dreams and saw into the future. "Divine Mother who Reveals the Law" was her name, for she brought them the holy *meh*, the divine Law, which she conquered from the God of Wisdom. As Lady of the Moon, "Great Mother of Serpent," they worshipped her, since she was wisdom, eternity, and cyclic regeneration of life from death from life (Baring and Cashford 1991, 91; Stone 1976, 199). In Egyptian hieroglyphs, the word *Goddess* was denoted by a cobra, a snake known as "The Eye" and as "a symbol of mystic insight and wisdom" (201). Like the cobra, the Goddess possessed the Glance.

Some of the most enchanting and moving stories about Inanna concern her passionate, yet turbulent, relationship with the shepherd Dumuzi, who was her brother, lover, husband, and son. Exciting her desire, the shepherd courted her with fabulous expressions of passionate admiration. With promises of his eternal love he gained her trust. He wooed and humored her vigorously until she cried "make your milk sweet and thick, my bridegroom. / My shepherd, I will drink your fresh milk." She declared that "he is the one my womb loves best" (Wolkstein and Kramer 1983, 38–39). Finally,

> He put his hand in her hand.
> He put his hand to her heart.
> Sweet is the sleep of hand-to-hand.
> Sweeter still the sleep of heart-to-heart.

$$(43)[3]$$

Inanna and Dumuzi's sacred marriage was the central ritual of every ancient Near Eastern culture and was celebrated by the sexual unity of the Goddesses' chief priestess with her chosen lover. In the latter sacred marriage, the chosen lover was made king and God, ruling at the priestess's side for one year, until the next sacred marriage.

When Inanna descended into the Great Below, the kingdom ruled by her sister, Ereshkigal, she was kept there for three dark days, and her consort sat on her chair, rejoicing.[4] For this, she condemned him to be taken into the underworld in her place. Yet she missed him and wept in mourning. She saved her lover, brought him back to life.[5] The young God's death and resurrection were annually celebrated and mourned in every Mesopotamian

---

3. Many of these incredible love songs greatly resemble the biblical Song of Songs.
4. For one version of the descent of Inanna to the Great Below see Wolkstein and Kramer 1983, 51.
5. For one Sumerian version of the myth of the death of Dumuzi see Kramer 1969. In this discussion, I point out only the most basic themes of the generic myth.

culture, as well as in many others.[6] Dumuzi's return from death "became the archetype of all deaths and of all resurrections in whatever plane they might occur" (James 1959, 237).

As the millennia passed, the Great Goddesses lost their powers to the rising male Gods. The worst fate awaited the Mother Goddesses, whose creative powers the young male Gods coveted. And so the myths of creation changed time and again: where at first the primordial Mother created all life, later on her son joined her, only to take her place and finally become the Father God, sole creator and ruler (Lerner 1986, 145). The *Enuma Elish* documents how the brave God Marduk defeated the primordial Great Mother, Tiamat, becoming king of the Gods. Tiamat's dead, now monstrous body was used by the young God to create heaven and earth.

Goddesses were clearly marginalized within the new mythological order, but not so Inanna. In the emerging patriarchal social order, Inanna (sometimes referred to as Ishtar) remained the "nondomesticated woman": the nonmaternal, unattached lover-warrior "woman in a man's life" (Frymer-Kensky 1992, 29). In fact, she "not only did not disappear, but continued to grow in importance" (77). She was the Goddess who served "the important function of modeling a role that women were *not* expected to fill and that was *not* considered socially desirable" (25; emphasis added). She remained an extraordinarily powerful Goddess, but "having a great variety of powers and roles, she nevertheless [did] not fit any of the niches that society has provided for its women" (27) and therefore was an "outsider" in both human and divine societies.[7] Women in Sumer were expected to keep house, but Inanna roamed the streets night and day (she was the morning and the evening star, as well as the moon).[8] Her restless roaming characterized her as "masculine" and allied her with the *harimtu*, the nocturnal streetwalkers (29).

Within the new male-oriented order, the more powerful Inanna/Ishtar was, the more Gods and men feared her and the more they fought and abused her. Their ultimate weapon was the strategy of "divide, tame and demonize." They slashed the Goddess, using her colorful components to create two distinct feminine images: one domesticated and powerless (Eve), the other a bloodthirsty night-stalker (Lilit). The attributes that once sym-

6. Most scholars believe that Dumuzi's annual death and resurrection was related to the seasonal "death" and "rebirth" of crop; for other interpretations see Gordon 1961, 184; Shuttle and Redgrove 1978, 64; James 1959, 237.

7. Not only did Inanna remain the powerful, attractive warrior Goddess, but, paradoxically, she "inherited" some of the older Goddesses' features: "Ultimately, she became a 'Great Goddess' to whom was attributed a wide variety of attributes and characteristics, including those of the mother goddess" (Frymer-Kensky 1992, 78).

8. "As the morning star she was the virgin, as the evening star the harlot, as the lady of the night sky the consort of the moon; and when extinguished under the blaze of the sun she was the hag of hell" (Campbell 1968, 303).

bolized Inanna's strength were reformulated as signs of the female stalker's
wickedness; women were taught to regard the domesticated female as their
only role model and to fear the female stalker as a mortal enemy. The effects
of this cultural maneuver, which continues within Western culture to this
day, are inseparable from our notion of female stalking. The fear, hatred,
longing and guilt collectively felt toward the degraded Goddess are the
emotions manifested in our notion of female stalking.

The Story of the *Huluppu* Tree: Decline of the Goddess and Creation of Eve

Let us analyze a Sumerian poem that performs this cultural, patriarchal
"scheme."

The Sumerians worshipped Inanna as early as 3000 B.C.E. and possibly
much earlier (Kramer 1969, 57; Stone 1976, 141). Written texts, on the other
hand, were not produced until a whole millennium later, some time after
2000 B.C.E. By this period, Inanna "still receives great reverence, [but] she has
clearly lost what was previously Hers" (Stone 1976, 83). Therefore, when the
text "Inanna and Gilgamesh under the Huluppu Tree" was written, the
Goddess's image was already being subjected to a manipulative patriarchal
reconstruction. In the Gilgamesh epic, written versions of which date back to
1700 B.C.E., Inanna/Ishtar is scornfully rejected and humiliated by Gilgamesh, and Enkidu, Gilgamesh's mate, slaughters her holy bull in an act of
disrespect (Dalley 1989, 3, 78). The text clearly testifies to Inanna's demotion
during that historical period and identifies Gilgamesh as the man responsible for her subordination. I suggest that the written version of the huluppu
tree story offers yet another illustration of Inanna's denigration at the hands
of Gilgamesh. A critical reading of the text reveals how the once almighty
Goddess was transformed into a whining maiden in distress. Furthermore,
her powerful features, now vilified, became associated with the image of the
female stalker.

Based on Professor Kramer's translation of a text narrating this myth,
Diane Wolkstein composed the following poetic version of this narrative:

> In the first days, in the very first days, . . .
> When the Sky God, An, had carried off the heavens,
> And the Air God, Enlil, had carried off the earth,
> When the Queen of the Great Below, Ereshkigal, was given
> the underworld for her domain,
> He set sail; the Father set sail,
> Enki, the God of Wisdom, set sail for the underworld. . . .

At that time, a tree, a single tree, a huluppu-tree
Was planted by the banks of the Euphrates. . . .
The whirling South Wind arose, pulling at its root . . .
Until the waters of the Euphrates carried it away.

A woman who walked in fear of the word of the Sky God, An,
Who walked in fear of the word of the Air God, Enlil,
Plucked the tree from the river and spoke:
"I shall bring this tree to Uruk.
I shall plant this tree in my holy garden."
Inanna cared for the tree with her hand. . . .
She wondered:
"How long will it be until I have a shining throne to sit upon?
How long will it be until I have a shining bed to lie upon?"

The years passed; . . .
Then a serpent who could not be charmed
Made its nest in the roots of the huluppu-tree.
The Anzu-bird set his young in the branches of the tree.
And the dark maid Lilith built her home in the trunk.
The young woman who loved to laugh wept.
How Inanna wept! . . .

Inanna called to her brother Utu . . .

Utu, the valiant warrior, Utu
Would not help his sister, Inanna. . . .

Inanna called to her brother Gilgamesh . . .

Gilgamesh the valiant warrior, Gilgamesh,
The hero of Uruk, stood by Inanna.

Gilgamesh fastened his armor of fifty minas around his chest.
The fifty minas weighed as little to him as fifty feathers.
He lifted his bronze ax, the ax of the road,
Weighing seven talents and seven minas, to his shoulder.
He entered Inanna's holy garden.

Gilgamesh struck the serpent who could not be charmed.
The Anzu-bird flew with his young to the mountains;
And Lilith smashed her home and fled to the wild, uninhabited places.

Gilgamesh then loosened the roots of the huluppu-tree;
And the sons of the city, who accompanied him, cut off the branches.

From the trunk of the tree he carved a throne for his holy sister.
From the trunk of the tree Gilgamesh carved a bed for Inanna.
From the roots of the tree she fashioned a pukku for her brother.
From the crown of the tree Inanna fashioned a mikku for Gilgamesh,
    the hero of Uruk.

(Wolkstein and Kramer 1983, 4–9)

The story mentions three mighty male Gods: the Sky God, An, who carries off the heavens, the Air God, Enlil, who carries off the earth, and the Father God of Wisdom, Enki. The great Sumerian primordial Goddesses, such as Tiamat, the first Mother creator of both the universe and the Gods (Dalley 1989, 233), Nammu, "the mother who gave birth to heaven and earth," and Nina, the Primeval Sea (Stone 1984, 236–39), are not mentioned. Even the Gods' female partners are absent: An, Sky, appears here without his wife Ki, Earth, and Enlil (An and Ki's son), the Air God, is not accompanied by Ninlil, the Air Goddess, his sister and mate.[9] The only feminine deity mentioned is Ereshkigal, queen of the underworld, who is said to have been put there against her will (unlike the male Gods, who actively seized their superior loot).[10] Ereshkigal's kingdom, the story indicates, was not one any male God cared to rule.

Unlike in other texts, which presumably document earlier accounts of creation, here the Goddesses are strikingly invisible. Inanna too is not introduced as a goddess. In the traditional Mesopotamian pantheon, Inanna was the granddaughter of Enlil and the great-granddaughter of An on both sides. Ereshkigal was her sister and/or her other, dark self (Wolkstein and Kramer 1983, 51; Baring and Cashford 1991, 193, 510). And yet the huluppu tree text highlights neither her divinity nor her lineage; Inanna is presented merely as a woman who fears the word of the ruling male Gods. How very different from the Great Queen of the Earth Gods, supreme among the Heaven Gods, whom we encountered in the hymns composed in her honor during the earlier days. How far away seem the days when she was the Loud Thundering Storm that made heavens tremble and the earth quake. How very distant indeed is this pitiful, human figure from

9. For a relatively simple genealogical map see Wolkstein and Kramer 1983, x. This map is, of course, only one version of the family relations in the pantheon. For discussion of the systematic erasure of the Goddesses from Mesopotamian mythology see Frymer-Kensky 1992, 71.

10. In Kramer's less poetic but probably more exact translation, Ereshkigal is said to have been "carried off into the nether world as its prize," and she is not called "queen" (1963, 200).

that of the fierce young Goddess who storms into her father's palace, where he, "afraid of his brutal daughter, has hidden in the innermost chamber," pleading, "I know thee to be impetuous, O my daughter, / For there is no restraint among Goddesses. / What dost thou desire, O Virgin Anath?" (Gordon 1961, 204).[11]

Moved by Inanna's feminine, helpless inability to cope with the creatures that populated her tree, the chivalrous Gilgamesh came to her rescue. Unlike Dumuzi, his predecessor, Gilgamesh did not court Inanna, nor did he aim to win her favors. Instead, he did away with her snake, with her lion-faced Anzu bird and with Lilit; he cut down Inanna's tree, turning it into her throne and bed.

Let us examine the huluppu tree and its creatures: the possessions from which Gilgamesh stripped Inanna naked. Generally, in antiquity, "the tree of Life was one of the primary images of the [typical ancient Great] Goddess herself, in whose immanent presence all pairs of opposites are reconciled" (Baring and Cashford 1991, 496). Earlier in this chapter, we encountered Inanna leaning against a tree, admiring her marvelous vulva. We also know that the Canaanite Queen of Heaven and Earth, Ashera, who may have been one of Inanna's Canaanite counterparts, was quite literally the Tree Goddess, *Ashera* being also the name of a tree.[12] I would like to suggest that the huluppu tree, which houses Inanna's treasures, may have symbolized the Goddess herself as much as her temple. In this context, it is noteworthy that in this story the tree is *not* Inanna's by right: she all but stole it (from the male Gods who forbade her to do so?). Symbolizing the male hero's overcoming of the Goddess, Gilgamesh quite literally cut the tree down.

As for the snake "who could not be charmed," Inanna, like most Great Goddesses, was identified with the snake, who (together with the full moon) symbolized the Goddesses' divine eye, wisdom, regeneration, fertility, free sexuality, and contact with the dead (Gimbutas 1989, 324). The snake was also the guardian of the Goddess's tree (Baring and Cashford, 1991, 490). The

11. Anath/Anat is, very likely, one of Inanna/Ishtar's Canaanite counterparts (for more on this topic see appendix 2.1). Her father is the Canaanite El (the Sumerian Enlil), and her brother-lover-son is Baal. Stories of Anat are outstandingly bloody, and we will probably never know whether that was her "original" characterization, and, if so, whether it was a sympathetic one, or if some of her monstrous violence was added later, as a means of demonizing her. For an example of Anat's brutality see appendix 2.11, note 10.

12. Although they may have started out as distinct entities, "all three major Canaanite goddesses (Ashera, Astarte, and Anat) tended to blend into each other" (Frymer-Kensky 1992, 159). Frymer-Kensky adds that the figurines in the shape of breasted tree trunks found in Jerusalem and Sumeria may be representations of the Goddess (Ashera/Anat/Inanna) as source of life and nourishment. She adds that in Egypt such tree images are identified with Isis, who was a Queen of Heaven and Earth very much like Inanna (160). As for the worship of the tree-Goddess by the Hebrews, Stone proposes that "the sacred branch being passed around in the temple, as described by Ezekiel, may have been the manner in which the fruit was taken as 'communion'" (1976, 220).

Anzu, a lion-faced bird, was a wise, ambitious mythological creature. I noted earlier that Inanna was often depicted with the wings and feet of a bird, and surrounded by lions and owls. The Anzu, a lion and a bird of prey, may have symbolized the Goddess, her wisdom, or some of her majestic characteristics. It may have also signified the sacred *meh*, the Laws of the Universe, with which the Anzu was linked (Dalley 1989, 203; Alster 1971, 120) and which were an important trophy in Inanna's temple (since she obtained them from the God of Wisdom).

Lilit was the last of the creatures Gilgamesh chased away. In Hebrew, *lilit* means "screech owl" and may well have also had the same meaning in Sumerian. (The Akkadian, i.e., Semitic Babylonian for owl was *kilili* [Gimbutas 1989, 216]). Typically associated with female deities, the owl was a "prophetic bird, death messenger, . . . [symbolizing] regenerative qualities" (324). "Nin-ninna," one of Inanna's many names, testifies that like other Great Goddesses she too was the Divine Lady Owl (216, 510).[13] Lilit, then, probably represented Inanna's "owl-like" aspects: she personified the Goddess's sexuality, wisdom, night-preying qualities, regenerative powers, and connection with death and the dead. A Sumerian fragment depicts Lilit as a young maiden, the "hand of Inanna," sent by the Goddess to gather men to her temple (Stone 1984, 158; Hurwitz 1992, 58). Was Lilit Inanna's priestess? In the story of the huluppu tree she is referred to as a "dark maiden." Was her hair dark? Her dress? Her character? Did she do her sacred work by night? Was she a holy streetwalking "prostitute" roaming the streets of Sumer?

Inanna's temple may have accommodated snakes, owls, the sacred *meh*, and the helpmate Lilit. If so, then in the huluppu tree story, the tree, the Anzu, the snake, and Lilit, taken together, may have represented Inanna. Viewed this way, the story narrates the stripping of Inanna of her divine self. Just as the preface demeans the Goddess by failing to acknowledge her divinity, so the plot relates the symbolic disempowerment of Inanna. Ingeniously, the process is disguised as a woman's salvation, as her deliverance from unbecoming, burdening features. The victimized Goddess herself is not only silenced but also claimed to rejoice in her new femininity. Severed from her sexuality, from her power and might, Inanna is now ready to become the feminine icon of patriarchy: a domesticated wife.

The happy ending of the huluppu tree story leaves us with two distinct feminine characters: the domesticated woman in the garden and the exiled dark Lilit. Genesis 3, the fall of Eve (Everywoman) in the Garden of Eden, is a modified version of the former's story, which has been incorporated into

---

13. Another phonetic similarity may have connected this "kilili-lilit" with Ninlil, which was Inanna's name (in Nippur) as Lady Air (Stone 1984, 127). (Ninlil was also the name of Inanna's "grandmother," wife and sister to Enlil, God of Air).

the canonized mythology of Western culture.[14] As in the huluppu tree text, a young woman is forbidden by a male God to come in contact with a primordial tree. Like Inanna, Eve breaches the God's "word" and reaches out for the tree despite an explicit warning. In both stories, a serpent is closely associated with the tree, the woman experiences pain, and she is eventually separated from both the tree and the snake. Furthermore, she is related to the first man (Gilgamesh is Inanna's brother, and Adam is Eve's brother-father-spouse). Her separation from the tree and the snake is related to her dependence on and subordination to that man. In both stories, the tree event leads the young woman to mature womanhood, represented, respectively, by the bed carved out of the huluppu tree and by the subordination to Adam ("thy desire shall be to thy husband, and he shall rule over thee," Gen. 3:16).

In terms of patriarchal indoctrination, Genesis, it seems, picks up where the Sumerian story of Inanna's tree left off. Although Eve's name still connects her with the Goddess ("Eve," *hava*, is said to stand for "the mother of all living"), she no longer carries any of Inanna's unique names; she is a mere woman now. Similarly, she no longer owns her garden and tree, nor her womanhood, sexuality, wisdom, or fertility. Genesis stresses that all are bestowed on her by the male God, as is her existence. All are handed to her with specific instructions and at a price. The woman's fear, at the outset of the Sumerian story, of the "word" of the male God(s) is finally explicitly justified in Genesis: she is severely punished for disobeying it. The allegorical nature of the Hebrew text presents Eve, the tamed part of Inanna, as the

14. It is widely held among Bible scholars that the biblical text is a later edition of four sources, referred to as J, E, D, and P. For a full discussion see Friedman 1989. E. A. Speiser offers a good, clear summary of the issue in the introduction to his Genesis (1964, especially xxii–xxxvii). Also see Coote and Ord 1989, 8–12. The third chapter of Genesis, which textualizes the most familiar and influential version of this story, is generally believed to have been part of the J source, composed in the tenth century B.C.E., approximately four centuries earlier than the P source's story of creation, which is documented in Gen. 1. (For other interpretations see Cassuto 1990; Rashkow 1993, 110.) I see no conflict between treating the text as four different sources for analysis of the ancient society that produced the Hebrew Bible, and as a literary text when discussing the book's influence on later history, or just as a text per se.

The composers of Eve in the garden, as well as the story's original audience, must have been familiar with some version of the story of Inanna and the huluppu tree. At the very least, their culture shared many of its underlying concepts and images with the Sumerian culture that told the story of Inanna and her tree. As an example of such common underlying concepts and images, consider that in Sumerian the same word, *ti,* meant both "rib" and "life," and that *Nin-ti* would have been "the lady who gives life" and also "the lady of the rib." Within Sumerian mythology this related to the "Paradise Myth," in which the Goddess Ninhursag cursed Enki (who ate plants she had planted) and turned her eye of life away from him. When she was persuaded to return and save his life, she healed him by creating eight deities, each fit to cure one of his ailing body parts. One of those deities was Nin-ti, lady of the rib, and also lady of life (Kramer 1945, 9, 21). Baring and Cashford convincingly claim that "the Yahwist writer of Genesis 2 and 3 was undoubtedly aware of this double meaning" (1991, 493).

monotheistic West's first Everywoman: no longer Great Goddess, just wife and mother. And Genesis, scholars believe, is "one of the most read and most influential of biblical books"; "Genesis 1–3, perhaps more than any other biblical text, has influenced the way men and women relate to one another in the Western world" (Fewell and Gunn 1993, 20, 22).

The striking differences between the two stories include the Hebrew replacement of the young woman's distress and liberation with her sin, punishment, guilt, and shame. But the most significant difference is Lilit's complete deletion from the biblical narration of Eve's story. In the Hebrew Bible, Eve and Lilit have been carefully separated into two distinct stories: that of the first woman and that of the female stalker.

As will be demonstrated in the next chapter, the ambivalent relationship between the images of the domesticated wife and that of the female stalker has played a significant role in the translation of the stalking story into moral panics.

Decline of the Goddess and the Substitution of Lilit, the Female Stalker

Even in the spring of her divine rule, Inanna/Ishtar may have always had her "dark aspects"; her glorious self may have always cast fearsome, deadly shadow images. But the more she was feared by the rising patriarchy, the more her powers were personified as evil mythological creatures, which grew strong and fearsome. One such personification of Inanna's deadly power was her dark other-self sister, Ereshkigal, queen of Hell and Death. Lilit, the owl-like maiden, was also a dark personification of Inanna's challenging sexuality, wisdom, and connection with the dead. Another devilish personification of the Goddess's power was Lamashtu, the mythological female night stalker, "the most terrible of all Sumerian demonesses" (Langdon 1964, 358). This wretched creature was not only the source of nightmares (371), but was also said to infest rivers and highways, to drink the blood of men, and to snatch human babies and kill them (Langdon 1964, 369; Frymer-Kensky 1992, 78).

Inanna and her monstrous shadow image, Lamashtu, were closely associated: Lamashtu, like Inanna, was said to roam about at night, entering houses at will; she also shared the Goddess's epithet *sahiratu* (Frymer-Kensky 1992, 78) and was even frequently referred to as "Ishtar" and "Inanna" (Langdon 1964, 368).[15] Wolfgang Fauth observes that "Lamastu, like Inanna,

15. Hurwitz argues that Ishtar (Inanna) and Lamashtu were two separate Goddesses, and that it was in the Hebrew image of Lilit that they were integrated (1992, 35–36.) I am more convinced by the scholars mentioned previously who claim that such a merger occurred earlier.

has a close association with lions, wears her hair loose, and is the daughter of An. She is quite possibly the feared side of Inanna" (Frymer-Kensky 1992, 232, n. 57). Accordingly, in one stone plaque Lamashtu is depicted as "the lion-headed demoness, holding a double-headed serpent in each hand. A dog sucks at her right breast, a pig at her left breast" (Langdon 1964, 367). In an amulet, "her feet are those of a bird of prey," like Inanna's (367; in some incantations she takes the form of a wolf). Not surprisingly, Frymer-Kensky concludes that "antipathy to Ishtar takes its extreme (though perhaps unconscious) form in the depiction of Lamashtu, the demon who kills newborn children. This demon . . . may very well be the fearsome side of Ishtar's character split off and demonized into a separate character, an evil doppelganger to the mighty Goddess" (Frymer-Kensky 1992, 78).

I propose that the demonized personifications of the Goddess's powers—Ereshkigal, Lamashtu, and Lilit—were ultimately combined into a single shadow image, a dark character that embodied a negative version of Inanna's once admired endowments. As the Goddess lost her divine might and became the biblical Eve, so her dark self grew strong and devilish, overshadowing her completely in the collective conscious and unconscious. The divine Goddess of Life and Death was thus substituted by her shadow image of a stalking demon.[16]

More vividly than any of the other female demons, Lilit personified the combination of the Goddess's most powerful, attractive traits, which were the most threatening to the patriarchy. Those traits, feminine sexuality, divine wisdom, and connection with death, have long been associated with every femme fatale. Lilit also inherited the Goddess's most prominent feature: her divine eyes. It is therefore not surprising that Inanna's shadow image, the mythological female stalker, greatly resembles Lilit and that, in the Hebrew culture, that image was named Lilit. For that reason I will from here on call the female stalker by her proper name: Lilit.

A Neo-Babylonian tablet dating from 600 B.C.E. contains the following incantation, which vividly depicts Inanna/Ishtar and her priestesses as monstrous, evil stalkers:

> Murderous witch, deceitful woman, sorceress, ecstatic exorcist, enchanting snake charmer, *qadishtu*, *naditu*, *ishtaritu*, *kulmashitu*,

---

16. Another step in the patriarchal subordination of these feminine images is the twentieth-century psychoanalytic depiction of Ereshkigal (as "old witch"), Inanna (as "young virgin"), and Lamashtu-Lilit (as "young witch") as fundamental universal eternal archetypes of the feminine. In his classic work *The Great Mother* (1974), Erich Neumann transforms the images of the denigrated Goddess into universal, "natural" inner images of (mostly negative) femininity, supposedly symbolizing irrationality and restrictive psychological limitations.

hunter by night, stalker by day, defiler of the heavens, who dirties the earth, who muzzles the mouth of the Gods, who closes the womb of the Goddesses, killer of men, unsparing of women, a sneering despoiler, whose spells and witchcraft none can fathom. (Emphasis added)[17]

The stalking witch in this incantation is referred to as "qadishtu, naditu, ishtaritu, kulmashitu." Ishtaritu and Naditu may have been priestesses, or otherwise related to the temples of the Goddesses, and thus symbolized Inanna/Ishtar. Qadishtu might have been "a wetnurse, a midwife, a functionary (primarily a singer) in the cult of Adad, occasionally an archivist, and in later times even a sorceress" (Gruber 1992, 42–43). Her name suggests a possible connection with the Semitic Qudshu, Holiness, which served among the west Semites (Canaanites) as an epithet for Ashera/Anat.[18] The incantation's title, *maqlu*, means "burning," and incantations of this category were "intended to counteract the evil machinations of people through black magic. Wax or wooden figurines of the . . . sorceress who bewitched the supplicant are melted or burnt in the fire, and the conjurations that compose Maqlu address . . . either these sorcerers—in effigy—or the fire God who is to destroy them" (Reiner 1958, 2–3). The subsequent lines of the incantation call on the male Gods Marduk and Ea to catch the witch and change her spell, to cause her to stagger and to hand her over to the hero Gira, who should break her knot and cast back onto her all the spells she had cast on others.

Thus it seems that by the middle of the first millennium B.C.E., the female characters who had once been revered as divine had become an evil stalker, associated with witchcraft. In most texts following this period, this stalking female devil is specifically referred to as Lilit (Stone 1984, 127). Furthermore, this incantation and others may document an ancient (perhaps the first?) stalking moral panic, in which women, perhaps women associated with Goddess worship, were accused of embodying Lilit, the mythological female stalker.

17. The incantation appears in Maqlu 3, lines 40–61. The original text, translated into German, was published by Gerhard Meier in Berlin in 1937. The translation into English of lines 40–55 cited here is Gruber's (1992, 40). For the translation from German to English of the whole text I thank my friends Sabine Lauer and Werner Zdouc.

18. Discussing a Phoenician pantheon of the city Tyre, Albright describes a beautiful stela "with 'Holiness' (Qudshu) in the center. She is standing stark naked on a lion, with a spiral headdress . . . and in her left [hand she is holding] stylized serpents" (Albright 1968, 127). Cross understands the Qudsu, "holiness," to have been an epithet of Ashera. "Of special interest is the Winchester relief on which three names, Qudsu, Astart, Anat, appear revealing the confusion of the three goddesses, but also using the Qudsu as the equivalent of Ashera" (1973, 34).

Moon, Owl, Eye: From Divine Symbols to Symbols of Stalking

The snake, the owl, the eye, and the moon were all once symbols and attributes of the Great Goddess and her divine powers. These symbols became associated with Lilit as part of the same process that reduced the Goddess to Eve and diminished her powerful features. It was Lilit, not Eve, who inherited the Goddess's symbolic iconography.[19] Accordingly, the ancient symbols were transformed from emblems of divine virtue into omens of stalking evil. The moon, for example, when identified with the Goddess, was a symbol of life and regeneration. But when identified with Lilit, the moon's cyclical appearance came to represent menacing stalking. Its return every month was felt to bind men to times and memories they would have preferred to leave behind; lunar cycles seemed to trap them in their ever-returning pasts. Thus, uncontrollable returns of primordial supernatural entities became a constituting element of our culture's notion of stalking, which evolved through the image of Lilit and the moon. It is no coincidence that the moon, and particularly the full moon and the lunar cycle, has played a prominent role in stalking stories throughout the centuries (narratives involving werewolves, witches, and vampires are obvious examples).

The eye is another prominent symbol that encountered a similar fate.[20] O. G. S. Crawford found that as early as the fourth millennium B.C.E., a feminine deity, which may have been Inanna/Ishtar, was portrayed in the image of staring eyes (1957, 27–28). He claims that the "eye Goddess" spread from the Fertile Crescent (Mesopotamia) to all corners of the world, including Greece, Italy, Iberia, Brittany, Ireland, Britain, Africa, and the Canary Islands. Embracing these findings, Gimbutas interprets them as testifying to

19. This iconographic point is well illustrated by the scholarly debate (or confusion?) concerning a terra cotta Sumerian relief dated 2000 B.C.E. and known as the Burney Relief. "This fascinating object depicts a nude female figure, only partially anthropomorphised. She has wings and owl's feet. She is standing on two lions couchant and is flanked by owls. Frankfort's long accepted judgment was that the figure is Lilith" (Trombley 1985, 3–4) See also Neumann 1974, plate 126; Liptzin 1976, 66–74; Zuckoff 1976, 7; Patai 1990, plate 31; Hurwitz 1992, 84; all interpret the relief as portraying Lilit. In 1983, however, a prominent Sumeriologist, Thorkil Jacobsen, announced that the figure in the Burney Relief portrayed not Lilit, but Inanna (Trombley 1985, 3–4). Later scholars adopted this reading (see Baring and Cashford 1991, 199, 217). I suggest these conflicting interpretations merely testify to the close link between the two mythological figures.

20. So closely was the eye associated with the image of the Great Goddess that at least in one language (Latin) the same word was used for both eye and vulva (de Vries 1974, 170). Some of the Goddess's other symbols, such as the full moon and the owl, clearly resembled the eye and referred to it. Gimbutas suggests that a decorative pattern relates the Eye Goddess to the Bird Goddess with her "characteristically owlish appearance. The round eyes so definitively establish her identity that often no auxiliary anthropomorphic features were deemed necessary" (1989, 51).

a universally held symbolic concept of Divine Eyes (Gimbutas 1989, 54). She claims that "the large eyes with which the Goddess is portrayed strongly suggest the epithet 'All-seeing' for her. However, the symbolism which surrounds the eyes speaks for an even more fundamental attribute, namely that the eyes, like the Goddess's breasts or mouth, are a Divine Source" (51).[21]

Crawford notes that "the use of the eye as a religious and magical symbol . . . is rare in Mesopotamia after the close of Early Dynastic III (about the middle of the 3rd millennium)" (1957, 78). I would like to propose that this decline in the eye's religious status was complemented by the rising fear of the "evil eye," which apparently originated, and certainly thrived, in Mesopotamia (Roberts 1976, 234; Dundes 1992, 39). This dual process coincided with the gradual decline of the Great Goddess and with the emergence of Lilit, the demon stalker. The Great Goddess's all-seeing life-giving eye has become Lilit's fatal "evil eye," bringing illness, death, destruction, and sorrow, especially to newborns and to their young mothers. Not surprisingly, Moss and Cappannari, who define the evil eye as one embodiment of the source of evil, found that the spirit of Lilit and the evil eye both hovered over the same cultural area (1976, 2).[22] (Another nonsurprise: since antiquity, the most universal sign used to guard against the evil eye has been the phallus and anything resembling it [Potts 1982, 7–11]; the phallic symbol of the male Gods was the natural remedy to counter Lilit's evil eye). From this cultural context the notion of stalking developed a close link with the image of a penetrating, controlling, potentially harmful gaze.[23]

The arresting quality attributed to the eyes of the stalker brings to mind the Greek myth of Medusa, the snake-coiffed Gorgon whose hideous gaze turned men to stone. In Hesiod's version of her story, Medusa had been a beautiful young maiden who was seduced (i.e., raped) by Poseidon in Athena's shrine. As punishment, Athena transformed Medusa's hair into snakes and gave her look its fatal effect. With Athena's help, Perseus decapitated Medusa as she slept, using a mirror to avoid looking directly at her face. The severed head was then placed in the center of Athena's shield, where Medusa's staring eyes maintained their deadly power, now in the ser-

---

21. Gimbutas describes a European figurine "with slit eyes from which streams flow down over full breasts" (1989, 51, fig. 86).

In the Sumerian "Paradise Myth" (see note 14), the Goddess's eye and look are clearly the divine source and nourishment of all life.

22. To this day, in the Middle East it is women among humans, and snakes among animals, that are particularly suspected of casting the evil eye (Spooner 1976, 80; Potts 1982, 5). For a variety of discussions of the evil eye see Dundes 1992.

23. It can be argued that even on an instinctual level, the gaze, the fixed staring eye, has deep psychological implications. Some advocate that the gaze might be a biological means of conveying and responding to dominance and submission. This line of thought complements the cultural analysis.

vice of the Olympian Goddess (Tripp 1974, 364).[24] This is Medusa's "official Olympian biography." But Medusa may have had an earlier life, previous to that narrated by Hesiod (Phillips 1984, 20). Medusa may have once been a beautiful, benevolent snake-and-eye deity of regeneration (Gimbutas 1989, xxiii). Maybe she started her mythological life as an independent pre-Olympian Goddess and was then denigrated and demonized by the patriarchal Olympians, who, threatened by her powers, associated her with the fearsome (originally Babylonian) image of the deadly staring head (Potts 1982, 30–31);[25] this association may have triggered the creation of the common biography, as narrated by Hesiod. If so, the monstrous Medusa was Lilit's Greek mirror image. Not surprisingly, much like Lilit's, Medusa's features in Greek art included, besides the staring eyes and the wild, snakelike hair, a protruding tongue and fangs (27).

Since Lilit and Medusa are twin mythological images raised by neighboring cultures, a mutual influence between them seems likely. It also seems likely that the two appeared in Western culture at the same time. The archetypal Lilit, as we know her, may therefore contain not only the Mesopotamian queen of Death (Ereshkigal), the baby-snatcher (Lamashtu) and the owl-priestess-"prostitute" (Lilit), but also elements of the Greek Medusa. The notion that the stalker's gaze is paralyzing, hypnotizing, may have originated in Medusa. It is fitting that "the drops of blood that fell from Medusa's severed head into the Libyan Desert were transformed into snakes" (Tripp 1974, 364) and likewise produced Lamia, the snake-woman, who was born as a queen and raised in the Libyan desert, raped by Zeus, and finally transformed, by Olympic mythology, into the fearsome paradigmatic succubus.[26] This Lamia was to be "officially" united with Lilit in the Vulgate (the Latin translation of the Bible). But in order to better understand the Hebrew Lilit, who was united by the Vulgate with Lamia, let us examine Lilit's image and history in the Hebrew culture and its religious texts.

24. Once fixed in Athena's shield, Medusa's fatal eyes served as a constant reminder of the danger the Medusa had posed as a fatal woman, and of her harsh fate. At the same time this was also a clear sign of Athena's glorious victory, and a statement that Athena was now the sole owner of the evil eye. (The owl figure, as well as the snakes, which accompanied Athena on many coins and other artifacts, may have served the very same purpose.) In the next chapter I show how, much as Athena placed Medusa's head on her shield, so YHWA took on Inanna's all-seeingness.

25. Works of art reveal that the Goddess Artemis (the Roman Diana), once a Great Moon Mother Goddess who was transformed in the Olympian era into the brutal virgin Goddess of childbirth and hunting (Tripp 1974, 105), received a similar treatment: her body too was sometimes combined with a deadly staring face (Gimbutas 1989, xxiii).

26. A succubus is a female demon that copulates with men, whereas an incubus is a male demon that copulates with women. These mythological creatures were incorporated into Christian theology and were widely believed to exist.

Lilit's Hebrew/Jewish Story

Mesopotamian mythology furnished Lilit with her basic attributes and symbols, but the Hebrew culture provided her with a full biography, a character and a story, which gave rise to the specific, unique components that we identify with stalking narratives.

The Hebrew Bible found Lilit in the wastelands, to which Gilgamesh had confined her in the story of the huluppu tree, and chose to leave her there. Isaiah 34:14 describes a forsaken land that "from generation to generation . . . shall lie waste; none shall pass through it for ever and ever. . . . The wild beasts of the desert shall also meet with the wild beasts of the island, and the satyr shall cry to his fellow; Lilit also shall rest there, and find for herself a place of rest." This is Lilit's single appearance in the entire Hebrew Bible. For just as Lilit was banished from (the story of) Eden, so the Hebrews barred Inanna's descendent from all their official, recorded stories. But surely not even the fiercest prophets could banish her away from men's dreams, or from their oral stories. And even if Lilit gradually faded from their collective memory, the Hebrew's exile in Babylon during the sixth century B.C.E (after the destruction of the First Temple) provided them with an opportunity to become reacquainted with Lilit and be reminded of her horrifying charm. In any event, even though Jewish authoritative texts before the Babylonian Talmud never mentioned Lilit by name, female creatures that may have been orally associated with her appear as early as the *midrashei agada* (legendary interpretations) documented in Bereshit Rabba (composed in Israel during the first two centuries C.E.). In Bereshit Rabba page 325, we read Rabbi Simon's playful speculation that during the 130 years when Adam was separated from Eve (after their banishment from the garden), the female ghosts (or spirits) came to be warmed and inseminated by him (whereas male ghosts did the same to Eve). This same legend appears later in the Babylonian Talmud (Bava Batra 73b), but this time the creatures "warming themselves" with Adam are called *lilin* and their offspring are devils. This tradition may have been added by Babylonian Amoraim (Talmudic scholars) influenced by Babylonian myth, but it may have already been attached, orally, to the earlier *agadaic* version.

The other context in which a Lilit-like female appears in scriptures is when references are made to "Adam's first wife." Gen. 2:23 (in a more literal translation than the King James version), quotes Adam as saying upon first seeing Eve: "this time bone from my bone and flesh from my flesh." Referring to Adam's "this time," Rabbi Yehuda Bar Rabbi said that before Eve, God must have created another woman for Adam, but because Adam had been awake to watch the whole bloody process of her creation, he was repelled by her, and God had to try again (Bereshit Rabba 271). This and other *midrashei agada* (legendary interpretations) established the legend of Adam's first wife, or the "first Eve."[27] Later sources testify that this "first Eve" was identified as Lilit. One other *midrash agada* attached to Gen. 5:2 ("Male and female created he them") adds another aspect to Lilit's story and character. Said Rabbi Shmuel Bar Nahman: when God created the first man he created him double with two faces; he then sawed him in the middle and making two backs, separated a male and a female. So the first man and woman were one and the same until violently torn apart. Closer than brother and sister, they were twins; sharing the same genetic makeup, they are literally each other's doubles; when torn apart, each was the other's missing half.[28]

Unnamed, Lilit also entered some noncanonized Jewish writings. In the Testament of Solomon, a Judeo-Hellenistic 3rd-century text (written in Greek), there appears "a female demon who is known by tens of thousands of names and moves about the world at night visiting women in childbirth and endeavoring to strangle their newborn babies" (*Encyclopedia Judaica* s.v. "Lilith"). This text had little if any influence on later developments within Jewish culture, but the Church fathers, such as Hieronymus, were well familiar with it.

Lilit made her first appearance in mainstream Jewish religious text in the Babylonian Talmud. In this canonical document, composed in Babylon during the second exile, (between the second and fifth centuries C.E.), Lilit is only mentioned in passing, but under her own name. We hear of her long hair (Eruvin 100b) and of her wings (Nidda 24b). Men are warned not to sleep alone, lest she come and seize them (Shabat 151b).

This is the Lilit that Hieronymus had in mind when, at the end of the fourth century C.E., in his Latin version of the Bible, he renamed Lilit Lamia (see the Vulgate, Isaiah 14). This combined image, coupling the Hebraic Lilit with her Hellenistic counterpart, became the official Catholic version of Lilit.

Lamia had once been the Libyan prehistoric Great Mother Snake Goddess, a queen of heaven and earth who was later reconstructed in Greek mythology as a devouring sexual monster (Edwards 1991, 208). In her later, Olympian life, Lamia was a vampiristic baby-snatching demon, with a

27. The "first Eve" helps explain the two biblical versions narrating the creation of the first woman: that in Gen. 1:27, and the better-known one in Gen. 2:21–22. Most modern biblical scholars attribute the version in Genesis 1 to a P source and the other (rib) story to E documents (see Speiser, 1964, xxiv, xxx).

28. For more on the theme of the double-faced androgynous first human in other cultures, see Rappoport 1966, 152. As for the twins motif, let me just add that already in ancient Egyptian mythology Isis and Osiris were twins (Kinsley 1989, 165). The Jewish sages were fond of the special closeness of twins, and they generously provided biblical characters with such siblings: Cain and Abel each received a twin sister (Bereshit Rabba 341), as did all twelve of Jacob's sons (Bakan 1979, 70).

woman's face and breasts and the body of a snake.[29] The Lamia lured men
and had intercourse with them by "riding" on top of them; she drank their
blood and ate their flesh. She also devoured the babies she snatched from
their mothers' arms. The Olympian mythologists furnished Lamia with a
narrative to explain her transformation into a stalking, vampiristic succubus: Once upon a time, Lamia was the beautiful queen of Libya, beloved
(raped?) by Zeus. When Hera, Zeus's jealous wife, killed all the children that
Lamia had borne Zeus, Lamia's pain transformed her into an ugly, old baby
snatcher (Hera was the protectress of childbirth and children, and Lamia
threatened her protégées). Lamia "finally became a beast and went to live in
a cave" (Lederer 1968, 62). It was there that she met Lilit and happily merged
with her.[30]

In light of Lilit and Lamia's histories, it seems only natural that in the
next known Jewish text containing Lilit legends, the Alphabet of Ben Sira,
Lilit is the First Woman, Adam's first wife, who flew away from the garden
when he refused to let her "ride" on top of him. She became the Devil's
lover, and to this night, so the story goes, she continues to stalk Adam's sons,
calling on them when they sleep alone, causing their wet dreams (symbolic
masturbation? fornication?) and stealing their semen (their source of fertility
and symbol of their patriarchal power) to breed her own demons. Of course,
she also stalks and attacks women in labor and abducts babies.

The Alphabet, probably composed in Gaonic Babylon around the ninth
century C.E. (Yassif 1984, 19–29), masterfully wove together many diverse
elements, forming a convincingly individuated character of Lilit and a full-
blown mythological story of stalking. Despite important later developments, the Alphabet deserves the credit for creating and canonizing the Lilit
archetype, an archetype that has grown to be a distinguished and persistent
member in the community that thrives within the Western collective unconscious.

The following is my reconstruction of a narrative that integrates two
versions of the Alphabet (as translated into Hebrew by Yassif), Genesis, and
the midrashic legends mentioned above.[31] I believe the account encapsulates
many elements and symbols of Lilit's story as it may have been known and
told within the Jewish world starting at the early Middle Ages. This Lilit

29. On the Lamia see Liptzin 1976, 67, 69; de Vries 1974, 289; Osborne 1994, 73; Abarbanell 1994, 26; Edwards, 1991, 207–14; and Lederer 1968, 62. Langdon has an interesting
take on the Lamia. He claims that she was a Sumerian demon, who was assimilated by the
Greeks into another Sumerian demon, called Gallu. "Gallu has survived to the present day
as one of the names of the demoness Lilith, and occurs repeatedly in Christian demonology
of the Middle Ages as Gaou, Gilou" (Langdon 1964, 365). He also identifies the Lamia as
Lamashtu (366). Hurwitz embraces this identification (1992, 43).

30. Like Medusa, Lamia did not cease to exist independently, but she took on some of
Lilit's unique features.

31. *Midrash* in Hebrew is "creative interpretation"; an authoritative, canonized
"Midrash" can be legendary, or legal.

found her way into the larger Christian European West, a development that plays a central role in the chapters that follow.[32] Ben Sira's linkage of Lilit with the Devil will prove especially significant there.

Lilit's Story: A Reconstruction

In the beginning God created in his own image Adam/Lilit, a double-faced human creature. Then God sawed them in two, female and male created he them, and he blessed them, saying, Be fruitful and multiply. Soon they quarreled about which of them would sleep on top of the other, both wanting and claiming the right to do so. Finally Adam lost his temper, at which Lilit remembered the Ineffable Name (of God), and thereby flew away.[33]

At Adam's request, God sent three angels to persuade Lilit to go back to the garden, but she refused, saying she had already had another (better) lover, the Devil, and that according to the biblical law a woman cannot return to a man after having slept with another. She added that she had also learned that her destiny was to kill human newborns. Finally, after some discussion, the angels made her promise that she would not harm babies protected by amulets containing the angels' names. They also made her agree to the death of one hundred of her devilish offsprings every day.[34]

And the Lord God said, It is not good that the man should be alone; I will make an helpmate for him. And the Lord God caused a deep sleep to fall upon Adam, and he took one of his ribs and made a woman, and Adam said this time she is bone from my bone and flesh from my flesh, she shall be called woman, for she was taken out of man.

And then the serpent woman, Lilit,[35] persuaded Eve to eat from the forbidden tree, and Adam imitated her, and their eyes opened,

32. Liptzin documents Jerome's writing that the Hebrews call the Lamia by the name Lilit.

33. The word "remembered" is a literal translation of the Hebrew version of the Ben Sira texts.

34. When creating Man out of the Earth, God signed a contract with Earth, promising her that one hundred humans would die daily and return to be part of her. Divorced from Adam, Lilit was now considered an independent entity and was required to pay her own taxes.

35. In Jewish Agada (such as Bereshit Rabba 278 and on), the snake in the garden was often portrayed as a male creature who tempted Eve and maybe even "polluted" her by having intercourse with her. The portrayal of the snake in the garden as feminine, and as Lilit, was probably a Christian development (see "Lilith, Winged and Crowned, with Serpent's Tail, Offers the Apple to Eve," Baring and Cashford 1991, fig. 14). As I implied, I believe this to be an outcome of the uniting of Lilit with the snake woman Lamia. In any event, in later medieval Judaism, and especially in the kabbalah, Lilit and the serpent became identified,

and they knew that they were naked. And they heard the voice of the Lord God walking in the garden, and hid themselves, but the Lord God saw and knew all. And the Lord God said unto the serpent woman, because thou hast done this, thou art cursed above all creatures; upon thy belly shalt thou go, and I shall put enmity between thee and the woman, and between thy seed and her seed. And since that day humans and demons have been enemies, and demons bring plagues unto humans.

Unto the woman he said, your sexuality will no longer be a source of joy and power; it shall cause your subordination to Adam, my son, and it will cause you the pains and bleeding of first intercourse, monthly menstruation, and labor.

And the Lord God drove out the man from the Garden of Eden unto the ground, to work and sweat and die there, and the man, blaming it all on his wife, knew her, and left her to live alone for 130 years. Then Lilit saw that Adam was good-looking, and so she came to him and knew him, and bore devils of his semen. And Adam returned to his wife Eve. And so to this night Lilit still preys on Eve's babies and takes their lives. She comes unto those of Adam's older sons who sleep alone, tempting them in their wet sweet dreams, bearing devils of their stolen semen. These devils bring misfortune and plagues on the children of Eve.

Lilit's reappearance in the story of creation parallels her mythological repetitive return to men's beds and dreams; both are highly "uncanny" in the full Freudian sense. To Freud, "uncanny" meant "that class of the frightening which leads back to what is known of old and long familiar" and which has been intensely suppressed (1919, 220). A significant factor of uncanniness is "involuntary repetition," such as the sensation of reliving the same experience several times (237). According to Freud, the uncanny repetitive return of one's childhood double, once "an assurance of immortality," as a thing of terror and harbinger of death, reveals suppressed infantile complexes connected with primitive beliefs (234–35). Freud asserts that "the quality of uncanniness can only come from the fact of the 'double' being a creation dating back to a very early mental stage, long since surmounted—a stage, incidentally, at which it wore a more friendly aspect. The 'double' has become a thing of terror, just as, after the collapse of their religion, the Gods turned into demons" (236). These notions uncannily describe the story of

---

and this is the basis for my adding this twist here (for Lilit's snake image see Tishby 1991, 538). Aschkenasy adds that "interestingly, an illustration in a sixteenth-century Italian translation of Josephus's Jewish Antiquities depicts Lilith with the face of a woman and the body of a snake lurking behind the trees in the garden and spying on Adam and Eve" (1986, 50).

Lilit, her place in both our private and collective unconscious and the concept of female stalking.

Lilit continued to reappear throughout the long history of Jewish culture.[36] In medieval Jewish mysticism she became Queen of Devils and was said to copulate with God in his temple in Jerusalem. She was represented as both a beautiful young temptress and an ugly old hag. She became Man's fierce prosecutor in the heavenly court. But it is her portrayal as the autonomous First Woman, Adam's estranged sister-lover, that best captures and establishes her most significant features as the archetypal female stalker.

After millennia of exile from her tree and her garden (the exile inflicted on her by Gilgamesh in the huluppu tree), Lilit returns to the garden; no longer an owl-like prostitute-priestess, she is now a confident, unruly, assertive woman. She is not only Adam's equal, but his braver, lost other-self. Her long, wild hair and fiery, dark eyes, her erotic night flights and her sensational affair with the Devil, her rebellious will and uncontrollable temper are legendary. She is totally free and completely *unknown:* visiting Adam in his sleep, she never allows him to know her (in that biblical sense he so craves). Her stalking of him subverts patriarchal sexual norms. Flying in and out of his bed and dreams in the dark of night, she never lets him control and objectify her. On the contrary, she reserves the power to gaze at him in his most vulnerable nakedness: in his sleep.

Lilit, Man's dark shadow and double (his "anima," if you like,[37] whom he prefers to present as Eve's shadow), makes him engage in every sexual practice prohibited by monotheistic patriarchy and its jealous God; mockingly she personifies them all. She is incest (being Adam's twin sister), masturbation (being his dark self), and night emission. She is sexuality for its own, nonprocreative sake. She lures Adam to do everything he was taught not to do, everything he knows he does not want to do—or doesn't he? Lilit offers Man an orgiastic gift, robbing him of control and eternity. She extends an invitation to return to their primordial, blissful unity, subverting the patriarchal language of distinctions and definitions. Beyond distinctions, she calls Man back to the legendary presexed, hermaphroditic human existence. She offers Man freedom from his responsibilities, from obligations, and from power; she can release him from Time and History. She symbolizes the ultimate alternative and also its ultimate price. This mature Lilit is an archetypal stalker because the fear and attraction she evokes in some men continue to be relevant and are at the heart of our culture's concept of female stalking.

36. For a short summary of Lilit's major appearances in Jewish culture see appendix 2.2.

37. For discussions of Lilit as masculine projection see D. L. Carmody 1992, 92; Schaafsma 1987, 59.

From the point of view of the social order, the stalking Lilit is at once deeply subversive and effectively disciplinary. While patriarchy was indoctrinating men and women in their social roles as Adams and Eves, Lilit allowed for the channeling of some men's (and maybe some women's) subversive fantasies into the imagery of the archetypal female stalker. She also frightened them all into conformity and thus served as a disciplinary mechanism. She was perfectly designed for the job. Deeply relevant to both men and women, she was, simultaneously, dreadful and a part of every secret attraction and sexual indulgence. Through Lilit, the female stalker became an uncanny double, an other-self phantom repeatedly returning to incite Man to forbidden non- or prepatriarchal freedom and to threaten his hegemony. The stalking woman came to represent oppressed (or repressed) non- or prepatriarchal femininity, lurking and potentially undermining patriarchal values and social order. It triggered a fascinating and frightening sensation, which society and patriarchy could, and can, bank on when necessary to establish solidarity among men.

Lilit's uncanny return throughout history is linked with outbursts of deep insecurities in the lives of men and in the history of patriarchy. Using Freud's phrase, these insecurities manifest patriarchy's "suppressed infantile complexes."[38] When these insecurities are overwhelming, such outbursts may incite moral panics.

---

38. A more Jungian formulation would have it that people call up negative shadow roles at times of social change, because they find the new roles they are expected to play unnerving (Zuckoff 1976, 9).

On the (Un)approachability
of Antiquity

Embarking upon the voyage into the past, let me address, briefly, the possibility of, and the perils in, any passage into antiquity in general, and into prehistory in particular.

J. J. Bachofen was the first nineteenth-century scholar of antiquity to propose a major, highly influential (and just as controversial) theory suggesting that a prehistorical matriarchy had preceded the patriarchal structure of culture and society.[1] He based his conclusions both on material archeological findings and on "deconstructive" readings of ancient texts.[2] Although Bachofen's theory was widely discredited by scholars a century later, the fierce controversy concerning prepatriarchy and matriarchy has not lost its edge, and any contemporary discussion of the Great Goddesses of antiquity must address it. This dispute remains unresolved because, as Bachofen himself admitted, "any penetrating and coherent understanding of antiquity is impossible" (1967, 75), particularly regarding prehistoric cultures. The difficulties in deciphering antiquity are manifold. One major obstacle is that the understanding of any historical period requires an understanding of the period that preceded it: "All historical institutions presuppose earlier stages of formation: nowhere in history do we find a beginning, but always a continuation, never a cause which is not at the same time an effect." Of course, such inescapable, endless regression must, to a large degree, be ignored if antiquity is to be approached. Another obstacle in deciphering antiquity is the bewildering inconsistencies one finds in ancient mythological texts, which often contradict each other or simply do not add up. A third obstacle is our natural tendency to perceive other cultures through our own contemporary concepts; this unconscious process superimposes later worldviews on earlier phases. Last, but not least, is the language barrier, which prevents us from fully grasping the exact meanings of words and phrases.

1. Anything before the beginning of written documents is "prehistory." Since documentation dates only to ancient patriarchy, anything that may have existed earlier (like matriarchy) is by definition prehistory.

2. There is a wide consensus among scholars of antiquity that any culture always contains traces of earlier ideas, and that if a transformation did occur from prepatriarchal Near Eastern cultures to patriarchal ones, then it "was not a replacement of one culture by another but a gradual hybridization of two different symbolic systems" (Gimbutas 1989, 318). It is therefore legitimate and essential to reconstruct earlier (prepatriarchal?) stories, voices, characters, and ideas based on "deconstructive" readings of ancient texts and ritualistic objects that consciously conform to patriarchic and/or monotheistic mythology. In my "deconstructive" treatment of ancient materials, I follow Bachofen's example.

The concept of virginity illustrates both the cultural and the linguistic obstacles that prevent us from fully grasping antiquity. Scholars believe that in ancient Near Eastern cultures virginity did not denote a biological condition, but rather an independent attitude to life, which did not in any way conflict with sexual practices.[3] Praise of virginity and representation of Goddesses as virgins may have had a different meaning to the ancients than we would expect based on our modern usage of the term. Similarly, scholars claim that in antiquity the snake symbolized neither temptation nor phallic imagery, but wisdom, longevity (or eternal life), regeneration, and good fortune, all of which were symbolically connected with the Goddess.[4] In ancient stories, therefore, the snake may have had a completely different symbolic role than we are likely to assume. As for the moon, Shuttle and Redgrove claim that it was not only used as a calendar, but was also thought of as the true lover of every woman (1978, 108, 148). Most other scholars, probably relying on different texts, think of the moon as a manifestation of the Goddess. Preferring one interpretation to the other is almost arbitrary. Time and life (like the moon and the snake) seem to have commonly been perceived in antiquity as circular rather than linear, consisting of ever-recurring stages of birth, maturity and sexuality, death, and rebirth; but scholars, interpreting different texts in different manners, do not agree on whether the time unit of the ritualistic cycle of regeneration was a week (Shuttle and Redgrove 1978, 233), a month (155), a year (Albright 1968, 110; Kinsley 1989, 121), or seven years (Gordon 1961, 184).

The concept of incest in antiquity is another example that can illustrate the obstacles mentioned above (while supplying us with background for the following discussion). Ancient mythology seems to describe sexual relations that we understand as incestuous. How are we to understand these testimonies? It may be that at some point in time the incest taboo did not exist (Albright 1968, 111; Abarbanell 1994, 167), or that it was constructed differently than it is today. Some scholars suggest that the ban on sibling incest referred only to siblings of a common mother (Bakan 1979, 67; Diner 1965, 80); if so, stories that we understand as involving incest may not have had that meaning in antiquity. Another possible interpretation of stories of sexual relations between siblings is that the word we translate as "sister" also meant "wife" (Albright 1968, 111), or "chief wife" (Rashkow 1993, 47). According to this line of thought, narratives that we read as depicting sexual liaisons between brothers and sisters may have referred instead to husbands

3. See Albright 1968, 113; Phillips 1984, 142; Baring and Cashford 1991, 197; Osborne 1994, 28–37; Shuttle and Redgrove 1978, 181.
4. See Gimbutas 1989, 121; Lerner 1986, 194; Phillips 1984, 41; Coote and Ord 1989, 64; Wolkstein and Kramer 1983, 142; Stone 1976, 67, 198, 199, 210; Baring and Cashford 1991, 488; Crook 1964, 16; Shuttle and Redgrove 1978, 140. The qualities of longevity and regeneration have to do with the snake's repetitive "changing" of its skin, which was interpreted as repeated rebirth.

and (chief?) wives. It is also possible that stories of sexual relations between siblings in ancient pantheons only testify to the legitimacy of such practices among deities, but not among humans. Referring to family ties among Canaanite deities, for example, Cyrus H. Gordon suggests that "the ambivalence of relationships in an ancient pantheon may be remote indeed from the familiar patterns of human society" (Gordon 1961, 196). Due to the linguistic and cultural barriers mentioned above, the ancient sources themselves shed little light on this enigma.

Let us briefly address the problem of inconsistencies among ancient texts. Various factors have been put forward to explain the baffling inconsistencies among ancient mythological sources. The deeply rooted oral nature of ancient cultures offers one such explanation, since "in oral tradition there will be as many minor variants of a myth as there are repetitions of it, and the number of repetitions can be increased indefinitely" (Ong 1991, 42). Every generic myth may have taken on numerous oral forms, and perhaps sources that appear to relate to a given myth cannot add up to one plausible story because they are remains of different versions of that myth (Dalley 1989, 39).[5] Another explanation is that the inconsistencies testify to the ancients' own confusion regarding, for example, the exact identities of Gods and Goddesses and the exact relations among them.[6] Yet another possibility is that different sources tell different stories because they were composed in different periods, and/or in different areas, and/or by different ethnic groups, and/or in different social settings. Perhaps neighboring communities each worshipped their local ancestors, some of whom were gradually adopted by other societies, who gave them new names and changed their biographies (Stone 1976, 82). These various speculations about inconsistencies of ancient texts, generate, in turn, new and unsettling doubts, such as which story was first; which text influenced which and how; which texts can be shown to directly derive from each other, and which are more likely parallel derivations of older common sources. We may never know whether the ancients all worshipped a single Goddess, who went by numerous names and whose story was told in many versions, or whether numerous

5. Referring to the many fragments of the *Epic of Gilgamesh* ("the longest and greatest literary composition written in cuneiform Akkadian"), Dalley finds that "each period and area had its own version of the story, so we cannot simply reconstruct a master version with variants in the way that Hebrew and Classical texts can be edited, and a new fragment may perplex us rather than elucidating an old problem" (1985, 39).

6. Cross notes "the confusion" of the four different entities Qudsu, Astart, Anat, and Ashera, which all appear in my discussion (1973, 34), and Albright states that "the coexistence of the three Goddesses, Ashera, consort of El, Anath, and Astarte, apparently both sisters and wives of Baal, not unnaturally confused the Egyptians. . . . they identified all three" (1968, 118). Frymer-Kensky claims that the three Canaanite Goddesses, Ashera, Astarte, and Anat, "tended to blend into each other" (1992, 159). Ackerman suggests that the Queen of Heaven worshipped in Israel was "a syncretistic deity who combines traits of east Semitic Istar and west Semitic Astarte" (1992, 9). Patai also speaks of "a confusion between Asherah and Astarte, which . . . began with the 14th century B.C.E." (1990, 58).

local deities greatly influenced each others' mythologies, and if so, why and how.[7]

In addition to the barriers listed above, another unresolved issue is that of the relations between mythological stories and social reality: do stories of powerful Goddesses indicate a society in which women of flesh were also powerful? Does the transformation of Goddesses from mighty independent deities to consorts and daughters of male divinities correspond to actual social changes, both mirroring and enhancing them? And this, of course, ties into the unresolved question of matriarchy: was there ever a prepatriarchal phase in the development of society, and if so, what was it like? Was it *matriarchal?*

Determining whether a prepatriarchal phase of society was matriarchal is very problematic, never mind trying to understand its nature. The fundamental difficulty is that written texts preserving firsthand evidence from antiquity were composed (at least in their written form) within a conquering patriarchy, presumably served its interests and conveniently adjusted the past.[8] Earlier oral traditions are largely extinct, and historians attempting to decipher the mysteries of prepatriarchy have only circumstantial evidence to rely on. There are enormous amounts of material to explore, such as personal belongings, burial sites, ritualistic figurines, drawings, and remains of buildings and temples. Texts written or edited by the patriarchy may still carry traces of earlier, abolished traditions, belief systems, and social structures. But both these types of sources require thorough interpretations, which must, to a large degree, be speculative.

Having stressed how treacherously unapproachable antiquity can be, I

---

7. Baring and Cashford's argument is typical of this approach, stressing the multilayered ethnic structure of ancient Near Eastern society as a source of conflicting cultural tendencies: "The mythology of the Sumerian goddesses and gods seems to reflect the uneasy fusion of at least four different cultures. It draws imagery that belongs to a people worshipping the Great Mother, who are closely concerned with earth and water, together with the imagery that reflects mountain and sky gods who rule the sky, air and storm (1991, 181). For more on the invading tribes and these four cultures see Stone 1976, chap. 4; Gimbutas 1989, 318; Kinsley 1989, introduction.

8. Here is Bachofen's poetic nineteenth-century analysis of ancient "patriarchal" texts:

Old features are overlaid by new ones, the venerable figures of the matriarchal past are introduced to contemporaries in forms consonant with the spirit of the new period, harsh features are presented in a softened light; institutions, attitudes, motives, passions are reappraised from a contemporary point of view. Not infrequently new and old occur together; or the same fact, the same person, may appear in two versions, one prescribed by the earlier, one by the later world; one innocent, one criminal; one full of nobility and dignity, one an object of horror and the subject of a palinode. In other cases the mother gives way to the father, the sister to the brother, who now takes her place in the legend or alternates with her, while the feminine name is replaced by a masculine one. In a word, maternal conceptions cede to the requirements of patriarchal theory. (1967, 74)

For more current and usually more specific uses of this approach see Kinsley 1989, xiv, 141; Phillips 1984, 3, 20; Baring and Cashford 1991, 171, Frymer-Kensky 1992, 72, 78; and Crook 1964, 23.

choose to approach it anyway, for antiquity is far too valuable to be left behind, and if we know not where we come from, we may never know where we are headed.

Not an archeomythologist or historian myself, in approaching antiquity I must rely heavily on professional experts for translations of the ancient texts (except for Hebrew ones), as well as for the historical and anthropological background. This being the case, I refrain from embracing any major assumption or argument about antiquity unless it can be supported by professional scholarship. Fortunately, many scholars do embrace certain notions about antiquity that allow for some discussion. Let me introduce some assumptions and perceptions that underlie the following discussion. For example, there seems to be no doubt that the orality of prehistoric cultures is responsible for variations on common narratives and themes; that "universal" deities were known by local names in different areas within the ancient Near East, and that different communities locally developed their own versions of universal mythologies. The massive mutual influences among the Sumerians, Babylonians, Canaanites, Egyptians, and even Greeks are by now taken for granted; indeed, in some contexts these ancient cultures are discussed as forming one conglomerate (much like our current Western culture). Equally common is the assumption that ancient Near Eastern culture deeply influenced the society that created the Hebrew Bible (Lerner 1986, 161). Albright expresses a commonly held scholarly belief, that "basic Hebrew conceptions were derived chiefly from Mesopotamia, but were later modified in detail by Canaanite terminology" (Albright 1968, 168).[9] Thus the "Hebrew Goddess" (as Patai named her), the feminine deity worshipped by the Hebrews and violently condemned and persecuted by the monotheism documented in their Bible, was probably closely related to the great Goddess(es) worshipped by the Sumerians and Canaanites: Inanna, Ishtar, Ashera, and Anat, who may have all been one and the same.[10] Patai suggests that

9. Mesopotamia includes both Sumer and (later) Babylon. Scholars emphasize different influences on the Hebrew Bible. Kramer, for example, reminds us that Hebrew is a Canaanite dialect. Canaanite paganism, therefore, "is of particular importance because Biblical religion in some ways continues it, and in others reacted violently and consciously against it" (1961, 184).

10. Anat seems to have been the most militant of these mythological characters. Particularly bloody are the stories of her battles in rescue of her brother Baal: "Anat, adorned with henna and rouge and scented (as she has been for the feast), closes the doors of the palace and falls on all who remain of Baal's enemies . . . slays guards and warriors alike, and girds herself with the heads and hands of the slain; then, wading through blood up to her knees, she drives away also even tottering old men. Proceeding thence to the palace, she joyfully lays about her right and left, smashing the furniture on the heads of her adversaries and slaying guards and warriors until the palace is swimming in blood. She then revives herself by the blood of her victims, distributes their flesh as portions (among her own followers), and . . . washes herself . . . clean with the dew and oils her body. Anat renews her make-up" (Driver 1956, 14). For more on the adventures of Anat and Baal see Driver 1956, 10–22; Gordon 1961, 185, 198; Cross 1973, 28, 43; Albright 1968, 112, 114; Patai 1990, 54, 58, 60, 136; Stone 1976, 109, 146, 165; Stone 1979, 121; Frymer-Kensky 1992, 156, 159; Diner 1965, 20.

this is what probably happened to Asherah, Astarte, and Anath: they arrived, at different times no doubt, among the Hebrews, and although foreign in origin, they soon adopted the Hebrews as their children, and allotted them all the benefits man finds in the worship of a goddess. There can be no doubt that the goddess to whom the Hebrews clung with such tenacity down to the days of Joshiah, and to whom they returned with such remorse following the destruction of the Jerusalem Temple, was, whatever the prophets had to say about her, no foreign seductress, but a Hebrew goddess, the best divine mother the people had had to that time. (1990, 31)

On the issue of matriarchy, I choose to assume only what is widely considered within the authoritative community of scholars as sufficiently established and documented; namely, in David Kinsley's extremely cautious words, that "in prehistory, cultures existed in which the worship of goddesses was central. . . . the number of images of females and their location in sanctuaries seem to indicate that females were central to the religion (or religions) of these cultures" (1989, xii–xiii). It is also quite plausible that some change (for the worse) in women's social status might very well have occurred over a long stretch of early history, which might have started in the late fourth or early third millennium B.C.E. A decline certainly occurred in women's status in religious ritual. It stands to reason that this long historical process went hand in hand with the establishment of monotheism and national monarchies, two value systems that are almost indistinguishable from patriarchy. Women's religious status clearly deteriorated tremendously within the evolving patriarchal tribal monotheism.[11]

---

11. Certain names that appear in this text (and especially those of Goddesses) are spelled in different ways; this is because different writers spell them differently and, when quoting, I did not change the spelling in my sources. Another issue is the capitalization of the words *God, Gods, Goddess,* and *Goddesses.* After serious consideration, I decided to capitalize them all.

Lilit's Return in Jewish History

In Jewish culture, Lilit played the role of a deviant female, who would not yield to the rightful, natural, sacred order of things. She threatened a system of meaning that prescribed women's subordination and subservience to men, and the submission of all people to a single male God, as represented by his abstract, scrutinizing language, logic, history and law, clear distinctions and hierarchy. She also personified the lonely fate of those who did not conform. All of these features must have made her wildly attractive, as well as deeply threatening, to some men and women. I welcome Aviva Cantor Zuckoff's historical suggestion that in exile, Jewish men felt disoriented, emasculated, and weak. At the same time, relying to a great extent on their women's survival skills, they became aware of women's strength. That ambiguous perception was accompanied by fear that women's strength might lead to a new allocation of power within the Jewish community. This insecurity manifested itself in the repeated revivals of the negative archetype of the powerful woman Lilit.

Lilit reappeared throughout the long history of Jewish culture. In the kabbalah (Jewish mysticism), she became Queen of Devils. Her spouse was still the Devil (now called Samael), but when the Shekinah, the feminine aspect of Godhood, was exiled (with the Jews) from the land of Israel, Lilit took her place as God's (or rather as the masculine aspects of the Godhead's) sexual partner. Now all three male images, God, Devil, and man, joined forces in satisfying her sexual demands. Of the many new features that were attributed to Lilit in the kabbalah, two are particularly relevant. In the Zohar (the thirteenth-century "Bible" of the kabbalah), Lilit returned to Adam's life only after, and as a result of, his (and Eve's) primordial sin (Tishby 1991, 541). As a temptress of men, she also became their fierce prosecutor, judge, and executioner (538–39). In this she took on the typical characteristics of her spouse, Satan,[1] and her evil eye became the horrifying eye of death.[2] The extraordinary passage from the Zohar quoted at the outset of chapter 2 demonstrates how fascinated some men were with her powerful image.[3]

1. For more on Satan see the discussion in chapter 4.
2. On the kabbalah see Scholem 1965, and for a short article (in Hebrew) on Lilit in the kabbalah, see Scholem 1948. In her kabbalistic incarnation Lilit "absorbed" more feminine images, such as the Queen of Sheba, the "strange woman" mentioned in Proverbs (see especially 7:11–12), and Helen of Troy (as incarnation of Venus). She was also explicitly associated with the waning moon and with menstruation; see Patai 1990, 231, 233, 240; Shuttle and Redgrove 1978, 21; Tishby 1991, 541–43; and Trachtenberg 1979, 257–58.
3. Compare the image of Lilit stalking men on street corners to the description of the biblical "strange woman." In Proverbs 7, for example, young men are warned that "she is loud and stubborn; her feet abide not in her house: Now she is without, now in the streets, and lieth in wait at every corner" (7:11–12). "Let not thine heart decline to her ways, go not

In Jewish folklore, Lilit seduced men away from their families and communities and, often, when kissing them farewell pumped their souls out of their bodies.[4] With the nineteenth-century revival of Hebrew literature in Europe, Lilit, like the ever-reviving phoenix, moved from folklore into literature.[5] But the most moving chapter in Lilit's life is being currently written by Jewish American women, who in recent decades have been claiming her as a feminist model. They publish a journal named after her and write stories and poems in her honor.[6] They tell her story and give her the voice that has always been denied her. They see in her a brave, heroic woman who would not be victimized. They give her what millennia of women may have wished to express: sympathy. They aim to lift the (Genesis) curses that have separated Eve and Lilit and reconcile them, in the belief that their unity can perhaps yet change and save the world.

---

astray in her paths. For she has cast down many wounded: yea, many strong men have been slain by her. Her house is the way to hell, going down to the chambers of death" (7:25–27). This description, in turn, brings to mind the earlier portrayal of Inanna, the Goddess of the Moon and Evening Star, as divine cosmic harlot. Later in this chapter, I show that the nineteenth-century prostitute was described along very similar lines, cast as a female stalker.

4. For such folk stories see Sadeh 1983, especially 64–76; Shenhar 1982, 83–102; Schwartz 1988, 140; Abarbanell 1994, 117.

5. For comprehensive discussions see Cohen 1990; Abarbanell 1994.

6. See Dame 1989; J. P. Goldenberg 1974; and David Schecter's musical comedy (music and lyrics by Margot Stein Azen) *Guarding the Garden* (1992).

CHAPTER 3

**"Female Stalking Moral Panics":
The Witch and the Prostitute**

*Witches appear evil because the persecutors of evil must justify their
persecutions.*
—Shuttle and Redgrove 1978, 220

Preface

Having seen how the Great Goddess of antiquity, through a process of denigration and demonization, was transformed into the archetypal female
stalker, Lilit, let us now address the consequences of her gradual reconstruction, in the Middle Ages and the Renaissance, into the witch of Christian Europe.[1] From the fourteenth through the seventeenth centuries, in
times of social apprehension, the ancient anxiety regarding the female
stalker, preserved in popular legends, burst into a series of moral panics par
excellence: the witch-hunts.[2] In these violent outbursts, the legendary image
of the witch became the site where the female stalker archetype (Lilit) was
imposed on actual women ("Eves"). European societies expressed their anxieties through the narration of Lilit's story; when narrated through the law,
this story was used to prosecute women as witches. This disciplined
"deviant" women, warned all women against deviancy, and reinforced the
monotheistic, patriarchal social order. From this perspective, the witch-
hunts were a legal acting out of the cultural fantasy associated with the
female stalker, as well as a war on femininity at large. In the last part of the
chapter I make an analogous argument regarding Victorian England's moral
panic concerning prostitutes.

Before presenting the argument, let me briefly sketch the relevant historical background. In Europe, the fourteenth to seventeenth centuries were
fraught with social instability and deep conflicts.[3] The social upheavals,

1. Although men were occasionally victims of the hunts, "the witch was almost by definition a woman" (Cohn 1975, 248).
2. In their book on moral panics, Goode and Ben-Yehuda dedicate a full chapter to the
"Renaissance Witch-Craze," presenting it as a classic case of moral panic (1996).
3. "Social factors such as growing mobility, with its impact on family structure and
style of life, provoked the first surge of witch accusations in the 14th and 15th centuries. The
intensified social disruption of the 16th century produced the witch-craze of the early modern period" (Kieckhefer 1976, 102). The sixteenth century's growing religious conflict
(between Catholicism and the younger churches) is said to have significantly contributed to
ecstatic witch-hunting (Trevor-Roper 1967, 131), as did the tensions generated by the political process of state-building (Levack 1989, 89–90).

widely believed to have caused frustration and anxiety, were bolstered by the recurring plagues that swept Europe, ravaging enormous sections of the population and annihilating at least half of Europe's inhabitants. Nachman Ben-Yehuda depicts the fifteenth century as "a time of great enterprise, bold thought, innovation, as well as one of deep confusion and anomie, a feeling that society had lost its norms and boundaries and that the uncontrollable forces of change were destroying all order and moral tradition" (1988, 43). Shifts in social stratification "vibrated the structure of the medieval order and directly threatened the Church's authority and legitimacy."[4]

> As a result of the severe socioeconomic stress, the entire feudal social order crumbled and "immense sadness and a feeling of doom pervaded the land" (Anderson 1970, 1733), intensified and aggravated by the severe climatological changes, demographical revolutions and the disruption of family and communal life, all of which were perceived as signs of impending doom. Furthermore, "the individual was confronted with an enormously wider range of competing beliefs in almost every area of social and intellectual concern, while conformity-inducing pressures of mainly ecclesiastical sort were weakened or discredited" (Rattansi 1972, 7–8). The existential crisis of individuals [was] expressed in terms of anomie, alienation, strangeness, powerlessness (O'Dea 1966) and anxiety. (Goode and Ben-Yehuda 1996, 171)

One development that particularly displeased the church was the change in women's status. Many women either could not or would not marry. On their own, many entered the job market. "[W]omen became increasingly active in the economy and gained much economic power. . . . the social role of women was in constant flux" (Ben-Yehuda 1988, 45). One such market was prostitution. A significant portion of women chose to not bear or raise children: "there was widespread use of contraception and infanticide, which the church strongly and fiercely denounced as most evil" (46). In this context, the church-encouraged witch-craze, which peaked in the sixteenth-century witch-hunts, was "a negative reaction to this emerging culture in the sense that its purpose was to counteract and prevent change and to reestablish traditional social-moral boundaries and religious authority." Faced with what it perceived as total war, patriarchal monotheism charged with full might. "By persecuting witches, society, led by the Church, attempted to redefine its boundaries" (43; see also Goode and Ben-

---

4. The European witch-hunts mostly flourished in the German states, the Swiss confederation, France, and Scotland; England and Italy lagged behind, and "eastern Europe, the world of Orthodox Christianity, was untouched by it" (Cohn 1975, 253). "[O]nly the most rapidly developing countries, and where the Catholic church was weakest, experienced a virulent witch-craze" (Goode and Ben-Yehuda 1996, 170).

Yehuda 1996, 174–80); by forcing women into limiting, stereotypical categories, monotheistic patriarchy sought to reestablish its full hegemony.

"It is obvious why the church 'needed' an opponent. But it needed a very special type of deviant-opponent to redefine its legitimacy. The opponent had to be widely perceived as a threat to society itself and to the Christian world view" (Ben-Yehuda 1988, 43). The European church's witch is a demonized reflection of the Great Goddess. Once again, monotheistic patriarchy called upon Lilit and her story of stalking to frighten men and women into conformity and submission.

The Witch's Likeness to Lilit

The witch was a familiar legendary figure in medieval and Renaissance Europe. In the numerous stories in which she appeared, the witch possessed every feature and characteristic attributed to Lilit. A few reminders suffice to illustrate this point. Like Lilit, she was either very young and attractive (to men) or very old and repulsive (to men). The young witch's lips were red and voluptuous, her hair jet black; the old witch's nose overshadowed the rest of her face, and she was as dark and ugly as sin. Her hair was long and wild (like snakes?), and her eyes were as bright as burning coals, enchanting and deadly. "The witch was most dangerous when she *looked* at you" (Osborne 1994, 86); she had the bewitching evil eye, the stalking, harmful gaze. Witches were associated with snakes and referred to as "pythonesses" (Kieckhefer 1976, 91). They were also "unnaturally" smart and strong.

The witch was characterized as being an obscenely sexual woman. Her reputed promiscuous sexuality *was* her witchery, cause and effect combined. Theologians never tired of preaching that "all witchcraft comes from carnal lust, which in women is insatiable" (Kors and Peters 1989, 127). The witch's unappeasable sexuality branded her as "a kind of supernatural whore" (Osborne 1994, 67). Similarly, the Babylonians and the medieval kabbalists referred to their Lilit as a "holy prostitute" and "Big Whore."

It was widely held (at least since the fourteenth century) that a witch could fly. She did not necessarily have (Artemis's) wings, but (like Lilit) she had other means to soar through the air. When not riding on animals, she was observed crossing the sky on a broomstick, or some other phallic object. Her riding position affirmed that she wickedly craved the intercourse position preferred by Lamia-Lilit. Like nocturnal predators, for example the owl, she flew mostly at night, when her powers were at full strength. Like Lilit's, her strength peaked on nights of a full moon or when the moon was imperceptible. One was especially likely to run into her at a crossroads.[5] The asso-

5. For Lilit's affinity for crossroads see Patai 1990, 233. Crossroads were also likely places to encounter the European vampire.

ciation of stalkers with crossroads, which symbolize sites of choice in human life, presents stalking as a dangerous temptation that awaits Man. Finally, like Lamashtu, Lamia, and Lilit, the witch stalked and threatened pregnant women and young mothers, abducting and devouring their young ones. Witches were "cannibals, with an insatiable craving for very young flesh; according to some writers of the time, to kill, cook, and eat a baby which had not yet been baptized was a witch's greatest pleasure" (Cohn 1975, 100).[6]

The Cultural Transformation of Lilit into the European Witch

The striking similarities between the image of the European witch and that of the archetypal stalker, Lilit, are not coincidental, nor do they attest to the existence of a universal archetype. Rather, I propose that Lilit and the European witch are culturally linked by one or more of the three subimages that, in their merger, constituted the European witch.

By the fourteenth, and certainly throughout the fifteenth and sixteenth centuries, the European witch combined three distinct subimages. (1) A witch was a woman believed by others, and/or by herself, to be a sorceress, that is, one who used magic to cause others harm (most typically death, disease, impotency, or passion aroused by "love potions"). (2) A witch was a "diabolist": a member of a Devil-worshipping sect. She entered into a pact with the Devil, who sealed it by branding her body with a hidden mark. She denounced Christianity, pledging allegiance to the Devil instead. She participated in nocturnal sabbat gatherings, where she took part in beastly orgies and copulated with the Devil.[7] In return for her profane devotion, she enjoyed the Devil's evil powers, which she could use to harm humans and animals (usually by activating her demon).[8] (3) A witch was "an uncanny

6. Jews were also widely accused of infanticide, as well as of diabolism, poisoning wells, carrying plagues, and, of course, having huge noses. And as Cohn reminds us, "the term 'sabbat,' like the term 'synagogue,' was of course taken from the Jewish religion, which was traditionally regarded as the quintessence of anti-Christianity, indeed as a form of Devil-worship" (1975, 101). Witchery was associated by medieval Europeans with Judaism, and so the linkage of witches with the "Jewish" Lilit seems only natural.

7. For a vivid description of the witch's flight to the sabbat see Trevor-Roper 1967, 124–25. For an account of a sabbat by a writer who believes in its existence see Summers 1966, chap. 11, 110–72.

8. The witch always had a *familiar* demon in the shape of a pet, whom she nursed with her blood; recall that in antiquity Lamashtu was portrayed suckling dogs and pigs, which were also the witch's favorite "familiars." The "tit" used for that purpose, and sometimes also to suckle the Devil himself, was widely confused with the Devil's mark on her body (the mark imprinted at the signing of the contract) until the two merged into one. It was this bodily mark that often gave the prosecuted witch away. "Any birthmark or scar would do to prove its owner a witch beyond question" (Williams and Adelman 1992, 155).

being who flew through the air at night for evil purposes, such as devouring babies, and who was associated with wild and desolate places" (Cohn 1975, 147).[9] Together, these three images constituted the European witch's unique character. The third image is the witch's main link to Lilit.

The origin of that third component, the witch as night rider, is complicated. Cohn argues that in European traditional folklore, with its long roots in pre-Christian eras, there were two distinct types of flying women: the evil Strix creatures and the benevolent protective "ladies of the night" (Cohn 1975, 206–24). The Strix (from the Greek "screech") were old women thought of as owls, whom Ovid described as having hooked beaks, grasping talons, "and eyes that stare fixedly out of big heads. . . . they fly about at night in search of babies" (207).[10] Petronius added that "particularly men who lose their potency, commonly think they are being eaten by a strix." European peasants often believed in the existence of the Strix, and certain women "assimilated the belief so completely that they imagined themselves to be night witches . . . living out, in their dreams, a collective fantasy" (210). Cohn traces the Strix back to the Roman period, determining that they mirrored the classical mythological creature known as Lamia (219). I believe that the Strix were Lilit-Lamia creatures, featuring the characteristics of both these mythological stalkers. Combined, they were the female stalker created by Hieronymus, who identified the two in the fourth century when he translated the biblical *Lilit* into the Latin *Lamia*.[11]

Let us now turn to the second traditional type of night riders, the good ladies of the night. A Christian judicial text from the ninth century, the *Canon Episcopi,* describes women who "believe and openly avow that in the hours of the night they ride on certain animals, together with Diana, the Goddess of the pagans, with a numberless multitude of women" (Cohn 1975, 211). These women, in Cohn's interpretation, "do not imagine themselves as night witches, addicted to murderous and cannibalistic enterprises, but as devotees of a supernatural queen who leads and commands them on their nocturnal flights" (212). He goes on to prove that the popular belief in these good nocturnal visitors persists, in some areas, to this very day.

The good ladies of the night are presented as followers of the Roman Goddess Diana, known to the Greeks as Artemis, the Virgin Goddess of the hunt, wild animals, and childbirth. She had large bird's wings and was sometimes painted with Medusa's head. She was a virgin Goddess in that she was completely independent, with no ties to a man, a family, or offspring. She was fierce, vengeful and ill-reputed for having turned Actaeon,

---

9. This portrayal of the distinct subimages is mostly influenced by Cohn's (1975) analysis. For a slightly different presentation of three types of witchcraft see Kieckhefer 1976, 5–6.

10. For the Ovid text see Hurwitz 1992, 45.

11. See chapter 2, pp. 37–38.

the man who accidentally saw her naked, into a stag. (He was immediately torn apart by his own dogs). It seems to be "generally believed that Artemis was originally a mother-Goddess similar to the Minoan 'Lady of the Wild Things' and the Phrygian Cybele" (Tripp 1974, 105). "The least civilized of all the Greek Goddesses, with the oldest lineage . . . Artemis . . . was the one who received the bloodiest sacrifices" (Baring and Cashford 1991, 322–23, 327). She was also believed to have been queen of the Amazons (Williams and Adelman 1992, 24, 150; Diner 1965, 126; Stone 1984, 183–210).

The New Testament, which describes how her dedicated devotees refused to listen to Paul, explicitly names Diana as Christianity's powerful rival.[12] When, throughout Europe, the temples of Artemis/Diana were transformed into shrines for the Christian Holy Virgin, the Goddess was stripped of her attributes and powers and was baptized under a new name: Mary. And just as Inanna's disturbing power was demonized and marginalized in the stalking Lilit, so too was Diana's, which became associated with the night-flying witches.

In the Middle Ages, Diana was also referred to as Herodias and as the Germanic Holda, a "supernatural, motherly being who normally lives in the upper air and circles the earth. . . . when Holda goes on her nocturnal journeys she is accompanied by a train of followers. These are the dead, including the souls of children and of babies who have died unbaptized" (Cohn 1975, 213). Her pet companion was an owl (Hurwitz 1992, 61). Among German-speaking Jews, the Jewish Lilit and the non-Jewish Holda were one and the same (Trachtenberg 1979, 42–43).

Finally, according to Leland, who conducted interviews with nineteenth-century Italian "witches," Diana was still worshipped as their Snake Queen of the Night, and her daughter, Aradia, also called Herodias, was the religion's female Messiah (1974, viii, 59, 102, 125). Cohn shows that in earlier sources Diana and Herodias were one and the same (1975, 212). Leland claims that the Messiah Herodias was clearly a derivation of no other than the Hebrew Lilit. He also claims that the church, as early as the sixth century, had already established that the two were identical (1974, 102). It seems that no matter which way we look at them, these legendary women all had connections to the night stalker, Lilit.

According to Cohn, peasants presumed that the good ladies of the night and the evil night witches were categorically separate. "But to the educated, looking at these fantasies from outside and from above, the distinction was not necessarily so absolute. . . . Here the two ideas—of the 'ladies of the night' and of night-witches who steal and devour babies—are ingeniously combined: both are commanded by the moon-Goddess or by Herodias, and the image of the nocturnal banquet merges into that of the cannibalistic orgy" (1975, 219). The European educated elite, combining the stories of the

12. "What man is there that knoweth not how that city of the Ephesians is a worshipper of the Great Goddess Diana" (Acts 19:35).

good and the bad night riders, made no distinctions between night riders, sorceresses, and diabolists.

Charges of diabolism (including secret Devil worship sessions, obscene orgies, infanticide, and cannibalism) had a respectable place in the history of European persecutions. As early as the first century C.E., Alexandrian Greeks applied the charge to local Jews. During the second century, the Roman Empire easily extended the accusation to Christians, who, thought to be members of a secretive conspiracy against traditional values and social order, were demonized and persecuted (Cohn 1975, 5–15). The church fathers documented the accusations made against their communities. Ironically, "when it came to discrediting some new religious out-group, monks would draw on this traditional stock of defamatory cliches" (56). And so, "again and again, over a period of many centuries, heretical sects were accused of holding promiscuous and incestuous orgies in the dark; of killing infants and devouring their remains; of worshipping the devil" (54). Thus, the medieval "learned tradition" was based on the long-documented tradition of using Satan's mythological character (together with Aristotelian demon theories) in order to associate dissent with diabolism.

Faced with bewildering stories of sorceresses and of various night-riding creatures, Europe's educated elite translated the "primitive" folktales into its own "learned tradition." All types of flying ladies, conveniently identified with the image of the bewitching sorceress, were redefined as heretic Devil worshippers. This union forever linked the European witch with the image of the female stalker, Lilit. The demonized shadow image of the Goddess Diana, mistress of the night-flying female stalkers, was replaced by the Christian male image of Satan, and her alleged worshippers, mostly women, became his stalking witches.

The cultural transformation of the archetypal Lilit into the medieval legendary witch was consequential. It consisted of three distinct elements: (1) a shift from an archetype to a legendary character, (2) a shift from a stalker to a Devil worshipper, when diabolism (but not stalking) was eagerly recognized as a legal offense, and (3) a close theological association between the witch and Eve (Everywoman). Combined, these elements facilitated the application of the stalking archetype to flesh-and-blood women and encouraged the legal prosecution of women for stalking, witchcraft, and diabolism. This combination paved the way for the translation of the patriarchal anxiety, as manifested in the archetypal image of the female stalker, into the fatal series of moral panics, the witch-hunts. Let us examine these elements more closely.

Lilit, Eve, and the Witch

In Eve, the early fathers of the Christian Church saw the image of the First Woman of Greek myth, Pandora, who was a divine creation designed to inflict sin and misery on mankind. This association also connected Eve with

Lilit, the Hebrew version of the dangerous Pandora. But in the church fathers' reconstruction of the female imagery, Eve and Lilit did not "add up" to a new Inanna. Rather, due to the influence of Greek misogyny, which viewed women as innately sexual and sex as inherently sinful, the church fathers' linkage between Eve and Lilit meant that the allegorical Every-woman was now linked to Lilit's sinful and despised sexuality.[13] The ideal-ization of Mary only served to hasten Eve's demotion to Lilit's status, since Mary, with her pure virginity and meek obedience, was hailed as the sec-ond, true Eve and, situated in binary opposition to both Eve and Lilit, sealed their "fallen" union. As Ruether phrased it, "Their depersonalized view of sexual relations gives three basic images of the possibilities of woman in the Church Fathers: woman as whore, woman as wife, and woman as virgin" (1974, 163). Woman as whore is Lilit, and woman as wife is Eve, the only dif-ference being that the first is "wrongly abused" for sexual pleasure, whereas the second is "used rightly" (i.e. for the sole purpose of procreation). In fact, they so resemble each other that "Lilith's story became confused with the story of Eve" (Phillips 1984, 39). Mary alone, the unachievable, and therefore frustratingly punitive, feminine ideal, was noncarnal, a nonwoman woman, whereas in contrast both devilish Lilit and wifely Eve shared the same debased category of nonvirginal women.[14] Lilit became a case of an extreme Eve, while Eve became a "diluted" Lilit.

As Lilit's incarnation in medieval Christian Europe, the witch inher-ently resembled Eve, the allegorical Everywoman, in many ways. Both Eve and the witch were inherently sexual, and despised for it. Eve's carnality, deemed evil, was identified with her fallen womanhood; the witch's sexual-ity was similarly evil and similarly identified with her wicked practices. Spe-cific feminine traits were used to reinforce Eve's association with the witch. Take menstruation. In medieval Europe, witches were believed to have deadly energy, manifested in their gaze; such a "Medusa trait" was also attributed to any menstruating woman (Osborne 1994, 86). Witches, like Lilit, were known to be particularly murderous regarding human babies— and so were menstruating women (Goode and Ben-Yehuda 1996, 173).[15] This suggests that the witch was a constantly menstruating woman; if so,

13. For a fascinating comparison of Jewish and Hellenistic concepts of femininity, and the gradual penetration of Greek misogyny into Jewish thought see Boyarin 1993, especially 82–106.

14. For detailed scholarly discussions of the issues summarized in this paragraph see Aschkenasy 1986; Boyarin 1993; Daly 1985; Phillips 1984; Frymer-Kensky 1992; McLaughlin 1974; Osborne 1994; Pagels 1988; Ruether 1974; and Warner 1976. For discussions of Catholi-cism versus Protestant Christianity see Henning 1974; Romero 1974; and Douglass 1974. (Although the Reformation belittled virginity and encouraged motherhood, it did not ele-vate either sexuality or womanhood, which remained bound to each other.)

15. Along this line, the witch's blood was also believed to be powerful and dangerous (Shuttle and Redgrove 1978, 218).

then every woman was potentially, or occasionally, a witch.[16] Womanhood and witchery thus became all but synonymous.

The additional, literary, element that helped bridge the gap between the mythological Lilit and human Eves was the witch's legendary (as opposed to mythological) nature. The single most significant difference between Lilit and the European witch is their fictional affiliations. Whereas Lilit is a full-blown, well-defined mythological image, the witch is a legendary, fairy-tale type. According to Bruno Bettelheim, although the same exemplary figures and situations are found in both mythology and fairy tales, and although equally miraculous events occur in both, there is a crucial difference in the way they are communicated. "Put simply, the dominant feeling a myth conveys is: this is absolutely unique; it could not have happened to any other person or in any other setting; such events are grandiose, awe-inspiring, and could not possibly happen to an ordinary mortal like you and me" (1977, 37). The portrayal of Lilit as a mythological being therefore relegated her to a unique realm of existence; she was the Strange Woman, clearly distinct from the human Eve and her daughters. The witch, on the other hand, being a fairy-tale character, is much closer to our human, everyday life: she can appear before us and become part of our reality; she can be any and every woman we encounter. And if, like Eve, all women are fallen and share the witch's wicked essence, then it is inevitable that all women are potential witches. Phillips rightly points out that the notorious *Malleus Maleficarum*, the witch-hunters' "gospel," targeted "an Eve responsible for carnal lust and death" (Phillips 1984, 70), an allegorical Eve that is personified in each and every woman. In the chapter "Why It Is That Women Are Chiefly Addicted to Evil Superstition," *all women* are said to be, among other things, weak and deceitful, liars by nature, faithless, feebler than men in mind and body, undisciplined, impulsive, and dangerous. "The crudeness of the misogyny in this section of the *Malleus* is astonishing" (70). And the *Malleus* was no negligible book: "This amazing document . . . was, through 30 editions and 200 years following its publication in 1486, the most prominent, the most important, and the most authoritative treatment of the questions of how witches were to be explained, identified, accused, tried, tortured, and exterminated" (70).[17]

By combining the imagery of Eve, Lilit, and the witch, womanhood was conveniently associated with witchery and women with witches; and as witchery was linked with female stalking, all women were suspect.

16. Shuttle and Redgrove in fact define the witch as a woman who adhered to "values of menstruation"; it was during menstruation that she was at her best, lively, imaginative, and active (1978, 78). They refer to "the persecution of the witches in the Middle Ages . . . [as] one enormous menstrual taboo" (218).

17. This important text is available in English in Kors and Peters 1989, 113–89. For astounding highlights and quotes from this document, see Williams and Adelman 1992, chap. 3, "The Hammer of Witches," 35–45.

Nevertheless, some women were more suspect than others. Medieval midwives, who also manufactured birth control aids, performed abortions, and sometimes delivered dead babies, were especially suspect as potential witches and thus also as potential stalkers (Phillips 1984, 72; Williams and Adelman 1992, 11).[18] Women thought to interfere with marital bliss are another example in point. Witches were said to cause impotence, especially in men who left their lovers to marry other women (Cohn 1975, 151; Kierck-hefer 1976, 57). Mistreated, abandoned mistresses, as well as their associates, were, therefore, obvious suspects of witchery and stalking. Similarly, wives of abusive husbands were in danger of being accused of witchcraft if their husbands suffered misfortunes (Cohn 1975, 196–97).

Thus the mythological Lilit was transformed into a witch, and the archetype was applied to real human beings. Releasing Lilit of her "bigger than life" dimensions, Lilit's fairy-tale caricature, the witch, made it possible for the sociocultural treatment of the archetypal night stalker to shift from the fictional instructive discourse to the real, legal one. It is hard to bring Lilit to trial; it was much easier to prosecute witches, to convict and execute them in numbers that are estimated anywhere between thirty thousand and more than one million (Daly 1985, 63).

The Legal Discourse

Several major developments that occurred within European legal systems during the thirteenth century enabled the legal witch-hunt (Levack 1989, chap. 3; Peters 1978, 151–54). "None of these legal developments, or even all of them taken together, amounted to a sufficient cause of the great witch-hunt, but each of them served a necessary precondition of that hunt" (Levack 1989, 64). Interestingly, the very changes that were widely considered as progressive facilitated the witch-hunts (Peters 1978, 176).

As Peters and Levack show, the thirteenth century in Europe saw a significant return to the Roman law, which had always prohibited sorcery. With the Roman law, interrogatory torture as a means of extracting testimony entered the European legal arena as well. Simultaneously, secular and regional courts received more powers (such as jurisdiction over witchcraft cases), and in continental Europe a new *inquisitorial* method replaced the older *accusatorial* system, which had used the *ordeal* as its "decision-making" procedure. The adoption of the inquisitorial legal procedure seems to have

18. Ancient Babylonian midwives, associated with Goddess worship, were also demonized as stalkers (see discussion in previous chapter).

The *Malleus Maleficarum* deals with midwives extensively. One of its chapters is titled "That Witches Who Are Midwives in Various Ways Kill the Child Conceived in the Womb, and Procure an Abortion; or If They Do Not This Offer New-Born Children to the Devils" (Jacob Sprengler and Heinrich Kramer, *Malleus Maleficarum*, in Kors and Peters 1989, 127).

been the most influential of these changes. Under the older accusatorial system, an accuser who failed to prove his allegation was exposed to the charge of unjustly libeling the accused and was severely punished. In the new (inquisitorial) system, the burden was eased away from the accuser: he was no longer responsible for the actual prosecution of his case, which was now performed by public officials, nor was he personally liable if the charges were not proved. This, of course, encouraged accusations, especially regarding crimes such as witchcraft, which could not be proved.

Another significant difference between the accusatorial and inquisitorial systems was the replacement of ordeals with a revolutionary, rational procedure: court officials now based their legal determination on evidence.[19] "Instead of presiding over a contest between two private parties in which the outcome was at least theoretically left to God, the officers of the court—the judge and his subordinates—took it upon themselves to investigate the crime and to determine whether or not the defendant was guilty" (Levack 1989, 67). Since evidence of events such as the sabbat (Devil-worshipping session) could only come from the accused, and since the accused was hardly willing to self-incriminate, the use of the new legal method of torture seemed essential.

But in the context of this work, the most significant aspect of the law's participation in the witch-hunts was the legal translation of night riders and sorceresses into diabolists. Examining depositions by witnesses in prosecutions for witchcraft, Kieckhefer established that "the overwhelming emphasis is upon sorcery," and "trials for bodily harm (bringing sickness or death to men or animals) rank among the most abundant witch trials in the period 1300–1500" (1976, 31, 48). But the educated elite, influenced by the "learned tradition," simply "could not acknowledge the efficacy of preternatural, magical forces except by postulating that they were in control of spiritual beings, whether angels or devil. . . . There was no place in their world view for causation that was neither natural nor fully supernatural" (79). In other words, stalking stories, as well as stories of the "evil eye," were simply not considered serious, respectable, or legal. In order for such stories to gain the necessary respectability for the elite to intervene, they had to be translated into learned terminology, such as that of diabolism. The legal discourse played a crucial role in turning the witch's dubious night riding and sorcery into Devil worship. Thus reformulated, witchery moved into the socially recognized realm of the rational and the reasonable, and enabled the fierce prosecution and condemnation of women. The process was simple and ingenious: "witnesses' charges of sorcery were followed by judicial interroga-

19. An ordeal, which was at the heart of the old, accusatorial system, was "a test that the accused party would have to take to gain acquittal. Either he would have to carry a hot iron a certain distance and then show, after his hand was bandaged for a few days, that God had miraculously healed the seared flesh; . . . or he would be thrown into a body of cold water and would be considered innocent only if he sank to the bottom" (Levack 1989, 65).

tion, in which [confessions] of diabolism were extracted from the suspects. Indeed, all valid and relevant evidence indicated that this pattern was typical" (78). More specifically,

> [W]hen the populace pointed to instances of maleficent magic, growing numbers of intellectuals could only see the influence of Satan. When these learned individuals entered the courtroom, they convicted suspects of diabolism—a charge more serious than that of sorcery, more sensational, and probably punished more frequently with death. . . . One must surely conclude that the increase in trials for sorcery came about primarily because of anxieties felt throughout society. The more fantastic charge of diabolism, then, built on a foundation that was already laid. The jurists and the theologians who suggested this charge supplied a new dimension to the craze that was already under way, adding fuel to an already blazing fire. (103, 105)

Cohn similarly determines that "left to themselves, peasants would never have created mass witch-hunts—these occurred only where and when the authorities had become convinced of the reality of the sabbat and of nocturnal flights to the sabbat. And this conviction depended on, and in turn was sustained by, the inquisitorial type of procedure, including the use of torture" (Cohn 1975, 252). It was necessary to torture the accused into supplying their prosecutors with details of their crimes. Torture supplied the sought confessions, which "proved" the accusations and substantiated the "learned" theories of diabolism. Convictions based on torture condemned the accused to harsh punishments, encouraged the judicial system to proceed in its course, and taught the public what type of stories to use when charging sorceresses, what stories worked best in court. Telling these powerful stories, the public surely internalized them, perhaps to the point of believing them.

An integral part of this legal translation of sorcery into diabolism was the careful delineation of "professional profiles" of witches. These profiles were based on women's confessions, which were coerced in inquisitorial investigations coupled with torture. The authorities used a set of standard questions that dictated, in detail, the stories the accused women were to "volunteer" in their confessions: accounts of their lustful, perverted sexual nature; of their beastly and masochistic desire to copulate with anyone, in any way, all the time.[20] This profile established the rational, scientific justifi-

20. "And all female witches maintain that the so-called genital organs of their Demons are so huge and so excessively rigid that they cannot be admitted without the greatest pain. Alexee Drigie reported that her Demon's penis, even when only half in erection, was as long as some kitchen utensils which she pointed to as she spoke . . . Claude Fellet . . . said that she had often felt it like a spindle swollen to an immense size so that it could not be contained by even the most capacious woman without pain. This agrees with the complaint of Nicole Morele" (from Nicholas Remy's reports in Osborne 1994, 70).

cation of the legal witch-hunts. The interrogative process used to confirm them enabled the prosecutors to *know* the women and control their sexual fantasies. It permitted them to create the witches by forcing their stories to follow a dictated, pornographic script.

It is inconceivable, from our historical perspective, how the Western legal profession of that time, and for much time following, failed to perceive the blind vicious cycle in which it was trapped. Expressing deep social anxiety in their search for Devil worship, the courts forced a diabolistic story out of defendants and witnesses alike, using their testimonies and confessions as evidence supporting the story's accuracy. Several centuries later, it is clear that once the required and acceptable story and imagery were defined by the legal system, it was inevitable that they would perpetuate themselves through legal procedures. The legal perception, plainly able to find only what it set out to find, established itself as social reality.

The particular content of the imposed legal story seems to us today not only diabolic, but absurd. With hindsight, it is not difficult to see that the "learned" images, superimposed by the legal discourse, were hardly more advanced than the popular tradition; they were just different. Diabolism did not rephrase sorcery charges in a more accurate, professional, objective, or value-free manner. It was not a better way of getting at the truth behind the sorcery accusations. The legal system with its "learned" views merely substituted one value-laden worldview for another. And yet, the more general insight, so clearly illustrated by this example, is that—no matter the culture or the historical period—the legal discourse and system can allow for *any* content, once embraced, to uncritically perpetuate itself and that other "learned traditions" may be as ideological and dangerous as diabolism. Our own contemporary legislation and judiciary systems no longer impose the image of the witch or the story of diabolism, but they have their own "learned" beliefs and mediating images, which often rely on psychoanalytic wisdom; these images and beliefs perpetuate themselves through the legal process in ways very similar to those discussed above. Analysis of the legal system's blindness to its role in promoting the witch-hunts can help us see our own legal system's fallacies. These issues will be further explored in chapter 8.

The Common Prostitute of Victorian England

To conclude, let me point to another series of moral panics, in which the legal system catered to public anxiety fueled by female stalking stories. In Victorian England, Lilit's story, expressing public apprehension in the face

---

"Margueritte . . . testifies that the Devil . . . always has a member like a donkey . . . It is so long and thick like an arm: when he wants to copulate with any of the girls or women he conjures up a bed of hay on which he makes them lie, which does not at all displease them" (from Pierre de Lancre's reports, Osborne 1994, 71).

of social change, was mediated by the image of the streetwalking prostitute. Like the witch, the prostitute enabled the female stalking story to burst out into a series of moral panics.

Victorian England was by no means plagued by explicit insecurity and turmoil. Nevertheless, changes in women's social roles were perceived to be threatening the social order. The prosperity enjoyed by the upper classes required strict regulation of female sexuality: "since property was passed on by the father, paternity could not be in doubt. Thus wifely infidelity was more a threat to the economic stability of society than to its morality" (Reynolds and Humble 1993, 6). Yet the "New Woman," encouraged by popular treatises and novels advocating women's rights, threatened to leave the confinement of the home and to neglect her role as the "angel in the house." Prostitutes, who were at the time a very visible sight on the streets of London, were a particularly unpleasant embodiment of the prospect that women could not only be sexually independent, but could also use sexuality to enter what was conceived, by patriarchy, as men's exclusive terrain: the urban public sphere of business and money. "The combined association of cash and the public sphere rendered the prostitute powerful and independent—qualities which were the unique privilege of the white, middle-class male" (Nead 1988, 95). This was perceived as intolerable, and patriarchy did not fail to respond.

Like the mythological Lilit and the legendary witch, the social type "common prostitute" was believed to be carnal in nature. Prostitutes *chose* sexuality and rejoiced in it; in their lust for carnal love they tempted men into illicit sex, infecting them with their dreadful diseases. It is not hard to see how this perception of the prostitute associated her with Lilit and the witch. One Victorian writer referred to streetwalkers as a "multitudinous amazonian army of the devil" (Walkowitz 1980, 42). Not surprisingly, the prostitute was a stalker, too, relentless in her pursuit of men.

> [A] young man "cannot pass along the street in the evening without meeting with, and being accosted by, women of the town at every stop." "His path is beset on the right hand and on the left, so that he is at every step exposed to the temptation from boyhood to mature age, his life is one continued struggle against it." (Walkowitz 1980, 34)

A convenient, tangible proof of the danger posed by the prostitute was found in the venereal diseases, syphilis and gonorrhea, that were spread by prostitutes as "consequence of unnatural vice and sexual excess" (56). Walkowitz finds that with no rational justification, "mid-Victorian statistics convinced medical and military authorities that an epidemic of venereal disease was sweeping the nation" (50). This contributed to elevating prostitution in the nineteenth century "to be *the* social evil, a particularly disruptive, singularly threatening vice" (Laqueur 1990, 230).[21] "Prostitutes had become the social lepers of the eighteenth century, as syphilis replaced leprosy as the symbol of one kind of dreaded social contagion" (Walkowitz 1980, 59). The supposed threat posed by prostitutes to public health triggered a moral panic that brought about their legal restriction. As early as 1824, the Vagrancy Act stated that a "common prostitute" who "wandered" in any public place "behaving in a riotous or indecent manner" could be imprisoned for one month. But it was the Contagious Diseases Acts, passed in the 1860s, that played a central role in creating "prostitution as a distinct legal category" (Bell 1994, 55). The 1866 act, replacing and extending a previous one of 1864, established a compulsory periodic medical examination for every "common prostitute." It specified compulsory detention (of up to six months) of any woman found to be infected with venereal disease, and refusal to be examined or treated was a criminal offense.[22] Section 12 declared that a hospital should not be certified to treat common prostitutes "unless at the time of the granting of a certificate adequate provision is made for the Moral and Religious Instruction of the Women detained therein." But the most striking feature of this act was that, whereas terms such as *police, superintendent,* and *justice* were legally defined, *common prostitute* was not. And rather than penalizing common *prostitution,* whatever that activity might include, the legislation allowed forced examination and detention when a magistrate found that a superintendent of police had "good cause to believe that a Woman therein named is a common Prostitute" (sec. 15). The legal category created by the act consists not of individuals who committed a defined act, but of women who, in the eyes of the superintendent of police and the judge, *were* "common prostitutes": evil, carnal, disease-carrying female stalkers. This essentialist legal standard brings to mind the law employed in 1641 by the Colonial Laws of Massachusetts: "If any Man or Woman *be a Witch* (that is hath or consulteth with a familiar spirit) they shall be put to death. Exod. 22:18, Levit. 20:27, Deut. 18:10, 11" (emphasis added).

Once again, a mediating category ("common prostitute") was used by the law to accuse women of personifying Lilit and to condemn them as female stalkers. This time the legal regulation of prostitution did not provide for the extermination of prostitutes, but it may well have promoted a public atmosphere in which private acts of retribution, such as Jack the Ripper's, were almost encouraged.[23]

21. The official position of the Victorian administration regarding the medical and moral responsibility for the venereal "plague" in the 1860s "clearly sets male and female sexuality apart: 'there is no comparison to be made between prostitutes and the men who consort with them'" (Bell 1994, 58).

22. The Contagious Diseases Act, 1866, Public General Acts 15, 29 Vic. Cap. xxxiv, p. 138. For a detailed discussion see Walkowitz 1980; and Bell 1994.

23. For a discussion of Jack the Ripper see chapter 5.

The legal panic regarding prostitutes was accompanied by a deep scientific ambition to measure and categorize them, to construct their "professional profile." Like the witches in the Middle Ages, Victorian prostitutes were a favorite object of man's lust for scientific knowledge. Shannon Bell finds that in the nineteenth century "the prostitute was territorialized as an 'object of inquiry' and defined as a distinct female body" (Bell 1994, 41). Scientific experiments, often brutally imposed on prostitutes imprisoned in lock hospitals (Walkowitz 1980, 55), established that they had distinguishable physical and mental characteristics. Their eyes, for example, "have been found to be decidedly darker than those of either respectable women or criminals. . . . Fronsari's study revealed that 'prostitutes were . . . of lower type than the normal individuals, having smaller heads and larger faces'" (Bell 1994, 68). The scientific study of streetwalkers was complemented by increasing control over and regulation of their lives and sexuality.

The primary victims of the Victorian prostitute craze were, of course, the wretched women forced to sell their bodies on the streets of London. But all women became suspect by association. The Victorians, on the whole, accepted the church's traditional alliance of female sexuality and sin. The Victorian version consisted of a firm belief that, whereas it is natural and normal for men to experience (hetero)sexual drives, women have no legitimate claim for sexual urges.[24] Sexual desire in women was considered unnatural, perverted, beastly, and unfeminine. Sexuality tarnished women's natural modesty and drove them to prostitution, which was deemed immoral, sick, and dangerous to individual men and the public order. (Indeed, any contact with feminine sexuality was considered sinful and therefore dangerous to men.) Through a naturalistic fallacy, the Victorians reasoned that if female sexuality and pleasure are morally evil, then they are not natural, and what is unnatural cannot be common, especially not in women who are not evil. Most women are not, must not, cannot be sexual, and the few others who are, therefore, are perverse. Nevertheless, they also believed that any woman could potentially, at any time, turn to carnal ways. This double-edged line of thought naturally generated the dread that any woman might potentially turn out to be sexually perverse, that is, a prostitute. Initiation of a woman into marital and motherly duties was therefore perceived as precarious, since sexual experience could possibly trigger a latent perverse tendency and bring about sin and retribution (Reynolds and Humble 1993, 49).

24. In *Making Sex*, Thomas Laqueur presents the argument that whereas in the Old World (starting with ancient Greece) Woman was viewed as an imperfect version of Man, the eighteenth century saw the transformation of the sexes into inherently different forms of being. "The dominant, though by no means universal, view since the eighteenth century has been that there are two stable, incommensurable, opposite sexes and that the political, economic, and cultural lives of men and women, their gender roles, are somehow based on these 'facts'" (1990, 6).

According to this philosophy, prostitutes were inherently perverse, for otherwise they would not have "fallen"; at the same time it was their "fall" into sexuality that made them perverse and evil. This vicious cycle is akin to the Christian theology applied to Eve and her seduction by the serpent. But since Victorian science established that men's sexual desire was natural, the Victorian fallen Eves, the prostitutes, had no snake to blame. As for other women, Victorian England established "that women were almost of two species" (Tropp 1990, 136): the asexual, good wife-mother and the sexual, evil prostitute. But despite the binary opposition with which wife and prostitute were conceptualized, the Victorians believed that

> immoral women were not the only ones to stimulate gonorrheal inflammation in men. The vaginal discharge of virtuous women could also generate "disease" in men. . . . designating all women as potential pollutants of men and reservoirs of infection . . . evoked a more general hostility and dread of females and female "nature." (Walkowitz 1980, 56)

Shannon Bell determines that in Victorian writings "one finds a sliding between the prostitute body and the mother body; between the prostitute as different, as contaminated other, and as the same, the same as 'our' mothers, daughters and wives—'honest women'" (1994, 42). Much like the witch, the "common prostitute" was not only a deviant female, but also the manifestation of feminine potential. She was Lilit, but also a threatening Eve.

Much like the medieval legendary character of the witch, the Victorian social type of the common prostitute mediated between the image of the mythological archetypal female stalker and real women. In times of social apprehension regarding women's status, Western legal systems used these mediating images and applied Lilit's story to real women. Thus the female stalking story materialized in moral panics. Women who practiced sorcery or carried out abortions and women who sold sexual services may have actually challenged the social order. There may have even been good reason for legal intervention in their conducts. But the legal measures that grew out of moral panics did not address the actual social problems. Instead, they labeled, stereotyped, and demonized unpopular categories of women.

CHAPTER 4

Male Stalkers

Preview

Like female stalking, male stalking is experienced as a lurking, watchful, uncontrollable, supernatural threat. This sensation is, however, less uncanny and less ridden with desire and longing. Male stalking is not necessarily perceived as following a pattern of repetitive return. It is not necessarily nocturnal, nor is it sexual in nature. It is ever-present, omnipotent, and overpowering. It controls, subordinates, objectifies, judges, and condemns. Unlike female stalking stories, those about male stalkers are not a subversive cultural element, but rather a disciplinary mechanism of the (patriarchal) social order. The most illuminating metaphor of male stalking is the biblical God's watchful, ever-present, and unseen eye, waiting to witness man's fall.

In this chapter I argue that when the Hebrew God succeeded the Great Goddess of antiquity, he appropriated her all-seeingness. The ancient symbol of divine nourishment, comfort, and wisdom took on additional attributes of total control, objectification, spying, and stalking. This patriarchal, Godly omniscience inspired the cultural creation of distinct patterns of stalking, which evolved closely linked with mythological male characters. Adam's burning ambition to resemble God through knowledge of the other (especially Eve) developed, in Christian medieval Europe, into the Faustian overreaching pursuit, experienced by its human objects as stalking and controlling.[1] Satan's character developed as the heavenly spying stalker, suddenly present at people's moments of weakness and failure, ever ready to seduce, report, and condemn. His sneaking, tempting, prosecuting reappearance constitutes a pattern of male stalking. The legendary vampire is my fourth and most powerful image of a male stalker. With his penetrating

---

1. Doctor Faust (most likely named after a Dr. Johan Faust, 1480–1540) is a legendary scholar who traded his immortal soul for superhuman knowledge and the power to practice magic. He achieved his ambitious and sinful desire by entering into a pact with the Devil, signed with his blood and, consequently, at the end of his earthly life, he was cast into hell. Goethe's version of the legend turned Faust into the prototypical Romantic overreaching hero. (Book 1 was published in 1808, and the second posthumously in 1832.)

I treat Faust as an overreaching Adam character. Another possible interpretation, suggested by Nehama Aschkenasy, is to see Eve as Faust's predecessor (1986, 41). Unlike Eve's desire to know good and evil, Faust seeks knowledge and power well "beyond" good and evil, and yet Eve's Judeo-Christian sinful weakness became Faust's Romantic virtuous ambition; *her* fall—*his* tragedy. While her curiosity and desire to overreach were traditionally associated with the fatal Pandora's, his overreaching elevated him in the eyes of the Romantics to the status of the tragic, heroic Prometheus. Whereas she was severely punished for tempting Adam, he was completely exonerated of tempting Margaret.

gaze, the vampire stalks his human prey (especially women), exposing and punishing carnal, sinful Eves. The vampire is not merely a male stalker; he appropriates the female stalker's symbols and pattern of stalking, thus subordinating the subversive notion of female stalking to the controlling, authoritative imagery of male stalking. Much like the son-God who replaced his mother-Goddess in ancient Near Eastern religions, this mythological male stalker gradually took on his female counterpart's powers, features, and symbols, sucking away her vitality, finally eclipsing and subduing her altogether.

In close proximity to its male stalkers, European folklore also nurtured "haunting images," of which the Wandering Jew may be the most elaborate example.[2] The Flying Dutchman (also known as the Ancient Mariner) and the Romantics' Cain can be seen as his descendants.[3] A brief reference to the haunting Wandering Jew may illuminate stalking and the fear of stalking through comparison with haunting and the fear of being haunted.

2. The legend of the Wandering Jew originated in the aftermath of the "Antichrist" hysteria at the turn of the first Christian millennium. (It was believed that the end of the first Christian millennium would bring both the Antichrist and Judgment Day [Gaer 1961, 18].) The first written account of it known today dates from 1250; it records the Wanderer's appearance to an Armenian archbishop in 1228 (15–18). During the following centuries numerous versions of the legend spread throughout Europe, but several basic features were common to most. The Wanderer was usually a Jew and most often his name was Ahasuerus. "He was inordinately tall and gaunt, with snowy white hair falling over his shoulders, and a beard reaching to his chest" (34). He was born in Jerusalem on the same day as Jesus and witnessed the Crucifixion. When, carrying the cross, Jesus stopped to rest, Ahasuerus exhorted him to keep going, in reply to which Jesus condemned him to wander restlessly until the day of judgment (i.e., Jesus' Second coming). Christ's reproach doomed the Wanderer to an eternal life of misery: he lived Christ's Via Dolorosa forever. Over and over again he aged normally, until, on reaching a certain age, he was always rejuvenated to his age on the day of the Crucifixion. "He felt compelled to wander from one place to another and from one country to another, stopping nowhere long enough to make friends or to feel at home. He wandered on in poverty and privation and in utter loneliness, year after year, decade after decade" (36). In some countries, Gaer records, "he appeared only in stormy weather, because storms and hurricanes surrounded him; and pestilence followed in his footsteps" (40). In Slavic Eastern Europe he could change himself into a dog, and his age correlated with the phases of the moon (60–61). In some versions of the legend, the Wandering Jew is identified as Cain (79).

3. In most folk tales, the Flying Dutchman, a legendary living-dead mariner, was doomed forever to sail the seas (usually around the Cape of Good Hope) on board his phantom ship. He was said to have brought this fate upon himself by trading his soul for the Devil's help in rounding the cape during a storm. Sailors allegedly believed that seeing the Dutchman on his phantom ship was a sure sign of approaching death. In Coleridge's chilling poetic variation on the theme, the "Ancient Mariner" sinned in needlessly shooting a harmless albatross. "Life-in-Death," a female character, won the captain's soul in a card game with "Death," and the man was thus condemned to roam forever, undead, cursed by all the sailors whose deaths he had caused. He roamed around the world telling of his fall and punishment, an undead symbol and warning (Magnuson 1974, 50–84). Coleridge's mariner resembles the Wandering Jew in his lack of compassion; the legend of the Dutchman manifests an obvious "Faustian" theme. As for the making of Cain (who was traditionally associated with the Wandering Jew) into a Romantic hero, see Byron 1986, 881.

The legend of the Wandering Jew is the story of a sinner (against God, love, and compassion) who cannot die and of his unbound wandering and homelessness. It is a story of repetitive, unhappy rejuvenation and recurring appearances. It was experienced throughout Europe as uncanny and haunting. Like stalking characters, the Wanderer was an undying, lingering reminder of antiquity, sin, and punishment. But unlike Lilit, Satan, or the vampire, the Wanderer was neither threatening nor harmful; he did not follow humans, spy on them, lie in wait for them, target, attack, or seduce them. On the contrary, he was a tormented, guilt-ridden wretch, carrying with him painful memories of bygone times in an ancient land and the misery of eternal punishment. It was merely his uninvited, unexpected appearances that disturbed the living's sense of security in their own time and space, and aroused their fear of being haunted.

This haunting image shows that what distinguishes haunters from stalkers is the active approach to the community of the living taken by the latter. Whereas the Wanderer merely reappears uncalled for, stalkers both reappear and actively initiate relationships, targeting individuals and pursuing them. Stalking, therefore, includes both haunting and active pursuit.

God as a Stalker

When the conquering male God succeeded the Goddess, he seized heaven and earth, land and sea. Taking over her powers and functions, he transformed them. He took charge of creation but, having no vulva, he created with his Word: he named things into being and wrote history. Inheriting the Goddess's Look, he transformed that divine source of life and protection into a controlling, disciplining weapon. The Hebrew God, YHWH, who tolerated no other and had no image, was unseen and unthinkable; his ever-seeing-all was invisible monitoring. His Look made his human subjects feel stalked. The biblical story of Eden amply illustrates this point:

> And the eyes of them both were opened, and they knew that they were naked; and they sewed fig leaves together, and made themselves aprons. And they heard the voice of the Lord God walking in the garden in the cool of the day: and Adam and his wife hid themselves from the presence of the Lord God amongst the trees of the garden. And the Lord God called unto Adam, and said unto him, Where art thou? (Gen. 3:7–9)[4]

The Lord God's Look, as represented by Adam and Eve's experience of their nakedness in the garden, is an omnipresent, spying eye that surveys

4. I read God's "Where art thou?" as a rhetorical question, implying control and reprimand.

their every move, witnesses their every fall, leaves them no space for privacy, intimacy, or autonomous personhood. Its unseen presence recognizes no boundaries. Adam and Eve feel there is no place for them to hide from this gaze; they are helpless, paralyzed, unable to look back at their watcher; they feel stalked. To use Sartre's terms, the Edenic scene establishes God as the ultimate Other and the ultimate Subject, his Look both shaming Adam and Eve and objectifying them. His complete, overwhelming Subjectivity, manifested in his unseen eye, forces them to conceive themselves as mere objects of his Look, denying them the opportunity to perceive themselves as autonomous subjects. (For a brief presentation of Sartre's relevant terminology see appendix 4.1.)

People subjected to the controlling mechanisms of totalitarian regimes often experience the kind of stalking that is described in Genesis through the image of God's watchful eye. The biblical, literary description of God's stalking can be read as manifesting and constituting the more worldly stalking of ruling authorities. This pattern is experienced as male stalking and is narrated through male images, because in our contemporary social order both God and state are male entities.

Faustian Pursuit of Knowledge as Stalking and Control

In Western culture, the desire for knowledge is manifested in the human pursuit of selfhood and control. Taken to its extreme, it is man's way of attempting to adopt the totalistic point of view of our culture's male God; to achieve the all-seeing, all-judging Look. It is the human means of categorizing, objectifying, "othering," and subordinating. When such one-sided, penetrating study is aimed at another human being in an attempt to *fully know* him or her, it can, much like the Godly Look, be experienced and described by the objectified other as stalking.

Because the extreme pursuit of knowledge threatens to blur the boundaries between the human and the divine, it is strictly forbidden by our culture's God and his human representatives; overreaching searchers of forbidden knowledge are condemned as sinners. In European folklore, the mythological Dr. Faust is the allegorical seeker of that knowledge. Faust sought to know nature's innermost secrets; he yearned to know all the hows and whys. He aspired to look at creation from God's unique point of view. Like the biblical God, he objectified and stalked his human objects. I therefore refer to this kind of stalking pursuit of knowledge as "Faustian." (Another notorious overreaching knowledge seeker is Don Juan, the "knower of women").

Women have always been the most vulnerable victims of the Faustian pursuit of knowledge. Even in the first days, having experienced God's stalking Look, Adam-Faust attempted to exercise similar power by *knowing* Eve, his wife (Gen. 4:1), penetrating her both sexually and intellectually (the Hebrew root *yda* denotes both knowledge and sexual penetration). Campbell demonstrates that Adam's attitude is culturally disguised as "natural," matter-of-factly noting that "woman in the picture language of mythology represents the totality of what can be known. The hero is the one who comes to know" (Campbell and Muses 1991, 116). Within this conceptual framework, in order to be a hero, Adam must be Faust and strive to know Eve; he must penetrate and control her, make her reveal her secrets, and leave her no space she can call her own. He must objectify and shame her. D. H. Lawrence insightfully observed that when fully successful, this knowledge-seeking results in the death of its human object; thus, stalking blooms into murder: "To *know* a living thing is to kill it. You have to kill a thing to know it satisfactorily. For this reason, the desirous consciousness, the SPIRIT, is a vampire."[5]

Faust's "courtship" of Margaret proved fatal (to her) because it was part of his overreaching attempt to know all. The pattern was, therefore, conquest, penetration, control, loss of interest, and (her) death.

Men's frustrated inability to fully know and control Lilit may have motivated the fierce Faustian stalking of women who were labeled as her incarnations. I mentioned in chapter 2 that both witches and prostitutes were subjected to extreme inspections, inquisition, and monitoring. Under the guise of scientific, theological, and legal justifications, the women's bodies were zealously ripped open, penetrated, and forced to reveal their concealed secrets. In both these cases, the social, collective Faustian stalking

---

5. In his analysis of both Edgar Allen Poe and the hero of his short story "Ligeia," Lawrence powerfully claims that to fully know a woman is to objectify and kill her:

> What he [the fictional husband] wants to do with Ligeia is to analyze her, till he knows all her component parts, till he has got her all in his consciousness. . . . she never was quite a human creature to him. She was an instrument, from which he got his extremes of sensation. . . . It is easy to see why each man kills the thing he loves. To *know* a living thing is to kill it. You have to kill a thing to know it satisfactorily. For this reason, the desirous consciousness, the SPIRIT, is a vampire. . . . to try to *know* any living being is to try to suck the life out of that being. Above all things, with the woman one loves. . . . To try to *know* her mentally is to try to kill her. . . . It is the temptation of a vampire fiend, is this knowledge. Man does so horribly want to master the secret of life and of individuality *with his mind.* It is like the analysis of protoplasm. You can only analyze *dead* protoplasm, and know its constituents. It is a dead process. Keep knowledge for the world of matter, force, and function. It has nothing to do with being. (1953, 78–80)

Edgar Allan Poe's cycle "The Death of a Beautiful Woman" includes six horror tales of women who are mentally "vampirized" by their lovers; in some cases they come back from the dead to "vampirize" the men in return. The most celebrated of the six is "The Fall of the House of Usher," in which Roderick buries his beloved twin sister Madeline in the cellar of their home, and when she returns to take him with her, the whole house crumbles and buries them both. But Poe's own favorite, and the story he thought his very best, was "Ligeia" (1976, 64; for a compact summary of the mesmerizing short story see Frost 1989, 41).

endeavor was portrayed as an innocent defensive means of combating women who were themselves constructed as threatening stalkers. It is plain to see how such manipulation of stalking imagery facilitates moral panics: the persecuted "folk-devils" are described as stalkers, and their persecution, which includes massive Faustian stalking by the community, is righteously defined as scientific, legal, moral, and an inevitable act of self-defense.

Satan, the Spying Stalker

The spying aspect of God has evolved into the mythological character of Satan, also known as Lucifer and the Devil. The biblical Hebrew name, Satan, implies "he who obstructs, persecutes, and engages in defamatory reporting."[6] In the book of Job, in his most renowned biblical appearance, Satan is a member of the heavenly court, who reports on his strolling the land to and fro.[7] Tur-Sinai explains that Satan's strolling mimics that of the Persian kings' secret police and intelligence agents, who, according to the historian Herodotus, were the king's "eyes and ears" throughout his kingdom (Forsyth 1987, 114).[8] The biblical Satan thus wanders about the land spying on people and seeing all; he witnesses moments of weaknesses; he gathers prosecutional information in order to condemn the fallen. In the New Testament, Peter warns Christians: "Be sober, be vigilant; because your adversary the devil, as a roaring lion, walketh about, seeking whom he may devour" (1 Pet. 5:8). This ancient image subsisted for many centuries and was especially prominent in medieval Europe.

The New Testament, as well as Jewish postbiblical legends, endowed Satan's image with an additional layer of meaning. Satan was portrayed both as a powerful, evil seducer and as God's bitter opponent. His powers of seduction are illustrated in his temptation of Judas Iscariot (John 13:2) and even of Jesus himself (Luke 4:5–7). The book of Revelation offers the following description of Satan as God's primordial opponent:

And there was war in heaven: Michael and his angels fought against the dragon. . . . And the great dragon was cast out, that old serpent, called the Devil, and Satan, which deceiveth the whole world: he was cast out into the earth, and his angels were cast out with him. (Rev. 12:3–9)

6. The Greek *diabolos* ("devil") is the literary translation of the proper name *Satan*.

7. "[T]he sons of God came to present themselves before the Lord, and Satan came also among them. And the Lord said unto Satan, Whence comest thou? Then Satan answered the Lord and said, From going to and fro in the earth, and from walking up and down in it" (Job 1:6–7).

8. Forsyth adds that the Hebrew root used to convey Satan's "strolling" *(hithallek)* is "cognate with the Akkadian word applied to the evil eye or to evil spirits that rove about seeking to harm" (Forsyth 1987, 114).

This last feature was greatly enhanced through the Latin translation of the Bible. The Vulgate used the name Lucifer to denote both the Hebrew Satan and the ancient Mesopotamian mythological character of the archangel who had rebelled against his father God and fallen from grace. In thus doing, the Vulgate identified Satan as that rebellious angel, the cosmic opponent of the heavenly God and rule (Forsyth 1987, 134–39).[9] Cast as God's adversary, Satan became his "mirror" reflection: cosmic Evil (and therefore also Sexuality) incarnate, King of Hell and Death, leader of other fallen angels and all demons and God's rival for domination over human souls. In his efforts to master human souls, Satan perfected his tempting skills, and became the familiar, seducing Devil.

In the legends of Satan as a primordial fallen angel, he was incited to rebellion by his jealousy of God's beloved creature, Man, and his arrogant refusal to worship this younger brother. Thus, jealousy was the motivation for the Devil's eternal hatred of Man, as well as for his spying and seducing stalking. His jealousy was manifested in his portrayal as an "evil eye," which, in popular belief, connotes jealousy, supernatural envy, and spite.[10] Within the Christian world, Satan came to be the focus of fear of this type of evil eye: if his seeking jealous eye were to see happiness, he would surely do his utmost to destroy it.[11]

Additionally, the Christian Devil is not merely God's opponent, but also a negative, shadow image of Christ. Furthermore, "The primary target of Satan's animus and envy is the Son. These two, the Son and Satan, are precisely and dramatically opposites" (Frye 1960, 31). Satan is, quite literally, an Antichrist.[12]

In conclusion, in light of Satan's complex character, his stalking combines spying in the service of God with rebellious seduction. It is laden with jealousy, hate, wickedness, and treacherousness. Satan's dubious relation to God makes his stalking both subversive and disciplining. Although his seductive power might have tempted some sinners, it must have also motivated fearful Christians to constantly monitor their behavior and thoughts. And lest any Christian forget the danger of the Evil lurking in the shadows,

9. Isaiah's famous ironic ridicule of the Babylonian monarch, cast in the ancient Mesopotamian image of the rebelling angel, was translated in the Vulgate into "How art thou fallen from heaven, O, Lucifer, son of the morning!" (Isa. 14:12–15). In the original Hebrew text, the rebel's name is not Satan, but *Hillel Ben-Shahar*, literally meaning "light, son of dawn."

10. "Its root is the pagan conviction that the gods and the spirits are essentially man's adversaries, that they envy him his joys and his triumphs, and spitefully harry him for the felicities they do not share" (Trachtenberg 1979, 54).

11. The mentioned legend also supported Satan's identification as the serpent who tempted Eve and caused the Fall of Man, which mimicked Lucifer's own, thereby suggesting an analogy between the two fallen heroes, Satan and Adam.

12. The Antichrist was a powerful negative concept, and he was expected to rise before Christ's Second Coming only to be defeated by the powers of light.

the church and the guilds organized annual stage performances of the Christian mysteries, or "miracle plays," a prominent one being *The Creation and the Fall of Lucifer*.[13] The English Corpus Christi plays always began with Lucifer's Fall, followed by the Fall of Man. They displayed the Resurrection and ended with the Last Judgment (Hardison 1965, 473). In this context, Satan's stalking is a fearful obstacle to be overcome by Christians aspiring to rejoice in the Second Coming; it is an ordeal to be endured.

The Vampire: Introduction and Overview

Of the mythological male stalkers, the vampire is the most complex and powerful.[14] Christian Europe's vampire is a reanimated corpse that leaves its grave at night to stalk and prey on the living and to suck their blood in order to sustain its "undead" condition.[15] The vampire of folklore has a deadly, pale complexion, dark hair, sharp teeth (sometimes fangs), rosy lips, and a diabolical, chilling smile. But his most significant physical feature is his wide open, fixed eyes, with which he stares at his victims, hypnotizing them "with a blood chilling gaze" (Copper 1975, 28). The vampire's all-seeing eyes remain "gazing open" even while he sleeps (Twitchell 1981, 12, 57). Bloodsucking stands out as the most definitive behavioral characteristic of the vampire at all times (although this trait is in itself neither necessary nor sufficient for the identification of a vampire). The vampire preys on living humans, most often women, usually his closest kin, and usually in their sleep at night. Being mostly nocturnal, his visits carry sexual connotations. He leaves distinct bodily marks of his bloodsucking (nowadays always on the victim's neck). The folkloristic vampire, if not stopped, would gradually drain all life from his victim. Vampires of the modern era can sometimes initiate their victims (or at least their preferred ones) into vampirism, but there seems to be no proof that vampires possessed this capacity before the late seventeenth century (Twitchell 1985, 106).

Vampires are photophobic night hunters. In the dark of night their powers increase dramatically, whereas during the day they are significantly weakened, and vampires often need to take refuge from the light by hiding or by sleeping until nightfall. At least since the turn of the nineteenth cen-

13. For the text of one such version, from York, England, see Cawley 1993, 1.

14. My discussion of vampires relies on the works of numerous writers. Many of my "factual" statements are considered "common knowledge" and are frequently repeated in any discussion of vampirism. I rely mostly on Twitchell 1981, 1985; Frayling 1987; Senn 1982; Leatherdale 1987, 1993; Florescu and McNally 1992; Frost 1989; Roth 1982; L. E. Walker 1998; Wolf 1975, 1997; Ursini and Silver 1975; Snef 1988; Carter 1989; and Copper 1975.

15. Vampires seem to exist in every corner of the world; my discussion here concerns only those who populated the legends of Christian Europe, and are, in this respect, "Christian." Just as the medieval European witch was typically female, so the folkloristic ("traditional") vampire was typically male; I will therefore refer to it as "he."

tury, moonlight miraculously revives and rejuvenates them (Twitchell 1981, 111). Vampires fly through the night in the shape of birds or bats; some can also cover great distances by changing into mist, fog, or storm. A vampire does not (usually) cast shadows, nor reflections in mirrors. He generally leads a solitary (noncommunal) life and is driven solely by self-interest, namely his urge to maintain his "undead" survival. Most vampires can enter a house (or a dream?) only when invited in by a living human. Vampires have always been accused of carrying diseases and spreading plagues of various sorts. They often frequent crossroads, like Lilit and the witch.[16]

The vampire personifies the coupling of the most uncouplable categories of our social order: life and death. He both "is" and "is not"; he is dead and alive and neither. The vampire also obfuscates the clear distinction between categories that are fundamental to human language and to our social and moral orders. The vampiristic (non)existence establishes an unthinkable (dis)association between such concepts as body and soul, nature and culture, beastly and human. By sucking a nourishing life-giving liquid from his female (sexual) partner the vampire blurs the sacred distinctions, the patriarchal boundaries between mother and wife, love and lust, familial intimacy and erotic bonding. He brings together the sexual woman and the nonsexual/motherly woman, thereby stripping both categories of their meaning. With his "feminine" traits (in which he resembles female stalkers) he transcends and confuses even the most fundamental binary distinctions between male and female. The returning vampire bridges the divide between present and past, carrying the latter into the former. He also adds an amusing twist to the doppelgänger motif of man and his mirror image monster. Casting no reflection, being both man and monster, the vampire undermines the very binary structure in which the idea of "double" is rooted. This brings vampire and man very close together.

By blurring the distinctions between basic, dichotomous concepts, the vampire subverts the whole structure of binary thinking, the structure often depicted as the underlying paradigm of patriarchal rationality and as the basis for Western culture as we know it. To put this in slightly less abstract terms: if death is an inherent part of life and vice versa, and if the same applies to many other categories, believed to constitute unbridgeable opposites, then perhaps our whole system of thought is tentative rather than absolute and exclusive.

The vampire's outstanding features and story seem to relate to a multi-

16. "Christian" vampires (those acknowledged and used by the church as symbols of evil) cannot cross running water and are unable to harm anyone protected by holy water or garlic or, best of all, the sign of the cross. The most effective methods of destroying them include decapitation, driving stakes through their hearts, and fire. It is, of course, advisable to combat vampires in daylight. Christian vampires are also closely related to Satan. Sometimes a vampire is a sinner's body, possessed by the Devil himself, and used by him to cause evil. Some vampires result from witches' carnal pleasures with the Devil (Leatherdale 1993, 30).

tude of human emotions and mental states, particularly fears. Some fears are addressed by the vampire myth almost explicitly: the dread of dying and of death, of the approach of death (thanatophobia), of being buried alive (or of having thus buried another), and of that which awaits us after death. The myth also clearly relates to fears of loss of vitality, of aging, of fatal hunger (or thirst), of uncontrolled epidemics and plagues, of being eaten (perhaps by stronger, superior beings), of being trapped (claustrophobia). It touches on fears of the unknown, of supernatural powers, of the inhuman, of the unholy, of nightmares, of nocturnal emission ("wet dreams"), and of incest. The vampire connotes people's fear of forgetting the dead (or of being forgotten by them) and their fear of the dead's envy and revenge. Within our contemporary frame of mind, it makes sense to read into the vampire legend multiple fears: fear of disorientation (both in time and place), of (co)dependence, of the "Other"; fear of ruthless tyrannical power, of omnipotence, of selfishness, of helplessness; fear of the incestuous father, of castration, and of returning to the womb (the womb being connected with death, coffin, grave, etc.). The vampire seems to express fear of sexuality, some men's fear of their attraction to and their need of the feminine (in women and in themselves) and fear that incest is inherent to intimacy with any woman. These fears are often inseparable from the hostilities they evoke.

Theorists did not fail to notice the vampire's symbolic potential, and they associated him with a wide variety of emotions, complexes, and mental states. For the psychoanalyst Ernest Jones, the vampire story portrays the Oedipal complex, personifying the transformation of love into hate and then into guilt (1951, 320). "The vampire," Twitchell suggests, "was variously used to personify the forces of maternal attraction/repulsion, incest, oppressive paternalism, adolescent love, avaricious love, the struggle for power, sexual suppression, homosexual attraction, repressed sexuality, female domination, and, most Romantic of all, the artist himself exchanging energy with aspects of his art" (1981, 5). To this long list of learned interpretations I add the proposition that the vampire is our culture's most popular and interesting stalker. As such, he links our experience of stalking with the long list of emotions and fears cited above. Fears of death, of incest, of a supernatural hungering fiend, and of the loss of conventional categories have all been associated with stalking through centuries of vampire stalking stories. Furthermore, the vampire appropriates the female stalker's traditional characteristics, recruiting them to the service of the ruling patriarchy, subjecting the anxious desire associated with female stalking to the fear of male stalking. The following section expands on this argument.

The Vampire as Both Male and Female Stalker

The vampire is a male stalker. His hypnotic gaze resembles that of an omniscient God. Moreover, the fact that mirrors cannot capture his reflection endows him with something of the biblical God's imagelessness (an absolute one-sidedness).[17] In a (Sartrean) world where the Look establishes its owner's subjecthood and reduces the looked-at to object, the mirror poses an inherent absolute threat. The vampire's reflectionlessness assures his subjecthood by guarding him from his own powerful gaze. He is so much a subject that even his own reflection does not look back at him.

As a male stalker, the vampire disciplines humans, especially women, into obeying patriarchal ideology.

In the ancient world it was the love of a divine woman, Inanna, that brought Dumuzi, her brother-lover, back from death. The Christian version of this myth, the story of Mary and Jesus, omitted this element, stressing, on the other hand, Eve's moral culpability for man's death in general, and for Christ's in particular. The Christian shadow story, the vampire legend, once again attributes man's resurrection to woman. Her blood is life-giving. But unlike Inanna, the vampire's Eve is sinful and fallen, and it is her sin that brought about the curse of death unto man, and thus also unto the vampire. This feminine character brings her man back from the dead through her persistent yearning; evoking his monstrous desire for her, she incites his passion—as well as his hunger for retaliation (for his death). In addressing the issue of retribution, the vampire story substitutes Christ's nonsexual return from the dead for a violent male version of a Lilit-like return to a reprehensible loved one. (For a full discussion of the argument in this paragraph see appendix 4.2.)

In this interpretive context, the vampire story becomes plausibly simple: woman, because she is sexually sinful, causes man's death; subsequently, she brings him back to life through her psychological attachment to him and by inspiring his vengeful desire for her. Man returns from the dead to reunite with his woman once again. In their reunion, he makes her the sexual woman she is, combining her crime and punishment, just like Eve's curse in Christian theology. He also tortures her to death as a just and punitive revenge for his own death. The vampire's story of male stalking thus becomes the story of woman's just punishment by man.

The centrality of the vampire's bloodsucking supports this line of thought. The bloodsucking implies the woman's lack of sexual virtue (loss of virginity), her sexual punishment (rape), and incest (sexual "breast-feeding"). It also alludes to menstruation, which in Western monotheism came to be a manifestation of Eve's curse for her sinful sexuality. The vampire inflicts menstruation on women as a shaming punishment that symbolizes their guilt.

The vampire is, therefore, a disciplining, patriarchal stalker whose female victims are presented as carnal women, guilty of both the vampire's

17. Of the interpretations offered to explain the vampire's "reflectionlessness" I particularly appreciate that given by Wolf, who claims that the vampire does actually appear in the mirror, "but we fail to recognize him since our own faces get in the way" (Wolf 1975, xviii).

death and his return, and deserving of punishment. Twitchell's point, therefore, is not at all surprising: "The rise of Christianity, ironically, did as much to nurture the vampire as the plague would later do, for the Christian Catholic Church found in the story of this fiend a most propitious analogy to describe the intricate working of evil" (1985, 106).

At the same time, the vampire, more than the other male stalkers I discuss, portrays every symbol associated with female stalking. Like Lilit, the vampire is a nocturnal sexual predator, who typically returns repeatedly to a loved-hated close kin. His supernatural night flights, his birdlike image, his close relation with the moon and the spreading of plagues all associate him with his feminine counterpart. So does, of course, his appearance: the pale face, the red lips, the menacing teeth, the fangs, the protruding tongue. As in Lilit's case, the "family" context—he targets his kin—intensifies the emotional impact of the vampire's uncanny sexual return.

The vampire, therefore, appropriates the female stalker's traditional features and symbolic role. He is a male image that submerges the concept of female stalking within that of male stalking. Having acquired Lilit's attributes, the vampire embodies many of the traits that defined the ancient female stalker. But, being a male, patriarchal stalker, the vampire is less subversive and less threatening to the dominant social order. This may explain why the vampire was preferred to Lilit and grew to be our culture's most popular stalking character. Just as in antiquity the young male Gods took over the Goddesses' powers and roles, so did the vampire unseat Lilit.

Moral Panics

The mythological characters presented in this chapter were linked with large-scale hysterical behaviors, including moral panics. Thus, for example, the Devil was used during anti-Semitic moral panics, such as the European blood libels (in which Jews were said to abduct Christian children and use their blood for Passover rituals) and the recurring accusations that Jews carried the plague. The Devil, of course, was also evoked during the witch-hunts. The vampire as well played a central role in times of public panic. When "whole cities of people would be coughing blood one week, gasping on the streets the next, and dying during the third or fourth," the vampire was often said to be the reason for the plague (Twitchell 1981, 19). Popular wisdom had it that "the first person affected and killed by the plague becomes the vampire; he sits upright in his grave, and feeds on his shroud. The plague lasts as long a time as he takes to be finished with it" (Rank 1975, 68).[18]

18. The reason for the vampire panics, according to most writers, was that during the medieval plagues, when the hasty interment of corpses was of vital importance, more people were likely to be buried "undead": in comas, in catatonic fits, and in shock. "Lively" looking contorted bodies, combined with the fear of premature burial, explain the perpetuation of the vampire legend.

In some moral panics, social groups who were associated with these mythological stalkers were labeled "folk devils" and fiercely persecuted. (In periods of anti-Semitic moral panic, for example, Jews were identified with the Devil). But, interestingly, in stalking moral panics, the disciplining, patriarchal nature of the mythological male stalkers may, paradoxically, facilitate the persecution not of stalking men, but of their women victims, who are identified as fallen Eves or Lilit women. In the moral panic surrounding Jack the Ripper, it was the prostitutes who were most demonized. I discuss this in the next chapter. In chapter 7, I illustrate how the mythological images of male stalkers are currently being used in the creation of the contemporary stalking moral panic.

Sartre's Objectifying God

Jean-Paul Sartre analyzes the biblical Edenic scene through the framework of the notions of self, object, and shame. In *Being and Nothingness,* the Look serves Sartre as a basic notion in the discussion of subject and object, self and other, power and shame. Sartre defines the perceiving human subject as "being-*for*-itself," which means "nothingness," unbound freedom, countless possibilities from which to choose. An object, on the other hand, is "being-*in*-itself": it just *is* that which it *is.* "The Other" is a look fixed on me, which "subjectifies" me in the sense that it allows me to reflect and perceive myself; "the being which is revealed to the reflective consciousness is for-itself-for-others" (Sartre 1966, 376). But, paradoxically, that same fixed look, the Other, also *objectifies* me, preventing my "being-*for*-itself," and thereby *shaming* me for my loss of freedom and mastery. For "we cannot perceive the world and at the same time apprehend a look fastened upon us; it must be either one or the other. This is because to perceive is to *look at,* and to apprehend a look is . . . to be conscious of *being looked at*" (347). Sartre stresses that it is the Other's look that both "spatializes and temporalizes us" (357).

The Other, therefore, the fixed look, undermines my subjectivity by forcing me to feel "looked at," like an object, rather than looking at the world like a subject. It restricts me as self in every possible way and prevents my "being-for-itself"; it overpowers and subjugates me (379); it kills me (if not as a material body, certainly as a subject). Shame within this framework is "the recognition of the fact that *I am* indeed that object which the Other is looking at and judging" (350). Shame is the degrading acknowledgment that one is but a "fixed and dependent being" for the Other; it is the feeling of an *original fall,* . . . that I have 'fallen' into the world in the midst of things and that I need the mediation of the Other in order to be what I am" (384).

God, in this analysis, is the ultimate Other, his Look the ultimate "objectifier" and "shamer." For Sartre, the episode of Adam and Eve's hiding in the garden, wrapped in their pathetic fig leaves, is

> a symbolic specification of original shame; the body symbolizes here our defenseless state as objects. To put on clothes is to hide one's object-state; it is to claim the right of seeing without being seen; that is, to be pure subject. This is why the biblical symbol of the fall after the original sin is the fact that Adam and Eve "know that they are naked." The reaction to shame will consist exactly in apprehending as an object the one who apprehended *my* own object-state. (384)

With the Lord God, salvation from shame by counterlook is not possible. The shame before God is "the recognition of my being-an-object before a subject which can never become an object." God, posited as "the absolute unity of the subject, which in no way can become an object," becomes the "eternity of my being-as-object and so perpetuate[s] my shame."

> The position of God is accompanied by a reification of my object-ness. Or better yet, I posit my being-an-object-for-God as more real than my For-itself; I exist alienated and I cause myself to learn from outside what I must be. This is the origin of the fear before God. Black masses, desecration of the host, demonic associations, etc., are so many attempts to confer the character of object on the absolute Subject. (385–86)

To rephrase Sartre in the context of my discussion, the "vulvaless," imageless male God cannot give birth to humans, nor create unity and intimacy; he, therefore, creates abstractly, using language. He creates categories, differences, and binary polarity. Creating subject, he must also create object. Creating self, he must create other, always in opposition, like himself and his creation. And if he defines himself as subjectivity, then by the "either/or" logic of his language he must doom us to existential "shame" of *being* (objects) for him, prey for his absolute Look. Because this God is wholly subject ("nothingness"), his absolute, one-sided Look, ever fixed on all that he surveys, "objectifies" everything, not allowing anyone a chance to be subject in relation to him. The Godly absolute, abstract, one-sided, dominating, controlling, "shaming-into-selflessness" Look: *this* is the look that turns men into stone.

Let me conclude this brief discussion of Sartre's ideas with a comment on his essentialistic description of the human condition. When axiomatically determining that while apprehending the Other's constituting look one cannot also look at that Other, Sartre assumes that the biblical, invisible, all-seeing God is the paradigmatic Other. But in a social reality free of such biblical imagery of the invisible, objectifying male God, people *can* look at each other compassionately, without rivalry and suspicion. It *is* possible to look into another's eyes and enjoy the feeling of being looked at without experiencing shame or submission; that is the joy of affection, intimacy, and trust. Being for others need not conflict with any other form of being, and certainly need not arouse what Sartre defines as "shame." Sartre quite accurately presents a possible, prevailing interpretation of our monotheistic, patriarchal world; but he fails to notice that the biblical text, as well as his own reading of it, does not merely depict this world as it "really is," but also constitutes it. It forms part of, and perpetuates, our worldview.

The Vampire as a Dumuzi Antichrist

In order to better understand the vampire's unique function as a male stalker, let me introduce him as Christ's shadow, cast in a Dumuzi role.

The myth of the periodic death and revival of Inanna's young son-lover, the God Dumuzi, was the most popular of ancient Near Eastern stories. The death and resurrection of the young God appeared in every ancient mythology, and the story is believed to have symbolized "one of the most ancient practices recorded—the ritual sacrifice of an annual 'king,' consort of the high priestess" (Stone 1976, 132).[1] The Hebrew Bible rejected the cyclic, lunar rhythm of this mythology, replacing it with the more linear, historical narrative of the creation, the Garden of Eden, and the Fall. Adam and Eve, the first Hebrew humans, replaced the divine Inanna and Dumuzi, gaining a father in heaven at the expense of a mother. But Hebrew women did not forsake the Goddess and her young, dying God, and even in the Temple at Jerusalem the women of Judah continued to mourn the death of the Goddess's son-lover, which had been completely expunged from the Hebrew's mythology.[2] So prevalent was this ritual that the summer month of Dumuzi's death was named after the young God; to this day, in the Jewish calendar, that month is called Tamuz.

Christianity embraced the story of the dying son-God: the narrative of Mary and Jesus clearly depicts the young God's birth, death, resurrection, and heavenly reunion with his mother.[3] The Christian identification of Jesus as the second Adam and of Mary as the second Eve united Inanna and Dumuzi's story with the biblical story of Eden; it also stressed the "family resemblance" between the story of Mary and Jesus and that of Inanna and Dumuzi. In the combined Christian story, the second Adam was son of the

---

1. "Most authors who discuss the sacrifice of the 'king' describe it primarily as a fertility rite, suggesting that his remains may have even been scattered over the newly sown fields" (Stone 1976, 135). According to this theory the death of Dumuzi is the "death" of crops in the heat of the Near Eastern summer. The phase of regeneration refers to the budding of new crops in winter, and the sacred rite is blooming spring. For a "lunar" interpretation of the myth see Baring and Cashford 1991, 147.

2. "Then he brought me to the gateway of the Lord's house which faces north; and there I saw the women sitting and wailing for Tammuz" (Ezek. 8:14). For a summary of the worship of the dying God in Israel see Stone 1976, 147.

3. Stone documents that the Anatolian version of the religion of the Goddess, in which Cybele and Attis feature as Inanna and Dumuzi, "was eventually brought from Anatolia to Rome. It was celebrated there in great processions and festivals until AD 268 and embraced by such emperors as Claudius and Augustus. We can only guess at the influence this had upon the Christian religion that was developing there at that time. Roman reports of the rituals of Cybele record that the son . . . was first tied to a tree and then buried. Three days later a light was said to appear in the burial tomb, whereupon Attis rose from the dead, bringing salvation with him in his rebirth (1976, 146). See also Baring and Cashford 1991, 607.

second Eve, Mary. His untimely, tragic death was related to Eve's role as Adam's wife and lover (Jesus died on the cross to redeem mankind from the original carnal sin, identified with Eve's sexuality). He returned to the second Eve from death and was finally reunited with her in heaven. This complex imagery retained all the elements of the ancient narrative of the young God's sexual relationship with his mother-wife-lover, his dying on her account and his return to her beyond life and death.[4]

Within the Christian context, the Inanna-Dumuzi relationship acquired new symbolic significance. In the ancient heyday of Inanna's rule, the concepts of life and death were relatively diffuse, and the notions of mother and lover seem not to have been mutually exclusive (at least regarding heavenly beings). Within the monotheistic patriarchal world, on the other hand, life and death, and motherhood and sexuality, were placed in strict binary oppositions, and their distinctions were sanctioned by the highest moral commands. Death and incest were the fundamental social taboos. In this context, the major elements of Dumuzi's story: death, resurrection, and the mother-son relationship, took on subversive connotations. Because these unholy aspects were ignored and repressed by the story of Jesus and Mary, they needed to be addressed in a parallel, shadow story. The vampire legend is that shadow story.

The vampire is Christ's negative mirror image. Accordingly, in the tradition of the Antichrist, the vampire refuses to die; his resurrection is unholy; he drinks the blood of Christians rather than letting them drink his own; he is associated with Satan; he selfishly sacrifices others for the sake of his own livelihood; and he is anticommunal. He is carnal, and his resurrection is associated with incestuous sexuality. In a word, he is a shadow-Christ Dumuzi.

4. In pre-Christian cultures the Inanna figure was mother, wife, and also Dumuzi's sister. My guess is that Mary's original Hebrew name, Miriam, carried with it strong connotations of sisterhood, because the biblical Miriam was introduced and remembered as "the sister of" Moses and Aaron. I find some support for this speculation in the Koran. In the chapter entitled "Mary," which narrates the story of Jesus and his mother, the Koran quotes Mary's people referring to her as "Sister of Aaron" (19:28).

CHAPTER 5

Stalking in Nineteenth-Century English Literature

Introduction and Preview

Chapters 2 and 4 presented male and female stalker archetypes as they were constructed and developed in Western mythology and folklore. Nineteenth-century European literature embraced these images, molding them to reflect and strengthen contemporary dispositions and superstitions. These literary interpretations became the basis for many of the concepts, both popular and "learned," that have been associated with stalking. This chapter focuses on English Gothic and Romantic literature, genres that played a significant part in this process of appropriation and modification.

In a backlash against the "progressive" era of "enlightenment," Gothic literature nostalgically idealized the medieval past, portraying it as primitive, savage, yet pure. The "rational" frame of mind was rejected and replaced by mythological reasoning, which focused obsessively on gory horror, taboo, and death (Panter 1980, 5–21).[1] The Romantic poets were enamored of the Gothic and were particularly fascinated with "the three principal symbolic figures which run through their Gothic work: the wanderer, the vampire and the seeker after forbidden knowledge" (99). They were also attracted by (their interpretation of) Milton's Satanic hero.[2]

The vampire was particularly well suited for the Romantics' needs, and "as part of the great mystery of love, life, death and the supernatural, the vampire became something of a vogue" (Leatherdale 1993, 45). The Romantic preoccupation with the vampire was such that by the end of the nineteenth century "the folkloric vampire of central and eastern Europe eventually metamorphosed into the British-built vampire of the Romantic literature." Similarly, in the same period, "the decadent Romantics made

---

1. David Panter describes Gothic culture as distinctly feminine. "To the dominant male-oriented ethos of Western society, love and sexuality display only an affirmative side: to the Gothic writers, they are the products and visible outcropping of darker forces, and thus the Gothics persist in trying to come to grips with their alternative forms—incest, sexual violence, rape—and in questioning the absolute nature of sexual role" (Panter 1980, 411).

2. Milton's Satan, in *Paradise Lost,* was the most acclaimed seventeenth-century English Satan. Unlike his notorious predecessors, "Milton's Satan has absorbed so many Promethean qualities that we are in danger of admiring him and sympathizing with him. Satan is in trespass and thus sinful; but at the same time he represents our (Greek and unregenerate) aspiration towards new and higher levels of existence, our human battle against heavy and indifferent odds" (Werblowsky 1952, xix).

Satan something of an esthetic fad" (Russell 1986, 218). Also intrigued by images I defined earlier as "haunting," the Romantics showed much interest in the Wandering Jew and his legendary "offspring": the Flying Dutchman, the Ancient Mariner, and their own version of the biblical Cain.[3] Don Juan, another Romantic favorite, often combined features of Faust, the Wanderer, and Satan.

Stalking (associated with haunting images) was, therefore, an underlying theme that was explored, developed, and redefined by this body of literary work.

This chapter explores nineteenth-century female and male writers' literary interpretations of stalking. I analyze Mary Shelley's *Frankenstein,* written in the early decades of the century, as a woman writer's subversive reformulation of stalking. Bram Stoker's *Dracula,* written at the end of the century, represents a man's perspective. A brief reference to Lady Caroline Lamb's *Glenarvon* serves as a prologue to the discussion of *Frankenstein.* The highly popular *Varney the Vampire* and Stevenson's *The Strange Case of Dr. Jekyll and Mr. Hyde* are treated as literary benchmarks arising between *Frankenstein* and *Dracula.*

In Shelley's fictional world, the target of stalking is an overreaching Faustian scientist; his stalker, "the creature," is the scientist's self-made other-self, that is, his literary double. The creature is explicitly linked with traditional male stalkers (Satan, the Wanderer, and the vampire), but, given a point of view and a voice, it is allowed to present itself as desperately trying to bond with its neglectful, egotistical creator. Sympathizing with the creature's torment and agony, Shelley holds the scientist responsible for his creature's "autostalking" (of its other-self, the scientist). She also holds the scientist responsible for the creature's killings of the scientist's closest kin, including his sister-lover. Nevertheless, the scientist, like his creature, is given both voice and point of view. This method of double first-person narration enables Shelley to illuminate both the psychological motivation underlying stalking and the victim's experience.

Bram Stoker's *Dracula,* on the other hand, reestablishes the male stalker as a modern, disciplining, patriarchal character. In Stoker's text, the male stalker is a bloodthirsty serial killer, presented as a Faustian, devilish vampire, who is considered to be a genetically defected individual of the "criminal type." This male stalker attacks women, distinguishing the pure Eves from the fallen ones and turning the latter into stalking Lilits who bow to his orders. The stalking and victimizing of women is part of a bonding game Stoker's vampire imposes on the community of men. In the heat of that game, the community becomes Dracula's double image, pornographically stalking and ripping women who are defined as dangerous prostitutes.

3. See chapter 4, notes 2 and 3.

Glenarvon

Lady Caroline Lamb's scandalous autobiographic novel *Glenarvon*, published in 1816, is said to portray her unhappy love affair with Lord Byron (which ended when he deserted her, leaving her to face humiliation and social ruin). It is also a sensitively depicted story of stalking, which presents both the (male) stalker's and the (female) victim's psychological affliction, highlighting the emotional torment of the victim.

' *Glenarvon* narrates the fall of an innocent young married woman, Calantha (presumably Lady Lamb herself), at the hands of a cynical Don Juan seducer, Lord Ruthven Glenarvon. Glenarvon was clearly modeled after Lord Byron, though embellished with explicit satanic, vampiristic, and "Flying Dutchman" features.[4] An older female character, Lady Margaret, is portrayed as an independent, strong-minded, attractive, sexual, overbearing mother and baby-murderer.[5] The satanic Ruthven is obsessed with this Lilit-like woman throughout the novel. Frustrated with her dismissal of his passionate approaches, he stalks and eventually murders her. Lord Ruthven stalks and kills while disguised as the dark, monstrous-looking Viviani.

The novel details Ruthven's torment, presenting the agony of rejection as the motivation for his desperate acts. "Viviani [Ruthven] had long and repeatedly menaced Lady Margaret with vengeance. In every moment of resentment, on every new interview, at every parting scene, revenge, immediate and desperate, was the cry" (Lamb 1816, 242). His stalking is presented as a pathetic, childish means of communicating with the motherlike woman with whom he is madly infatuated and who completely rejects him. But *Glenarvon* also narrates the stalking from the victim's point of view, inviting the reader's sympathy for her. In the following scene, Lady Margaret, alone at sunset in an isolated spot, realizes she is being followed.

> She thought she had been alone; but she heard a step closely following her: she turned around, and to her extreme surprise, beheld a man pur-

---

4. Glenarvon is frequently described by phrases containing references to death, diabolism, or evil, such as "deadly wit," "demonic smile," "spirit of evil." His eyes are dark, his cheeks pale, his lips red. His gaze, compared to that of a rattlesnake (Lamb 1816, 104), is often described as deadly and fixed: "in his look there was all the bitterness of death; his cheek was hollow" (328). Glenarvon refers to himself as a cursed harbinger of death and destruction (115, 161), and other characters refer to Glenarvon as "a pestilence which has fallen on the land" (78). His predecessor "John de Ruthven drank hot blood from the skull of his enemy and died" (86). In one instance he is described thus: "From the sepulchre the dead appeared to have arisen to affright her" (89). And like a vampire, Viviani strikes the fatal bloody blow on her neck. In the last chapters of the novel, Ruthven, sailing his lost ship, literally becomes the Flying Dutchman.

5. The widowed Lady Margaret plots to kill her brother's son, so that her own son can inherit the family estate. (Ruthven Glenarvon takes upon himself to fulfill her wish, in the hope of pleasing her.)

suing her, and just at that moment, on the point of attaining her. His black brows and eyes were contrasted with his grizzly hair; his laugh was hollow; his dress wild and tawdry. If she stopped for a moment to take breath, he stopped at the same time; if she advanced rapidly, he followed. She heard his steps behind, till passing near the convent he paused, rending the air with his groans, and his clenched fist repeatedly striking his forehead, with all the appearance of maniac fury, whilst with his voice he imitated the howling of the wind. Terrified, fatigued and oppressed, Lady Margaret fled into the thickest part of the wood, and waited till she conceived the cause of her terror was removed. She soon perceived, however, that the tall figure behind her was waiting for her reappearance. She determined to try the swiftness of her foot, and sought with speed to gain the ferry:— she durst not look behind:— the heavy steps of her pursuer gained upon her:— suddenly she felt his hand upon her shoulder, as, with a shrill voice and loud laugh, he triumphed at having over taken her. She uttered a piercing shriek, for on turning round she beheld . . . His name I cannot at present declare; yet this I will say: it was terrible to her to gaze upon that eye—so hollow, so wild, so fearful was its glance. From the sepulchre, the dead appeared to have arisen to affright her; and scarce recovering from the dreadful vision, with a faltering step and beating heart, she broke from that grasp—that cold hand—that dim fixed eye—and gained with difficulty the hut of the fisherman. (89)

The scene is set in a space open enough for the victim to stand a reasonable chance of evading the trap; at the same time the predator's age and gender give him an advantage over his prey. This combination signals to the reader that the outcome of the conflict is not predetermined and that there is room for tension and hope. The whole incident is narrated exclusively from Lady Margaret's point of view (i.e., it is "focalized by" the victim). It conveys *her* terror and stress, inducing reader sympathy while fomenting the hope that she will escape. The stalker is only portrayed through Lady Margaret's eyes—although she discovers his identity, it is not explicitly disclosed to the reader; during this scene he is not a character in his own right, but an anonymous threat.

Caroline Lamb's narrative offers original psychological insights and ideological claims. In her text, the stalker is at once satanic, vampiristic, haunting (the Flying Dutchman), and overreaching (Don Juan). He has two faces: the distinguished lord and his dark shadow, the monstrous Viviani. While the target of his "Don Juan" behavior is Eve-like, the target of his stalking is Lilit-like. He is both sexually and emotionally obsessed with the latter. His stalking is motivated by deep desire, longing, and an acute pain caused by rejection. It expresses both his desperate need and his vengeful violence, which inevitably leads to her murder. To him, stalking her is a means to attain a close relationship with her, to which he believes he is enti-tled. For her, stalking is a threatening, dark menace that limits her move-ment and obstructs her normal course of life. Calantha, the young, wifely Eve character, is presented in this context as an innocent bystander, victim-ized in the course of this game, which is played by a vampiristic man and aimed at Lilit.

Lamb's construction of the Lilit-like woman as a *victim* of stalking, as opposed to a stalker herself, and her compassionate portrayal of the fallen Eve as a victimized bystander, results from the writer's feminine point of view. Her ability to convey the emotions of both predator and prey is as groundbreaking as her integration of the "doubling" motif into the stalking story and her unification of the images of the overreacher with the vampire. She paved the way for Mary Shelley's acclaimed treatment of similar themes. At the same time, despite her compassionate portrayal of her female characters, her male protagonist is a traditional male stalker in the sense that he targets Lilit, exposes the fallen Eve and punishes her because she is carnal and, therefore, sinful. In spite of Lamb's sympathy for the victim, she con-tinues the tradition of representing the stalking male stalker as a tool of patriarchal discipline.

Mary Shelley read *Glenarvon* as she was working on her novel *Franken-stein*, published in 1818. Her treatment of the issues just mentioned is in dia-logue with Lamb's. (For a short summary of the Lamb-Shelley connection see appendix 5.1.)

Frankenstein: The Double Motif

> Almost every critic of *Frankenstein* has noted that Victor and his Mon-ster are doubles. The doubleness even enters some of the popular ver-sions and is un-self-consciously accepted by everyone who casually calls the monster "Frankenstein." The motif of the Doppelganger was certainly in Mary's mind during the writing. (Levine 1979, 14)

> If we had any doubt about the doppelganger relationship between Vic-tor and the monster, the last quarter of the book resolves them. For from now on Victor pursues the monster to set things right, just as earlier the monster had dogged Victor for what he felt was just. First the shadow chases the man, then the man chases the shadow. (Twitchell 1981, 172)

Mary Shelley's *Frankenstein; or, The Modern Prometheus* narrates the story of a young scientist, Victor Frankenstein, who creates life but—appalled by the ugliness of his creature—abandons it. Wandering in streets and forests, the agonizing creature observes people from afar, educating itself in their lan-guage and manners. In desperate need of family, the creature attempts to reunite with its creator and asks him for a mate, only to be rejected and refused. Turning violent, the creature kills Victor's father, brother (William), bride (Elizabeth), best friend (Clerval), and an innocent servant girl. Determined to take its life, Victor chases the creature to the North Pole, where he dies after telling his story to Walton, an ambitious ship-captain; the creature then promises Walton to take its own life.

Frankenstein is overlaid with mythological, biblical, and legendary imagery, inviting practically endless interpretative approaches. Victor is presented as Adam, the allegorical everyman, in his innocence, ambition, and fall.[6] In accordance with the title, which calls for a reading of Victor Frankenstein as an overreaching Greek Titan, the text clearly places this "mad scientist" "in the tradition of Faustian over-reachers" (Levine 1979, 9).[7] The creature, on the other hand, repeatedly associates itself with Satan (Shelley 1992, 97, 127, 213). In its cursed wandering and brother-slaying, it relives the tragedy of the biblical Cain, who was associated in medieval Europe with the Wandering Jew, and whom Lord Byron established as a Romantic archetype.[8] Above all else, Victor explicitly calls his creature "vampire" (74), and the text supplies many details to support this accusation.[9]

But Victor is not merely Adam-Faust, and his creature is not merely a satanic, vampiristic wanderer; each is also associated with his antagonist's mythological roles. Shelley's epigraph from Milton's *Paradise Lost*,[10] and the creature's references to itself as Adam and to Victor as its creator,[11] clearly establish the analogy to the story of Genesis, associating the creature, not

6. Gilbert and Gubar point out that "in the Edenic coziness of their childhood, . . . Victor and Elizabeth are incestuous as Adam and Eve" (1979, 229).

7. "So much has been done, exclaimed the soul of Frankenstein,—more, far more, will I achieve: treading in the steps already marked, I will pioneer a new way, explore unknown powers, and unfold to the world the deepest mysteries of creation" (Shelley 1992, 47).

8. The creature has no brother to slay, but it does murder Victor's brother, and its motivation for so doing is not very different from Cain's. For reference to Byron's Cain see chapter 4, note 3.

9. Victor composes his creature of dead body parts, and in this sense the creature is a vampire. Like the traditional legendary vampire, the creature preys on and drains the life out of all his (Victor's) relatives and loved ones: Victor's brother, his lover-sister, his best friend, his father, and finally Victor himself. Victor notes that the creature, his vampire, is "forced to destroy all that was dear to me" (Shelley 1992, 74). The death marks left by the creature on William, Clerval, and Elizabeth are on their necks (70, 169, 189). William's cry of fear at the sight of the monster is, "You wish to *eat* me" (138; emphasis added), and Victor's dying wish regarding the monster is that Walter should thrust his sword "into his heart" (202). The creature itself plans to burn itself on a stake (215). In addition, like all vampires, the creature is excluded from human society. It is lonely, it does not belong. Time and again it explains: "My vices are the children of a forced solitude that I abhor" (142).

10. "Did I request thee, Maker, from my clay / To mould me man? Did I solicit thee / From darkness to promote me?"

11. "I ought to be your Adam, but I am rather the fallen angel" (Shelley 1992, 97); "God, in pity, made man beautiful . . . but my form is a filthy type of yours" (127). The creature frequently addresses Victor as "creator" (132), and Walter calls Victor "godlike" (203).

Victor, with man. By quoting a passage from Coleridge's poem, Victor suggests that there is an analogy between the Ancient Mariner and himself (Shelley 1992, 58). Walton, who is both a potential Frankenstein and a potential Flying Dutchman, contributes to this allusion (see 29, 195, and 205). During his deadly nocturnal work of making the creature, which takes place under the gaze of the moon, Victor feels a "resistless and almost frantic impulse" that urges him forward; he later admits that at the time he "seemed to have lost all soul" (53). There are other hints of Victor's vampiristic inclinations. For example, he dreams that his kiss drains the life from his beloved Elizabeth:

> I thought I saw Elizabeth in the bloom of health, walking in the streets of Ingolstadt. Delighted and surprised, I embraced her, but as I imprinted the first kiss on her lips, they became livid with the hue of death; her features appeared to change, and I thought that I held the corpse of my dead mother in my arms; a shroud enveloped her form, and I saw the grave worms crawling in the folds of flannel. I started from my sleep with horror . . . when by the dim and yellow light of the moon . . . I beheld the wretch—the miserable monster whom I had created. He held up the curtain of the bed; and his eyes, if eyes they may be called, were fixed on me. (57)

After a long separation from Elizabeth, during which Victor created his creature, he is reunited here with his sister-lover, who (like Inanna to her returning Dumuzi) takes on the role of his "mother." But instead of returning to her joyously like a loving Dumuzi, Victor returns in the form of a deadly vampire, like his unnatural creature. Elsewhere he calls himself the murderer of his relatives, and speaks of the "never-dying worm" in his bosom (Shelley 1992, 85). Most tellingly, he calls his creature "my own vampire, my own spirit set loose from the grave" and "the fiend that lurked in my heart" (90).

Thus, Frankenstein, who embodies imagery connected to Adam, Faust, Satan, the Wanderer, and the vampire, is trapped, together with his mirror-double creation, in a cycle of autostalking. Mary Shelley's remarkable presentation of male stalking suggests that Satan, wanderer, and vampire together comprise the Faustian creation: that of one's own monstrous shadow. Stalking is Faust's doing, and Faustian stalking is vampiristic, performed by undead creatures who are Faust's dark mirror images.

Frankenstein illustrates that the overreaching, Faustian zeal is individualistic, vain, irresponsible, loveless, and, therefore, vampiristically fatal, particularly for women. For Victor, scientific knowledge is knowledge gained through penetration. In describing his passionate thirst to know, Victor speaks of "a fervent longing to *penetrate* the secrets of nature" (Shelley 1992, 39; emphasis added), and of becoming the disciple of "men who had *pene-*

trated deeper and knew more" (emphasis added). The obvious subject of this kind of masculine penetration is Woman: the secret of creation and generation.[12] Victor's scientific endeavor optimizes the aim to explore Woman, the foundation of generation. This pursuit is meant to substantiate his belief: "To examine the causes of life we must first have recourse to death" (50). And so it is Man's arrogant, egotistic lust to know Woman scientifically, his cold penetration of her as a theoretical principle of generation, that breeds the monster that kills her. Man's loveless passion to know (Woman) begets his vampire self that destroys Woman.

Moreover, the only real participants in Mary Shelley's male stalking game are Man and his self-made double. The creature's predation is a manifestation of Victor's split existence: his dark self stalks his distinguished self. Elizabeth, just like Victor's brother, William, and his friend, Clerval, is not the ultimate subject of stalking: she is pursued and killed as part of the shadow's stalking of its creator, which is all part of their private bonding ritual. Elizabeth's murder is described only from Victor's perspective: two screams and a silent body (Shelley 1992, 188–89). In this homosocial, male-bonding ritual, women, children, and other living things are mere objects caught in the crossfire: they are incidental to the central drama of man versus his twin. (To the contemporary reader, *Cape Fear* may come to mind.)

Shelley's (Absent) Lilit

Several literary analysts have already stated that Victor and his creature "play all the neo-biblical parts over and over again" (Gilbert and Gubar 1979, 230).[13] In the context of this study, the creature's most illuminating neobiblical role is his emulation of Lilit. Like her, the creature is forced to leave its "Eden" and human society when it fails to live up to Adam's demands. Like her, it is outcast, feared by all, and forced to dwell in isolated wastelands. Like her, he is a creature of the night, and although he does not fly, he runs with superhuman speed. Lilit was traditionally believed to stalk men and to kill their women, usually at the time of conception; the creature stalks Victor and kills Elizabeth just before her initiation into procreative sexuality (on her wedding night). Just as Lilit was believed to come between man and wife, so too does the creature obstruct the union between Victor and Elizabeth ("I shall be with you on your wedding night," it promises Victor, and it kills Elizabeth in her bridal suite [193]). Both Lilit and this creature are child killers. Lilit begat devils, and Victor fears that the creature, too, will

12. Maurice Hindle observes that "the sexual metaphor is no accident [since] it is Frankenstein's desire 'to penetrate the secrets of nature' . . . through the appliance of the new masculinist-made god, Science" (1992, xxxvi).

13. See also Wilt 1979 and Knoepflmacher 1979.

become the progenitor of a new "race of devils" (160). Like Lilit, the creature is partially subhuman and partially superhuman, as well as an uncannily familial ever-returner. Also, like Lilit, the creature is strong, free, and smart.[14] Plainly put, *Frankenstein* casts a male stalker in Lilit's story, thus exposing Lilit's true nature as Adam's self-made same-sex shadow.

In *Frankenstein*, the double, the Lilit, is not a woman. In fact, the novel suggests that Lilit never was a woman, but Adam's dark double. The legendary Lilit, the text implies, does not exist. Inanna is thus redeemed from the demonization inflicted on her through association with Lilit's character, and Adam is held responsible for Lilit's creation, as well as for the fatal outcomes of "her" stalking. *Frankenstein* features no stalking females; stalking is associated uniquely with male characters. And yet, since in Shelley's fictional world women are all innocent, none of the stalking is male stalking, as defined in the disciplining, patriarchal sense.[15] It does not reinforce the ruling social order. Rather, it is a deeply emotional means of self-expression for the stalker and a haunting nightmare for its victim.

Shelley's Double Vision of Stalking

Mary Shelley presents her stalking story in a double first-person narration. This structure furnishes her reader with an awareness of both the pursuer's and the target's point of view. Shelley's double narration is an important, innovative contribution to the understanding of stalking, illuminating the tragic lack of communication between stalker and victim.

Frankenstein is narrated in the form of letters to a beloved sister, written by the adventurous Captain Walton, who, on his way to the North Pole, finds Victor Frankenstein chasing his creature. Walton's narrative records a second narration: Victor's story, as he tells it to Walton. Victor's account, in turn, brings forth the creature's story, as Victor heard it from the creature itself (after it murdered Victor's brother William). Finally, after Victor's death on board Walton's ship, the creature appears to pay its last respects, revealing to Walton the epilogue to its story, which includes the creature's promise to kill itself by fire.

The story of the creature's stalking of Victor appears in both Victor's and the creature's narratives, and is thus related twice, in two levels of nar-

---

14. The title, referring to Frankenstein as Prometheus, suggests an analogy between Victor's creature and the disastrous Pandora. Pandora with her box of misfortune was sent by the Olympian Gods as punishment and revenge for Prometheus's "treason" in giving humans the sacred fire. Pandora can be viewed as a Greek Eve, or Lilit, or both, as can Frankenstein's creature.

15. It is noteworthy that featuring only innocent Eves, Shelley's fictional world lacks real, interesting female characters.

ration, that is, in two diegetic levels.[16] Each time, the stalking is narrated in the first person by an inter-homodiegetic narrator-focuser.[17] The first narration is the victim's (Victor's), told in the second diegetic level; the second narration is the stalker's (the creature's), relayed mostly in the third diegetic level (the last part of the creature's story is narrated directly to Walton and is therefore in the second diegetic level; Walton's own "frame story" constitutes the first level). The victim's story is disclosed to a very sympathetic audience (Walton), whereas the stalker's story is narrated to two hostile audiences (Victor and Walton). On the other hand, the creature's version follows Victor's, thus giving the creature the advantage of having the last word. Furthermore, narrated in the third, innermost level of narration, the creature's story is introduced as the last, deepest, hidden truth (at the very heart of darkness, so to speak). Structurally speaking, therefore, the accounts are presented so that they lay equal claim to the reader's trust and empathy. One account sheds light on the motivation and experience of stalking, while the other captures the feeling of the stalker's victim. Let me begin by introducing Victor's narration of his experience of being stalked by the creature.

Victor first becomes aware that he is being pursued by his creature in Geneva, after his brother William's funeral:

> I perceived in the gloom a figure which stole from behind a clump of trees near me; I stood fixed, gazing intently: I could not be mistaken. A flash of lightning illuminated the object, and discovered its shape plainly to me; its gigantic stature, and the deformity of its aspect, more hideous than belongs to humanity, instantly informed me that it was the wretch, the filthy daemon to whom I had given life. What did he there? . . . The figure passed me quickly, and I lost it in the gloom. (Shelley 1992, 73)

Later, in the village of Chamonix, where Victor has traveled from the Frankensteins' house in Belrive, he again glimpses the unwelcome presence:

> I suddenly beheld the figure of a man, at some distance, advancing towards me with superhuman speed. . . . I was troubled: a mist came over my eyes, and I felt a faintness seize me. (95)

16. In Genette's terms, Victor's narrative is the text's "diegesis," and most of the creature's story (not including the epilogue) is "hypodiegetic," that is, subordinate to the diegetic level and once removed from the reader. Walton's narrative is the text's "extra-diegetic" level of narration, as it is the highest level, the one immediately superior to the diegesis and concerned with its narration. For a clear explication of these narratological terms see Rimmon-Kenan 1989, chap. 7.

17. In other words, both Victor and the creature tell a story in which they participate, and in their respective stories each of them is both the narrator of the story and the character whose point of view focuses it.

This time the creature approaches Victor, narrates its experiences to him, and finally demands, "You must create a female for me, with whom I can live in the interchange of sympathies necessary for my being" (140). Victor consents and after a long journey through Germany, England, and Scotland, finds an almost deserted, remote island, where he sets to work to create a female creature. "I did not doubt but that the monster followed me, and would discover himself to me" (158). And so it does:

> I trembled, and my heart failed within me, when, on looking up, I saw, by the light of the moon, the daemon at the casement. . . . Yes, he had followed me in my travels; he had loitered in forests, hid himself in caves. (161)

Horrified by the prospect that the two creatures will procreate, Victor destroys the female, and, in return, the creature murders Henry Clerval, Victor's traveling companion and best friend. Victor returns to Geneva to marry Elizabeth, but the creature kills her on their wedding night. By now Victor knows that he will never be free: "I do not doubt that he hovers near the spot which I inhabit" (Shelley 1992, 193). He determines to spend the rest of his life chasing the creature and ridding the world of it, but dies before the completion of his task.

In Victor's story, the stalking takes place between Man and his self-made shadow, his dark double, his externalized other-self. (Recall his dream and the phrases quoted earlier: "my own vampire, my own spirit," "I, the true murderer," "I called myself the murderer." He speaks of "the fiend that *lurked in my heart*" (90; emphasis added), a phrase clearly carrying a double meaning.) In Victor's own mind, the creature is not clearly distinguishable from himself, and its predation seems to be an aspect of *his* "dual existence." Victor experiences the stalking as a punitive reminder of his own monstrosity, and the creature's persistent presence as an ugly self-reflection. It frightens him, paralyzes him, fills him with guilt, shame, and frustrated rage. He perceives his stalking creature as a dreadful secret that alienates him from the rest of humanity. He feels trapped.

The stalker's perspective offers a different story altogether, in which a cruel creator is pursued by his desperate, abandoned creation, which justly seeks acceptance, affection, and reconciliation.

The creature's story is as follows: after a short period of happiness in the woods (near the De Lacey family), the creature is forced to flee and, having no companion and nowhere to go, chooses Geneva: "You had mentioned Geneva as the name of your native town; and towards this place I resolved to proceed" (Shelley 1992, 135). There, the creature runs into young William Frankenstein. When it learns that this is Victor's brother, it kills the boy. Avenging its own misery, the creature makes a discovery.

I too can create desolation; my enemy is not invulnerable; this death will carry despair to him, and a thousand other miseries shall torment and destroy him. . . .

For some days I haunted the spot where these scenes had taken place; sometimes wishing to see you, sometimes resolved to quit the world and its miseries forever. (138, 139)

And this is the creature's portrayal of his killings of Clerval and Elizabeth:

After the murder of Clerval, I returned to Switzerland, heart-broken and overcome. I pitied Frankenstein; my pity amounted to horror: I abhorred myself. But when I discovered that he, the author at once of my existence and of its unspeakable torments, dared to hope for happiness; that while he accumulated wretchedness and despair upon me, he sought his own enjoyment in feelings and passions from the indulgence of which I was forever barred, then impotent envy and bitter indignation filled me with an insatiable thirst for vengeance. I recollected my threat, and resolved that it should be accomplished. I knew that I was preparing for myself a deadly torture; but I was the slave, not the master, of an impulse, which I detested, yet could not disobey. Yet when she died!—nay, then I was not miserable. I had cast off all feeling, subdued all anguish, to riot in the excess of my despair. Evil thenceforth became my good. Urged thus far, I had no choice but to adapt my nature to an element which I had willingly chosen. The completion of my demonical design became an insatiable passion. And now it is ended; there is my last victim. (212)

The creature's account of its pursuit of Victor documents the evolution of the stalker's motives and emotions. When it first heads toward Victor's home town, the creature is seeking only a home for itself; it yearns to belong, to break with the intolerable solitude forced upon it, and Victor's is the only home where it can hope to belong. But once in Geneva, the creature is bluntly rejected by young William Frankenstein, and its sorrow is transformed into fury and rage. In killing William, the creature asserts itself as powerful and capable of initiating meaningful action: it proves to Victor and to itself that, if nothing else, it can be as cruel as its creator. But it also hopes to attract Victor's attention and to evoke his compassion. It hopes to bring Victor to Geneva, so as to at least see him from afar. Following its creator across Europe, the creature joins its "father" as a secret traveling companion. At the same time, it also reinforces its mastery over Victor's consciousness. It longs to be a part of Victor's life, and by keeping Victor constantly aware of its potentially dangerous presence nearby, it ensures that Victor can never stop thinking of it. By forcing itself upon Victor's mind, the creature will never again be completely alone.

The creature becomes violent when Victor refuses to acknowledge it as part of his life, when he disclaims it and refuses to assume responsibility for it. Killing William is the creature's only means to rejoin Victor, who has abandoned it "at birth." The killing of Clerval is in response to Victor's refusal to assume responsibility for the creature's happiness and to supply it with a female partner. Elizabeth is murdered to prevent Victor from pursuing his own happiness without the creature. The message is, "If you don't make sure I am happy, I'll make sure you are not," combined with "If I cannot have you, nobody will."

The creature seeks Victor's attention and obtains it in full by stalking him and his relatives. Elizabeth's death provokes Victor to dedicate the rest of his life to chasing his shadow: "My first resolution was to quit Geneva forever; . . . And now my wanderings began, which are to cease but with life. . . . I pursued him, and for many months this has been my task" (195–96). Victor thus becomes the stalker of his monstrous image.

Mary Shelley may have been the first to associate stalking with hideous monstrosity, a linkage now so widely accepted that we have come to take it for granted. At the same time, her monster does not conform to the folkloric, one-dimensional portrayal of monsters as beastly, supernatural forces of darkness. If the creature is monstrous, it is because it was neglected, rejected, and misunderstood. Its monstrosity is not a mere fact, but a completely human psychological response to unfair social treatment. Its stalking is not beastly, but a manifestation of deep pain and unattended emotional need. Further, Shelley's monster stalker is a tormented wretch, doomed to follow a compulsive obsessive pattern of behavior: "I was the slave, not the master, of an impulse, which I detested, yet could not disobey" (212). The generous allowance for the creature's point of view to be expressed and for his voice to be heard enables *Frankenstein* to capture and portray the stalker's innermost secrets.

Concluding Remarks on *Frankenstein*

Like Caroline Lamb's, Mary Shelley's narration of stalking, her original reworking of ancient materials, and her sensitive, subversive treatment of stalking characters disclose her feminine as well as her humanistic point of view. (For a brief summary of Shelley's life see appendix 5.1.). In Shelley's world, women are all innocent Eves, victimized by men. Lilit, the demonized female predator, does not exist; stalkers are uniquely male. And yet Shelley's male stalker does not reinforce traditional, patriarchal values; on the contrary, the monster is revealed as a sensitive, hurting, lonely creature, in pursuit of the male creator who rejected and abandoned it. This creator is accused of bearing responsibility for his creature's rampages. It is his masculine, unfeeling, overreaching ambition that is exposed as the tragic flaw and the main cause of ruin for many. Shelley's sympathetic sensitivity to the unique psychological experiences endured by both stalker and victim is unparalleled.

Some of the literary images that Lamb and Shelley introduced into their narrations, such as the imagery of doubles, the "mad scientist," and the agonizing, tormented monster, became essential elements in subsequent stalking stories. But these images were quickly detached from the subversive (i.e., feminist) social connotations they carried in *Glenarvon* and in *Franken-stein*. In later literary treatments by men, these elements were adapted to fit a more authoritarian and conventional worldview. Similarly, Lamb's and Shelley's sympathetic identification with the victim, as well as their portrayal of the stalker's torment, were discarded. Tales written by male writers portrayed stalking as thrilling woman-hunting, inviting readers to participate and take delight in the predator's excitement. Such literary treatment of stalking was voyeuristic and often pornographic. It conformed with dominant patriarchal perceptions, establishing vampirism and stalking as sensational mass entertainment.

Varney the Vampire

Varney's extremely popular adventures were published anonymously in weekly editions of English magazines throughout the 1840s and were later collected into a lengthy book. His was the most widely published and read nineteenth-century English vampire story. Before his sinful death, Varney was the close friend of his first victim's father; this positioned him as a "patriarch's shadow." His victims were virginal young women on the verge of womanhood: Eves on the verge of their potential fall. Summarizing Varney's plot, Frayling describes three ingredients:

> Sir Francis Varney's attempts to seduce the innocent heroine; the local villagers' realization that Varney is a vampire, and organization of a mass counter-attack; and a wedding scene, where Sir Francis is denounced in the nick of time, and chased out of the area. This extremely simple story is rewritten at least five times during the 868 pages of *Varney*. (1978, 41)[18]

The opening scene is a good illustration of how stalking can be, and was widely narrated as, sensational, voyeuristic pornography. (See the text in

18. For a most helpful summary of *Varney* see Twitchell 1981, 207–14.

appendix 5.2.) The scene features Varney stalking the child-woman Flora in her bedroom, trespassing into her intimate space, intimidating and humiliating her. Varney captivates and paralyzes her with his stare, depriving her of the power to look away or to call for help. (Having been her father's friend, Varney is shown in a portrait that hangs on the wall of her bedroom; Flora is thus trapped between the vampire and his mirror image, both gazing at her.) The scene culminates in sexual assault, depicting stalking as leading to the inevitable climactic rape.

Much of this opening scene is narrated from the point of view of young Flora, whose privacy, intimacy, control, dignity, and security are being crudely violated. But rather than identify with the terrified girl, the reader is invited to indulge in the vampiristic stalking. The child-woman and her nightmarish fascination with the nocturnal visitor are heavily eroticized. The text evokes thrilling excitement when it invites its reader to follow the stranger's slow advance toward the young hapless maiden trapped in her bed. Her terror is designed to provoke sensation and stimulation; there is increasing expectation of the inevitable violence and violation to come. That she is doomed to be victimized is clear from the start, and thus the reader's suspense is directed toward the violent climax, in which the girl's exploitation will materialize. To maximize the voyeuristic exhilaration aroused in the reader by the girl's terror, the description is narrated in the present tense, just as if the scene were taking place right before the reader's eager eyes.

Because nineteenth-century magazines published factual news alongside fictional stories, Varney's story paralleled those of real criminals and celebrities, adding a sense of reality and relevance to his image. Furthermore, the serial pattern of his appearances turned Varney into a returning element in his readers' lives. Unlike a book character, he did not fade away into the past, but was always fresh in their memories, lurking in the backs of their minds, stalking them in their imaginations, in the dark streets of London. Moreover, since the form of a continuous series defines as its hero the character who survives every episode, Varney's reappearances made him into the hero, one with which readers could identify.

Jekyll, Hyde, and Jack the Ripper

> The attraction of Dr. Jekyll is . . . that it is a playing-out of buried desire. . . . it has been made allegorical in the manner of pornography—it projects repressed desire not to censure it, but to experience it.
>
> —*Twitchell 1981, 241*

Robert L. Stevenson's *The Strange Case of Dr. Jekyll and Mr. Hyde,* published in 1888, is the nineteenth century's best-known variation on *Frankenstein.* The similarities between the two stories of stalking are plain to see. Frankenstein's creature is the tragic manifestation of the murderous, Faustian other-self; Hyde's ugly character is Faustian man's dark, evil, atavistic inner self, who lurks in the shadows behind man's civilized mask, awaiting the opportunity to leap out and take over. Like Shelley, Stevenson holds the over-reaching scientist responsible for the male stalker's fatal stalking, and for this sin he pays with his life.

The significant differences between the works include the two stalkers' different motives in committing their act. Whereas Shelley's tormented creature stalks to solicit his neglectful kin's affection, Stevenson's Hyde is simply evil—he performs his ugly deeds for the mere pleasure of it. The difference in narration is of particular interest. *Jekyll and Hyde* narrates the elements of Shelley's story in a *Varney*-like, pornographic manner, inviting the reader to secretly join the stalker in his thrilling exploits. Whereas the detailed torments of Shelley's creature and his creator invite empathy, Stevenson's inexplicit narration of Hyde's dark villainies evokes horror combined with fascination. Hyde's prohibited exploits excite the reader because the dreadful acts are intriguingly absent from the page: "the veil drawn over the most shocking moments ostensibly protects the readers, but actually gives them freedom to indulge their most private fantasies in the solitary landscape of the mind—the real domain of Jekyll's alter ego" (Tropp 1990, 111). Male stalking becomes a thrill.

In 1890, two years after the sensational publication of *Jekyll and Hyde*, five prostitutes were murdered and extravagantly mutilated in Whitechapel, London. Their killer was never found. Notes sent to the London police by the anonymous murderer were signed "Jack," and he became known as "Jack the Ripper." England's new popular press was relentless in reporting the sensational atrocities (Walkowitz 1982, 546). Jack became a Varney-like media hero. The public's hysterical response quickly developed into a moral panic. Preoccupation with the mystery endured a very long time, and attempts to resolve the mystery continue to this day.

Victorian society needed some organizing principle, some orderly rationale that would make sense of the atrocities. "[U]nable to find historical precedents to the Whitechapel 'horrors,' commentators resorted to horrifying fictional analogues," such as Stevenson's tale (Walkowitz 1982, 550). Under the influence of the Shelley-Stevenson imagery, the media referred to the Ripper as "man-monster," and "half-beast half-man" (Tropp 1990, 544). Tropp similarly finds that "the reading public used the pattern of Dr. Jekyll's story to piece together a narrative from the horrifying evidence left behind by Jack the Ripper" (110).

In the anxious public's mind, "the Ripper murders seemed to replay the fantasy of Dr. Jekyll's mysterious and brutal secret life in the reality of London's East End" (Tropp 1990, 99), and the elusive character of Jack the Ripper was explained in light of Jekyll and Hyde. He, like Hyde, stalked his women. Having killed them, he "opened up" their bodies, penetrating, seeing, investigating, and knowing them—just as the Faustian Dr. Jekyll would have. Tropp points out that "dissecting a woman and removing her sexual organs—is the ultimate reduction of body to thing, the exercise of an unfettered will, the end of all dehumanizing pornographic fantasy" (130). Jack's brutal assaults were as pornographically thrilling as Hyde's. And just as Stevenson's reticence about describing Hyde's crimes had incited curiosity, the newspapers' refusal to supply the specific gory details of Jack's horrifying acts, their mere hints of the butchered, sexually mutilated, badly disfigured bodies, only enhanced the public's titillation.

In turning to the mythological male-stalker imagery and in interpreting the serial killer as a Jekyll-Hyde image, the Victorian public created a mediating image that allowed for the persecution of real people as stalkers. Doctors, Freemasons, mentally disturbed vagabonds, and Jewish immigrants were suspected of being the Ripper. However, unlike in other moral panics, such as those discussed in chapter 3, no one actually prosecuted and punished. Instead, the moral panic took a different course.

The fact that Jack's victims were all prostitutes attracted much public attention and response. Walkowitz quotes a contemporary Victorian (Canon Barnett) who expressed the opinion that the "disorderly and depraved lives of the women" were more "appalling" than the crimes committed by the Ripper (Walkowitz 1982, 569). Newspapers of the day did not hesitate to blame the "women of evil life" for bringing the murders upon themselves, while at the same time stressing the similarities between all women by warning the public that no woman is safe (560). Some went so far as to accuse prostitutes of committing the murders, and "suspicion also extended to midwives and medical women inasmuch as the 'knowledge of surgery . . . has been placed within female reach'" (561).

Instead of targeting the male stalker, the moral panic concentrated on his victims: the prostitutes, the fallen Eves, the stalking Lilit women. The Whitechapel murders triggered rage and anxiety about female sexuality and predation. In this social process, the popular version of the "Jekyll and Hyde theory" took an interesting turn. Stevenson's story featured a male stalker, but no Eve or Lilit. In the new "Jack, Jekyll, and Hyde" story, it was no longer Jekyll's Faustian overreaching that caused Hyde's stalking and murders; it was the sinful lifestyle of the fallen Eves and the Lilits that brought about Jack's attacks. It was the prostitutes who turned Jekyll into Hyde; his bloodcurdling deeds were, thus, no longer merely evil: they were righteous.

The Jack-Jekyll-Hyde moral panic established the male stalker as the scourge of woman's carnal nature. He became persecutor and prosecutor of the fallen Eves, the plague-carrying, stalking Lilits. He "knew" these wicked women, exposing them as open, submissive, disgusting bodies; he removed their dangerous sexuality. He distinguished evil women from pure ones, warning them all of their sexuality and of his revenge. His image reaffirmed the male stalker's role as a patriarchal, disciplining character, adorning him with pornographic allure. This version of the stalking story received its canonical literary treatment in *Dracula*, written at the century's end.

Dracula: Vampire, Satan, and Faust

Bram Stoker's *Dracula*, published in 1897, presented Jack the Ripper as a contemporary incarnation of Vlad IV, the bloodthirsty fifteenth-century ruler and warlord of the Wallachian province of Muntenia.[19] More than any other literary character, Dracula embodies male stalking. Above all he is, of course, a vampire, featuring typical vampiristic attributes adopted from European folklore into English Gothic and Romantic literature.[20] His aristocratic background and title make him a "Byronic vampire," descendent of Lord Ruthven and Lord Varney. Similarly, he features every aspect of the Devil's image: he is the fallen archangel, king of Hell, leader of the dead, prince of evil, Mephistopheles, and the silk-tongued seducer.[21] The name Dracula, which was the historical Vlad IV's nickname, literally means "son of Devil" (Florescu and McNally 1992, 9–10; Senn 1982, 44). The legendary, haunting Wandering Jew and Ancient Mariner are also woven into his character.[22]

Just as explicitly, Dracula is also portrayed as a Faust. Van Helsing (*Dracula*'s fictional "exorcist") reveals that the vampire was once "an alchemist, which was later the highest development of the science-knowledge of his time" (Stoker 1975, 267). Further still, he was a student in the

19. Vlad, who was widely known as "The Impaler," was allegedly responsible for the brutal murder of one hundred thousand people. Aside from impaling his victims, "Dracula decapitated them; cut off noses, ears, sexual organs, limbs; hacked them to pieces; burned, boiled, roasted, skinned, nailed, and buried them alive; exposed them to the elements or wild animals. If he did not personally drink blood or eat human flesh, he compelled others to practice cannibalism" (Florescu and McNally 1992, 71). The cruelest punishments of all were imposed on unfaithful wives and unchaste maidens and widows (79). For full accounts of the horrors, and (contradictory) analysis on the relationship between Vlad the Impaler and Stoker's Dracula, see Leatherdale 1993; Florescu and McNally 1992, particularly chap. 6, "The Historical Dracula"; and Senn 1982, particularly chap. 4, "Dracula."

20. A detailed list of Dracula's vampiristic features is narrated by Van Helsing (Stoker 1897, 213).

21. See Van Helsing's learned lectures in Stoker 1897, 211, 267; Leatherdale 1993, 104; and Dracula's temptation of Renfield, echoing the Devil's temptation of Christ: "all these lives will I give you, and many more and greater, through countless ages, if you will fall down and worship me!" (247).

22. "[L]ike the Wandering Jew, Dracula cannot die and speaks of nations long extinct as though personally acquainted with them" (Roth 1982, 96). Like him, Dracula is an ancient sinner, doomed to wander eternally, lonely and feared, bringing storms, and repeatedly miraculously rejuvenating (Wolf, 1975 158). Physically, too, Stoker's tall, gaunt, pale, bearded, "beaky"-nosed Dracula resembles the Jew. See also chapter dedicated to the Wandering Jew in Stoker 1910. Dracula's famous phantom sea passage to London clearly echoes those of the Flying Dutchman and the Ancient Mariner.

Devil's *scholomance* school, where the Devil taught ten specially selected students the secrets of nature and of his magical powers. The "tuition fee" was that one of the ten would become the Devil's "dragon-riding storm-fixing" helper (214).[23] Thus Dracula, that tenth student, literally sold his soul to the Devil in return for forbidden knowledge.[24] In his undead state, Dracula is no longer a Faustian scientist, only his other self, evil Hyde.

Stoker's 1897 depiction of Vlad the Impaler clearly evoked Jack the Ripper.[25] Dracula-Vlad-Ripper was the "eternal Ripper," reappearing throughout human history. Through Dracula's character, Stoker presented the Ripper as the paradigmatic male stalker. But this identification of the serial killer as a mythological predator did not satisfy Stoker; he needed to supply his readers with a scientific, "foolproof" explanation of the phenomenon. Thus he labeled his creature as a distinct social type. The count, as Van Helsing says to the community, "is a criminal and of a criminal type. Nordau and Lombroso would so classify him, and *qua* criminal he is of imperfectly formed mind. Thus, in a difficulty, he has to seek resource in habit" (Stoker 1975, 300).

The serial killer, then, is a stalker who is strictly evil and is scientifically labeled as clinically deviant; his pattern of behavior is explained as a consequence of an "imperfectly formed mind." The male stalker is no longer a tormented, neglected, unnatural creation, a cursed sinner, or a precivilized inner self; he is a genetically defective person, as determined and identified by science. No Faustian overreaching mind is morally responsible for his murderousness: it is a purely scientific fact, beyond good and evil.

Eve and Lilit in *Dracula*

Dracula's fictional world features two sisterlike Eve characters: Mina and Lucy, both on the verge of adult womanhood.[26] Dracula attacks both, putting their true feminine nature to the test. Mina is a wholesome Eve: smart, strong, good, and thoroughly nonsexual. She is not too pretty, not too rich, but wholly devoted to one man (Jonathan). She is "the nearest thing to a saint that Stoker can conceive of" (Leatherdale 1993, 143). This Mina, although fiercely attacked by the vampire, is bravely defended by her community and, at the end of the ordeal, is fully established as a holy mother-

---

23. For background see Leatherdale 1987, 116–17.

24. In his insatiable womanizing he is also a Don Juan. For a direct reference linking Dracula with Don Juan, see Wolf 1975, 176.

25. "Jack" is a noticeable name throughout the novel. Doctor Seward is referred to as "Doctor Jack"; the notorious criminal, John Sheppard, is called "Jack" (Wolf 1975, 102); and the restaurant where the novel's heroes dine is "Jack Straw's Castle" (177).

26. Stoker has Mina-Eve admit explicitly that "some of the taste of the original apple . . . remains still in our mouths" (1975, 166).

virgin. "[T]he child which eventually does grace her life is named after those who fought Dracula on her behalf, as if a multi-platonic love affair has conceived it. This offers another link with the Virgin Mary, for Mina's son can be seen as the product of immaculate conception: she has not defiled her body through succumbing to the sexual act" (149).

Lucy, on the other hand, is an attractive and wealthy woman of liberal mind who walks in her sleep. In Victorian terms, her sleepwalking signaled sexuality and madness (Leatherdale 1993, 151). Those qualities make Lucy "an ideal 'Eve' for the visiting serpent" (140). When attacked by the male stalker, this Eve falls and becomes a voluptuous night-stalker, who drinks blood, preys on infants, and endangers her own kin. At the touch of the powerful vampire, Lucy's former sweetness

> was turned to adamantine, heartless cruelty, and the purity to voluptuous wantonness.
> . . . the lips were crimson with fresh blood, and the stream had trickled over her chin and stained the purity of her death-robe. . . . [She had] Lucy's eyes in form and colour; but Lucy's eyes unclean and full of hellfire, instead of the pure, gentle orbs we knew. . . . There was something diabolically sweet in her tones. . . . [Arthur, Lucy's fiancé] seemed under a spell . . . the eyes seemed to throw out sparks of hell fire, the brows were wrinkled as though the folds of the flesh were the coils of Medusa's snakes. . . . If ever a face meant death—if looks could kill—we saw it at that moment. (Stoker 1975, 189–90)

Lucy's beauty "changes from that of a virgin to that of a whore" (Leatherdale 1993, 161). As in a holy ordeal, Dracula exposes the fallen Eve for what she is, distinguishing between good and bad women. Reaffirming patriarchal social order, he rightly punishes the fallen woman: he turns her into Lilit, a witch and his slave.

Once, Lilit fled from Eden and chose the Devil as her lover. In *Dracula,* much as God and Adam created their Eve, so Dracula creates Lilit in his own image. This new Lilit is as sexual and dangerous a stalker as her predecessor, but, unlike the ancient and independent character, she is completely submissive to Dracula. She is his daughter, mistress, and servant. In Stoker's world, even Lilit is not an independent woman.

The Community as the Vampire's Double in *Dracula*

Much like Frankenstein's creature, Dracula provokes the community of men to join in his deadly game (Stoker 1975, 255–56, 271). The adversarial relationship he initiates with the men gradually becomes mutual. He stalks and victimizes their women, and they, in turn, chase and destroy the women who have joined his tribe of vampires. Lucy's brutal ripping by the community of men is the ultimate bonding ritual, in which the men not only accept Dracula's game and its rules, but also manifest the deep similarity between themselves and the male stalker. In that horrible moment, they become the monster's double.[27]

> Arthur took the stake and the hammer, and when once his mind was set on action his hands never trembled nor even quivered. Van Helsing opened his missal and began to read, and Quincey and I followed as well we could. Arthur placed the point over the heart, and as I looked I could see its dint in the white flesh. Then he struck with all his might. The Thing in the coffin writhed; and a hideous, blood-curdling screech came from the opened red lips. . . . But Arthur never faltered . . . his untrembling arm rose and fell, driving deeper and deeper the mercy-bearing stake, whilst the blood from the pierced heart welled and spurted up around it. . . . Then we cut off the head and filled the mouth with garlic. (Stoker 1975, 194–95)[28]

The assault of Lucy by the community of men is what we currently refer to as the victim's "second rape" by society's authorities. In Stoker's world, the men treat Lucy's body, now Dracula's prize, with the same violence Dracula used to snatch her away from them. The result is a sort of warped bonding ritual, wherein the men admit that their premises are not different from his. In other words, when Dracula succeeds in making their Lucy into his Lilit, the men take on the mission previously performed by Jack the Ripper: they stalk Lucy, the prostitute, in the dark of night, and upon seizing her, they slash open, mutilate, and punish her wicked body. They indulge in the ultimate, pornographic dehumanization of a woman. By imitating the Ripper, the men exonerate him and claim him as one of their own. Paradoxically, here the Ripper of women, defined as a deviant criminal, is not merely a patriarchal, disciplining character, but also society's double and role model.

The Victim's Experience of Stalking in *Dracula*

Irrespective of its ideology, *Dracula* is especially insightful in its portrayal of the feelings of the target of stalking. Dracula's figure is a big dark shadow, flapping its wings outside the window at night. It is incomprehensible and bewildering to the "normal" mind, that is, to anyone but its victim. It is a

27. Other noteworthy bonding rituals are the men's mixing of their blood with Dracula's through Lucy (their blood is transfused into her, and Dracula drinks it out of her), and the blending of Jonathan's semen with Dracula's blood in Mina (who drinks the count's blood and later conceives a child, supposedly Jonathan's).

28. For the similar treatment of the other vampire women, see Wolf 1975, 325.

threatening, often unseen, constant presence. The stalked woman is afraid to fall asleep, because *he* will surely be there to take advantage of her vulnerability. She is alone in her plight: others see only birds or bats and cannot sympathize with her inexplicable anxiety. She feels trapped in a never-ending nightmare. She begins to doubt her senses, her understanding, her sanity. She grows nervous and tired. A war of nerves is imposed on her by an obscure threatening force, whose motives and aims are unclear to her.

Dracula's stalking of Lucy and Mina is timeless and nonlinear in nature. The men's pursuit of the count, on the other hand, is progressive, straightforward, and rational. The count hypnotizes his prey into an uncanny, dreamlike state that lies outside of time. There is no past, present, or future. The rhythm of the victim's life becomes that of anticipation, terror, and renewed anticipation. Every evening resembles the previous one, once again bringing her closer to his lurking presence. The men's chase is hurried. They feel they have no time to lose, whereas Dracula has spread his revenge over centuries: he has all the time in the world.[29]

29. Martin Tropp rightly notes that by traveling into Transylvania Jonathan "has clearly crossed the border that separates the modern world, the place where trains run on time, from a place where time has little meaning" (1990, 140). When stalked and attacked by the vampires in Dracula's castle, Jonathan seems to have lost his sense of (linear) time. After his escape Mina writes that "the poor dear . . . cannot think of the time yet, and I shall not wonder if at first he mixes up not only the month, but the year" (Wolf 1975, 105).

The Literary Summer of 1816:
Lamb, Shelley, Byron, and Polidori

The Summer of 1816

Lady Carolyn Lamb was one of Lord Byron's many lovers. In 1816, Byron apparently lost interest in her and left her to endure public scorn. In response, Lamb published her autobiographic novel *Glenarvon,* which attracted great public interest. Soon after, Byron, offended by the unpleasant public reaction to his affair with his sister and to his separation from his wife, left London and traveled to Geneva, accompanied by Dr. John W. Polidori as his personal physician. On Lake Geneva, Byron's party was joined by the Shelleys. Percy B. Shelley, having forsaken his wife Harriet, had fled London together with Mary Godwin (whom he later married). The third member of the Shelley group, Mary's half sister (Claire Clairmont), who was at the time carrying Byron's child, apparently initiated the historic reunion, which had profound literary consequence: Mary Shelley's *Frankenstein,* Byron's *Fragment of a Vampire Story,* and Polidori's *Vampyre.* All three works were written in the shadow of the sensational publication of Lamb's *Glenarvon.*

Polidori, who felt ill treated by his employer, composed his short vampire story in Geneva, shortly after reading Lamb's novel together with Byron. Polidori named his vampire Ruthven; his story's plot relied, to a great extent, on that of Byron's *Fragment of a Vampire Story,* which Polidori summarized as follows:

> Two friends were to travel from England into Greece; while there, one of them should die, but before his death, should obtain from his friend an oath of secrecy with regard to his decease. Some short time after, the remaining traveler returning to his native country, should be startled at perceiving his former companion moving about in society, and should be horrified at finding that he made love to his former friend's sister. (MacDonald 1991, 89)

Polidori's story is commonly considered to be the most influential literary vampire story next to *Dracula* and is also the main source of inspiration for all nineteenth-century vampires, including the popular Varney. Unlike Lamb and much like Byron, Polidori allows us no insight into the stalker's emotional world, nor does he narrate the stalking from the victims' perspective. Polidori's sole interest is the horror—if mingled with fascination—of the vampire's young male companion, the human double of the "monster." Polidori's treatment of the subject, although less complex, was far more influential than Lamb's, or even Shelley's.[1] (The most celebrated descendent of Polidori's vampire is Bram Stoker's Dracula.)

It is noteworthy that in 1816, Coleridge's *Christabel,* Goethe's *The Bride of Corinth,* and Tieck's *Wake Not the Dead* comprised virtually the whole literary corpus of vampire tales, and in all three the bloodsucking monster is a woman. In the three stories composed by Byron, Mary Shelley, and Polidori, the vampire is a man. It is tempting to claim that both the "real" Byron and his literary description (in *Glenarvon*) impressed the creative imagination more than the fictional *Christabel* woman, horrifying as she might have been. In this respect, the historical Byron may be significantly responsible for the creation of the literary male vampire. If so, it may be that in addition to deep, sociocultural ideological tendencies, mere personal coincidence led to the demise of the literary female stalker and the rise of her male counterpart.[2]

Mary Shelley

Here are the basic facts that are widely believed to have molded Mary Shelley as a woman and a writer. Her mother, Mary Wollstonecraft, the renowned author of *A Vindication of the Rights of Woman,* died while giving birth to Mary, whom she expected to be a boy, and planned to name William. Mary read her mother's book while she was working on *Frankenstein,* in 1817. Mary Shelley's father, William Godwin, a radical thinker and writer, was the author of the "all-male" stalking story *Caleb Williams.* It was to him, and in that capacity, that Mary dedicated *Frankenstein.* Godwin is said never to have quite recovered from losing his beloved wife, and it is widely held that, at least in her own mind, Mary was made to feel guilty for his loss. Mary married Percy Shelley, the celebrated poet and her father's disciple, after his wife Harriet's suicide in 1817.

While working on *Frankenstein* (1816–17), the nineteen-year-old Mary, already mother to William (born in 1816), and to a prematurely born daughter who died unnamed (in 1815), gave birth to her Clara (1817). Mary's sister, like Harriet Shelley, committed suicide in 1816. In 1818 and 1819, Mary would lose William, baby Clara, and later her husband. Hence the widely held opinion: "The sources of this Gothic conception, which still has power to 'curdle the blood and quicken the beating of the heart,' were surely the anxieties of a woman, who as a daughter, mistress and mother, was a bearer of death" (Moers 1979, 86).[3]

1. For more on Polidori's *Vampyre* see in particular Polidori 1819; MacDonald 1991; and Frayling 1978.

2. For more details regarding this fascinating summer on the lake see Polidori's *Diary* (1911); Mary Shelley's introduction to *Frankenstein* (1992); Frayling's (1978) introduction; MacDonald 1991, chaps. 6–10, 17.

3. For more dates and details see Maurice Hindle's introduction to *Frankenstein* (1992, liii–lvi); and Peter Dale Scott's chronology (1979, vii).

Varney the Vampire, Chapter 1

The bed in the old chamber is occupied. A creature formed in all fashions of loveliness lies in a half sleep upon that ancient couch—a girl young and beautiful as a spring morning. Her long hair has escaped from its confinement and streams over the blackened coverings of the bedstead; she has been restless in her sleep, for the clothing of the bed is in much confusion. One arm is over her head, the other hangs nearly off the side of the bed near to which she lies. A neck and bosom that would have formed a study for the rarest sculptor that ever Providence gave genius to, were half disclosed. She moaned slightly in her sleep, and once or twice the lips moved as if in prayer—at least one might judge so, for the name of Him who suffered for all came once faintly from them.

She has endured much fatigue, and the storm does not awaken her; but it can disturb the slumbers it does not possess the power to destroy entirely. The turmoil of the elements wakes the senses, although it cannot entirely break the repose they have lapsed into.

Oh, what a world of witchery was in that mouth, slightly parted, and exhibiting within the pearly teeth that glistened even in the faint light that came from that bay window. How sweetly the long silken-lashes lay upon the cheek. Now she moves, and one shoulder is entirely visible—whiter, fairer than the spotless clothing of the bed on which she lies, is the smooth skin of that fair creature, just budding into womanhood, and in that transition state which presents to us all the charms of the girl—almost of the child, with the more matured beauty and gentleness of advancing years.

A shriek bursts from the lips of the young girl, and then, with eyes fixed upon that window, which in another moment, is all darkness, and with such an expression of terror upon her face as it had never before known, she trembled, and the perspiration of intense fear stood upon her brow. "What— what was it?" she gasped; "real, or a delusion? Oh, God, what was it? A figure tall and gaunt, endeavoring from the outside to unclasp the window. I saw it. That flash of lightning revealed it to me. It stood the whole length of the window. . . ."

A tall figure is standing on the ledge immediately outside the long window. It is its finger-nails upon the glass that produces the sound so like the hail, now that the hail has ceased. Intense fear paralysed the limbs of that beautiful girl. That one shriek is all she can utter—with hands clasped, a face of marble, a heart beating so wildly in her bosom, that each moment it seems as if it would break its confines, eyes distended and fixed upon the window, she waits, frozen with horror. The pattering and clattering of the nails continue. No word is spoken, and now she fancies she can trace the darker form of that figure against the window, and she can see the long arms moving to and fro, feeling for some mode of entrance. What strange light is that which now gradually creeps up into the air? red and terrible—brighter and brighter it grows.

The lightning has set fire to a mill, and the reflection of the rapidly consuming building falls upon that long window. There can be no mistake. The figure is there, still feeling for an entrance, and clattering against the glass with its long nails, that appear as if the growth of many years had been untouched. She tries to scream again but a choking sensation comes over her, and she cannot. It is too dreadful—she tries to move—each limb seems weighted down by tons of lead—she can but in a hoarse faint whisper cry,— "Help—help—help—help!" And that one word she repeats like a person in a dream.

The red glare of the fire continues. It throws up the tall gaunt figure in hideous relief against the long window. It shows, too, upon the one portrait that is in the chamber, and that portrait appears to fix its eyes upon the attempting intruder, while the flickering light from the fire makes it look fearfully lifelike. A small pane of glass is broken, and the form from without introduces a long gaunt hand, which seems utterly destitute of flesh. The fastening is removed, and one-half of the window, which opens like folding doors, is swung wide open upon its hinges.

And yet now she could not scream—she could not move. "Help!— help!—help!" was all she could say. But, oh, that look of terror that sat upon her face, it was dreadful—a look to haunt the memory for a life-time—a look to obtrude itself upon the happiest moments, and turn them to bitterness.

The figure turns half round, and the light falls upon the face. It is perfectly white—perfectly bloodless. The eyes look like polished tin; the lips are drawn back, and the principal feature next to those dreadful eyes is the teeth—the fearful looking teeth—projecting like those of some wild animal, hideously, glaringly white, and fang-like. It approaches the bed with a strange, gliding movement. It clashes together the long nails that literally appear to hang from the finger ends. No sound comes from its lips. Is she going mad—that young and beautiful girl exposed to so much terror? she has drawn up all her limbs; she cannot even now say help. The power of articulation is gone, but the power of movement has returned to her; she can draw herself slowly along to the other side of the bed from that towards which the hideous appearance is coming.

But her eyes are fascinated. The glance of a serpent could not have produced a greater effect upon her than did the fixed gaze of those awful, metallic-looking eyes that were bent on her face. Crouching down so that the gigantic height was lost, and the horrible, protruding, white face was the most prominent object, came on the figure. What was it?—what did it want there?—what made it look so hideous—so unlike an inhabitant of the earth, and yet to be on it?

Now she has got to the verge of the bed, and the figure pauses. It seemed as if when it paused she lost the power to proceed. The clothing of the bed was now clutched in her hands with unconscious power. She drew her breath short and thick. Her bosom heaves, and her limbs tremble, yet she cannot withdraw her eyes from that marble-looking face. He holds her with his glittering eye.

The storm has ceased—all is still. The winds are hushed; the church clock proclaims the hour of one: a hissing sound comes from the throat of the hideous being, and he raises his long, gaunt arms—the lips move. He advances. The girl places one small foot from the bed onto the floor. She is unconsciously dragging the clothing with her. The door of the room is in that direction—can she reach it? Has she power to walk?—can she withdraw her eyes from the face of the intruder, and so break the hideous charm? God of Heaven! is it real, or some dream so like reality as to nearly overturn the judgment for ever?

The figure has paused again, and half on the bed and half out of it that young girl lies trembling. Her long hair streams across the entire width of the bed. As she has slowly moved along she has left it streaming across the pillows. The pause lasted about a minute—oh, what an age of agony. That minute was, indeed, enough for madness to do its full work in.

With a sudden rush that could not be foreseen—with a strange howling cry that was enough to awaken terror in every breast, the figure seized the long tresses of her hair, and twining them round his bony hands he held her to the bed. Then she screamed—Heaven granted her then power to scream. Shriek followed shriek in rapid succession. The bed-clothes fell in a heap by the side of the bed—she was dragged by her long silken hair completely on to it again. Her beautifully rounded limbs quivered with the agony of her soul. The glassy, horrible eyes of the figure ran over that angelic form with a hideous satisfaction—horrible profanation. He drags her head to the bed's edge. He forces it back by the long hair still entwined in his grasp. With a plunge he seizes her neck in his fang-like teeth—a gush of blood, and a hideous sucking noise follows. The girl has swooned, and the vampyre is at his hideous repast!

CHAPTER 6

Stalking Movies in the First Half of the Twentieth Century

Preview

In the twentieth century, popular and high culture, as well as common and educated wisdom, were very closely integrated. One factor in this integration was the influence of psychoanalytic discourse on the social sciences, humanities, arts, and popular media. Through the media, this discourse became a common ground, facilitating an ongoing discussion among the social sciences, the humanities, the arts, and the public. Psychoanalytic concepts influenced the arts, which influenced both popular beliefs and the social sciences, and vice versa. The images, concepts, ideas, and stories of stalking—the legacy of previous centuries—were adapted and reformulated through that interaction. Among the arts, film has undoubtedly been the most influential.

Examining the development of stalking imagery in cinema through the 1960s, this chapter proposes that film trains viewers in voyeuristic stalking; that at the same time, it subjects the viewers to the intense experience of being stalked; that these experiences accompany viewers out of the cinemas and into their daily lives; and that this influences attitudes and behavior in the real world. Three influential groups of films in particular are considered here: silent German horror films, Hollywood's horror classics, and Hitchcock's thrillers.

In silent German horror films, stalking is committed by living-dead serial-killing creatures in the service of tyrannical authorities. In Hollywood's classics, stalking is commonly committed by serial-killing creatures in the service of evil fathers and by overreaching male spouses. In Hitchcock's world, mothers use their castrated sons to stalk young "fallen women," preventing the sons' sexual maturation. These diverse ideas of stalking have deeply influenced public sentiment and imagination, leaving their marks on popular beliefs and learned traditions alike.

The Viewer as Stalker and Victim

One of film's most powerful traits is its rare capacity of simultaneously allowing the viewer to experience the sensations of both stalking and being stalked. As Metz rightly observes, film allows and trains its viewer to be present in the world viewed, both *not* being on screen and simultaneously being there as an unseen perceiver (1985, 793). This fundamental aspect of the experience of film is commonly thought of as voyeurism; I suggest that it is *voyeuristic stalking*. It offers the viewer an armchair, worry-free, simulated experience of stalking.

Film as a medium inherently *performs* stalking. The movie camera furtively pursues the characters on screen, and the viewer, sharing the camera's point of view, is not only a passive beneficiary of these acts of the camera, but also a consenting collaborator. He is seated quietly, hidden in the dark, unseen by the film's characters, and, together with the camera, stalks them throughout the viewing.[1] In comparison to any other form of art or communication, film conveys the most realistic experience of time and movement. Characters move on the screen in what seems to be "real time," and the camera continually moves closer to or farther from them. This creates a feeling of constant change in distance between the viewer and the screen characters, enhancing the viewer's realistic feeling of movement, as well as his realistic sensation of stalking. The film viewer is conveniently supplied with moving targets, and he himself is "moved" behind or toward them by the camera's tracking and zoom shots, drawing closer to them, taking a step back, all within a "real life" experience of time and changing speed.[2]

The movie enables the viewer—man—to mimic God, whose all-seeing gaze spies on the inhabitants of his created universe, witnessing their every moment, following them, judging them, and objectifying them at his pleasure.[3] Like God, man is invisible to the eyes of the characters—he is immune to their look. This construction establishes him as an absolute Subject and them as mere objects in his world. In chapter 4, I defined such Godly gazing as the ultimate symbol of male stalking; man as film viewer becomes that same stalking God, the ultimate male stalker. The use of the subjective camera in on-screen stalking scenes enables the viewer, enjoying his God-like off-screen safety, to also indulge in a more personal, on-screen stalking.[4]

1. My usage of the male pronoun when referring to the film viewer alludes to the classic feminist theoretical claim that the mainstream movie industry constitutes a male viewer. My discussion of film relies on and assumes feminist film theory, which also holds that women are portrayed in film mostly as objects for men's visual pleasure.

2. A tracking shot is a shot taken from a moving vehicle, and a zoom shot implies a change from a wide-angle to a telephoto shot "in one continuous movement, often plunging the viewer in or out of a scene rapidly" (Giannetti 1982, 486). The tracking shot conveys a very real feeling of the viewer's own movement.

3. For the film viewer's "God-like" point of view see Metz 1985, 789; and Baudry 1992b, 307.

4. The term *subjective camera* refers to "any shot which is taken from the vantage point of a character in the film: what he sees" (Giannetti 1982, 482). Beaver adds that "the camera becomes the eyes of the character, revealing what is being seen as the character moves through or surveys a scene. A combined pan and tilt shot is a commonly used method of suggesting a character's surveillance of an area; a moving camera shot conveys in a subjective

Thus viewers simultaneously enjoy the sensations of two types of stalking: that practiced by God and that practiced by Satan. And as long as movies give us mostly female objects to watch, they train men in male stalking of women.

Constructed as the modern, scientific mirror of man, film allows him to watch and stalk women without being exposed to their gaze. Like the brave Gorgon-slayer Perseus, man can now pursue even a Lilit woman without meeting her "evil eye"; without fearing that, Medusa-like, she might look back at *him* and subject *him* to *her* gaze. It provides its viewer with a luxurious, worry-free experience. Furthermore, film is a mirror that reflects for man all that he cares to view, but without disclosing his own face; it is a mirror that enables man to be the reflectionless, stalking vampire.[5]

Training its viewer in voyeuristic stalking, film teaches him not to seek his object's active consent. As Metz puts it, the characters, without "presenting" themselves to be seen, all "let" themselves be viewed; their mere presence is an implicit invitation. "What is necessary in this fiction for the establishment of potency and desire is presumed to be sufficiently guaranteed by the physical presence of the object: 'since it is there, it must like it'" (1985, 801). Film viewers, therefore, practice stalking when they assume their targets' inherent consent. And as the cinematic object is usually a woman, movies train their viewers to pursue women, assuming their implicit consent. Every on-screen woman is always available to the viewer. If the viewer needs reassurance, movies make sure to have their women viewed and stalked on screen by male characters.

Although film shares the elements of real-life stalking, such as the changing distances between viewer and object, it cannot provide a union of (viewer) stalker and (screen) object: crossing the barrier of space is not a possibility. A movie viewer cannot approach his on-screen object, converse with her, and initiate a relationship. A permanent distance between viewer and object is inherent to the cinematic experience (Metz 1985, 979).

The film viewer is trained to feel that distanced stalking is the only mode of communication available to him in relation to his on-screen objects. A fantasy of unity between stalker and object can, therefore, only take place in a different realm, beyond their "normal" existence; perhaps in death. This may explain why, when obsessed fans stalk film actors, they may feel that only in death can they consummate their pursuit. And what such stalkers feel may be an exaggeration of what other stalkers experience as well.

Training the viewer as stalker, film also submits him to the experience of being stalked. Editing, the process of film creation, the reassembling of

---

manner a character's movement through space" (Beaver 1983, 281). ("Tilt" is "the movement vertically (up or down) of the camera resting on a fixed base" [292].)

5. "Although everything may come to be projected, there is one thing and one thing only that is never reflected in it: the spectator's own body" (Metz 1985, 785). See also Prawer 1980, 79.

"separate shots into an illusion of continuity," has been described as "a mechanical equivalent of the Frankenstein Monster" (Nestrick 1979, 303). I suggest that editing resembles Victor Frankenstein's creation of life; film resembles the creature. The world constituted of moving pictures projected onto a screen is, much like Frankenstein's creature, the glorious achievement of man's imagination, science, and technology. Like the creature, film is man-made, a creation, as well as a double image of the viewer's own reality (Metz 1985, 278). And like the creature, film stalks its father-self: film's vivid images insinuate themselves on the viewer in the darkness of lonely nights, its traces lying in wait to shape the viewer's real-life experiences with conventions and expectations induced by the moving images. And the more it resembles its creator, the more its creator-viewer regresses to derive his own identity from his creature. (The 1998 film *The Truman Show* comes to mind.)

Movies encourage the viewer to identify with the uncanny unease of *being* viewed and stalked. From his own practice of cinematic stalking, the viewer cannot help but realize how exposed anyone may be to another's gaze. True, in his relationship with the world on screen he knows that the controlling gaze is his and his alone, but stepping out of the theater and into the dark streets of his threatening, alienating metropolis, alone in his silent room, he is likely to experience a creepy suspicion that he may not be completely alone; that someone may be following and watching him, just as he and the camera followed and watched the characters on screen. He may become conscious of himself as an object of another's stalking gaze; such self-awareness adds a measure of artificiality of play-acting to one's otherwise spontaneous behavior. This uncanny sensation may be reinforced if a stalked character in the film has elicited the viewer's sympathy and identification. If that character is presented as one of the film's heroes or heroines, then, disregarding the camera's points of view and the character's gender, the viewer may identify with him or her, just as, according to Freud, "the person who plays the main part in dream scenes is always the dreamer himself" (Baudry 1992a, 699).[6]

Theorists suggest that the uncanny is "normal experience of film," explaining "that a visual version of the uncanny is almost a natural temptation of film, that an apprehension of a degree of weirdness in the seen world is what films often gravitate towards" (M. Wood 1975, 116). Much of film's uncanniness surely derives from its inherently paradoxical, phantomlike nature. It is real enough for our senses to perceive and yet unreal in that none of what it presents really exists there: it is, in reality, "absent."[7] It con-

6. For identification with a fantasy hero see Baudry's discussion of Freud's *Supplement to the Theory of Dreams* (1992a, 699). For more on cross-gender identification with screen characters see Creed 1993b, 154; and Clover 1992.

7. "[T]he activity of perception which is involved is real (the cinema is not a fantasy), but the perceived is not really the object, it is its shade, its phantom, its double, its *replica* in a new kind of mirror" (Metz 1985, 785).

veys the sensations of immediacy and closeness, and yet it is intrinsically twice removed: the world presented on screen is but an imitation of reality, and the projected pictures are merely an imitation of that imitation.[8] Film characters are "immortal, but they are always already dead. The beings projected on the screen are condemned to a condition of death-in-life from which they can never escape" (Rothman 1982, 241).[9] Film and its characters thus have much in common with the mythological image of the living dead.

Additionally, film's uncanniness, like a dream, like Lilit, repeatedly returns us to our personal and collective pasts, stalking us with bygone images and memories. "Movie" implies constant change, motion, and the replacement of one thing with another. Nothing lasts. The present vanishes to make way for new visions. But the ever-new is often uncannily familiar, as if we had seen it before. Film often restores characters and narratives that once lived among us or among our ancestors. It reanimates and transforms them, setting them free once again into the streets of our imagination. It depicts scenes by which we experience primordial memories and fears. (Film genres, as such, greatly enhance this aspect of uncanny return, by repeating their formulas in film after film.) To Eisenstein, cinematic art was "a return to prelogical Eden" (Andrew 1976, 57). From a more Freudian perspective, it may be thought of as a set of compulsive repetitions of primary traumas. As in a dream, film allows regression of the libido "back to a previous period of hallucinatory satisfaction of desire" (Baudry 1992a, 699). Such emotional regression, observed Freud, triggers uncanny feelings of familiarity,[10] much like Lilit.

Thus, the emotional manipulation of film teaches viewers to indulge in the voyeuristic (often pornographic) male stalking of their celluloid doubles, women in particular, while at the same time training them to expect that stalkers, both male and female, might hunt them in real life.

Horror Film Techniques

To some degree, every film engages its viewers in a form of stalking. But some films are more focused on this than others. Certain film plots contain explicit stalking elements; some involve their audiences in more "cinema stalking" than others (by using assorted camera and editing techniques); some use cinematic conventions to enhance their viewers' identification with the targets. And, of course, there are films that combine all of the above.

8. Metz refers to this phenomenon as "a double withdrawal" (1985, 799).

9. "The image we see on the screen is a kind of spectral double, the simulacrum of landscapes and townscapes filled with human beings that seem to live, to breathe, to talk, and are yet present only through their absence. Their originals, indeed, may already be dead" (Prawer 1980, 83).

10. See reference to Freud's essay on the uncanny in chapter 2.

Such movies are usually classified as horror films, chillers, thrillers, or stalker-slasher films (for reasons of convenience I use the term *horror films* to denote all these categories).

Inducing the Viewer's Fear of Stalking

Horror films specialize in manufacturing dread: the perpetual anticipation of shock and horror. Viewers identify with on-screen fictional characters, regularly expecting that in the next scene the evil monster, which they know lurks in the shadows of the film's fictional world, will appear and attack their heroes (Tudor 1974, 208). A horror film viewer, aware of the genre's conventions, knows that, in the film's fictional world, the monster's pursuit takes place continually, and if the monster is not on screen, then it must be off screen and will reappear to shock characters and viewers alike. (The major function of a horror film's musical score is to remind the viewer of the lurking monster and to signal his nearing approach.) In other words: the primary effect of watching a horror film is the viewer's persistent experience of being stalked. Furthermore, while the monster is off screen, it shares the same space occupied by the viewer, thus enhancing the viewer's "realistic" feeling that he is a potential target (Sevastakis 1993, 187).

Horror films employ a variety of cinematic techniques to enhance these sensations. A simple, yet efficient technique was used as early as 1913, in Paul Wegener's *The Student of Prague*. In this early German classic, the hero's mirror image, which eventually stalks him to death, is repeatedly superimposed on scenes and then fades out.[11] This produces in the viewer an uncanny sensation (also experienced by victims of real-life stalking) that a stalker may appear and disappear anywhere, at any time, unexpected and unrestricted by ordinary norms and conventions.

A common method of enhancing the viewer's feeling that he is a victim of stalking is to encourage his identification with a stalked character, while informing the viewer, but not the character, of the predator's existence. In such a setting, the viewer, instead of the on-screen character, feels stalked. To achieve this result, a film may limit the viewer's knowledge to that of the stalked character. This technique places the viewer in the character's shoes, facilitating their bonding. But the viewer's familiarity with the genre's codes, enhanced by the film's musical score, places him in a position of privileged information: he knows that the on-screen character is in danger. Such privileged information invites the viewer to fear for the oblivious, unsuspecting character with whom he identifies and to acutely experience the sensation of being stalked in her place.[12]

11. *Superimposition* is "an optical technique in which two or more shots appear within the same frame, one on top of the other" (Beaver 1983, 282). "The fade-out is the snuffing of an image from normal brightness to a black screen" (Giannetti 1982, 478).
12. *The Eyes of Laura Mars* is a good example of such manipulation.

Another common method is to use scenes set at night. In the context of the cinema, the darkness on screen merges with the darkness of the theater, extending the atmosphere of menace from the film world to the viewer's real life (Sevastakis 1993, 183). That films are usually seen in the evenings links the darkness of the theater with the darkness of night, and with the closely related world of dreams. The horror film blurs the boundaries between its dark on-screen fictional world, the theater, the night, and the viewer's dreams, making the viewer's cinematic experience of being stalked a part of his real life.

The technique of rapid "cross-cutting," when used in horror films, can enhance the viewer's sensation of being stalked by subjecting him to the uncanny feeling, experienced by victims of stalking, that time both rushes and stops.[13] An example occurs in the final, unforgettable sequence of the 1921 German silent *Nosferatu*, the first film version of *Dracula*.[14] Having followed Mina's husband (Jonathan) from Transylvania to the city of Bremen, the ghastly vampire moves into a building across the street from her window, and stalks her with his hypnotic presence and penetrating gaze. The last sequence begins with a series of shots separated by cuts.

> Mina sleeping
> The vampire standing at his window, intensely gazing across the
>   street into hers
> Mina awakens
> The vampire gazes through the window
> Mina, clasping her breast, approaches the window
> The vampire at his window
> Mina struggles with his hypnotic command (or is it with herself
>   that she battles?)
> The vampire, gazing
> Mina opens her window
> The vampire leaves his post, moving to cross the street
> Mina collapses, Jonathan asleep
> The vampire approaches
> Mina
> The vampire approaches
> Mina sends Jonathan to fetch the professor, then stands by the
>   window in anticipation
> The vampire's huge, bent shadow climbs the stairs
> Mina startled by a sound on the staircase

13. *Cross-cutting* is "the alternating of shots from two sequences, often in different locales, suggesting that they are taking place at the same time" (Giannetti 1982, 476). For the use of cross-cutting to enhance tension see Sevastakis 1993, 187; and Tudor 1974, 124.

14. *Sequence* is "an imprecise structural unit of film, composed of a number of interrelated scenes, and leading to a major climax" (Giannetti 1982, 483).

The shadow reaches for the door knob
Mina clasps her breast and retreats to her bed
The vampire in her room, slowly approaching her

This extended cross-cutting illustrates film's capacity to convey the unique way victims of stalking often experience the passage of time. The number of cuts makes each second seem to endure forever. As he watches the scene, time seems to stop for the viewer—as it does for Mina. And yet simultaneously, time is also rushing, at a speed of dozens of cuts per minute, toward a terrifying, inevitable end. Subjected himself to this paradoxical sensation of a speeding yet frozen time, the viewer identifies with the stalker's victim, and associates her terror with the described experience of time. Furthermore, many of the shots in such scenes are reaction shots that portray the target's horror at the presence or sight of the stalker. This repeatedly illustrates the terror of stalking, inviting the viewer's identification with the target.

Another horror film technique designed to convey the sensation of being stalked is the employment of panning shots to "find" fiends lurking within on-screen spaces.[15] In Universal's 1931 *Dracula*, for example, the fiend is almost never shown entering a space; the camera repeatedly pans through spaces to find him present there. This device helps make the count seem always present everywhere. A victim often feels her stalker is omnipresent; the use of panning shots evokes this feeling in the viewer.

A minor, but not insignificant, horror film technique is the magnification of the effect of the predator's gaze. In the classic *Dracula*, for example, the fiend's (Bela Lugosi's) evil eyes are highlighted throughout the film, often with methods such as pinpoint lighting (to make them seem radiant), extensive close-ups (sometimes enhanced by cross-cutting to reaction shots conveying horror), and the shadowing and/or covering of the rest of the face (as in the carriage scene). Lugosi's dominating, paralyzing gaze has been stalking viewers for many decades.

The portrayal of hypnosis is another point of interest in this context. Many on-screen stalkers hypnotize their victims, much as the film hypnotizes its viewer (Tudor 1974, 75). The horror film thus creates an analogy between the viewer's situation qua film viewer and the situation of the victim, reinforcing the viewer's unconscious identification.

Watching horror films, viewers enter a fictional world where they constantly experience stalking. Being stalked becomes a mode of existence,

15. *Panning shot* is "short for panorama, . . . a revolving horizontal movement of the camera from left to right or vice versa" (Giannetti 1982, 482). For example, Dracula's hand is shown reaching out of a coffin; then the camera moves elsewhere, until panning through the vault it eventually "runs into him." In another instance, a bat is flapping its wings outside of Lucy's window. Cut to the sleeping Lucy, and panning from her—once again the camera meets the count standing by her bed.

which lingers on well beyond the theater. One consequence is that stalking and horror have become all but inseparable; itself acquiring undertones of horror, stalking has become a crucial aspect of horror. A wider consequence is that to the large public of horror film viewers, stalking has become a part of daily life.

Inviting the Viewer to Perform Stalking

Horror films also explicitly cast viewers in the role of the stalker. They accomplish this by encouraging viewers to identify with on-screen stalkers. The subjective camera, capturing the stalker's point of view, is a powerful tool toward this effect.[16] The most dramatic classic example of this method is Reuben Mamoulian's 1931 *Dr. Jekyll and Mr. Hyde,* produced by Paramount. Twitchell remarks that "this is the first Hollywood film in which we in the audience are forced to become stalk-and-slasher" (1985, 247). The film's opening scene is shot entirely from Jekyll's point of view.

> We become Jekyll, thanks to the justly famous panning shots in which we merge, via the subjective camera, into his consciousness; we link our fate to his. We move with him as he pounds the Bach fugue from his organ; those are our hands; we rise and travel to the lecture room. Then the camera pans 360 degrees and now, for the first, we are outside and we see him straightaway. Again and again we hear his heartbeat, see with his eyes, and, thanks to the most artful use of a central image in all the Jekyll/Hyde movies, watch in the mirror as the self—ourself, in a sense—comes apart. (Twitchell 1985, 247)

Through the use of the subjective camera, when Jekyll becomes Hyde, the viewer, too, is transformed into a beastly stalker.

> For after Jekyll has raised the effervescing potion to our lips, the room whirls around us, we look in the mirror, and there Hyde is coming out of us. And what does Jekyll do now that he has been transformed? Almost immediately he starts to chase women. (Twitchell 1985, 247)[17]

The casting of popular stars as stalkers increases viewer identification with the fiends even further. Film stars have always been the main focus of the audience's identification.

> The relatively fixed persona of a star, created through the movies themselves and through the publicity machine, was a central element in

16. See note 4 above for definition of the term *subjective camera.*

17. To mention another classic example, in Universal's 1931 *Dracula,* Dracula stands above the sleeping Lucy, "and as he starts to crouch down and steal towards her the camera pans with him and moves in once he reaches her face" (Sevastakis 1993, 16).

audience involvement. The audience is able to identify with its favorite in a range of different story circumstances, and project its desires and frustrations into this intimately accepted character. . . . A large group of movie-goers explicitly recognize that they "put themselves in the place of" the star. (Tudor 1974, 78–79)

Cinematic stalkers such as Karloff, Lugosi, Lon Chaney, Christopher Lee, Robert Mitchum, Robert De Niro, Jack Nicholson, and Gary Oldman are clearly "stars," and, as such, they attract audience identification and strengthen viewers' ties with their fictional personae. It is significant, in this context, to note that "audiences are attracted to stars of their own sex" (Tudor 1974, 78–79).

Horror Films: Stories and Images

Horror movies have been an integral part of the film industry from its earliest days, and stalking stories and images have always been at their heart.[18] These images and stories often echo those crafted in nineteenth-century English literature. Contemporary notions of stalking are grounded in these variations on classic themes. For viewers who, in viewing the films, experience both sides of stalking, these films' presentation of stalking is inseparable from personal experience.

Early German Horror Films

The first important horror movies originated in Germany, where a rich heritage of horror tales (Gothic, Romantic, and others), facilitated by Expressionistic artistic trends, gave birth to "the first wave of terror films" (Dettman and Bedford 1976, 4; Prawe 1980, 9).[19] As early as 1913, Paul Wegener's *The Student of Prague* told the story of a Faustian student who sold his mirror reflection to the Devil, only to be uncannily stalked to death by this abandoned other-self.[20] In this story, man and his reflection are inseparable; they are unable to let each other go. Paradoxically, each seeks to eliminate the other, each wishing to be the exclusive self. In a Jekyll-like gesture, the protagonist finally shoots his monstrous mirror image, only to die of his own shot.

   The Cabinet of Dr. Caligari (1919), written by Hans Janowitz and Carl Mayer, is probably the best-remembered of the German silents and widely

18. See discussions in Hardy, Milne, and Willemen 1985, 16–18; and Prawer 1980, 9. For a list of Frankenstein films see Lavalley 1979, 286; for Jekyll and Hyde films see Geduld 1983, 195; and for Dracula films see Sklar 1975, 201; Wolf 1997.
   19. See also Prawer 1980, 9, 32; and Tudor 1974, 158–59.
   20. The film also features a subplot of an unnoticed, jealous "romantic rival," a young maiden who stalks the student and his beloved countess.

held to be the finest cinematic example of the Expressionistic style.[21] It also offers the most interesting interpretation of stalking. The *Cabinet* features a living-dead Frankenstein creature of sorts, Cesare, who commits serial murders in the service of his mad Faustian creator.[22] During the day, the evil Dr. Caligari exhibits this undead somnambulist at the fair, and at nightfall he sends him to stalk and murder townspeople. When sent to stab a young maiden (after having killed one of her two suitors), Cesare carries her away in his arms, but is chased by the townspeople and forced to drop her in order to flee (unsuccessfully) for his life. When his body is presented to Caligari, the doctor collapses into raving madness.

The most interesting insight offered by this Frankenstein story is that Dr. Caligari in fact directs an asylum, where the victimized young maiden and her remaining suitor, the story's narrator, are both locked away. The mad, overreaching, devilish Frankenstein-Dracula who is responsible for the serial killer's stalking and murders represents the "authorities," the government, the leader. The serial killer, Cesare, meanwhile, is portrayed as the system's abused, dehumanized, "remote-controlled" soldier, who does the ruling order's cruel, dirty work.[23] The stalker's targets and victims are institutionalized as inmates, their story silenced, their testimony doubted.

The *Cabinet* also echoes *Dracula*'s formula of male rivalry over a young woman. Cesare's rampages, particularly the attack on the young woman, are a challenge to the community of men, composed of the girl's father, her suitors, and the townspeople. As in *Dracula,* they chase and kill the stalker. But, unlike Dracula or Victor Frankenstein, Caligari lives on. In fact, despite losing his "soldier," he wins his war, defeats the community, and enslaves the young woman, who becomes a sleepwalker and joins the living dead in his grim world. She is in a realm beyond human reach. Neither her virtue, nor the community's efforts, can keep her in the community of the living or secure her union with her appropriate mate. This film's depiction of a community's abdicating its power and future to a mad overreacher was a dark foreshadowing of what was to befall Germany in later years. The film's political insight, as well as its portrayal of stalking in this context, are frighteningly credible to this day.

The *Cabinet*'s treatment of stalking addresses other issues as well. Dr. Caligari is presented as the evil shadow of the maiden's father. He appears

21. For a discussion of the making of this movie, see the fifth chapter of Kracauer's classic study *From Caligari to Hitler* (1966). See also Price 1992, 332.

22. The caption that assures the viewers that they are about to witness "a tale of the modern re-appearance of an eleventh-century myth involving the strange and mysterious influence of a mountebank monk over a somnambulist" associates Caligari with the haunting Wandering Jew.

23. "According to the pacifist-minded Janowitz, they had created Cesare with the dim design of portraying the common man who, under the pressure of compulsory military service, is drilled to kill and be killed" (Kracauer 1966, 65).

on the scene when the young woman is about to leave her paternal home for a mature, sexual relationship with a young man. From a Freudian perspective, the father's dark shadow operates his stalking monster in an attempt to prevent the young woman from leaving the father and enjoying sexual maturity with another man. Suggesting Freud's myth of the primal horde, Caligari's stalking can be interpreted as the father's attempt to hold on to the young woman and prevent her union with the next generation: her suitors, his "sons."[24] In these terms, the challenge posed by the male stalker to the community of men is the primordial patriarch's shadow's attempt to undermine modern society and its fundamental coupling norms. Stalking, in this context, intervenes with society's most essential structures of family, intimacy, and allocation of young women. It threatens to deny young men access to young women. In order for society to secure its future, it must rid itself of this threat. In the *Cabinet*, the community fails, and the evil father succeeds in destroying the community's family structure as well as its future. As the evil father is also the tyrannical authority, the film seems to imply that the mad leader's tyranny is a reinforcement of the precivilized system of the primal horde, a system in which young women and men have no intimate lives and society has no future. (Stalking is similarly presented as an element of the primal-horde theme in other early classic German horror films, such as Wegener's *The Golem*, circa 1920.)[25]

The *Cabinet* also left its mark on the cinematic imagery of stalking. In a striking scene, the tall, gaunt, pale-faced zombie, Cesare, dressed in black, steals through the dark streets and enters the girl's bedroom, his shadowlike image growing larger and larger as he slowly approaches her bed. Awakened by his touch and terrified by his evil facial expression, she screams, faints, and is then snatched and carried away by the fiend. This (Varney-like) image of the undead predator approaching a girl in the dark while she lies in bed became a commonplace of stalking films—so much so that even vampires, who traditionally cast no shadows, became cinematic shadow stalkers. Two of the *Nosferatu*'s most memorable sequences feature the vam-

24. The "primal horde" myth was introduced by Freud (in *Totem and Taboo,* 1913) to explain the evolution of human civilization. In essence, it tells the story of a paternal clan where the father had exclusive rights to all women until the sons united, killed him, and ate his flesh. Their guilt over this deed generated the creation of God and culture.

25. The film imaginatively adds a complex romantic plot to a Jewish folktale about the animation of a giant clay automaton, designed by Rabbi Loew to save the community from the devastating consequences of blood libels. In Wegener's version, the rabbi's jealous assistant seems to be in love with Miriam, the rabbi's daughter, who is in love with a gentile. It is in this context that the vengeful assistant unleashes the potentially evil forces of the father's creature, and brings about the stalking and killing of the young gentile suitor, and Miriam's kidnapping. She is eventually rescued at her father's magical intervention. In light of my analysis of the *Cabinet*, here the stalking by the evil father's creature prevents Miriam's "assimilation" into the world of the living.

pire's oversized shadow stealing up the stairs and entering a bedroom in his castle, and then in Bremen, again creeping up stairs and into Mina's bedroom. A slowly approaching shadow on the screen (accompanied by the right musical chords) has become a convention of horror films. In other words: film has taught us to envision stalking in the image of lurking, advancing, dark shadows.[26]

To a large extent, *Nosferatu* narrated Stoker's story. Improvising on Stoker's Mina, it defined a new role for the heroine. In this film's fictional world, "The Book of Vampires" reveals that "only a woman can break his [Nosferatu's] frightful spell, a woman pure in heart who will offer her blood freely to Nosferatu and will keep the vampire by her side until after the cock has crowed." The "pure-hearted" woman is thus both empowered—she is the vampire's only real adversary—and sacrificed. Although a tragic heroine, she is allowed to be an active instead of a passive victim.

All the films mentioned thus far featured male stalkers and pure-hearted heroine-victims. G. W. Pabst's 1928 *Pandora's Box* cast the American Louise Brooks as Lulu, a full-fledged Lilit. Magnetically sexual, free of any cultural restraints, Lulu "bewitches" every man (and some women), including the film's patriarchal figure, Dr. Schon. He leaves his fair, respectable fiancée and marries Lulu, only to die at her hands on their wedding night.[27] Lulu is smuggled out of court by Schon's infatuated son, who flees with her abroad. In London, as the young Schon withers away, Lulu night-stalks strange men, initiating sexual liaisons. Eventually she encounters Jack the Ripper, who like her is lurking in the foggy streets, and in his arms she meets her death, as young Schon weeps.[28] Before Jack kills her, he is shown struggling with himself in an effort to overcome the deadly urge that seizes him. But Lulu's inviting sexuality, combined with a commanding force that is stronger than his will, seals her fate.

In Pabst's story, Lulu—Lilit, the witch, the prostitute—provokes her own death at the hands of the serial male stalker: she has come between man and wife, snatched Schon's son, and caused ruin to both father and son. Her uncontrollable sexuality undermines the foundations of patriarchy. Because the legal system could not win justice by prosecuting Lulu, Jack the Ripper, functioning as society's avenger, had to execute the patriarchal social task.

In Pabst's version, the Ripper, young Schon's shadow image, is father Schon's Frankenstein-Cesare creature. Avenging the patriarch, he prevents Lulu's union with young Schon. But unlike the *Cabinet,* the later film does

26. In Coppola's 1992 adaptation of *Dracula,* the count's shadow leads an independent life, performing its own stalking of Mina in London, and strangling Jonathan Harker in Transylvania.
27. Upset by her immoral behavior, he places a gun in her hand, asking her to take her own life. She refuses, a bullet goes off, and he dies.
28. This fateful meeting occurs on Christmas Eve; Jack rips Lulu as young Schon, weeping, joins a procession that carries a Christ icon.

not condemn the patriarch for interfering with the family structure and society's future. The blaming finger is explicitly pointed at the Lilit woman.[29]

An insightful examination of the psyche of a tormented, compulsive serial stalker and murderer of little girls is presented in Fritz Lang's celebrated *M* (1931). At the climactic scene of his trial by the city's underworld, the notorious stalker, superbly played by Peter Lorre, delivers the following speech:

> "You all are criminals because you want to be! But me . . . What choice do I have? I can't help myself! This evil thing inside me . . . The fire, the voices, the torment!"
>
> "You mean you've got to murder?"
>
> "Always there's this terrible force inside me—driving me on. I'm always afraid of myself—of people, of ghosts. I must always walk the streets alone. And always I am followed—soundlessly. Yet I hear it. It's me pursuing myself. I want to run—to escape from myself. But I can't. I can't escape. I must obey! Forced to run endless streets—pursued by ghosts. Ghosts of mothers—And of those children. They are always there—Always—except when I— [here his hands move in a strangling gesture, and his face takes on a tormented expression; then the hands drop]. Then I can't remember anything. And afterwards when I see those posters I think—Did I do this? But I don't remember it! But who would believe me? How I'm forced to act—How I must—*must*—Don't want to—but must! And then—a voice screams—I can't bear to hear it, I can't go on, I can't go on, I can't go on!"

This motif—the tortured reluctance of the compulsive killer, the human agony of the monster—would also be a motif in the horror films produced in the early days of Hollywood.

The Classic Horror Films of Hollywood

The early German horror movie industry influenced its American counterpart in two ways: First, the American admirers of the German classics used them as models for their own creations. Second, a number of German cinematographers and performers crossed the ocean to participate in the making of the films of the 1930s, and Hollywood became the new leader of the industry (to mention only one example of many, Karl Freund, photographer of the *Cabinet* and the *Golem*, was also the photographer of the American

29. For a full, feminist analysis of *Pandora's Box* see Doane 1992. Interestingly, in the historical context of 1928 Germany, a menorah in Lulu's apartment implies her Jewishness. The triumphant Christmas procession at the film's end contrasts with this Jewish symbol. This Lilit is thus both woman and Jewish, and must be overcome by Jack the Ripper on Christmas Eve.

Dracula (1931) and the director of *The Mummy* (1932), two of Hollywood's most influential classic horror films).[30] The European origin and orientation of Hollywood's leading American producers (in Neal Gabler's terms: the "Hollywood Jews") account for the strong presence of European cultural themes and motifs in the American film industry. Carl Laemmle, the founder and head of Universal Studios, which produced most of Hollywood's classic horror films, was himself a Jewish immigrant from Germany, and in such films as *Dracula* and *Frankenstein*, both the monsters and their hunters were played by European actors (the Hungarian Bela Lugosi as Dracula, the Russian Boris Karloff as Frankenstein's creature and the Dutch Edward Van Sloan as the vampire hunter Van Helsing [Prawer 1980, 133]).[31] The stalking monsters of Europe thus crossed the Atlantic not only on celluloid, but also in the European minds that re-created and reanimated them on film in the New World.

During the 1930s, Universal was the major producer of Hollywood's horror films. This was the studio that created that distinctive, familiar fictional world of classic horror, where, in a semi-Expressionistic setting, vampires, werewolves, monsters, and overreaching scientists relentlessly stalked their female victims.[32] In this world of fairy-tale horror

> the settings were interchangeable, the ambiance unchangeable. This was the secret of the Universal universe. It gave the great films a continuity that was comforting to come back to, whatever the horror that walked abroad. Familiar faces, familiar places: a sort of security in a world of fear. . . . The impossible took place in a tight false world of studio-built landscape, where every tree was carefully gnarled in expressionistic fright, every house cunningly gabled in Gothic mystery, every shadow beautifully lit into lurking terror; and where every actor was caught in the closing ring of horrors, untouched by the possibility of a normal world beyond. (Gifford in Prawer 1980, 130)

Universal's world of horror eagerly adopted the stories and characters bequeathed by the nineteenth-century Romantics. Dracula, Frankenstein, Jekyll and Hyde were its most prominent citizens. Hollywood offered its own interpretations of their stalking, though.

Several of Universal's earliest classical horror films featured stalking as

30. See Prawer 1980, 17, 32, 37; Lavalley 1979, 252; Gabler 1988; and Dettman and Bedford 1976. For full credits for both early German and American films of horror, by year of production, see Hardy, Milne, and Willemen 1985.

31. In his annual trips to his tiny home village in the south of Germany, Laemmle touched base with the world of film in the "old continent," bringing back with him to America both ideas and personnel (Gabler 1988, 72–73, 48; Dettman and Bedford 1976, 4–5).

32. Other studios, such as RKO, Paramount, Warner Brothers, and MGM also contributed to Hollywood's classic world of horror, but Universal Studio's dominant contribution justifies the name "Universal's world."

an element in the Freudian myth of the primal horde. *The Phantom of the Opera* (1925), *Dracula* (1931), and *The Mummy* (1932) are the most notable of these films (Warner Brothers' 1933 *Mystery of the Wax Museum,* although not produced by Universal, also belongs in this distinguished category). In each of these films, as a young suitor "threatens" to introduce the film's young heroine to matrimonial intimacy and sexuality, an "evil father" or his creature appears on the scene and stalks the young woman in an attempt to prevent her union with the young man.[33] In the *Phantom,* the *Mummy,* and the *Wax Museum* the stalker is himself an evil father figure. In *Dracula* and the *Mummy,* the young heroine is a motherless "daddy's girl," and the stalking fiend is not merely an older, "fatherly" man, but also one brought to life by the maiden's (overprotective?) father, hence—"the father's creature."[34] In the tradition of the *Cabinet,* stalking is thus portrayed as a sinister threat to civilized social order, that is, to the foundation of what America views as its "family values." As in the *Cabinet,* the attacks challenge the whole community and the female victim is wholesome and blameless. But in contrast to the *Cabinet,* the "evil father" is not associated with state authorities. And, of course, Hollywood provides happy endings: the monster is always defeated, the heroine is always saved, she is reunited with her young, eligible mate, and the social order is repeatedly reestablished.

In the mentioned films, as well as in their abundant "look-alikes" and remakes, Lilit women play no part in the presentation of stalking; furthermore, they do not even exist in Hollywood's fictional world of horror. Even Dracula's daughter in the film from 1936 by that title and the cat woman in RKO's *Cat People* from 1942, two of classic horror's most conspicuous female stalkers, are not Lilit women. Rather, they are portrayed as tormented, pitiable creatures desperately trying to overcome the uncontrollable bloodlust with which they were cursed through no fault of their own. Both these stalking females are presented as sympathetic victims rather than beastly sexual fiends. Too complacent or too worried to even suggest their existence, Hollywood found no use for truly dangerous women in its world of horror.

In the absence of political connotations that would identify the evil father with the state, and of moral, patriarchal connotations that would link the monster with feminine sexuality, Dracula-type films, although they reestablished social order, were neither socially critical nor disciplining. Their treatment of male stalking was ideologically benign. It was Holly-

33. Interestingly, in the *Phantom of the Opera,* the "evil father stalker" encourages the young woman to prefer her musical career over family life at the side of her young suitor.

34. In Universal's version of Dracula, Dr. Seward, who in Stoker's version was Lucy's suitor, is Mina's father. His home is situated in the lunatic asylum that he directs. Dracula attacks Mina because Reinfield, her father's "pet looney," invites him in. The *Mummy* offers an interesting twist: the mummy is an ancient corpse brought back to life by the heroine's suitor's overreaching scientist father. Here the mummy is the creature of the young man's father.

wood's treatment of Jekyll and Hyde that integrated "bad women" into the stories, inviting patriarchal moral implications.

Stevenson's *Jekyll and Hyde* featured no women. I suggested earlier that the public's association of Hyde with Jack the Ripper may have encouraged the popular reading of the Ripper's victimized prostitutes into the story. In a very successful 1887 stage adaptation of the story, no "evil women" were presented, but Dr. Jekyll received a fiancée. The young woman's (widowed) father prevented his daughter's wedding, causing the transformation of the frustrated Jekyll into Hyde. This transformation eventually led to Hyde's fatal attack on the tyrannical father. In the sense that the father's action caused Hyde's generation, Hyde was the young woman's father's creature. Only in Hollywood's classic remakes of the play does the fallen woman appear on screen.[35] In those versions, Dr. Jekyll encounters a young prostitute, and it is her seductive behavior that contributes both to his transformation into Hyde and to Hyde's deterioration into a cruel, sadistic, "pornographic" ripper. In Mamoulian's 1931 version, a disturbing scene shows a cat stalking, attacking, and finally killing a bird. Just as the bird prompts the cat's natural stalking impulse, so the fallen woman brings about her fate. Hyde cannot help it: it is in his nature.

From here on, Hyde is not merely an evil "father's creature," but also a male stalker forced into action by the sexual behavior of a fallen Eve. Thus, in Hollywood's classic horror films, Hyde was finally united with the Ripper. In Hollywood, the prostitute did not merely provoke the Ripper: she was to blame, together with the evil father, for Hyde's genesis out of the good Dr. Jekyll. The pornographic thrill at the sight of her torment was thus made acceptable, and the male stalker was reestablished as a tool of patriarchal discipline.

MGM's attitudes about women and stalking are encoded in the casting of Victor Fleming's *Jekyll and Hyde* of 1941.

> The core of this film is that the women are switched: the "bad"—i.e., sexual—woman is played by a lady, Ingrid Bergman, while the "lady" is played by a woman with a screen history elsewhere, Lana Turner. . . . the trick was a stroke of genius and luck: it worked. It worked because in a psychosexual sense the women are interchangeable. They are, after all, just like Jekyll and Hyde, parts of the same human. When Hyde attacks Ivy [Bergman, the fallen Eve], a part of Jekyll is really attacking Miriam [his fiancée]. (Twitchell 1985, 250)

In some of Hollywood's classic horror films, then, (fallen) Eves cause the transformation of Dr. Jekyll into Mr. Hyde, who stalks, rapes, abuses,

35. I refer to Paramount's 1921 and 1931 versions of *Dr. Jekyll and Mr. Hyde,* and to MGM's 1941 version. For a full discussion of the story's film versions see Twitchell 1985, chap. 5.

and rips them in turn. Interestingly, even here, the prostitute is merely a fallen Eve and not a full-blown Lilit, as Lulu was in *Pandora's Box*. One of the British Hammer Studios' many "neo-horrors," *The Gorgon* (1964), featured a young woman who, on nights of full moon, became a Medusa, turning men who looked at her into stone. Despite her final decapitation by the film's monster slayer, audiences did not approve, and the film, a dismal commercial failure, was never sequelized (Hutchings 1993, 83). The public knew well what the *Gorgon*'s makers overlooked: that the classic world of horror does not accommodate Lilit characters.[36]

If Dracula and mummy films linked stalking with evil father and creature, and Jekyll and Hyde films depicted the male stalker as a Ripper provoked by both evil father and fallen women, the Frankenstein, and some werewolf, films associated male stalking with overreaching, emotionally incompetent male spouses. This theme had already been found in Shelley's novel, but some Hollywood classic horror films brought it to the fore. The best representative of this group is Universal's *The Werewolf of London* (1935).

The film's first scene is set in Tibet, where a vigorous British botanist is searching for a unique flower that "takes its life from the moon." The scientist disregards all warnings that the flower, an antidote for lycanthropy (werewolfism), is beyond his reach. Eventually, he finds the flower, and as his hand reaches out to it, he is attacked and bitten by a wolflike monster. Back in London, the botanist fails to revive the Tibetan flower by artificial means (he later discovers that all the flower needed was moonlight). Obsessed by this project, he grossly neglects his lovely young wife, pushing her to spend more time with her former suitor. Learning that "the werewolf instinctively seeks to kill those he loves best," the botanist mocks this as an "old wives' tale." But alone in his laboratory one night, when the moon is full, he sees that his arm is changing into a beastly, hairy limb. He also learns that the touch of the flower removes the symptoms.

That night, when the botanist's wife and her friend leave for a party, the botanist refuses to join, but his jealousy and rage turn him into a hideous monster. Grabbing his cloak and a tall hat, the botanist rushes out after his wife and her suitor. Under the light of the full moon, he steals along the foggy, empty streets of the London night. Unable to enter the party, the werewolf hides by a wall. When a young woman walks toward him, he jumps at her, and her screams fill the night air while he drags her off screen. The newspapers report that fatal wounds were found on the young woman's neck.

36. It is telling that, unlike *The Gorgon*, in Hammer's typical "lesbian" vampire films, the female vampire is usually subordinated to, and activated by, an evil male creature, who lurks mysteriously in the background. Like Bram Stoker's vampire women, the cinematic "lesbian vampires" are mostly "tamed Lilits," who are initiated into vampirism by a powerful male vampire and prey mostly on traditional female victims. For lesbian vampire films, see Creed 1993b and Ursini and Silver 1975.

In a desperate attempt to save his wife, the botanist locks himself up in a room at an inn. But when the moonlight reaches him, he again is transformed into a beast, jumping out the window howling. At the zoo that night, he happens upon a common young woman who is seducing the zoo's night watchman, tempting him to leave his wife and children for her. The beast stalks the young woman and attacks.

The next night, the botanist locks himself up again, but upon seeing his wife and her friend together from his hideout, he is transformed once again into a beast, and attacks. The friend's intervention prevents the wife's murder. The next evening, the werewolf overpowers and kills a fellow scientist-werewolf who had been continually begging him to share the antidote flower. Once again the werewolf hunts his wife, who is trapped in their home. Finally, shot dead by Scotland Yard, he regains his human form. (The widow and the friend fly to the New World.)

This tale of predation is almost explicitly presented as an allegory for the domestic drama, simultaneously defamiliarizing the domestic arena and domesticating the supernatural. The protagonist's scientific overreaching is made to look much like a typical man's compulsive preoccupation with his career; it leads him simultaneously to the allegorical ends of the earth and to the prosaic neglect of his wife, which are portrayed as one and the same. "Beastliness" is presented as a cursed, supernatural state, symbolizing the materialization of the protagonist's dark and dangerous lesser self. The flower's need for moonlight is constructed as analogous to the wife's need for attention. The protagonist's lack of sensitivity threatens to destroy both of them. His attempt to scientifically know the flower correlates with his inability to love his wife. The protagonist's incapability to share the flower symbolizes his jealous need to exclusively own his knowledge and his wife. The moon, the natural, cyclical, "feminine" order of things, is presented as a force that could have brought life to the flower and happiness to the human couple (the botanist's wife adores strolling in the moonlight). The scientist's insensitive overachievement (in obtaining the flower), which is also his underachievement (in maintaining his relationship), turns the moon into a fatal trigger of lycanthropy.

Put together, all these elements indicate that *Werewolf in London* tells the story of an obsessive overreacher who undermines his marriage by not accommodating his wife's basic need for his attention. His neglect pushes her into (what the protagonist believes to be) a relationship with another man, a situation that causes the protagonist's tormented insecurity and triggers his aggressive jealousy and agonized revenge. Suspicion, humiliation, pain, a sense of betrayal and despair all drive him to stalk his wife and the other man, whom he perceives as his rival. His stalking expresses a host of confused urges: to reinforce his control over the situation, to not be left out, to get his wife back, to get back at her and at his male rival. His killing of other women in the street is a displacement of the protagonist's hostility from his wife to her evil, sexual doubles. In stalking the prostitute and the seductress, the protagonist allegorically punishes the "betraying" traits of his wife.

The stalking of the wife includes feudlike homosocial communication with the other man in her life. The protagonist's inability to form any relationship with another man except rivalry over a woman excludes the option of creating a harmonious community and leads to the inevitable confrontation and to the protagonist's tragic destruction.

In short, the husband's obsessive pursuit of knowledge takes over his life and correlates with his failure in the more complicated world of human emotions and relationships. Stalking, in this context, is the desperate, inherently futile means of the man-turned-monster protagonist to cope with a crisis that he refuses to acknowledge and treat. It is a beastly manifestation of frustration that claims unnecessary victims.

This nearly feminist treatment of ancient and classic stalking stories as allegories of spousal dramas is Universal's most original and significant contribution to the conceptualization of stalking. Another interesting contribution is the reinforcement of the motif, familiar in vampire folklore, that the relationship between the monstrous male stalker and his female target is an everlasting bond, beyond life, death, and linear time. In *The Mummy*, one of Universal's most popular and sequeled horror films, the young woman targeted by the stalking mummy is a reincarnation of the mummy's ancient Egyptian lover. Thousands of years ago, the film explains, she was a royal princess, and his forbidden love for her was punished by his being buried alive. This chilling, eternal "blood tie" makes the pursuit not only uncannily supernatural, but also inevitable, almost justified. Only the most fundamental social convention, such as the suitable young man's entitlement to win the girl, can overcome the mummy's powerful claim.[37] A version of this motif was adapted into Francis Ford Coppola's remake of *Dracula* in 1992. Here Mina is the reincarnation of the count's fifteenth-century wife, who took her own life when she believed he was dead. Like Romeo and Juliet, stalker and target share a history of eternal love, stronger than life and stronger than death. He stalks her because they belong together.[38] Unlike the *Werewolf in London*'s treatment of the theme, this romantic presentation neutralizes stalking, redeems the stalker, and all but blames the targeted victim.

Universal's *Invisible Man* (1933), which resonates with the earlier *Phantom of the Opera*, offers yet another important presentation of stalking, vividly portraying it as the threatening *unseen* presence of a tyrannical other. In this film, an overreaching scientist experiments on himself, becomes invisible, and discovers that "an invisible man can control the world! Nobody will see him come and nobody will see him go. He can hear every

37. *The Wax Museum* and its sequels feature a similar theme.
38. An interesting take on this theme is Eddie Murphy's 1995 *Vampire in Brooklyn*, which links this motif with race politics.

secret. He can rob and wreck and kill!"[39] Clearly, *The Invisible Man* portrays what I have been referring to as "satanic spying," combined with "ultimate male stalking": a godly, objectifying gaze. Unable to see the invisible man, the viewer identifies with the victim who cries, "He may be here now, beside us, in the garden, looking through the window, or at the corner of my bedroom waiting for me, waiting to kill me." The film does not offer a way to appease the invisible stalker, but rather mandates his death.

In Hollywood's classic horror films, Dracula, Frankenstein's creature, the phantom of the opera, the mummy, the invisible man, Hyde, and many others shared the same fictional world. Each film invited the viewer into a world where *all* of these characters lurk in the shadows. The repeated appearances of stars such as Boris Karloff and Bela Lugosi helped to connect the different stalkers and their stories, thus fusing together the different social themes and interpretations of stalking.

In this fictional world of horror, the evil father and the evil women were always potential causes of stalking and serial killing; the fiend's female target was assumed to be an incarnation of his eternal, long-lost love; overly ambitious spouses were suspected of expressing their sexual jealousy through stalking and random killings of fallen women, and unseen stalkers were expected to lurk where they were not seen. Male stalkers roamed unleashed, spying, "knowing," and disciplining.

These images remained with viewers, following them into their dreams and into their everyday lives. The boundaries between Universal's fictional world and the world inhabited by real people were not always clear. Thus, "fallen women" in the real world could easily be understood as provoking stalking; jealous, overachieving spouses could be viewed as potential stalkers and serial killers; respectable-looking "Dr. Jekylls" could be suspected as potential Hydes; empty rooms could suggest the presence of predators. Universal's images and stories were reinforced in the public's imagination through numerous sequels and remakes. They continue to influence our own world through their reappearances on television and on videotape and through their pronounced influence on later films and on the contemporary social sciences. They played an important part in the twentieth century's understanding and conceptualization of stalking.

In conclusion, let me mention one other masterpiece of the genre. In 1962, Universal made the classic chiller *Cape Fear*. Instead of one of the stable of supernatural monsters, Robert Mitchum plays an ex-convict, Kaity, who has spent eight years in jail (for brutal rape) planning his revenge on the lawyer, played by Gregory Peck, whose testimony had put him behind bars.

---

39. He enslaves his colleague, who also happens to be his romantic rival over their older professor's (motherless) daughter, and when the colleague betrays him, he vengefully (and literally) stalks him to death. At the happy end, which inevitably entails the "monster's" death, he becomes visible once again, a human trait he lost through his "scientific" overreaching ambition.

Upon his release, Kaity abuses a sexually liberated young woman and maliciously stalks the lawyer, his wife, and their maturing daughter. He follows them wherever they go, forcing himself into their lives, trying to live his own life through theirs. Having studied law in prison and making the lawyer actively participate in his cruel stalking game, he attempts to become the lawyer while forcing the lawyer to resemble him. He is determined to ruin the lawyer's life, since he believes the lawyer has ruined his own, and only direct confrontation will stop him. Like Dracula, the "undead" Kaity returns from "death" to "drink the life" of the living. He is also an evil "father's creature," threatening to prevent the young woman's decent maturation. Like Hollywood's Hyde, he is the lawyer's evil other-self, brutalizing fallen women and threatening the social order. Like Frankenstein's creature, Kaity stalks to demand attention, to communicate, and to avenge himself on the man who (in his own mind) "made him." Like the creature, he too becomes a murderer in the process. In other words, even when no longer featuring its classic horror characters, Universal found an effective way of "remaking" its old horror films and perpetuating their stalking themes in other, more sophisticated film genres. The spellbinding *Cape Fear* inspired many imitations, as well as a powerful remake in 1991.

Hitchcock's Stalking Stories

The fictional world of Alfred Hitchcock is as distinct, and has been as influential, as Universal's.[40] It is also equally fraught with stalking. To mention only a few examples: *The Lodger*'s (1926) protagonist stalks Jack the Ripper by stalking the women the Ripper is likely to attack. *Rebecca* (1940) is the story of an (un)dead, evil first wife who (together with her loyal, living housekeeper) stalks her young, innocent substitute. In *Shadow of a Doubt* (1943), the vampiristic "Uncle Charlie" stalks and attacks his young, innocent namesake niece. *To Catch a Thief* (1955) features Cary Grant, "the cat," stalking his young, female imitator. *Vertigo*'s (1958) overreaching, knowledge-seeking James Stewart character stalks a living-dead woman with whom he becomes obsessed. The first four examples constitute autostalking, since the character, in each case, stalks his or her double image: a fellow stalker, a substitute, a niece by the same name, and an imitator.

   Rear Window (1954) is Hitchcock's allegory of the human condition and of film viewing. The James Stewart protagonist, Hitchcock's representative of "a race of Peeping Toms," is a voyeuristic male stalker. Living his life through his neighbors, whom he perpetually watches, the protagonist objectifies them, spies and informs upon them, judges, trespasses (with the assistance of his woman partner), traps and condemns them. More explicitly than

40. For full discussions of Hitchcock's films mentioned here see M. Wood 1989; Rothman 1982; Modleski 1989; Truffaut 1985; Price 1992; Žižek 1992; Samuels 1998; and Horwitz 1986.

some of Hitchcock's other films, *Rear Window* establishes Hitchcock's theory of stalking: the protagonist stalks because he is a "castrated" man, in the psychoanalytic, Freudian sense of the phrase.[41]

In Hitchcock's fictional world, which is deeply and manifestly Freudian, stalking is frequently a manifestation of castration. *Strangers on a Train* (1951) is a good example. In this version of the Frankenstein story, Bruno, attempting to become a part of Guy's life, stalks him. While pursuing Guy, Bruno stalks and kills Guy's unfaithful wife, a fallen woman, and threatens her innocent mirror image, Guy's fiancée's sister. Finally, Guy is provoked to chase Bruno. The chase culminates in a dramatic confrontation and in Bruno's death. Bruno's sense of rejection and neglect, his torment, and Guy's horror echo Shelley's story. But unlike any other Frankenstein story, Bruno is not a product of Guy's Faustian nature, but a castrated mama's boy. Rather than "Guy's creature," he is a "castrated stalker," motivated by the combined ambition to murder his father and to unite with Guy, a mature, sexually active man. Nine years later, Hitchcock perfected Bruno's character, as well as his mother's hold on him, when he created the castrated Jack the Ripper, Norman Bates (superbly played by Anthony Perkins).

Psycho (1960) is "without a doubt, the quintessential suspense-shocker of modern cinema, and a touchstone for almost everything in the genre that has since followed. Thirty years later, the famous shower scene is still firmly embedded in the cultural imagination" (Bloch 1989, 318). *Psycho* is also one of Hitchcock's most refined analysis of stalking, offering a full theory of the serial-killer male stalker.

As Lesser points out, "Hitchcock, as director, is his films' own psychoanalyst, consciously pointing out all the symbols for us" (Lesser 1991, 123). *Psycho* is a case in point. Norman Bates is a gentle, intelligent, childish, timid, tidy, lonely young man who, because he felt neglected, murdered his mother and her lover. He lives in a deserted motel with his dead mother, whom he has stuffed (and with several stuffed birds, including an owl); occasionally, he murders young women who happen by. In the famous shower scene he murders Marion, who stole from her employer to assist her lover. As he always does, Norman commits his murder dressed up as his mother. In fact, each time he murders a young woman to whom he is attracted, he *becomes* his mother, who takes over his personality. As the film's psychiatrist explains in detail, Norman was unable to live with the unbearable burden of guilt of having killed his mother. He therefore denied her death and found a way to bring her back to life in his own mind:

> [H]e began to think and speak for her, give her half his life, so to speak. At times he could be both personalities, carrying on conversations. . . . And because he was so pathologically jealous of her, he assumed that

41. The Stewart character's broken leg, which restricts him to his chair and to his window, is only the most obvious sign of his castration. For discussion see Samuels 1998, 109.

she was as jealous of him. Therefore, if he felt a strong attraction to any other woman, the mother side of him would go wild. When he met your sister [says the psychiatrist to Marion's sister], he was touched by her, aroused by her. He wanted her. That set off the jealous mother, and *mother* killed the girl. . . . You see, when the mind houses two personalities, there's always a conflict. A battle. In Norman's case, the battle is over, and the dominant personality has won. These were crimes of passion, not profit. (Rothman 1982, 332)

Norman the stalker is Mother's castrating force; he is also Mother's son, who performs her stalking and his own castration on her behalf; he is also the living-dead, vampiristic Mother herself, who has taken over her son's body and soul. In short, *Psycho*'s serial-killing stalker is the vampiristic, undead, castrating Mother, embodied in her castrated and self-castrating son. His serial attacks on young, fallen women, such as Marion, are his means of self-castration.

In *Psycho*, Hitchcock retells every story of male stalking, explaining them all as allegories of (Freudian) castration. Mother is what I defined as the ultimate, "godly" male stalker. Through the gazing eyes of the stuffed, dead birds that fill his home, especially the owl, she constantly watches Norman, knowing, controlling, and castrating.[42] In his overreaching attempt to stalk others (young women) in turn, he finds that in order to control his targets, just as Mother controls him, he must kill them. Thus, he becomes the serial killer of his own potential mates. Norman is also Mother's Frankenstein creature. She is the indifferent creator, and he is the tormented, rejected son who stalks to gain intimacy, as well as to punish and avenge. Like the Frankenstein creature, he is his own castrating monster. Simultaneously, Mother(-Norman) is also the vampiristic Dracula, who punishes the community's young fallen women, endangers the innocent ones, and castrates the community's young men, that is, Norman Bates. Of course, Norman and Mother are also Jekyll and Hyde, sharing the same body. Jekyll/Norman transforms into Hyde/Mother when a fallen woman attracts Jekyll/Norman. Hyde/Mother then stalks and kills her as a means of preventing the consummation of his desire.

Hitchcock started exploring the theme of serial killers in his first film, *The Lodger* (1926), an homage to Jack the Ripper. The film's protagonist, a gentle young man, was sent by his mother to avenge the murder of his sister. In his mother's service, he follows young women who resemble his sister, lying in wait for the serial killer. Although it finally unites him with one of these young women, the film leaves unresolved whether he himself is the

42. "Owls belong to the night world; they are watchers, and this appeals to Perkins' masochism. He knows the birds and he knows they're watching him all the time. He can see his own guilt reflected in their knowing eyes" (Truffaut 1985, 282). See also Samuels 1998, 135.

Ripper and the murderer of his own sister. Over the years, Hitchcock created numerous serial killers, castrating mothers, and murderous castrated sons. Thirty-four years of perfecting these images resulted in *Psycho:* in this adaptation of the story of the serial killer Ed Gein, Hitchcock's Ripper has evolved into Norman Bates. No wonder the film, and its portrayal of the serial killer, has had tremendous influence on the modern perception of stalking as well as on the analysis of serial killers. (It may have even strengthened the public's Freudian frame of mind.)

The Birds (1963), arguably Hitchcock's most powerful treatment of stalking, is yet another version of the Frankenstein-Hyde-Ripper stalking story.[43] Here, Melanie, a young "fallen woman," pursues a mama's boy, Mitch. In turn, the overwhelming, castrating jealousy of Mitch's mother brings about the birds' brutal attack of Melanie—she must be destroyed so that Mother can secure her hold on Mitch, that is, perpetuate his castration.[44] The murderous birds are, therefore, Mother's stalking creature, and as such they are her castrating mechanism, designed to prevent Mitch's independence and sexual maturity.

In *The Birds*, the Ripper image is a (super)natural extension of Mother, indicating that she herself is "Mother Nature" or the "Great Mother" (Price 1992, 201). In using medieval parlance, the serial-killing birds are also Mother's "intimate" or "familiar"; that is, Mother is a witch. Significantly, this witch's intimate is a flock of birds, which for Horwitz calls to mind the legendary flock of evil, flying women, the Strix (or "Harpies," as she refers to them [1986, 281]). Thus Mother represents the queen of the flying women of the night, also known as Artemis, an incarnation of Lilit. But Mother is not the only female character associated with birds and with Lilit. Price notes that Hitchcock referred to Melanie's character using the phrase "fly-by-night," which is British slang for a prostitute (Price 1992, 199). This term, read together with Melanie's provocatively sexual character and her interest in (love) birds, associates her both with the birds and with Lilit. At the same time, Melanie is also explicitly likened to Mother herself: there is a clear physical resemblance between the characters, enhanced by their similar hairstyles and by their rivalry over Mitch and over the "mothering" of his younger sister (Horwitz 1986, 280, 283). The flying Lilit women/birds are, thus, Mother/(old) Lilit's stalking creature, provoked into destructive, murderous action by the seductive behavior of (the young) Lilit. In this reading, *The Birds* presents a story of autostalking that is a gender reversal of Shel-

43. For a reading of the birds as Jack the Ripper see Price 1992, 191–99.

44. For a full analysis of the birds as representing the mother's jealousy see Horwitz 1986. She rightly argues that "the bird attacks function primarily as extensions of Lydia's [the mother's] hysterical fear of losing her son" (279), and that "the perverse mother's love portrayed in this film is responsible for a kind of castration" (284). She goes on to say that "the wild birds are the expression of a form of 'surveillance.' . . . It is as if Lydia [the mother] 'followed' Melanie back, the birds functioning as an extension of her" (280). See also Žižek 1992, 5; and Samuels 1998, 123.

ley's. In Shelley's novel, the Faustian "father" (Victor) stalks himself through his creature. Elizabeth is the innocent victim. In Hitchcock's version, the Lilit Mother stalks her (young) self through her creature(s). Mitch is portrayed as an innocent, castrated victim. In Shelley's text, Lilit is, in fact, a male character; in Hitchcock, Jack the Ripper is, in truth, Mother('s creature).

In any event, whether or not we read this layer of meaning into the film, the repetitively gathering birds, preparing quietly for their attacks, is one of the most uncanny images of stalking in the history of film.

In a case study first published in 1964, four years after *Psycho*'s sensational release, and republished (in an anthology) in 1992, psychiatrist Robert S. McCully analyzes what he labels an "autovampiristic" patient. This patient was "a young adult, unmarried, white male" who repeatedly cut his neck and drank his own blood. He also frequently masturbated while indulging in "fantasies of sucking blood from the necks of young boys" (Noll 1992, 40). McCully portrays the subject as struggling with his "fear of castration," as striving for "masculine self-esteem," and as suffering from "primitive oral fixation." Declaring that his subject's bloody sexual habits constitute an "affirmation of the life principle" while he is "simultaneously flirting with death," McCully finds that the subject violates the taboos of his society and that he is, therefore, "not unlike the vampire." McCully then investigates the ancient archetype of the vampire and finds that, according to Neumann's Jungian analysis, this primal creature is related to the negative aspect of what Neumann called "the great mother":

> Earliest mythology has associated the vampire with the destructive side of the feminine. . . . Artemis Orthia, the powerful goddess of ancient Sparta, was known as the winged lady, ruler of the kingdom of the beasts. She, as well as Hecate, was not without highly negative traits comparable to vampirism. . . . As ruler of primordial mysteries of the feminine, her role was intimately bound up with the sacrifice of blood, or she may have had the power to transform blood into milk. . . . It is her negative side (often vampiristic) that takes many forms and may demand the bloody sacrifice of castration. (50)

McCully leaves no room for doubt that it is the ancient, unconscious archetype of the negative mother that creeps out of the darkness, seizes his patient, and turns him into a vampire:

> There are many parallels between some of the qualities ascribed to her and some of the behavioral effects apparent in the present subject. What has happened to him seems not dissimilar to demands required by the negative side of Artemis-Hecate when their destructive forces demand sacrifice. Some mysterious force from the unconscious had sucked away a large part of the life principle in him. . . . Neumann called atten-

tion to the youth not strong enough or developed enough to resist the forces symbolized by the overpowering mother, and that his behavior may express flight from incestuous fears. . . . the primary expression of "flight" in one under the dominance of the destructive forces of the feminine is self-castration. This, of course, is tantamount to capitulation. The frightening aspect of the powerful mother becomes repressed, but the price required is a ban on sexuality. The son-victim may turn to masturbation or self-castration. . . . Perhaps, then, the vampirism which had him in his clutches hid (or symbolized) . . . the negative, destructive mother complex. A hostile animal replaced the image of the hostile side of the mother, and the subject virtually acted out the contents of what had been repressed, which is to say, he had taken on the role of the negative aspect of the terrible mother (whose archetype had sucked him in), and like Hecate, he sucked blood from young boys. . . . he may be said to have been under the curse of Hecate, or had developed a "Hecate complex." (51)

Offering a scientific analogue to the theory of stalking Hitchcock develops in *Psycho* and *The Birds,* McCully reveals Mother's true identity: she is Lilit. Lilit, it seems, is alive and well, and is stalking McCully's subject in the depth of his unconscious. She possesses him and has turned him into a bloodthirsty vampire. Thus, in 1964, in the *Journal of Nervous and Mental Disease* (where McCully's paper was first published), Lilit (referred to as "Hecate") was rediscovered and associated with a "complex." Through the mediation of film and psychoanalytic mythological discourse, she has found a new home in the person of McCully's young male vampire, a (potential) serial killer. Or, if you like, in the 1960s, psychoanalysis exposed Lilit's victimization of her son (once known as Dumuzi and later as Norman Bates) and declared her responsible for turning him into a monster. She is the living-dead within, which stalks his soul in the shadows of his being. Once upon a time, Inanna was a Great Goddess and Dumuzi was her son-lover God. Then Lilit became a mythological stalker, and her sons were said to be devils. Finally, she became Mother, the new mythological stalker, her son being Norman Bates, the victimized creature, the vampiristic serial killer. Mysterious, no doubt, are the ways of storytelling.

In our contemporary mass-media culture, diverse discourses are combined into something more than a dialogue: they are intertwined, forming an inseparable web. Through McCully's professional analysis of a real case study, Norman Bates, a fictional stalker, was implicitly declared a psychiatric vampire. Hitchcock's fictional Mother was similarly appropriated into the psychoanalytic discourse, to be explicitly identified there as the female stalker Lilit. She was found to be the real killer, preying on innocent victims through the victimization of her tortured Oedipal son. The combination of McCully's analysis with that of Norman's analyst "authenticates" the film's psychoanalytic interpretation. At the same time, it imports fictional characters and stories of stalking into social science, our modern "learned tradition."

This chapter discussed film as the primary medium that molded our notions and experiences of stalking in the twentieth century; in the twenty-first century, the equivalent medium may be the Internet. Cyberspace shares some of the features through which film subjects its viewer to the sensations of stalking and being stalked. For example, "the term 'lurk' . . . has entered standard computer vernacular to refer to what a computer user does when he or she observes, but does not participate in, a virtual chat room" (Lee 1998, 406). In the twenty-first century, cyberspace techniques and "plots" may reformulate familiar motifs into new sociocultural reality.

CHAPTER 7

Contemporary Erotomanic Serial Killers

Preface

During the 1970s the patriarchal social order and men in the United States experienced deep insecurity. The unheroic end of the Vietnam War had diminished public confidence and induced the nation to affect a "castrated" demeanor. Referring to the defeated, antiheroic postwar mood, Ray Raphael argues that the war was "an abortive rite of passage for an entire generation of American males, even for those who stayed behind" (1988, 146–47). He adds that, in general, men who were made to fail their initiation into manhood become highly insecure, and that "the frustrations of unfulfilled masculinity . . . are potentially dangerous" (187). The Watergate affair undermined the public's trust in the system and in "good old American values." Relative economic insecurity and racial conflicts generated anxiety on a nationwide scale. Strange occurrences of inexplicable, outrageous crimes, particularly serial killings, which were sensationalized by the media, added to the confusion. Simultaneously, a "second wave" of feminism gained visibility and brought about deep changes in social structures and values. During this period, traditional concepts maintained by the sociopolitical order, such as the images representing femininity and masculinity, were examined and criticized.

Many men felt threatened, attacked, and disoriented. Many felt that they were expected to fulfill roles and maintain order in a society in which they had no confidence. The traditional roles seemed suffocating, unattainable, and insufficient, while the new roles remained unclear. This condition of social disintegration led to anxiety and paralysis. In 1976, psychologist Herb Goldberg published his widely read *The Hazards of Being Male*. In it, he defined an identity crisis among American men, whom he calls tormented "zombies" and "sleepwalkers," "machinelike," "dehumanized things," and "role robots." Observing that "castrated men" would explode if they did not reclaim their masculinity, he claimed that modern man must embrace his "underlying rage toward the endless, impossible binds under which he lives" (1979, 5). Raphael speculated that today "society as a whole is facing its mid-life crisis, where the classical image of man as a hunter and warrior—an image best realized in young adulthood—must now be transcended" (1988, 195). But, certainly in the 1970s, a new image had not yet materialized.

Cultural anxiety during the 1970s was, thus, manifold. People feared Vietnam War veterans, the young men who had returned frustrated and disoriented from "the heart of darkness"; these men seemed to mirror the deep crisis of American masculinity and to reflect men's collective, castrated state: they represented their generation's failure to pass from childhood into manhood. People feared serial killers, whose actions seemed to lie beyond human understanding. They feared the new women and their radical demands for change. People feared the unknown, and they feared the repressed rage within themselves.

In this atmosphere, stalking stories, always a convenient venue for the narration, experience, and interpretation of contemporary existential insecurity, offered a familiar address where real-life crisis could be explained. It is not surprising that Vietnam veterans, serial killers, and liberated women were cast in such stories, where they could be identified, molded, and explicated in reference to fictional stalkers and their stories. Social sciences, the media, and the movies all participated in this cultural process, offering professional terminology and cultural insights while reformulating these new images into social categories. These categories, mediating between real people and archetypal images of stalking, culminated in a contemporary moral panic that focused on stalking.

Beginning with a discussion of *Taxi Driver*, a film that presented the most powerful and influential image of the period's castrated, disintegrated American man, this chapter shows that the media, the film industry, and social scientists (including psychologists and psychiatrists) joined forces to establish *Taxi Driver*'s protagonist, Travis Bickle, as the contemporary incarnation of the archetypal male stalker, and to render him as a psychological profile: the "erotomanic serial killer." The chapter further suggests that, in a parallel cultural process, fictional independent career women (such as Alex in *Fatal Attraction*) were portrayed as manifestations of the contemporary Lilit; this Lilit was also recast in the form of an erotomanic serial killer. This profile thus mediates between contemporary individuals and archetypal images of male and female stalkers.

Contemporary Images of Male Stalkers

The Stalking Veteran: *Taxi Driver*

In 1976 Martin Scorsese and Paul Schrader introduced the American public to a unique character, Robert De Niro's Travis Bickle. Travis, a shy, lonely marine veteran, is trapped in the meaninglessness of his alienated life as a New York taxi driver. Unable to sleep, he drives his taxi every night, ceaselessly prowling the city. From his taxi window, "Bickle understands the city solely as a place of corruption, filth, violence, dread—an open sewer, filled with garbage and inhabited by human vermin. Only pimps and pushers and prostitutes walk the streets; . . . it is a city of dreadful night and the night's creatures" (Martin 1988, 46). Bickle documents the city's moral guilt, awaiting supernatural intervention that will cleanse it from the filth. Developing an infatuation with a fair, virginal political campaign worker, Betsy (Cybil Shepherd), Travis follows her and succeeds in attaining her attention for a short while. When she rejects him, he purchases three guns, drills himself in their use, changes his appearance, and stalks the presidential candidate for whom she works, in an attempt to assassinate him. Failing in this, he takes on another mission, that of saving an underaged prostitute (Jodie Foster) from her pimp. In the execution of his mission he shoots and kills three men. These avenging murders turn him into a media celebrity and allow him to reenter his previous life on the ugly streets and resume his original appearance and personality.[1]

Travis Bickle shares the qualities of the legendary, literary, and cinematic male stalkers that I have discussed. Vampire-like, he returns from war, the world of death, to lead a lonely, nocturnal living-death, in which he absorbs the lives of others, develops a murderous taste, and sheds human blood. Like the vampire, some of his violence is aimed at those whom he loves most (Betsy and the candidate, whom Travis claims to admire). His aimless roaming lies outside the axis of linear time, trapping him in a repetitive cycle of endless nights. Like Dracula, he pursues the community's "pure woman" and declares war on the body of men who reject him.

Satan-like, he spies on the fallen city, documenting its sins, awaiting the day of judgment. Like the Angel of Death, he actually passes judgment and executes it. A modern Faust, he wants to change the unchangeable world, to become a hero, and to win the unattainable, perfect woman. This exaggerated ambition leads him to become a stalker and a killer. Like Frankenstein's creature, he rages against what he perceives as unjust rejection. In his stalking he calls for attention as well as takes his revenge. Like Norman Bates, he is a lonely, castrated man-boy. And of course, the transformation of this polite, timid character into a murderous, head-shaven beast and his subsequent change back to his original state evokes the story of Dr. Jekyll. Instead of prostitutes, this Hyde-Ripper murders their pimps and johns.

On one level, Travis's stalking is explained in the context of his delusional, pathetic infatuation with an unattainable, virginal love object. It is she who rejects (and castrates) him; she is his target, and it is in his attempt to impose himself on her life that he pursues her, while also stalking and killing others. But on a deeper level, Travis's monstrous features are all manifestations of his "veteran character"; that is, it is his existential state as a con-

---

1. Travis's film character was modeled by the scriptwriter Paul Schrader on Arthur Bremer, a man who had attempted to kill George Wallace. Bremer himself claimed to have been inspired by Kubrick's *Clockwork Orange* (1971) (Martin 1988, 49).

temporary American man that renders him vampiristic and Hyde-like. Travis is not a supernatural or mythological creature. He is a soldier who, on behalf of a whole generation of American men, failed to achieve mature manhood for himself and for his nation.[2] Travis had been trained (as a marine) to stalk and kill the enemy, the Other. The war was supposed to transform him into a mature man, a successful hunter, capable of ruling the world. But this masculine initiation rite went awry, and Travis himself became the dangerous Other, the enemy; the transformation failed, leaving him lonely, rejected, immature, and castrated. He returned from a hellish place changed into a dehumanized "living-dead." Having crossed the lines into the world of death, he can no longer find his place in the community of the living. The Vietnam experience, which lies outside society's boundaries, has given him new, critical eyes. He, like Frankenstein's creature, is society's victim, its source of failure and shame. He murders to gain attention and affection and to exact revenge. He is the community's Hyde in that he is its dark, shadowy mirror image set free. In this sense, his stalking represents the community's stalking of itself.

The Vietnam veteran was clearly the focus of deep social guilt, shame, anger, and fear. The "vets" were a symbol of the identity crisis in American society. In this context, Travis's infatuation with Betsy is more than a romantic delusion. His attempt to enter her life is also Travis's attempt to regain entrance into the national community. His need to impress her is his need to redeem himself in the eyes of society. His stalking, attempted assassination of the presidential candidate and murder of the pimps are designed to redeem the failure of Vietnam. By proving himself a hunter, a warrior, and a man, Travis hopes to win Betsy, but he also hopes to achieve his own, and by extension his society's, manhood. His acts are an attempt to achieve his community's pardon and acceptance. Betsy, the blond, virginal, "apple pie" political activist, is a metaphor for American society. Travis targets society at large. It is this element that makes him the source of an overwhelming anxiety.

In a complex cultural process, Travis, the new American male stalker, is transformed into the "erotomanic serial-killing stalker."

Son of Sam

The same year that the fictional Travis first stalked America on screen (1976), a real predator was stalking it on the streets of New York City. Son of Sam, as he called himself, shot thirteen people, killing six and wounding seven, in seven incidents between July 1976 and June 1977. He usually attacked young

2. In 1978, Robert De Niro played a tormented soldier turned veteran in *The Deer Hunter,* associating Travis with the deer hunter and stressing his social role. It is interesting to compare De Niro's Vietnam veteran roles with his veteran of World War II in *New York, New York* (1977).

couples in parked cars late at night. Most of his victims were young women with long brown hair. In his sixth shooting, a note was found. In part, it read:

> I am the "Monster"—"Beelzebub"—the Chubby Behemoth. I love to hunt. Prowling the streets looking for fair game—tasty meat. The women of Queens are prettiest of all. . . . I live for the hunt—my life. Blood for papa. (Breslin and Schaap 1978, 143)

The assassin also sent letters to a *New York Daily News* reporter Jimmy Breslin, one containing the following passage:

> I am deeply hurt by your calling me a women hater. I am not. But I am a monster. I am the Son of Sam. . . . Sam loves to drink blood. "Go out and kill," commands father Sam. Behind our house some rest. Mostly young—raped and slaughtered—their blood drained—just bones now. . . . Papa Sam keeps me locked in the attic. . . . I feel like an outsider. I am on a different wavelength than everybody else—programmed to kill. (Breslin and Schaap 1978, 143)

One of the letters was signed "Sam's creation."

His notorious actions made Son of Sam a contemporary Jack the Ripper. His letters explicitly portrayed him as a hunter, a vampire's slave, and a Frankenstein's monster. It was almost inevitable that both the public and the media would associate him with the fictional Travis Bickle. Two common speculations that appeared in the newspapers were that Son of Sam was a veteran and that he drove a taxi. A century earlier, in London, Jack the Ripper had been socially constructed as an embodiment of literary figures, Jekyll and Hyde. Similarly, "throughout the long manhunt for him, Son of Sam was generally expected to be a Jekyll and Hyde type" (*Newsweek*, 22 August 1977). In 1976, the fictional association of choice was the delusional veteran of *Taxi Driver*. The list of Son of Sam's victims was relatively short, and his deeds were not half as gruesome as those committed by other serial killers, but the combination of the killer's teasing, chilling letters, his self-description as a vampiristic creature, and his popular association with the murderous protagonist of a powerful film touched an open nerve. The press described and analyzed his exploits relentlessly. The American public was obsessed and fascinated. Son of Sam became a household name and a national celebrity.

When he was finally caught, the media portrayal of Son of Sam (David Richard Berkowitz) confirmed the popular suspicion that he was a "Travis come true." Berkowitz was described as a "well-mannered, 24-year-old postal worker who lived alone. His apartment was filthy . . . and the walls were scratched with graffiti" (Hickey 1991, 172)—just as in *Taxi Driver*. This army veteran's "main character trait seemed to be that he was introverted and liked to roam the streets alone at night" (172). Like Travis, he was a keen consumer of pornography and owned two guns (his notorious .44, and a machine gun). Like the taxi driver, he documented his exploits in writing and was fascinated with the newspaper coverage of his escapades.

Upon Son of Sam's arrest, *Newsweek*'s reporters offered the following summary:

> It was a strangely mundane conclusion to one of the largest and most publicized manhunts in history. In the later days of Son of Sam's year long career as gunman and night-stalker, New York lived in fear of him and a world looked in fascination . . . "I only shoot pretty girls," he said with a note of pride. . . . And then describing the weird "voices" that made him kill in a tone he might have used to describe the Bronx post office where he worked. . . . Moments after singling out Sam Carr, Berkowitz told police that Sam was actually a 6,000-year-old man who spoke to him through Carr's dog, Harvey. The suspect also directed some "blame" in the murders toward his downstairs neighbor . . . [and] accused him of being a "master" who was commanding the killer to fill the streets with blood. . . . Throughout the long manhunt for him, Son of Sam was generally expected to be a Jekyll-and-Hyde type, someone who *stalked his victims by night* and then faded into the texture of the city as a mild-mannered innocent by day. . . . Some fellow postal workers and old friends did claim to be shocked when their "quiet" acquaintance was arrested as the .44 killer. But in retrospect, at least, it appeared that Berkowitz has strewn his lonely, troubled life with seeds of the paranoia that eventually boiled up. . . . Berkowitz organized an unofficial volunteer fire department. . . . "[I]t was like he just wanted to be recognized for something," says Shilkraut [a neighbor]. . . . During 1972, his year in Korea, his letters changed drastically. The kid who had signed his name "Doughboy Dave" switched to "Master of Reality." . . . In his apartment David entertained himself with pornography and a growing collection of Son of Sam clippings. His bookcase contained only a few volumes, including one on Jack the Ripper and an army manual called "Survival, Evasion and Escape." (*Newsweek*, 22 August 1977; emphasis added)

All the elements were there: the vampiristic lust for blood; the quiet young man who was transformed during his military service overseas into a Jekyll-and-Hyde Jack the Ripper; the lonely, alienated Travis who "just wanted to be recognized for something." The killer himself claimed that he represented society's dark mirror image.

> I will always fantasize those evil things which are part of my life. I will always remain a mental pervert by thinking sexual things, etc., How-

ever, almost everyone else is like me, for we commit numerous perverted sexual acts in our minds day after day. (Hickey 1991, 173)

Son of Sam Labeled "Stalker"

In its coverage of the story, the printed media linked Son of Sam, his character, and his pattern of behavior with the term *stalking*, which, until then, had not been associated with such events. Initially, in American newspapers the root *stalk* was confined to the sports columns, appearing principally in articles on deer hunting and fishing. Hank Burchard's usage of the term, in a *Washington Post* article titled "The Stalker Is Seldom the Slayer" (23 December 1977), is typical:

> The hunter . . . was trying to use the least effective and most demanding method of hunting deer: solo stalking. It requires, a man he admires had told him, total concentration, alertness to all the sights, sounds and shapes around you, an ability to read terrain from the point of view of the animals who inhabit it, and "more patience than I think you've got." If you simply want to kill deer, the man had said, use a tree stand or go with others and take turns driving the animals toward waiting guns. It is the difference between hunting and harvesting.

In this article, as in others, stalking is depicted as a characteristic of a traditional image of manhood: man as hunter. Stalking is a solo activity. It combines motion in space with purposeful lying in wait. It requires alertness, concentration, determination, persistence, endurance, and patience. It takes physical toughness and exceptional eyesight. It demands quick responses. It is conducted in complete silence. It is risky and therefore fair play. It takes nerve. It is an outdoor skill. It is the skill of a predatory animal. It is about self-control, self-assurance, and control of another's movement. It is ritualistic. When conducted properly, it is rewarded with a kill and a trophy. The appreciative tone in which it is described promotes it from a method of animal killing to a heroic skill in its own right. Stalking, as presented by Hank Burchard, fits in perfectly with the traditional characterization of the American hero: the lonely rider, the fastest gun in the West, the silent tough guy. (The image of Clint Eastwood in good old westerns and his *Dirty Harry* films comes to mind.)

The term *stalking* came to be applied to another "manly" sport, boxing. "Holmes, moving in for the kill, stalked Weaver along and nailed the challenger with a hard right to the head" (Jack Cavanaugh, Reuters item, 23 June 1979); "Green, who shuffled ahead flat-footed as he stalked Leonard most of the fight" (Michael Posner, Reuters item, 1 April 1980). Boxing is linked with another major traditional image of manhood: man as warrior. In this hand-to-hand combat, man faces not an animal but a human opponent. One man's victory is another's defeat. The hunt-related term, when transferred to the boxing ring, took on a slightly metaphoric meaning. In this context it no longer implied silent lurking behind bushes, but quick, forceful, face-to-face encirclement of the rival. Determination, endurance, persistence, and skill continued to be inherent elements of the stalking enterprise. As in hunting, stalking was ritualized into a professional skill in its own right.

Stalking was occasionally used, metaphorically, to describe photographers, associating them with hunters, and making the eye and the gaze into deadly weapons. On 12 September 1977, photographer Ron Galella was described as a man who "made a career of stalking [Jackie Kennedy] with a camera until she went to court to keep him at a distance" (Bill Roeder, *Newsweek*). A month later, under the title "An Eye Made for Stalking," Hank Burchard wrote in the *Washington Post* that "stalking with the skill and knowledge he developed in his hunting days, but shooting only with his camera now, Blacklock is a delightful enthusiast" (21 October 1977). The metaphor was expanded when *stalking* was used in reports of conflicts in Central and South America. "Terrorism stalks the country" was the formula; it made "the stalker" into an abstract, invisible source of public terror in wild, faraway countries.

In reporting Son of Sam's mayhem, the media repeatedly described him as "stalking" (emphasis added in all selections):

> The mad gunman who calls himself Son of Sam claimed a sixth life today. . . . The 44-caliber killer's reign of terror has frustrated police, . . . and ruined business at discotheques, which are thought to be a favorite *stalking ground* of the killer. . . . the shadowy threat of Son of Sam is disrupting night life in areas where the killer has struck. *(Washington Post,* 1 August 1977, first section)

> Police shooed lovers from secluded byways this weekend in a stepped-up effort to clear them of potential targets of "Son of Sam," the *night-stalking killer* who has slain six persons. *(Washington Post,* 7 August 1977)

> Even as fear spread in the middle-class neighborhoods where he *stalked his prey,* some girls had joked hollowly about bleaching their hair . . . dread and curiosity were turning into obsession with Son of Sam. (Pete Axthelm, *Newsweek,* 15 August 1977, National Affairs section)

Son of Sam was thus defined "a stalker," and as a flesh-and-blood Travis was associated with traditional American images of manhood, as well as with "terror" in foreign, distant lands.[3] His linkage—through the

---

3. In a parallel manner, Robert De Niro's film persona linked the hunter (*Deer Hunter,* 1978), the boxer (*Raging Bull,* 1980), and the lonely, deadly veteran (*Taxi Driver*).

stalking terminology—with respectable masculinity, revealed that his actions were perceived as attempts at manly initiation rites. The linkage also constituted him as the shadow, mirror image of traditional American masculinity. In so doing, it awarded Son of Sam some prestige, while adding a sinister undertone to the traditional image of manhood.

Following Son of Sam, *stalker* and *stalking* quickly became common terms in newspaper reports of serial killing, rapes, and celebrity assassinations. The perpetrators of these acts were now labeled *stalkers*. Simultaneously, the term began to flourish in newspaper reviews of paperbacks and films: in the couple of years immediately following the Son of Sam murders, it appeared in reviews of such films as *Halloween* (1978), *The Psychic* (1979), *When a Stranger Calls* (1979), *Fog* (1980), *The Shining* (1980), *Dressed to Kill* (1980), and *Prom Night* (1980). Together with the news media and the social sciences, which published a seemingly endless stream of reports, these films processed and formulated the emerging social category of "stalkers."

In 1979, a television film by Dan Curtis that depicted the bloody adventures of a vampire, proved so popular that it grew into a television series that remained on the air for several years. It was called *Night Stalker*. Serial killers were thus united with vampires by way of linguistic association. When, in 1985, Richard Ramirez "terrified suburban Los Angeles with an orgy of 13 murders plus the shooting, stabbing and sexual abuse of many other victims" (Wilson and Seaman 1990, caption to Ramirez's photograph), he was dubbed "The Night Stalker," and thus the linguistic identification between serial killers and vampires was sealed.

The Professional Making of Serial Killers

Son of Sam's trial took place in the summer of 1977 and received widespread media coverage. In February 1978 another notorious serial killer, Ted Bundy, was recaptured, and the media reporting of his exploits was at least as sensational. Bundy was first convicted of aggravated kidnapping in December 1976 and was sentenced to one to fifteen years in prison. A year later he escaped and immediately struck again. In January 1978, he attacked five women students at the University of Tallahassee, Florida, killing two. A month later he abducted and murdered a twelve-year-old. Several days later, he was found and arrested. The shocked and fascinated American public was then presented with the image of this eloquent law student who had tortured, raped, mutilated, and murdered at least thirty young women (some say as many as one hundred) over the course of five years. One of them was attacked coming home from a Halloween party (Wilson and Seaman 1990, 264–65).

Ted Bundy was described as having had a deprived childhood. Fatherless, he suffered at the hands of a violent grandfather. Poor, frustrated, and always feeling unwanted, he dreamed of leaving his mark in the world.

Ted began to delve deeper into a world of sexual fantasy that became increasingly violent in nature. He consumed quantities of pornographic material depicting sexually violent acts. . . . He fed his sexual fantasies through voyeurism. For years he peeped through windows to watch women undress. . . . Like some other serial-killers, Bundy began to act out his fantasies by stalking his women and then attacking them. . . . The victims were all young, attractive females, who appeared to come from middle or upper class families, and many were students. He killed victims in at least 5 different states between 1973 and 1978, usually leaving the bodies in secluded wooded areas. . . . Ted was usually able to lure the intended victim to his car by asking them for assistance. . . . At other times he was known to lurk in dark shadows and attack women who were alone. . . . He raped most if not all of his victims; several were subjected to sodomy and sexual mutilation. . . . He had absolutely no remorse for his crimes. . . . Talk shows, newscasters, and newspaper editors all began exploring the life of Ted Bundy and the phenomenon of serial murder in general. . . . The execution in many respects took on the atmosphere of a circus. (Hickey 1991, 158–59)

The tremendous anxiety and fascination aroused by Son of Sam and Ted Bundy inspired the professional investigation and research of "serial killers" (Hickey 1991, 9; Wilson and Seaman 1990, 26).[4] Serial killing was the crime of the decade, and its perpetrators were its "heroes." Despite the diverse theoretical treatment of the subject, the typical "professional profile" of the serial killer closely resembled both Bundy and Son of Sam; stalking was one of its fundamental elements.

Unlike individual or mass murder, serial killing, and especially serial lust killing,[5] is generally said to be a modern phenomenon, particularly prevalent in twentieth-century America, where it gained prominence after the 1970s (Hickey 1991, 76; Wilson and Seaman 1990, 32, 114). Hickey's definition of a serial killer is typical:

[S]erial murderers should include any offenders, male or female, who kill over time. Most researchers agree that serial killers have a minimum of 3–4 victims. Usually there is a pattern in their killing that may

4. In this section I rely mostly on the following texts: Cameron and Frazer 1987; Norris 1988; Wilson and Seaman 1990; and Hickey 1991.
5. Lust murders are those in which the murderer finds sexual gratification in the act of killing itself, or in the victim's dying or death, whereas other sex murders may be committed, for example, by a serial rapist trying to silence potentially dangerous victims. Guttmacher's (1973) alternative label for serial murderers who derive sexual gratification from killing is "sadistic serial murderers" (Hickey 1991, 9).

be associated with the types of victims selected or the method or motives for the killing. (1991, 8)[6]

Most serial killers are men;[7] "most serial murders are sexual in nature" (10); and victims are mostly women, typically "young females alone: prostitutes, hitchhikers, students, women at home selected randomly, women seeking employment, nurses, models, waitresses" (140).[8] According to Hickey's statistics, a vast majority of male serial killers, 69–84 percent, kill strangers. The ratio rises to over 95 percent for the solo male serial killers who kill exclusively women (1991, 139, 156, table 7.4).

Experts have determined that stalking plays a central role in serial killing. According to Norris, there is a typical pattern, a series of phases, associated with such murders. The first is the "aura stage," during which the killer withdraws from everyday reality, replacing it with a search for a companion "who will act out a role in the killer's primal ritual" (1988, 23). The next, the "trolling stage," begins when the killer actively begins searching for his victim. "His earlier observations, fantasies, and perverted needs direct him to the likeliest spots where the fatal stranger will cross his path" (24). It is during this stage that the killer is revealed as a stalker.

[T]he latter part of the trolling phase involves the identification and stalking of the victim. Once he has identified his intended prey, the killer begins his pattern of stalking from a distance. Carlton Gary kept watch on his victims' houses for weeks, stalking these elderly women as he traveled through their neighborhood delivering drugs and meeting young women for sexual encounters. He memorized his victims' schedules and habits. So when he did finally strike, he was able to move through the area silently, knowing what entrances could be penetrated without much trouble, and knowing how to leave the scene quickly after the victim lay beaten and strangled upon her bed. He knew which women in Wynnton lived alone. He attacked only widows and spinsters, women who reminded him of the mother he never had and the rich white women who employed his aunt and grandmother as domestic servants. . . . Richard Begenwald, another recently convicted serial

6. According to Hickey's findings (described in Hickey 1991, 135, table 7.2), most (male) serial killers (almost half) operate within a city or a state, and only 14 percent restrict themselves to their homes. Most women serial killers, more than 70 percent, are "place specific" (115, table 6.7).

7. In 140 cases of serial murders examined by Hickey, 88 percent were committed by men (1991, 133). Cameron and Frazer determine that sexual murder is "exclusively male" (1987, 19, 25). Serial killers are usually in their twenties; and, according to Hickey's data, their average age is twenty-eight (1991, 133).

8. The second most vulnerable population, according to Hickey's data, is children alone, particularly boys. The third category of preferred victims consists of travelers: people in cars, and campers (1991, 133).

killer, stalked his victims along the country roads of affluent New Jersey suburbs. Spotting pretty high school cheerleaders as they walked home from school, Begenwald tracked them day after day until he knew which ones would be alone in isolated spots and which ones had to walk the last stretch of road without companions. It was then that he would strike, freezing his victims at first with the glare of his headlights. Then he lured them into his car with offers of rides. His next step was to spring the trap, overpowering them quickly and violently, finally savoring their moment of death and his moment of triumph. (25–26)

In his discussion of the fourth, "capture" stage (which follows the third, "wooing stage"), Norris adds that

the trolling and stalking phases served to heighten his expectation of the event itself, and the capture, when the victim has finally been ensnared in the trap, is the penultimate moment. This is the moment he savors because he believes that he has closed off all possibility of the victim's escape and can take all the time he wants to prepare the victim for the ritual that will follow. (28–29)[9]

Social scientists have sought explanations of the serial killer in "maternal deprivation or control" (Norris 1988, 181), child abuse, and paternal absence. Wilson and Seaman refer to such killings as crimes of self-esteem (1990, 137). Many of these murderers, they report, express a longing to be "important," and mistake "fame for notoriety" (58). They propose that when some people's "'urge to heroism' and self-assertion is frustrated, it turns into resentment," and the resentment, in some, leads to serial murder (20). Serial killers are also viewed as irrational "avengers." Wilson and Seaman further suggest that when certain people feel unable to get back at those who they feel deserve to be punished, they satisfy their need for revenge by taking the rage out on others (1990, 21). Similarly, Hickey states that "the underlying pathology of serial-killers typically is frustration, anger, hostility, feelings of inadequacy, and low self-esteem," and points out that the psychological term *psychopath* seems to fit this profile (1991, 51). The fact that most serial killers follow some distinct, repetitive pattern has been characterized as evidence of their obsessive-compulsive personality (Norris 1988, 224–26). Psychologist Jay Martin suggests that many serial killers are "fictive

9. The next stage after the capture is the murder itself, followed by the "totem phase," in which "the victim has been transformed from symbolic creature to symbolic trophy, an object which, the murderer hopes, can transmit to him the fleeting feeling of power and glory at the moment when his private ritual reached its climax" (Hickey 1991, 33). The seventh and last stage is the "depression phase," caused by the fading away of the excitement of the purposeful, ritualistic stalking and killing.

personalities." They are "empty" people, devoid of identity. To escape their unbearable "lack," they adopt the personalities of others. Some "become" other people and may end up killing their "doubles," whose identities they have appropriated. Others adopt the personalities of fictional characters, performing the type of murders attributed to film or legendary characters (Martin 1988).

The serial killer's profile seems to be that of an empty young man with a history of parental abuse, lacking in self-esteem, lonely, angry, frustrated, vengeful, and in need of attention and recognition. He is consumed with fantasy and leads a double life: as an ordinary citizen and as a murderous beast. His stalking is a compulsive cry for identity, attention, and self-worth and an irrational means of avenging himself on his abusers. He challenges society by killing off its women. He is an obsessive-compulsive psychopath. In other words, the serial killer is a Travis with a history of parental abuse, a contemporary incarnation of the vampire, Jekyll and Hyde, Frankenstein's creature. He is a deranged version of the traditional image of the male stalker. The idiomatic terminology used by experts stresses this cultural association. For example, one of the chapters in Wilson and Seaman's book (1990) is entitled "The Jekyll and Hyde Syndrome." Norris, when describing the first stage of the serial killer's ritualistic murder, the "aura phase," states that "whatever is human in him recedes for a while, and he enters into a shadowy existence, a death in life" (1988, 23–24). In his chapter "The Disease of Serial Murder" he speaks of the phenomenon as "the infection" that "has been allowed to spread through society like a plague: the emerging serial-killers are the carriers, transmitting the syndrome from one generation to the next" (36). He notes the serial killer's "double life" (38) and establishes that "first and most obvious is the subject's animal-like, primal approach to the act of murder" (39). When seized, "the killer is simply a biological engine driven by a primal instinct to satisfy the compelling lust" (23). Martin speaks of killers who, vampire-like, kill "as a way of seizing their victims' lives and turning them into identities of their own" (1988, 56). He claims that "the fictive personality can also feel like a *mort-vivant*, one of the living dead: for such a person, fictions are used to find reflections. In extreme instances, the self has undoubtedly experienced some kind of traumatic death at an earlier period" (141). In other words, due to a traumatic mental death, the serial killer is a living dead. Lacking mirror reflections of his own identity, he therefore "becomes" other people and kills as a means of attaining mirror reflections. Richard Noll, in his anthology of psychiatric essays *Vampires, Werewolves, and Demons: Twentieth Century Reports in the Psychiatric Literature,* proposes that the "sexual blood-fetish syndrome defined here as a clinical vampirism should bear a new eponymous label in future psychiatric treatment and be renamed Renfield's syndrome in honor of the character in Bram Stoker's *Dracula*, who bore many of the classic signs and symptoms of the disorder" (1992, 18).[10]

The popular perception of serial killers clearly echoes this cultural identification. "Because of the wide publicity given to serial murderers, a stereotype of this type of killer has formed in the mind of American society. The offender is a ruthless, blood-thirsty sex monster, who lives a Jekyll-and-Hyde existence—probably next door to you" (Hickey 1991, 1). The epithets given serial killers are particularly telling. They include Jekyll/Hyde, Ripper, Night Stalker, Bluebeard, Nebraska Fiend, Torture Doctor, Moon Maniac, Sex Beast, Mad Biter, Angel of Death, and Red Demon (129–30).

Thus, through the media and professional literature, Travis Bickle, Son of Sam, and Ted Bundy were defined as stalkers and serial killers. Their stalking was established as an essential element of their serial killing, and their serial killing was portrayed as the ultimate expression of their stalking. They became a social category, a type of people who shared a scientific profile. Closely associated with the traditional imagery of the male stalker, the serial-killing stalker became a mediating social category: at a time of deep social anxiety, it associated a small, defined group of people with the archetypal male stalker.

Incorporating the Serial Killer in Literature and Film

While social scientists were establishing the social category of serial killers, writers and filmmakers were processing it culturally, fastening its ties with the classic stories of stalking.

In 1978, the year following Son of Sam's exploits and Bundy's sensational trial, two true-crime novels appeared that paved the way for later films about serial killers (*The Eyes of Laura Mars* and *Halloween*). In Jimmy Breslin and Dick Schaap's *.44*, the killer is a lonely New York taxi driver who spends his nights searching for prey in the streets of the metropolis. He is a childish man, trapped in deranged rape-and-murder fantasies, which the text describes in great length. The novel's character calls himself a monster, corresponds with the press, and is compared to Jack the Ripper. He is also the human, not yet undead slave of a vampire. Like Stoker's Renfield, he helps his master obtain the blood he needs, sometimes attempting to rebel, but always succumbing to his supernatural superior. He is what some professionals define as a "psychiatric vampire."

Dan Greenburg's *Love Kills* is more sophisticated.

In this very savvy Manhattan chiller, five young women are murdered by a quiet maniac who stalks his quarry for weeks before he moves in

10. In *Dracula,* having been bitten by Dracula, Renfield became his human slave and a potential vampire.

for the kill—training binoculars on them, sifting their garbage, taking meticulous notes, sidling up to eavesdrop on lunch-counter conversations and Bloomingdale transactions. When his researches are completed, he gains entry by posing as a delivery boy. . . . Enter the sixth young woman, Babette, who is embarrassed by her psychic powers . . . she has precognitive dreams of two of the homicides. . . . Soon Babette has an even more unnerving flash: she foresees her own murder. . . . "Love Kills" induces genuine, sweaty panic. . . . Greenburg's is a witty, scary invention. (Walter Clemons, *Newsweek,* 14 August 1978, Arts section)

Like a werewolf and a vampire, the protagonist attacks those he believes he loves most. His last intended victim, Babette, whom he attacks at exactly midnight, visualizes him as "a snarling hyena with long fangs about to puncture her neck" (Greenburg 1978, 306). A modern Jekyll and Hyde, this gentle, shy character combines Norman Bates's obsessive tidiness with some of Ted Bundy's widely publicized characteristics: he is a Peeping Tom who uses various disguises to enter his victims' apartments, stealing a pair of underwear from every woman he rapes and murders. Like Frankenstein's creature, he stalks his prey as a means of bonding with them, of finding the recognition and love that he feels he is due. He suffers from low self-esteem and lives in a fantasy world. According to the twisted logic of Greenburg's killer, each of his victims drove him to violence; they were all guilty, and he could not help but give them what they had coming. As the book's fictional psychological authority explains,

This guy feels terrible ambivalence toward women. Terrible anger. Terrible hurt. And a terrible need to be close to them, too. He's got to be pathologically shy with women. Some woman or women hurt him badly a long time ago. A mother, an aunt, a girlfriend. And now he's acting out his revenge. (249)

In the book, the media refer to the killer as "the animal . . . lurking in the shadows and stalking his prey like a hyena . . . a beast" (162). Being a "fictive personality," the killer proudly accepts the hyena metaphor, taking on the identity created for him by the press, which likens him to "the assassin who stalked Charles de Gaulle in *The Day of the Jackal.* You couldn't find a better man than that to model yourself after, now could you?" (164). Planning his next attack, he wonders, "[W]hat means would the Jackal have used? What means will the Hyena use?" (165).

Clearly, this true-crime novel portrays a serial killer who is identical to the type constructed by the professional literature of the day. It suggests the same sociological classification, offers the same psychological profile, and invites the same cultural association with archetypal male stalkers. Additionally, it features three important elements: the reader's participation in the killer's stalking, the role of the "final girl,"[11] and the unique experience of time in the context of stalking.

Like Frankenstein's creature, the Hyena in *Love Kills* is given a narrative point of view. Much of the text is narrated through his subjective perspective. Although the reader sees the world through his eyes, the killer himself is never described, either by the narrator or by another fictional character. He is not visible; he has no face. The reader *participates* in the Hyena's stalking but cannot *identify* with him in any emotional or moral sense, because the Hyena is an absent entity. The reader does, however, clearly identify with Babette, the novel's "final girl." She is a devout Catholic, a pure, virtuous virgin, as well as a dutiful, responsible person. Like Stoker's Mina, this innocent young woman, attached to the policeman who is investigating the Hyena's crimes, is beyond the monster's reach. Furthermore, she is the only one capable of beating the beast at his own game. For she is not merely pure, but also (in)sightful: she sees him better than he sees her. Armed both with purity and the power of vision, she conquers him, thus liberating her community.

In the media treatment of serial killers, as well as in the professional literature, young women were presented mostly as the killers' victims. When they were sexually active (as in the case of Son of Sam) they may have been associated in the public mind with Jack the Ripper's prostitute victims. They were also linked to some extent with the killers' mothers, who were constructed as likely abusive and thus guilty of their sons' crimes. Greenburg's novel offers a good illustration of the role of the "final girl."[12] But this "final girl" is not simply the stalker's opponent; she is also his double. Babette's powerful vision does more than simply see the Hyena; it takes on supernatural dimensions, compelling her to see the murders, in her mind's eye, before they are actually commited.[13] This involuntary sight makes her the murderer's other-self and accomplice. She becomes "guilty by sight." The novel enhances this element by introducing other similarities between Babette and the killer.[14] Her identification with him is such that when he

11. Clover coined the term "final girl" in reference to the stalker films' character of the young, nonsexual woman who is the only one to survive the serial killer.

12. "When the Final Girl assumes the 'active investigative gaze,' she exactly reverses the look, making a spectacle of the killer and a spectator of herself. . . . The gaze becomes, at least for a while, female" (Clover 1992, 60).

13. This is a fascinating development of a documentary element. Jeffery Iverson records that "as Son of Sam continued to gun down his victims, a Canadian psychic, Terry Marmoreo, gave details about him in a series of telephone calls to a New York detective, Rodney Roncoglio, and a parapsychologist, Dr. Karlis Osis, who were working as a team on the fringe of the official manhunt" (1992, 12).

14. They are both repeatedly portrayed as engaging in superstitious sign seeking. During their final encounter, the Hyena explicitly says, "That's the sort of thing that I would have done, you know that? We are somewhat alike, you and I" (Iverson 1992, 298).

finally attacks her, she almost feels she had it coming as punishment for her part in the killings. This fascinating twist makes Babette both the virginal heroine and, at the same time, a psychic witch, the serial killer's feminine double.

The text also illustrates the altered nature of time as experienced by stalkers and their targets. The strange premonitions make Babette feel as though she lived in two periods of time simultaneously. "She says it's like she's in the past and in the present at the same time. Or in the future and the present" (Greenburg 1978, 229). She perceives each moment of the killer's attacks as eternal and repetitive as they "reoccur" in her life before and after the actual murders take place. The repetition of these moments undermines Babette's perception of time as linear. Interestingly, Greenburg does not merely describe Babette's unique experience of time, but goes on to legitimize it. The doctor, as a representative of White Science[15] in the novel's fictional world, acknowledges that time might be very different from what the West believes it to be. Thus, feelings of circular time and eternal return, which have been associated with the sensation of being stalked since the earliest days of Lilit, are being restated and scientifically validated in this fictional story of the serial killer.

The thematic and narrative elements *Love Kills* added to the serial killer's story resurfaced in the films *Halloween* and *The Eyes of Laura Mars*. *Halloween* established the unseen "point of view stalker" and the "final girl" as fundamental elements of stalker films. *The Eyes of Laura Mars* established the independent, career woman's guilt in serial, murderous stalking through psychic vision.

Halloween

John Carpenter's *Halloween* (1978) opens with a murder committed by a six-year-old wielding a kitchen knife. The victim is the boy's teenage sister, who had spent the evening with a boy in the parents' bedroom. The murder takes place on the night of Halloween in 1963, and the little boy, Michael, is wearing a clown costume and a mask. When his parents return home that night, they find Michael still wearing his costume and holding the bloody knife in his hand. In the next sequence, fifteen years later, one night before Halloween 1978, Michael escapes (in a thunderstorm) from the mental institution where he has been confined and heads back home. He spends Halloween day stalking Tommy, a young boy who looks much as Michael himself did fifteen years earlier, and Laurie, the teenager who is to babysit Tommy that night. Michael sits in a car outside Laurie's classroom; he awaits Tommy by the school entrance and follows him home; he drives slowly by Laurie and her friends, Annie and Lynda (who, unlike Laurie, are

15. For Clover's definition of "White Science" and "Black Magic" see Clover 1992, 66, and further in this chapter.

vulgar, shallow, unpleasant, and explicitly sexual). Michael lurks behind bushes and, watching Laurie from behind clothes drying on a line in a neighbor's yard, looks into her room. While Michael is stalking, his psychiatrist roams the little town, hunting for his patient and trying to warn the unbelieving authorities that evil has returned to their jurisdiction.

As night falls, Michael, wearing a mask, stalks and murders Lynda and Annie. One is indulging in sexual activity while the other actively plans to frolic. Worried by her friends' disappearance, Laurie, who is watching over Tommy as well as Lynda's young sister, embarks on an active search for Annie and Lynda. She finds Annie lying dead in bed with Michael's sister's tombstone placed on her pillow. The suspense peaks when Michael attacks Laurie herself, but she manages to return to Tommy's house across the street. Later, she not only survives another attack, but succeeds in killing Michael by stabbing him in the neck with a wire she pulls from a sofa. Or so we, and she, are led to believe. But Michael rises again, and then once more, after Laurie has stabbed his eyes with a metal clothes-hanger. In the final face-to-face combat between Michael and Laurie, she snatches his mask off (although we do not see his face), and when he stops to put it on again, he is shot by his psychiatrist, who had been hunting him all day and finally arrives on the scene. While Laurie is sobbing, the camera follows the psychiatrist as he looks out the window only to discover that the body he shot (six times at very close range) has walked away and disappeared. The sound of heavy breathing assures us that Michael will return once again, as indeed he did, in sequels released in 1981, 1983, 1988, and 1998.

This modern legend of the Ted Bundy serial killer narrates his exploits as manifesting every male stalker's story. *Halloween*'s narration of the legendary vampire story is precise and faithful. Michael, one of the living dead, who returns from his deathlike existence in the asylum, "died" because of his sister's sexual nature and returns to punish female carnality. His pursuit of his sister's doubles carries incestuous undertones. By killing as he does, Michael embodies the vampire who attacks those whom he "loves" most. He distinguishes between "good," virginal women, and "evil," sexual ones. His psychiatrist, Dr. Loomis, is a vampire-hunting Van Helsing character, and Michael's attacks challenge the doctor's little community. Like Mina (particularly in *Nosferatu*'s interpretation), the pure virgin-mother Laurie battles the bloodthirsty vampire, survives his attacks, and liberates her community.[16] But in contrast with previous versions of such stories, here the vampire is not destroyed, and Laurie is not delivered into a mature relationship with a suitable young man. In *Halloween*'s world, vampire hunters are incapable of overcoming evil, vampires never die, and young women are all

16. In certain respects, Laurie particularly resembles Mina in *Nosferatu*. Like this Mina, Laurie is asked to risk her own life in order to liberate society of the fiend. As in *Nosferatu*, Michael "window stalks" Laurie, and does not attack until she initiates the face-to-face contact.

alone, because there are no suitable young men around. Likewise, there is no father figure, and Dr. Loomis's townspeople are not really a community. At the end of *Halloween*, Laurie is all alone, weeping, while Dr. Loomis helplessly realizes that he cannot save her.

It is easy to see that Michael, the outsider, is also a Frankenstein creature of sorts. Michael's otherness instills fear and hatred. As in the film version of Shelley's creature, he never utters a word. Dr. Loomis refers to Michael as "it." Family, society and the psychiatric profession are all to blame for having created the monster; their combined efforts, their "project," is unnatural and destructive. Deserted and rejected by family and society, abandoned to years of institutionalization and psychoanalytic treatment, Michael, like the creature, becomes a ruthless murderer. He returns home to bond (with Tommy and Laurie), and to take his murderous revenge.

As for the Jekyll and Hyde metaphor of stalking, *Halloween* presents a Hyde that has no Jekyll component; a Hyde that is pure, total evil. Dr. Loomis makes this point bluntly clear when he declares: "I spent 8 years trying to reach him and another 7 trying to keep him locked up, because I realized that what was living behind that boy's eyes was purely and simply evil." After a whole century of struggle, in 1978, Michael-Hyde has finally overcome his Jekyll, eliminating him completely at childhood.[17]

Interestingly, unlike most modern stalking stories, *Halloween* explicitly links its killer with the Devil. (In this context, his angelic name is of course ironic.) Michael's murders all take place on Halloween, the Devil's holiday. And according to his psychiatrist, even at the age of six, Michael was already a devil: "I met this 6-year-old with a blank, pale, emotionless face, and the blackest eyes, the Devil's eyes."[18] Like Satan, Michael spies on frail humans, witnessing their (sexual) "falls." This Angel of Death also swiftly sits in judgment and delivers their death sentences. This medieval undertone is reflected in the film's moralistic stand. Sex, in Michael's world, is equated with death; women, or at least most women, are closely connected with sexuality and, therefore, with death. Only a pure young woman, a virgin-mother, can be a "final girl" and survive. The traditional, patriarchal categories of womanhood are firmly reestablished. This message comes through so vividly that in later stalker films any sign of sexual activity is a clear signal that death is lurking and sure to strike.

In a masterful, self-conscious manner, Michael is similarly associated with various other images of male stalkers. His masked face brings to mind

17. Both Dika and Clover see a Jekyll-and-Hyde relationship between Laurie, the superego, and Michael, her raging id (Dika 1990, 50–51; Clover 1992, 48–49). I do not see Michael as Laurie's inner, secret voice set free. Michael has no "Jekyll."

18. Dr. Loomis is played by Donald Pleasance. In Carpenter's *Prince of Darkness* (1987), an occult film dedicated to the Devil, Pleasance plays the leading role of the priest who fights and conquers Satan.

the Phantom of the Opera; the detailed planning of his return and revenge echoes *Cape Fear*.[19] Above all, features such as obsessive voyeurism, a kitchen knife, a house of horrors, an interpreting psychiatrist, and allusions to the musical score of the "shower scene" make *Halloween*'s Michael the Norman Bates of the 1970s (Dika 1990, 40).[20] The dominant mother and her torn, tormented son are replaced by a young woman on the threshold of adulthood and a monstrous, immature young man. During the violent conflict that develops between them, the evil stalker loses his superior position and the power of *the gaze* to the young woman, who matures into a strong, brave woman who *sees*. The stalker, no longer mama's castrated boy, is now evil incarnate, overpowered by a stronger woman of his own generation.

Although *Halloween* relates a new version of the serial killer's story, which includes every previous cultural image of male stalking, the new male stalker presented is almost two-dimensional. He is evil incarnate, with no reason nor cure. Michael is a simplified, fairy-tale version of Travis. He simply lurks out there, with nothing to prevent his perpetual, repetitive return. A product of contemporary society and its White Science, a child in a man's body, he cannot be reached, understood, or treated. Although he must be destroyed, he is invincible. Perhaps he cannot be killed because there is no faith, or because there are no sets of rules that would provide for his destruction. Maybe Dr. Loomis is simply no Dr. Van Helsing. Or, perhaps it is because there is no alternative male image in the film's fictional world to take his place and win the girl. *Halloween*'s treatment of the serial-killer phenomenon is not an optimistic one, but its popularity was unparalleled. Repeated, communal viewing of this new film was, for a whole generation of teenagers, an initiation rite that integrated them into the alienated, disintegrated world of grownups.

Halloween's most salient cinematic device, which has become the definitive trademark of the stalker cycle, is the extensive use of a handheld camera to create point-of-view shots. Much of the film is shot from Michael's subjective point of view, from behind his shoulder. The technique is used so often that the viewer sees the killer's face only once, at the end of the opening scene. Instead, the viewer is compelled to share his visual perspective. *Halloween* explicitly identifies the point-of-view shot with stalking, and this became a paradigmatic element in a whole cycle of highly popular films.

19. The perpetual reliving of his past and future crimes is also a twisted version of the Wandering Jew's story. Of course, unlike the medieval mythological sinner, Michael feels no remorse and is made to pay no price for his sins.

20. "The appointed ancestor of the slasher film is Hitchcock's *Psycho*," states Clover (1992, 23); "the notion of a killer propelled by psychosexual fury, more particularly a male in a gender distress, has proved a durable one, and the progeny of Norman Bates stalk the genre up to the present day" (27). Dika points out that even the casting relates *Halloween* to *Psycho*: Jamie Lee Curtis, who plays Laurie, is the daughter of Janet Leigh, who played Marion. "Ms. Curtis's presence in the film makes reference . . . even to Hitchcock himself" (Dika 1990, 47). Interestingly, in a 1998 sequel, Janet Leigh herself appears next to her daughter.

Vera Dika rightly states that these films are "best identified by a predominantly *off-screen* killer who is known primarily by his/her distinctive point-of-view shots" (1990, 14). It was this very feature that led her to define *Halloween* and its descendants as "stalker films." She points out that this approach of presenting the killer's point of view though he is absent from the screen results in the viewer's "identification with the killer's vision while simultaneously disavowing it as belonging to an unknowable 'other'" (124). She explains that "in this way the viewer can identify with the killer's vision but not with the killer's character, taking pleasure out of watching acts of sex and violence while not participating in the attending fear and guilt" (67).[21]

Although the point-of-view shots put us in the stalker's shoes, it is Laurie, his innocent target, who dominates the screen and easily wins the viewer's sympathy and emotional identification. Dika convincingly argues that both the "Laurie" and the "Michael" of the stalker films "share the position of the film's center of consciousness"; the "Laurie" character "dominates the on-screen space, serving as our point of 'moral' identification, while the killer dominates the off-screen space, serving as the point of our visual identification" (Dika 1990, 70). Another way of phrasing this is to say that the visual identification with Michael, combined with the emotional identification with Laurie, makes the viewer both stalker and prey. The stalker film allows us a simultaneous experience of both stalking and being stalked, inciting both terror and guilt-free, voyeuristic, pornographic thrill. If film, as such, is capable of generating both these sensations; *Halloween* fulfills this potential.

The ability to generate both of the sensations, and the tight combination of the compelling stalking narrative with the stalking camera, made *Halloween* a spectacular box office success and the paradigmatic stalking movie, a model that was imitated by subsequent stalker-film classics and their numerous sequels: *Friday the 13th, Prom Night,* and *Terror Train* (1980), *Graduation Day, Happy Birthday to Me, Friday the 13th Part 2, Hell Night,* and *The Burning* (1981).[22] Cashing in on Carpenter's hit, most of the stalker movies repeated exactly the combination of elements that had proved so effective, creating a rigid, highly conventionalized genre. To a large extent, all the subsequent stalker films are remakes of *Halloween*. In this respect, Michael reappears in all of them.

During the 1980s and the 1990s, the principal elements of the stalker genre, by now widely familiar, found their way into mainstream films such as *The Shining, Dressed to Kill, Fatal Attraction, Cape Fear,* and *The Silence of the*

21. The *Blair Witch Project* (1999) offers an interesting variation on this theme. Here, the hand-held camera is held by the victims, allowing the off-screen stalker no point of view. The viewer is invited to identify exclusively with the victim and is not offered to share the stalker's perspective.

22. *Friday the 13th* alone was successful enough to carry six sequels by 1985 (Dika 1990, 64). *Halloween*'s latest sequel was released on Halloween 1998.

Lambs.[23] The modern male stalker and his cinematic point of view became commonplace.

The vocabulary and imagery of serial killer accommodated much of Travis's disturbing character. But it could not offer a convincing motivation for his obsessive infatuation, enhanced by his delusional perception of reality and of his relationship with his love object in particular. (The obsessive and delusional aspects of the Travis character were once again brought to the fore in De Niro's unforgettably obsessive, infatuated stalking fan, Rupert Pupkin, in the *King of Comedy*, from 1982).[24] The appropriate social explanation of these features was to be found in the psychiatric portrayal of "erotomania." Let me present this psychiatric concept, which is essential for the discussion of the contemporary film image of the female stalker.

Erotomania

A paper on erotomanic patients published in 1990 began, "Erotomania—the delusional belief that one is passionately loved by another—has long been a symptom in search of adequate conceptualization and has been incorporated into diagnostic systems in many different ways" (Rudden, Sweeney, and Frances 1990, 625).[25] The paper concludes that "our study suggests that erotomanic symptoms in themselves do not predict either diagnosis or clinical course" (627). But other psychiatrists have not necessarily shared this minimalist approach.

According to Meloy (1989, 478), Elienne Esquirol was the first to describe the syndrome, in 1838. Segal (1989, 1261) attributes the first "systematic understanding" of the phenomenon to Emil Kraepelin, in 1921. But it was Gaeetan Gatian de Clerambault who gave the syndrome its name. De Clerambault, who published his case studies in France in 1921, attributed the delusion primarily to single, aging women. Simultaneously, "the British psychiatrist Bernard Hart identified what he called 'old maid's insanity,' a syndrome identical to erotomania" (Segal 1989, 1261). According to Singer, the syndrome can be described as follows:

23. Interestingly, both Brian De Palma's *Dressed to Kill* (1980) and Jonathan Demme's *Silence of the Lambs* (1990) (starring Jodie Foster) cast a psychiatrist in the serial killer's role.

24. In his obsessive aspiration to become a comedian and a celebrity, Pupkin aggressively stalks a celebrated comedian (Jerry Lewis) and, kidnapping him, demands to appear on his show. For a full analysis see W. I. Miller 1994, 323–44.

25. For psychiatric articles on erotomania, see Dietz et al. 1991a, 1991b; Fein et al. 1998; Goldstein 1986; Hall 1998; Harmon, Rosner, and Owens 1995; Hollander and Callahan 1975; Kienlen 1998; Lion et al. 1998; Lipson 1998; Lloyd-Goldstein 1998; Mohandie et al. 1998; Meloy 1989, 1990, 1992, 1998; Meyers 1998; Persaud 1990; Rudden, Sweeney, and Frances 1990; Saunders 1998; Segal 1989; Singer 1991; Skoler 1998; L. E. Walker 1998; Wood and Poe 1990; Zona, Palarea, and Lane 1998; and Zona, Sharma, and Lane 1993.

In erotomania, the fundamental postulate states that the subjects believe that they are in an amorous union with a person of a higher social rank, who is the first to fall in love and to make advances. There are a number of derivative themes: the object is unable to be happy or have a sense of self-esteem without the subject; the object is free or the marriage is invalid; the object makes attempts to contact, has indirect conversation, and exerts continual surveillance or protection by means of phenomenal resources; there is almost universal sympathy or support for the relationship; and the object shows a paradoxical or contradictory attitude toward the subject. This last theme was accorded singular importance and was felt to be always present, while the others were only rarely all found in any one patient. (Harmon, Rosner, and Owens 1995, 189)

De Clerambault seems also to have been the first to distinguish two types of erotomania: "a pure or primary form, in which the onset is sudden and the disorder is limited entirely to the erotomania and a secondary form, in which the onset is gradual and the process superimposed on a preexisting psychosis of a paranoid type" (Hollander and Callahan 1975, 1574).

The distinct existence of the first of these types, "pure erotomania," became the focus of a psychiatric debate in the United States, "as to whether erotomania represents a discrete paranoid mental disorder, or is a manifestation of another type of mental disorder, for example, schizophrenia" (Harmon, Rosner, and Owens 1995, 189). In 1987, the Diagnostic Statistical Manual of Mental Disorders (DSM-III-R) classified erotomania as a delusional disorder, thus recognizing the existence of erotomania as distinct from schizophrenia.[26]

In 1975, Hollander and Callahan estimated that "since 1942, fewer than 15 additional patients with the syndrome have been described in the psychiatric literature" (1574). They quote Pearce, who, in 1972, thought it likely that "this particular syndrome will become an even greater rarity than it is at the moment" (1576). But the following decades brought with them a dramatic increase in public fascination with, and anxiety regarding, irrational behaviors such as serial murder, and a new awareness of and interest in domestic violence. Bewildering media stories of inexplicable passion and violence were sweeping the country. Gradually, erotomania, the romantic "old maid's insanity," became an appealing explanation for inexplicable, disturbing conduct.

In 1980, John Hinckley, who had been deeply influenced by David Chapman, John Lennon's killer, consciously "became" Travis Bickle. He stalked President Carter, shot at President Reagan, and planned to kidnap

---

26. "According to both DSM-III-R (1987–1993) and DSM-IV (1994), there are five specific types of Delusional Disorder: erotomania, grandiose, jealous, persecutory and somatic" (Harmon, Rosner, and Owens 1995, 188).

the actress Jodie Foster, marry her, and become the president of the United States (Martin 1988, 43–56). In Hinckley's trial, Dr. Park Elliott Dietz presented the defendant as an erotomaniac, although there was no indication of erotomanic delusion. The argument failed in court; it succeeded, however, in inspiring Dr. Reid Meloy, another prominent Los Angeles forensic psychiatrist, to develop a new, wider definition of erotomania that would more successfully accommodate Hinckley and Travis alike (Meloy 1989, 478–79).

Like de Clerambault, Meloy identifies two types of erotomania. His first type is similar to de Clerambault's pure erotomania; Meloy names it "delusional erotomania." His second type, however, differs dramatically from de Clerambault's. De Clerambault's second type captures individuals who manifest delusional erotomania as well as other psychiatric disorders (such as schizophrenia). Meloy's second type includes individuals who *do not manifest delusional erotomania* and yet persistently pursue their love objects. To distinguish it from delusional erotomania, he called this type "borderline erotomania." "The former implies the presence of psychosis; the latter indicates a gross disturbance of attachment or bonding, but not necessarily a loss of reality testing" (Meloy 1989, 480).

> In contrast to delusional erotomania, borderline erotomania usually involves some history of actual emotional engagement with the object. This relationship may vary from a friendly glance and smile to a terminated relationship that included emotional and sexual dimensions. . . . Borderline erotomanic individuals view separation as abandonment, and rejection by the object evokes abandonment rage. . . . rejection in the mind of the borderline erotomanic person is usually a grandiosely elaborated and distorted childhood abandonment fantasy that is recapitulated in the present by the object. (481)

> The genotypic defensive operation of splitting underscores the blatantly contradictory perceptions and affect states of the person with erotomania: the love object is initially idealized, but then ragefully devalued; intense love and intense hatred exist concurrently, but are experienced only in alternate, split-off affect states; and the narcissism and grandiosity of the violent act betray the defensive projection of devalued parts of the self into the victim. . . . Other erotomanic individuals may, through aspiring narcissism, seek a twinship alliance by their acts of violence and eventual identification in history with the famous, unrequited love. In other words, erotomanic individuals pursue a narcissistic wish to be like the love object to enhance their own grandiosity. (482)

Erotomaniacs, including borderline ones, sometimes combine erotomania with other psychiatric disorders.

An infantile personality . . . may express erotomanic desires in a more oral-aggressive, demanding, desperate, and inappropriate manner. . . . The erotomaniac's competitiveness with another person of the same sex suggests oedipal rivalry for the affections of the unattainable maternal or paternal object. (485)

The "dirty and disgusting" scatological character of sexuality in the mind of the hysterical person may be at least partially denied by the "long distance touching" of the unavailable object: looking, viewing, calling, or perhaps other scoptophilic or paraphilic pursuits within which the sexual arousal pattern toward the erotomanic object is consciously denied. (486)

One of erotomania's paranoid traits is jealousy (486); a psychopathic erotomaniac may engage in

stalking the victim over extended periods of time, rehearsal fantasies prior to the violence, a fueling of narcissistic characteristics to steel themselves for the task, and the use of transitional objects in fantasy as preparation for the violence itself. Transitional objects not only help maintain the illusion of omnipotent control over the erotomanic object, but they also function as a Janus-faced object that facilitates both distancing and disidentification with reality. (487–88)

Thus, Meloy's definitions of his diverse erotomanias supply infatuated stalkers with several psychiatric profiles to choose from. Meloy's description of erotomania has little in common with de Clerambault's; but it accounts perfectly for both Hinckley's and Travis's infatuations and their deadly outcomes.

Meloy's definition of erotomania has, by no means, been widely accepted by the psychiatric community. Segal's response is telling:

I feel that Dr. Meloy's term for this syndrome ("nondelusional or borderline erotomania") is confusing and should not come into general use. In the first place, "nondelusional erotomania" is a contradiction in terms, as erotomania's delusionary nature has, for the last 100 years, been considered its very essence. In addition, the word "borderline" has at least two meanings.[27]

In a research of celebrity fan behavior in Los Angeles, Zona, Sharma, and Lane substitute for Meloy's "borderline erotomania" (1993, 901) two categories: "love obsession," and "simple obsession." The "love obsessional"

27. See Segal's response (1990) to Meloy's response (1990) to Segal's article on erotomania (1989).

usually knows his love object only through the media; he may harbor an erotomanic delusion, but if so, it will be accompanied by other psychiatric disorders; if he is not delusional, then he is obsessed with the love object and
will begin a campaign to make his existence known to the love object (896).
The "simple obsessional" had some relationship with the love object,

> from customer, acquaintance, neighbor, professional relationship, dat-
> ing, and lover. In all of these cases, obsessional activities began after
> either 1) the relationship had gone "sour," or 2) the perception by the
> subject of mistreatment. The subject usually then begins a campaign
> either to rectify the schism, or to seek some type of retribution. (896)

Meloy's erotomania and borderline erotomania and Zona, Sharma, and
Lane's love obsession and simple obsession were categories designed to
explain, label, and catalog the Hinckleys, Travises, and Pupkins of American
society. These formulations were in demand, eagerly accepted and applied
in reference to these "stalkers" (see chap. 9). They fit nicely with the serial-
killer profile and completed it. Notorious Travises, celebrity fans and assas-
sins, on and off screen, can easily be construed as possessing both the features of the serial killer and erotomanic/obsessional impulses; this links the
two definitions in the public mind. And so Travis became an
erotomanic/obsessional serial killer, a scientifically defined social category
with a clear psychiatric profile. This new Travis is still extremely frightening, but not as guilt inducing as the alienated, disoriented Vietnam veteran
pointing an accusing finger at society. Robert De Niro's Kaity in *Cape Fear*
(1992), his creature in *Mary Shelley's Frankenstein* (1994), as well as his stalking fan in *The Fan* (1996) can be neatly defined as erotomanic/obsessional
serial-killing stalkers, and that is how the audience probably understood
them. Accordingly, people who seem to be manifesting erotomanic tendencies or serial-killer features are likely to be thought of as stalkers, and vice
versa. This confusion has led to the modern moral panic surrounding stalking.

As this book is being edited, a new collection of articles, titled *The Psychology of Stalking: Clinical and Forensic Perspectives*, has been published. It is
largely dedicated to the systematic translation of the described erotomanic
serial killer into the emerging professional category labeled "stalker." Influenced by the antistalking legislation of 1990 and thereafter, and by the wide
popularity of the term *stalker*, leading psychiatrists and psychologists would
now officially call Travis-Michael a "stalker." Satisfied with the new terminology, some no longer advocate the usage of "erotomania." Thus, Meloy
argues, "Delusional disorder, erotomanic subtype, is an unlikely primary
diagnosis among stalkers, contrary to early research assumptions" (1998, 4).
Others counter, "The most prevalent [delusional disorders] in stalking cases
are [of] the erotomanic, jealous, or persecutory subtypes" (Zona, Palarea,

and Lane 1998, 71). But whether or not they are referred to as "erotomanic," the new "stalkers" have been given scientific characterizations that associate them with the cultural stalking characters discussed throughout this chapter. So, for example, stating, "There is no single profile of a 'stalker,'" Kristine K. Kienlen goes on to argue, "Stalkers tend to be older, educated men with unsuccessful relationship and employment histories. . . . most stalkers experienced severe disruption in childhood caretaking relationships. Disturbances in early attachments may contribute to unstable adult relationships and stalking behavior" (1998, 52). As Dorris M. Hall rightly points out,

> To date, the most extensive research in the field focuses on stalkers who have had criminal charges brought against them or who have come to the attention of law enforcement due to their activities. All of the studies on this subject have used nonrandom samples of convenience. . . . Further, these same studies underrepresented stalkers who have been involved with the victim, such as ex-boyfriends or ex-spouses. (1998, 114).

Nevertheless, professionals do not refrain from molding detailed stalker profiles. Judging by the tendency apparent in many of these newly published articles, the erotomanic serial killer will soon be officially renamed and labeled "stalker." Significantly, stalking is prohibited and sanctioned by criminal law.

In "The Dangerous Individual" (1978), Michel Foucault links the early-nineteenth-century public preoccupation with a series of inexplicably horrifying murders to the concurrent rise of the psychiatric category called "monomania." (The term *moral panic* perfectly fits his description of the public's attitude.) Stories of brutal, irrational, and seemingly unmotivated crimes created a public demand for some explanation that would restore society's peace of mind, sense of order, and security. The psychiatric discourse, claims Foucault, seized the opportunity and defined monomania as a concealed mental illness that manifested itself only in the patient's horrendous crime. Monomania was a diagnosis that was used to explain every bewildering act of violence. Simultaneously, argues Foucault, it also established psychiatry as a familiar discourse and allowed its entry into the world of law and judicial proceedings. As the sole experts on monomania, psychiatrists became indispensable in judicial proceedings of bizarre crimes. As a result, defendants started being analyzed for mental illnesses, rather than being tried for unacceptable conduct.

Times have changed. Monomania is no longer a mental illness. But bewildering social behaviors still create public demand for professional, scientific solutions, and the legal system is still tempted to adopt these solutions. A critical perspective may prevent an unnecessary repetition of a historical mistake.

Contemporary Images of Female Stalkers

Over the last three decades, women, particularly the new, "second-wave women," have been viewed as a fundamental threat to the male ego. Just like men, who were portrayed as erotomanic serial killers, women were associated with stalking in two distinct ways. One way was inspired by the Hitchcock legacy: women, particularly the strong, independent, "new women," were portrayed as responsible for the stalking and serial killing committed by men. Like Norman Bates's mother, the contemporary woman was constructed as the male stalkers' "Frankenstein" and "Dr. Jekyll." Another cultural avenue was the construction of the contemporary Lilit as an erotomanic serial killer. *The Eyes of Laura Mars* is a good example of the first process; *Play Misty for Me* and *Fatal Attraction* represent the latter.

The Female Dr. Jekyll: *The Eyes of Laura Mars*

In 1978, as *Halloween* was presenting the public with the image of the contemporary American male stalker, *The Eyes of Laura Mars* offered a serial killer who was the "stalking creature" of an independent, successful business woman, one who possessed the power of vision. Starring Faye Dunaway, the film tells the story of a highly celebrated photographer, Laura Mars, whose (lesbian) models are being murdered by a mysterious killer. The murderer turns out to be the police officer in charge of the case, with whom Mars has been conducting a passionate affair. The young officer, a Jekyll and Hyde personality, is obsessed with a (Travis-type) mission to rid the world of the human filth that fills and corrupts it.

The film's most interesting and powerful proposition is the photographer's implication in the recurring murders. Exactly like Greenburg's Babette (in *Love Kills*), Mars experiences unexplained and uncontrolled visions of the murders just before they take place. At such times her sight is taken over by the killer's, and she can only see what he sees as he stalks his next victim. Although she does not perform the actual killings, she participates in the stalking phase of the murders through her psychic visions. Thus, Mars is constructed as the murderer's female double and accomplice, and when he turns out to be her lover, her association with him is significantly increased. Further still, Mars stages and photographs images that combine sexuality with extreme violence; her murdered models are all found in disturbing positions that are identical to those she had staged and photographed prior to the killings. The models had been portrayed as "prostitutes" and, therefore, as classic prey for serial killing. More significantly, the uncanny similarity between the models' positions in death and in their photographs underlines Mars's moral responsibility in the bloodshed. It is explained, in the film's fictional world, by the telepathic, premonitionary connection between Mars and the murderer. This telepathy symbolizes the inherent connection between Mars's violent sexual fantasies and their dangerous execution in reality. Her profession, which involves female vision, is clearly associated with the serial killer's fantasy world, and her images trigger his fatal exploits. This pornography—her carnality—causes his "disease."

The killer in *Laura Mars* is clearly a man, but it is his helpmate, a modern woman, who is responsible for bringing the horror about. He may be the murderer, but she is the real stalker, the vampire, lurking in the shadows of his psyche. In the last sequence, when she almost becomes another of his victims, it is hard not to feel that, like Babette, she "had it coming." If that were not enough, one other woman is held responsible for the killer's deeds: his prostitute mother. The film's serial killer is trapped between a whoring mother, whose behavior traumatized him at an early age, and a modern woman lover, whose powerful and sick imagination triggers and activates the lethal fantasies that his mother had provoked when he was a child. Travis, Son of Sam, and Bundy may all be men, this movie seems to say, but much as in *Psycho*, it is the staring woman within that instigates the violence. This inner woman combines the prostitute mother and the successful businesswoman. Behind every serial killer, it seems, stands at least one woman, if not two.

The Eyes of Laura Mars is mostly a realistic film, but the female protagonist's inexplicable visual powers relate it to the horror genre and make it a junior member of the modern occult-horror subgenre that emerged and boomed in the 1970s. Analyzing a long list of occult films, Carol Clover argues that by associating women with a variety of extremely hysterical behaviors and with evil, supernatural powers, these films actually deal with a crisis in the contemporary American masculinity's view of itself, offering a solution to this plight.[28] These films, Clover observes, depict a fundamental clash between White Science, identified with Western rational tradition and represented by white men, and Black Magic, associated with a variety of social minorities (such as Native Americans, Africans, old people, priests), but above all with women (Clover 1992, 66). The inevitable lesson of the modern occult film, says Clover, "is that White Science has its limits, and that if it does not yield, in the extremity, to the wisdom of Black Magic, all is lost." In other words, the problem of modern masculinity lies in its overidentification with rationality, science, and technology. If white man is to survive, he must reexamine his Western, rational identity and explore new territories. But since these regions are traditionally associated with femininity, they must first be cleansed of women to enable men to enter them without risking feminization. In occult films since the 1970s, Clover argues,

28. The films she cites include *Witchboard, The Fury, Carrie, Friday the 13th, VII, Firestarter, The Exorcist, Poltergeist, Don't Look Now, The Godsend, Rosemary's Baby, Deadly Blessing, Nightmare on Elm Street, Shivers, The Entity, It's Alive, The Hidden, Night of Creeps, Prince of Darkness, The Brood, Beyond Evil,* and *Audrey Rose* (Clover 1992, chap. 2).

women and femininity are pushed to the extremes of irrationality, so that the more mainstream, "normal" realms of emotional life can be appropriated by men in the making of their new masculinity.

> Crudely put, for a space to be created in which men can weep without being labeled feminine, women must be relocated to a space where they will be made to wail uncontrollably; for men to be able to relinquish emotional rigidity, control, women must be relocated to a space in which they will undergo a flamboyant psychotic break; and so on. (104–5)

In their treatment of women's "extreme" femininity, Clover says, these films rely heavily on familiar Early Christian and medieval imagery, including Eve as the Devil's gateway, woman's body as sexual and sinful, menstruation as a sign of feminine evil, and women as Satan's sexual partners. Possession by evil, impregnation by the Devil, female genitals gone berserk, and dangerous telekinesis are common stock of this subgenre. In other words, these films discuss modern masculinity in the medieval discourse of diabolism. And where there are witches, there is inquisition and persecution.

> The female side of the dual focus narrative, then, is a body story with a vengeance. Film after film interrogates what *Beyond Evil* calls the "physical presence" of a woman: forces it to externalize its inner workings, to speak its secrets, to give a material account of itself—in short, to give literal and visible *evidence*. It is remarkable how many of these films in fact put the female body to some sort of trial. . . . As in the medieval ordeal, skin is made to speak the truth it hides. (83)

The Eyes of Laura Mars inspired many remakes and influenced cinematic treatment of contemporary women and serial killers.[29]

The Erotomanic Serial-Killing Lilit: *Play Misty for Me*

In 1971, Clint Eastwood's *Play Misty for Me* featured the new, independent Lilit. The male protagonist, David, is the host of a radio program. Deserted by his fair girlfriend (for sleeping around too much), the melancholic Eastwood character has a one-night stand with Evelyn, a fan who picks him up at his bar, promising that no strings are attached. But when David attempts to win back his fair woman, his nocturnal, dark acquaintance hangs on to him, acting as if they have shared a significant relationship. She phones him despite his "Don't call me, I'll call you" demand; she surprises him at his

---

29. An interesting case in point is *Vampire in Brooklyn*, where the (African American) Laura Mars character is her stalking vampire's psychic double.

home with unwarranted gestures of familiarity; she phones him repeatedly at work and shows up at his neighborhood bar. She drives away a potential female business associate and tries to commit suicide in his home. When she does not receive the hoped-for responses, Evelyn violently attacks David and his housekeeper, destroying the interior of his house. She is hospitalized for mental treatment, but escapes, kidnaps the girlfriend, violently stabs out the eyes in David's life-size portrait, kills a policeman who tries to interfere, attempts to kill David once again, and is finally stopped when he manages to throw her into the ocean.

Evelyn is depicted as a sexually voracious woman who lurks in the dark, spying; she lies in wait, intrudes, clings, and endangers modern man's hegemony and self-perception. As a result of the sexual revolution of the 1960s, in 1971, Evelyn's sexual appetite is not deemed dangerous per se. But her behavior is linked with a feminine attempt to assume a masculine social role, upsetting the basic structure of patriarchal order. Eastwood's David struggles to leave the macho ("western") image behind and to come to terms with the new world order. He tries to create a new masculine identity for himself. Evelyn "appears as a threat precisely because she has taken on traditional masculine characteristics, of the very type David is being forced to give up, and in this way she is simultaneously a return of the masculine repressed" (Knee 1993, 91). For David, who is relinquishing the traditional masculine arsenal, the emancipated Evelyn is clearly confusing and threatening. There can be little doubt of the castrating, Freudian meaning of her attack on his portrait's eyes.

Eastwood's screen persona is particularly telling here. Adam Knee notes that "what is ultimately most provocative about *Play Misty For Me* is the extent to which Eastwood's tough guy persona is forced into a contemporary context and is cast into doubt" (Knee 1993, 100). Eastwood's screen persona is an icon of traditional American manhood, and Evelyn constrains his cherished freedom and independence. She challenges his definitive characteristics of autonomy, control, and detachment. She forces herself into his sacred space.

Evelyn is a modern-day Lilit. Her distinctive contribution to, and interesting twist on, the image is her refusal, in complete contrast with the ancient Lilit, to abandon her male prey and fly away at daybreak. Although Adam's first wife refused to stay and keep house for him, Evelyn is tired of flying; she is a Lilit that will not go away. Like a typical Lilit, Evelyn strips her Adam of his precious symbols of masculinity, but instead of flying away once she has had her way with him, she decides to stay and claim his respect in the morning. No longer content to make her lonely nest in the desolate wilderness outside the Garden of Eden, the new Lilit now demands to return home and take her place as Adam's respectable and equal partner. She settles for nothing short of full personhood. In Evelyn, Lilit abandons her separatist attitude and becomes a radical feminist. No longer accepting the role of the eccentric at society's fringe, she now demands to determine her own identity. She wants to be what she may once have been, Inanna, the Queen of Heaven and Earth, Inanna as she was before her sons slashed her body in order to divide and rule the monstrous Lilit and the domesticated Eve. It is little wonder that the film constructs her as a hysterical, deranged, revenge-seeking female who must be eradicated. The film goes even further, portraying this modern Lilit, the liberated new woman, as a clinging (borderline) erotomaniac or simple obsessional, who develops into a psychotic, potential serial killer. Neither borderline erotomania, simple obsession, nor serial killing were scientifically defined in 1971. But Evelyn manifested all the features that would later be explained by these professional labels. She was the frightful, collective nightmare; the "learned tradition" needed only to formulate the adequate terms to define her profile.

Fatal Attraction

Alex, the character portrayed by Glenn Close in Adrian Lyne's *Fatal Attraction* (1987), is the Evelyn of the 1980s (Knee 1993, 91). A single, professional, sexually initiating woman, she is portrayed as a contemporary Lilit who refuses to go away, a witch and a female erotomanic serial killer.

Sixteen years after *Play Misty for Me,* in the conservative 1980s, Alex's Adam, now called Dan (Michael Douglas), is a married man whose fair wife is a perfect homemaker and mother to their daughter.[30] When his wife and daughter are away for a weekend, the naive Dan is seduced by the independent, professional Alex, who promises that no strings are attached. When she instead insists on continuing a relationship, he feels trapped, helpless, and terrified. She appears constantly, in his office, by his car, and even in his home, demanding his recognition and affection. Feeling mistreated, she resorts to violence and even kills (although her victim is the family's pet rabbit). Like Evelyn, she attempts suicide to arouse the man's compassion, is frequently seized by extreme fits of hysteria, and rapidly deteriorates into destructive, uncontrolled lunacy. Dan's terror peaks when she notifies him of her pregnancy and when she makes contact with his wife (by pretending to be a prospective buyer of their house). If Eastwood's David was a modern man trying to make a new identity for himself, through Douglas's screen image, Dan in *Fatal Attraction* is the prototypical new man; he is the ideal type of the tormented, "politically correct" American man of the 1980s and 1990s, who, although not faultless, nevertheless invites nothing but sympathy and understanding. Alex is his nightmarish Lilit.

Alex is a Frankenstein creature: she feels unjustly abandoned by the man who she claims made her what she has become, but who refuses to take responsibility. She desperately stalks him as a means of simultaneously call-

30. Susan Faludi documents the moviemakers' search for the right "fair woman" to play the wife's part (1991, 120).

ing his attention, bonding with him, and punishing him. She demands that he acknowledge his responsibility for her suffering. She stalks and hurts the people most dear to him. She expresses deep pain, which evokes sympathy for her predicament—if not for her outbursts of rage and vengeful deeds. And she gradually becomes a raving monster. But as the raving monster, she is a hellish female demon of occult horror, as well as the deranged Michael character. Alex's ugly hysterical fits, combined with her alleged pregnancy, which from Dan's perspective is a nightmarish curse devised by Alex to ruin him, associate her with the satanic women of the occult horrors. Her persistent returns to Dan's life, sometimes shot from her peeping perspective outside his window, associate her with Norman Bates and Michael. This is particularly clear in the final scene. In Dan's new family home in the country, Alex ambushes his wife in the shower (yes, the shower) and tries to kill her with a large kitchen knife. When, in the nick of time, Dan comes to the rescue, he and Alex battle fiercely, until, just like Eastwood's David, he manages to drown her, this time in the bathtub. Recalling *Psycho,* in which Marion, lying at the bottom of the shower, stares fixedly at the camera, Alex's dead eyes are fixed on the tormented Dan for a very long time. And then, just when the tension begins to fade, Alex returns from death, leaping on Dan like a demented vampire armed with a knife. Luckily, as in all stalker films, the "final girl," here the good wife, arrives on the scene to shoot the monster down. Interestingly, the script's original ending left Alex to take her own life, but audiences demanded the killing, not suicide, of the monster (who then returned in remakes, such as *Fatal Instinct*).[31] Alex does not actually kill serially; but through her association with previous fictional murderers she joins the social category of serial killer. Her bisexual name stresses her association with the category of male stalkers.

Alex is also quite deliberately made to be an erotomaniac. Gelder reports that Glenn Close "consulted three separate shrinks for an inner profile of her character, who is meant to be suffering from a form of obsessive condition known as de Clerambault's Syndrome" (Gelder 1990, 93–94). Interestingly, however, at least four significant features of the classical definition of erotomania were reversed and reshaped in her interpretation of the character. First, erotomania is a delusion, in which the patient believes herself to be loved by a complete stranger (of a higher social rank). In Alex's case, she pursues a man with whom she actually had an affair. Second, the erotomanic delusion "usually focuses on idealized romance or spiritual union rather than sexual attraction" (Meloy 1992, 21). Alex, on the other hand, displays overwhelming sexual attraction toward her victim. Third, erotomanic women were traditionally described as mostly passive and not dangerous, whereas Alex is a raging femme fatale; an amazon, if you like. Fourth, writers agree that erotomaniacs are frequently unattractive women,

31. For a full discussion of *Fatal Attraction* see Gelder 1990, 91.

and not of high intelligence or social standing (Hollander and Callahan 1975, 1574–75). Glenn Close's Alex in undeniably attractive, intelligent, and successful.

Alex, therefore, has very little in common with what psychiatrists defined as erotomania. She is merely a single, sexual career woman who insists on continuing a relationship with an uninterested man. Two years after the film's release, Meloy published his definition of "borderline erotomania," which seems to account for every one of Alex's features. The persistent Lilit thus became a scientifically classified type of erotomaniac.

Fatal Attraction is a uniquely powerful stalking film. It succeeds in conveying the deep, nerve-wracking anxiety of the victim, which erupts at every ring of the phone, at every touch on his shoulder. It quickly became a tremendous success. The film was nominated for five Academy Awards, including one for best picture. Peter Van Gelder included it in *That's Hollywood: A Behind the Scenes Look at Sixty of the Greatest Films of All Times*.

The public was preoccupied, if not obsessed, with *Fatal Attraction. Time* magazine noted that "people just can't stop talking about this movie." Judging by surveys of audience response, the film seems to have aroused in male viewers strong feelings of anxiety, hatred (toward the woman stalker) and revenge (Faludi 1991, 113; Gelder 1990, 92).

> The film was perfectly timed for the market. . . . The gross in North America had topped $150,000,000 by the end of the year, and it broke box office records in Britain, taking 1,000,000 pounds in the first week. In analyst-ridden New York it was reported that 70% of patients with marital problems were claiming to be obsessed with *Fatal Attraction.* (Gelder 1990, 92)

As Susan Faludi reports, the press

> declared the movie's theme a trend, and scrambled to find real live women to illustrate it. Story after story appeared on the "*Fatal Attraction* phenomenon," including seven-page cover stories in both *Time* and *People*. A headline in one supermarket tabloid even dubbed the film's single-woman character the MOST HATED WOMAN IN AMERICA. (1991, 117)[32]

In an example of this "trend" identified by the media, on 25 December 1987, the *Los Angeles Times* reported, "In a case that smacks of the movie 'Fatal Attraction,' a former San Diego State University student had been charged with stalking her ex-lover for months, renting an adjacent apartment and

---

32. Gelder adds that "after completing the part Close had herself to seek psychoanalytic help as the pressures at home were exacerbated by her public identification with someone dubbed the most hated woman in America" (1990, 94).

then shooting him to death when he refused to rekindle their affair." The media's coverage of "fatal attraction" cases suggested to the public that the phenomenon had become a common occurrence. If the response to the film was not, in itself, a minor moral panic, it surely marked the development of such a social phenomenon.

Perhaps the best-known "real-life fatal attraction" story was that of Amy Elizabeth Fisher, the "Long Island Lolita." On 19 May 1992, the seventeen-year-old Fisher shot her lover's wife in the head. Her story, publicized immediately, included reports of childhood abuse and rape, teenage prostitution, an affair with an older, married man, her obsessive stalking of him, and, finally, the attempt to murder his wife. "The story has attracted lurid publicity and a Hollywood battle for film rights because of the 'Fatal Attraction' story behind the shooting."[33] The story became a hit, and Amy Fisher became the stalking Alex. In one of the television movies about her that were repeatedly shown during prime time, the following conversation takes place between two journalists: the first exclaims, "She became obsessed with him and tried to kill his wife; it was a near *Fatal Attraction*," to which the woman reporter replies, "Great, she's being charged with a movie" (*The Amy Fisher Story*, 1993). Amy Fisher *was* "charged with a movie," if not in court, where she received five to fifteen years, then certainly in the media, where she was deemed to be an immoral whoring homewrecker and ruthless killer—the stalking Lilit.

33. Hugh Davies, "*Fatal Attraction* Teenager Jailed," *Daily Telegraph*, 2 December 1992.

CHAPTER 8

Legal Moral Panic

Preview

The previous chapter described the process by which, since the 1970s, the ancient anxiety concerning stalking has been transformed into the contemporary fear of "erotomanic serial-killer stalkers." This chapter suggests that the legal response to the ensuing moral panic served only to amplify it.[1]

The first antistalking statute was legislated by the State of California in 1990, after the murder of actress Rebecca Schaeffer by a fan who was presented by the media as a "Travis-Hinckley" character, that is, a "serial-killer type," and was promptly classified in a psychiatric report as an erotomaniac. California's legislation was intended to protect the public from the threat allegedly posed by this "profile" of stalkers, that is, from archetypal images; no attempt was made to investigate and analyze the *real* social phenomenon of stalking. Addressing mythological images rather than social reality, the legislature did not adequately conceptualize the prohibited behavior, and the "panicky" drafting rendered an imperfect law. Most states followed suit and adopted California's formulation. Some legal scholarly literature added insult to injury by explicitly associating the prohibited behavior with the cultural images of stalkers. Some writers further advocated that the law subject stalkers to psychiatric analysis and treatment.

Popular culture quickly responded to the new learned formulations, molding the fearsome erotomanic serial killer accordingly. In turn, California's legislature amended the law, empowering the courts to recommend that stalkers receive psychiatric treatment. Culture and law were thus trapped in the dynamics of moral panic.

The Origins of California's Antistalking Law in Moral Panic

Robert Bardo

On 18 July 1989, Robert Bardo shot and killed Rebecca Schaeffer in Los Angeles. The murder immediately became a media event. The story was retold and analyzed ceaselessly. On 23 July, the *Los Angeles Times* published

---

1. In her law review article from 1994, Rosemary Cairns Way argued, similarly, that the Canadian antistalking legislation was the outcome of a moral panic.

a 2,910 word story entitled "Victim, Suspect from Different Worlds; Actress' Bright Success Collided with Obsession." The story's opening paragraph reads as follows:

> From his parents' house in a treeless, sun-parched subdivision in Tucson, Robert John Bardo wrote letter after letter to actress Rebecca Schaeffer, missives to another world. Scrawled shakily in pen, the letters were Bardo's way of reaching out from the boredom and insignificance of his young life. At 19, a janitor at a succession of hamburger stands, he was on the cusp of manhood, but going nowhere. Filling page after page, Bardo detailed his chaste devotion to the fresh-faced young woman who appeared to him only when his television set glowed.

In the story's subsequent paragraphs, the reader is informed that Bardo, despite being "a 'straight A' student," "stepped out of the legion of nowhere people"; that he was a "slack-jawed, ember-eyed young man shambling the streets like a phantom," "somebody who doesn't look right." He had been arrested three times, once for disorderly conduct and domestic violence. Inevitably, a quoted neighbor describes him as a "real 'Psycho' guy." Similarly, Bardo is explicitly compared to the serial-killer stalkers, the men who stalked Jodie Foster (John Hinckley), John Lennon (Mark David Chapman) and Theresa Saldana.[2] A quote from a letter Bardo wrote to his sister reads: "I have an obsession with the unattainable and I have to eliminate (something) that I cannot attain." One of his many letters to Schaeffer herself "told her how he identified with a *My Sister Sam* episode in which her character voiced yearning for the life of a celebrity." The newspaper story highlights the finding of "a final piece of evidence," which connected Bardo not so much to the murder as to other celebrity serial killers: "a red paperback copy of the novel 'The Catcher in the Rye,' the same book John Lennon's assassin, Mark David Chapman, had carried to the scene of the crime."[3] Robert Bardo is portrayed as a serial killer.

The story of Bardo's unhappy meeting with Rebecca is short and dramatic. From his treeless home Bardo arrives in Los Angeles, "a disheveled sight in a yellow shirt, spectacles and sandals," with "short kinky hair." For some hours he roams the streets of Rebecca's neighborhood, showing her picture to passers-by. "Robert Bardo was a stranger in this neighborhood, just as he was in Tucson. . . . When her door buzzer rang at 10:15 A.M. Tuesday morning, Rebecca Schaeffer was not prepared for it. . . . Rebecca was in her bathrobe. Her clothes were laid out for an 11 A.M. meeting with Coppola. Richard Goldman, a writer across the street, heard what sounded like an automobile's backfire. He heard two screams."

---

2. Theresa Saldana played the part of De Niro's wife in *Raging Bull* and was stalked and attacked.

3. For an interesting interpretation of this element see the 1997 film *Conspiracy Theory*.

Schaeffer, as the headline promises, is portrayed as everything that Bardo was not. She belonged to "an affluent community of well-kept homes with peaked roofs and sloping lawns. At Lincoln High, the city's most elite public school, Rebecca joined the 'talented and gifted' program. She talked of becoming a rabbi, but by her junior year she was swept up by the promise of a modeling career." On the night before her murder "she had thrown a 71st birthday party for her grandfather." "On screen, wide-eyed and luminous beneath a corona of curls, Schaeffer projected a kid sister's helplessness." "She was perfect for the part as Pam Dawber's sister [in *My Sister Sam*], a mixture of youthful radiance and dizzy charm." She was also perfect for the part of the "final girl." She did not deserve to die: because it broke the rules of the (Hollywood) game, her murder was insufferable.

Reporting Bardo's sentence, the *Los Angeles Times* story (from the Associated Press) concluded with two professional opinions:

> Deputy Dist. Atty. Marcia Clark said Bardo's true motivation was to gain fame as a celebrity killer. "A normal person does not stalk and murder an actress," the prosecutor said. "But this was less than extreme psychosis." Psychiatrist Park Elliot Dietz testified that Bardo had been schizophrenic since childhood. Dietz, who worked on the case of John Hinckley, who shot President Reagan, said he considered Bardo far more disturbed than Hinckley. He also said Bardo tried to emulate Mark David Chapman, the assassin of John Lennon, and visited the New York site of Lennon's killing. (*Los Angeles Times*, 22 December 1991, from the Associated Press)[4]

Reid Meloy took the professional diagnosis a step further, defining Bardo as a borderline erotomaniac. He stated, "The vivacious and wholesome star of the TV sitcom 'My Sister Sam,' Becky Schaeffer, became the sudden fixation of her assailant" (1992, 22).

Mike Tharp's story of 17 February 1992, "In the Mind of a Stalker," published by *U.S. News and World Report*, is frequently quoted in legal discussions of stalking. In this story Robert Bardo "is a symbol of a spreading national menace" and "an archetypal stalker." Bardo, Tharp emphasizes, was diagnosed in 1985 as being "'severely emotionally handicapped,' and [as] coming from a 'pathological and dysfunctional family'"; "he never made more than $3,000 a year, never had a date, and never lost his virginity. 'He began to live a fantasy life, . . . to give him some sort of relief from the mental pain and torture.'" In junior high school

---

4. The story read as follows: "The obsessed fan who stalked 'My Sister Sam' actress Rebecca Schaeffer and shot her on the doorsteps to her apartment house was sentenced Friday to life in prison without possibility of parole. . . . Bardo followed Schaeffer for nearly two years, hired a detective to get her address, repeatedly sent her letters and got his brother to buy him a gun before he killed her in 1989. . . . The defense argument that Bardo was too mentally ill to premeditate murder was rejected by the judge."

he never talked to other students, preferring to stand alone, nodding, on the school sidewalks. He began writing letters, often three times a day, to one of his teachers, signing them "Scarface," "Dirty Harry Callahan," and "James Bond."

At that time he exhibited traits common to autovampirism, stabbing "himself in the wrist with a pen." Concerning the actress, he is said to have written in his diary, "when I think about her I feel that I want to become famous and impress her." He is also said to have traveled to the studio where she worked twice—once carrying a teddy bear and a letter, and the second time carrying a knife. It is said that Bardo based his search for Shaeffer's home on the methods used by Theresa Saldana's stalker, which had been reported in the press. He is quoted as saying, "Hollywood is a seductive place. There are a lot of lonely people out there seduced by the glamour," and, about Schaeffer, that "she was going to call me."

Myriad press accounts around the country reinforced the same message: Bardo was a Travis character: an empty, fictive personality, a misfit on the lonely fringes of nowhere, a serial-killer type, an erotomaniac, a stalker. Hopelessly infatuated with Schaeffer's sisterly screen persona, as well as with her celebrity aura, and driven by a similarly hopeless ambition to be somebody, he sought the only avenue he saw open to him, and connected with Schaeffer by way of stalking and, finally, by taking her life. Bardo was unable to break away from his pathetic role as an eternal outsider. In his desperate, "creaturelike" attempts to connect, he embraced the fictional world of a television series. This fictional attachment became Bardo's only connection with, and source of, life, but when the mere illusion was no longer enough to fill the emptiness inside him, he demanded Schaeffer's blood. The story of Bardo's arrival at Schaeffer's youthful, sunny world bears a striking resemblance to Michael's arrival in Laurie's hometown in the paradigmatic stalking film *Halloween*. Robert Bardo's appearance in Los Angeles is the reappearance (from "death") of the contemporary stalker, known by many names: David Chapman, Travis Bickle, Son of Sam, John Hinckley, Ted Bundy, Michael, and Jason (the monster of *Friday the 13th*).

According to the endless press stories, Bardo did very little stalking, if any at all. Even in Mike Tharp's detailed story, all Bardo did before the murder was write letters and appear at the studio twice, which is less than many other fans do without being labeled stalkers. Although he was carrying a knife the second time he came to watch Schaeffer, he did not attempt to come close to her, to communicate with her, or to threaten her. Clearly, it was not his actual actions that made Bardo a stalker; it was his strong cultural ties with the contemporary images of male stalkers. He murdered the virtuous "final girl" at a time when the moral panic was ready to erupt. The "final girl," Rebecca Schaeffer, should have survived the monster's attacks, as Jodie Foster had. Her death at the hands of the lurking outsider was outrageous and unacceptable. It left the "audience" (the public) feeling confused, cheated, and angry. In overcoming the purity of the "final girl," the monster broke the rules of the game. Firm action to restore the public's sense of security and justice was in order. In this sociocultural context, Bardo was the trigger that brought about the legal intervention. The public and the media demanded that the erotomanic serial-killer Bardo and his story be outlawed. The legislature complied.

Schaeffer was murdered in July 1989. The National Institute of Justice clearly connects that event and the legal response:

> As a criminal justice problem, "stalking" captured public attention in the wake of 1989 murder of actress Rebecca Schaeffer and reports of a fan's persistent harassment of comedian David Letterman. California enacted the first anti-stalking legislation in 1990. (U.S. Department of Justice 1993, 5)

This view of the role of Schaeffer's murder in generating the antistalking legislation is almost unanimously held by the press and the legal world alike:

> Many state legislators consider California the leader in combating stalking, since the issue first came into the national consciousness when 21-year-old Rebecca Schaeffer was killed there by an obsessed fan in 1989. (C. Carmody 1994, 68)

To Matthew Goode, writer of a law journal article on stalking, "it is clear that, while some concerns have been prompted by domestic violence, the original California initiative was probably due to the 'stalking' of celebrities by crazed fans. Perhaps the most notorious of these (and there are quite a number), was John Hinckley" (1995, 21–22). He rightly notes that "it is rare to read an American article on the subject of stalking which does not commence with an outraged account of some horrendous case. An account of the murder of actress Rebecca Schaeffer appears to be the *de rigueur* first paragraph."

The Influence of *Fatal Attraction*

In 1990, the public reaction to *Fatal Attraction* was still hysterical enough to be considered a minor moral panic in its own right. Accordingly, a great number of press items and law review articles describing the legislation in California associated it with *Fatal Attraction*. One such news story, titled "California Law Targets Obsessed Fans, Vengeful Lovers" and published in *State Legislatures* in October 1991, contained the following sections:

[T]he most sensational stalking cases involved celebrities harassed by obsessed fans. David Letterman, Michael J. Fox and Sharon Gless were recent victims; and two actresses, Rebecca Schaeffer and Theresa Saldana, were brutally attacked by men who lay in waiting for them. Schaeffer died. The legislation was strongly supported by groups representing Hollywood stars.

The usual stalking victim, however, is a woman terrorized by a vengeful ex-husband or boyfriend. . . . Although men are stalked less often than women, male victims of harassment received some notoriety in the movie "Fatal Attraction."

Articles such as this probably reflect California's legislators' frame of mind at that time. They also helped to induce legislatures in other states to follow California's lead and to outlaw the phenomenon of Fatal Attraction. To mention just one example, in October 1991, the counsel of Michigan's House Judiciary Committee received and filed a copy of the *State Legislatures* article quoted above. When, in January 30, 1992, State Representative Dianne Byrum introduced the bill that eventually became Michigan's stalking law, she explained her motivation to the press by paraphrasing the quoted article:

In recent years, the most sensational stalking cases have involved celebrities such as David Letterman, Michael Fox and Sharon Gless, who were followed and harassed by obsessed fans. In the most tragic case, the young actress Rebecca Schaeffer was brutally killed by a man who stalked her across the country.

But the usual stalking victim is an average woman who is terrorized by a vengeful ex-husband or boyfriend, and in some cases a man who is pursued by a woman with a "fatal attraction."

The association of antistalking legislation with *Fatal Attraction* became so strong that in the following years antistalking laws were sometimes referred to as "*Fatal Attraction* laws." Reporting a court decision, David Peterson wrote in a *Star Tribune* story, "The case apparently marked the first time that someone had attempted to use the state's 'Fatal Attraction' antistalking law to keep the news media at bay" ("Judge Rules WCCO-TV Report Not Intrusive," 8 July 1994, Metro ed.).

Hossein Ghaffari, an "Erotomanic Serial Killer"

The murders of four Orange County women were also associated with California's antistalking legislation. All four were murdered by men who had been ordered by the court to stay away from them. Three of the murderers were estranged spouses, each described in the media as having been unable to accept the separation from his partner. The fourth, Hossein Ghaffari, committed the most sensational crime and received more media coverage than the others. He "drove his own car into the victim's car, . . . then threw sulfuric acid and poured a flammable liquid onto the victim. He ignited it and the victim burned to death inside her car" (Meloy 1992, 302). Ghaffari, who had followed his victim for ten years, had never had a real relationship with her, despite his repeated attempts. His attachment was mostly delusional. Yet, when he heard of her intention to marry, he killed her. In his court-ordered evaluation of the case, Meloy wrote that

> Hossein formed an immediate, erotomanic attachment to the voice of the victim on first telephone contact. . . . His relationship with her . . . was also the product of a primitive defense called projective identification, in which he attributed to her certain qualities, and also needed to control her and be controlled by her. When she rejected him in December 1989, he was filled with abandonment rage. . . . He also lost control of her, and felt she no longer controlled him, a source of dependent and maternal reverie. The generic roots of his erotomania probably lie with his attachment to his mother in what we would consider a very symbiotic relationship. Little is known of this relationship, however, so this is only speculative. . . . Paradoxically, his relationship with the victim has been renewed through her death. He now experiences her, once again, as an idealized object in his mind, when in sleep he can suspend the "reality tested" knowledge of her death and can be with her in a pleasant, isolated place. He has intrapsychically come full circle: he initially idealized her, she rejected him, he devalued her and killed her, and now, once again, he can idealize her. . . . It is my opinion that Hossein meets the legal criteria for insanity in the State of California. (1992, 322–25)[5]

This image of Ghaffari is the profile of a "Norman Bates erotomanic serial killer." In his psychiatric analysis, mother, erotomania, and serial killing were professionally united. California's new legislation was designed to banish the combination.

The Antistalking Law as a Flawed, Moral Panic Law

"A Hodgepodge of Flawed Statutes"

Because the antistalking legislation of 1990 was hastily enacted in response to a stalking moral panic, its inadequate wording rendered it incapable of properly addressing many types of stalking, including those very types it

5. In the postscript, Meloy adds that "the jury believed that he was mentally ill, but not legally insane" (1992, 326). Hossein Ghaffari was sentenced to life in prison without the possibility of parole.

supposedly set out to address. California's original legislation included the following paragraphs:

(a) Any person who willfully, maliciously, and repeatedly follows or harasses another person and who makes a credible threat with the intent to place that person in reasonable fear of death or great bodily injury is guilty of the crime of stalking, punishable by imprisonment in a county jail for not more than one year, or by a fine of not more than one thousand dollars, or by both that fine and that imprisonment.

(d) For the purposes of this section, "harasses" means a knowing and willful course of conduct directed at a specific person which seriously alarms, annoys or harasses the person, and which serves no legitimate purpose. The course of conduct must be such as would cause a reasonable person to suffer substantial emotional distress, and must actually cause substantial emotional distress to the person. "Course of conduct" means a pattern of conduct composed of a series of acts over a period of time, however short, evidencing a continuity of purpose. Constitutionally protected activity is not included within the meaning of "course of action."

(e) For the purposes of this section, "a credible threat" means a threat made with the intent and the apparent ability to carry out the threat so as to cause the person who is the target of the threat to reasonably fear for his or her safety. The threat must be against the life of, or a threat to cause great bodily injury to, a person as defined in section 12022.7. (Cal. Penal Code #646.9)[6]

This legal formulation defined stalking as the behavior of a stalker who maliciously and repeatedly follows or harasses his target, makes a credible threat against the target's life, or causes great bodily injury to the target. The threat had to be made with the intent to place the target in reasonable fear of death or great bodily injury; it had to seem credible, and the target, as well as the "reasonable person" in her place, had to actually suffer substantial emotional distress. It is evident that this definition of stalking could not encompass the types of stalking performed by such killers as Ted Bundy or Son of Sam; neither did it include erotomanic behavior, as defined by psychiatrists, or even the patterns of behavior of many borderline erotomaniacs, as described by Meloy. Further still, Travis Bickle, John Hinckley, or Robert

6. After four amendments introduced into this text in 1992, 1993, 1994, and 1995, the most significant difference between the original text and the current one is that the credible threat need now only be made with the intent to place the victim in "reasonable fear for his or her safety or the safety of his or her immediate relatives." For the original text and the full texts of all the amendments see California Penal Code #646.9 (West Supp. 1998).

Bardo would not, under California's law, have been considered to be stalking their victims. Had the law been enacted earlier, it could not have prevented them from committing their murders (or attempted murders). None of them threatened his victims with the malicious intent to place them under reasonable fear for their lives, and none of the victims actually suffered substantial emotional distress. Rebecca Schaeffer was not seriously distressed; Bardo never threatened her. In fact, she may not even have been aware of his existence. The law, similarly, failed to address the behavior of the three men who murdered their ex-partners in Orange County during the months preceding the legislation. Although all three may have actually threatened their former spouses, it is not clear, judging by the accounts of the murders, that any of them acted willfully and maliciously with the intent to place his former spouse in reasonable fear of death or great bodily injury. It is more likely that at least some of them acted, as their friends described, out of enraged jealousy and despair, with the intent of reestablishing the terminated relationships, or at least of preventing their former spouses from creating new intimate friendships with other men. Even if each of these men could be described as having harbored the intent to place his target in reasonable fear of death or great bodily injury, surely this intent was not the major motivation in any of these cases.

It is not clear why California's legislation was thus worded. According to Susan E. Bernstein, "Judge Watson [who drafted the statute's first version] suggested that the language of the law be drawn from California's Penal Code section 422, which defines terrorism" (1993, 544). California's definition of prohibited terrorism did (and still does) mention a threat and the victim's reasonable fear for his or her safety. But section 422 of the Penal Code, which was enacted in the years 1988–89, is much broader than the 1990 antistalking legislation. California's crime of terrorism does not require the following or harassing of the victim, nor does it require that a "reasonable person" would have been deeply frightened if he were in the victim's place. It merely requires (1) a credible threat made with the intent that it be taken as such, "even if there is no intent of actually carrying it out," and (2) the victim's reasonable fear for his or her own safety or for his or her immediate family's safety.[7] It is, therefore, hard to see what the new antistalking legislation added to the already existing prohibition. Whatever reason lay

---

7. "Any person who willfully threatens to commit a crime which will result in death or great bodily injury to another person, with the specific intent that the statement is to be taken as a threat, even if there is no intent of actually carrying it out, which, on its face and under the circumstances in which it is made is so unequivocal, unconditional, immediate, and specific as to convey to the person threatened a gravity of purpose and an immediate prospect of execution of the threat, and thereby causes that person reasonably to be in sustained fear for his or her own safety or for his or her immediate family's safety, shall be punished by imprisonment in the county jail not to exceed one year, or by imprisonment in his county in the stated prison." California Penal Code #422 (West Supp. 1998).

behind the wording, it is clear that the legal wording was inadequate to deal with the complex issue of stalking.[8]

Nevertheless, "California's actions produced a domino effect and within two years the remaining forty-nine states created the new crime of 'stalking'" (Salame 1993, 67). In October 1993, the National Institute of Justice (NIJ) presented Congress with an official report on the states' stalking laws, and with a Model Anti-Stalking Law for States (U.S. Department of Justice 1993). The report examines and compares the various laws criminalizing stalking in forty-six states and the District of Columbia. It finds that

> states typically define stalking as willful, malicious, and repeated following and harassing of another person. . . . Many states require a pattern of conduct. Provisions often require that the victim have a reasonable fear of death or bodily injury. The two chief elements of most stalking statutes are threatening behavior and criminal intent of the defendant. Fourteen states require that the perpetrator make a threat against the victim. . . . Thirty three states and the District of Columbia include in the definition of stalking actions that would cause a reasonable person to feel threatened, even if there has been no verbal threat by the perpetrator. . . . Many states require that the defendant have the criminal intent to cause fear in the victim. (U.S. Department of Justice 1993, 13–14)[9]

Most states followed California in not making adequate reference to various types of stalking. Only very few states conducted research and drafted definitions that captured wider varieties of stalking patterns.[10] "Ironically, it was state legislators' desire to address highly publicized stalking incidents quickly that resulted in 'a hodgepodge of flawed statutes,' some of them completely unworkable" (Bradfield 1998, 245 n. 84, quoting

8. Several law review articles criticize different antistalking laws for not affording stalking victims the needed protection. Particularly interesting is Jennifer L. Bradfield's (1998) account of her own stalking as a law student, and how Colorado's antistalking legislation failed to protect her.

9. According to the NIJ's detailed charts, in 1993, thirty-six laws required the stalker's specific intent to cause reasonable fear, implying that the victim was also, effectively, required to prove that she endured such fear. As for the course of conduct, forty-three laws included "pursuing or following" in their definitions of stalking behavior, twenty-eight include "harassing," twenty "non-consensual communication," eight "trespass," seven "surveillance," six "presence," five "intimidation," five "disregard of warning," four "approaching," four "possess or show weapon," four "confine/restrain," four "bodily harm," three "lying in wait," and two "vandalism" (U.S. Department of Justice 1993, 16–20, chart 2; 25–27, chart 4).

10. Michigan, Illinois, and the District of Columbia are interesting examples. See Michigan Comp. Laws 750.411(h) and (i), 600.2950(a), 600.2954, 764.15(b), 771.2, and 771.2(a); Ill. Ann. Stat. Ch. 720, par. 5/12–7/4; District of Columbia Code #22–504 (b).

Carmody). In short, the moral panic legislation resulted in inadequate laws.

Although several law review articles claimed that antistalking laws were too narrow to be sufficiently effective, most argued that the laws were unconstitutionally vague and overly broad.[11] (Overbroad legislation attempts to criminalize conduct that is constitutionally protected, such as free speech.) Stalking laws were criticized for being overbroad largely due to their possible implications regarding protected communicative speech and freedom of movement. Writers suggested that stalking be defined more narrowly, using carefully defined, constitutionally tested terms. Whereas relatively effective laws may not be constitutional, "the danger inherent in drafting a statute conservatively to avoid constitutional problems is that the result may be too narrow to achieve the original purpose" (Faulkner and Hsiao 1993, 56). Given this choice, all voted for constitutionality.

> Proponents of the current laws will argue that such changes [in breadth] will render the statute less effective against some types of stalkers, especially the delusional lovers. This point must be conceded; however, as the laws currently exist, they are unconstitutional and therefore offer no protection. (Wickens 1994, 209)

Most legal scholars, therefore, suggested that stalking be redefined so that the law would capture even fewer types of stalking than California's 1990 legislation.

However, a detailed NIJ report published in 1996 suggests that courts have, so far, been more sympathetic to the legislation than most writers expected.

> By January 1996, the Justice Department had identified 53 constitutional challenges to stalking statutes in 19 states. Generally, the courts are upholding the laws. . . . Courts rarely strike down anti-stalking statutes on vagueness grounds. . . . While there have been several overbroad challenges to anti-stalking statutes, no court to date has struck down a State's anti-stalking statute on this ground. (U.S. Department of Justice 1996, 6–7)[12]

11. A representative list of law review articles on stalking includes Anderson 1993; Bernstein 1993; Boychuk 1994; Bradfield 1998; Copelan 1994; C. Carmody 1994; David 1994; Diacovo 1995; Dietz 1984; Faulkner and Hsiao 1993; Gilligan 1992; Goode 1995; Guy 1993; Kolb 1994; Kruger 1995; Lee 1998; Lingg 1993; McAnaney, Curliss, and Abeyta-Price 1993; R. N. Miller 1993; Montesino 1993; Morville 1993; Perez 1993; Phipps 1993; Salame 1993; Sloan 1994; Steinman 1993; Strikis 1993; Tucker 1993; J. M. Walker 1993; Walsh 1996; Way 1994; and Wickens 1994. Most of the articles' titles refer to the efficiency of the laws and/or to their constitutionality.

12. Only three states' definitions of stalking were found unconstitutionally vague (U.S. Department of Justice 1996, app. A).

But, encouraged by the analysis offered by the majority of legal scholars, some states were quick to narrow their definitions of stalking: "In general, the revised laws include specific intent and credible threat requirements, broaden definitions, refine wording, stiffen penalties, and emphasize the suspect's pattern of activity" (4).

According to the report on antistalking legislation, forty-one states required that stalking involve "explicit or implicit threat," twenty-nine required "intent to [cause fear] and [behavior that] actually causes reasonable fear," and fifteen required behavior that "actually causes reasonable fear" (U.S. Department of Justice 1996, app. E). At the end of the first decade of the antistalking legislation, stalking is still commonly defined as willfully, maliciously, and repeatedly following or harassing a person with the intent to cause substantial fear, while making a credible threat that causes the victim and would cause the "reasonable person" substantial fear.

The Reasonable-Person Test

Of the antistalking laws' problematic features, I wish to focus on one that has not drawn much critical attention. The "reasonable-person test," as established by California and many other states, subjects the victim (rather than the defendant) to judicial scrutiny; it leaves the determination of the social damage of stalking to the "reasonable person" and, above all, invites uncritical import of cultural images into the legal discourse, thereby potentially allowing moral panic to penetrate the law.[13]

"Reasonableness" is a fundamental term within the Anglo-American legal discourse. Over the course of at least 140 years, it "has gained a prominent position in almost every area of American law" (Unikel 1992, 327). A common, traditional justification for using the concept is that "'reasonableness' aids the legal system in its attempt to reconcile the tension between individual autonomy and community harmony by providing an objective means of superimposing community standards upon individual behavior" (329–30; see also P. B. Johnson 1993). A fascinating manifestation of the reasonableness principle is its personification in the fictional figure of the "reasonable person," who is better known by the name he carried until the 1970s: the "reasonable man."[14] This fictional character is so conspicuous in legal thought that "we can hardly function without this hypothetical figure at the

13. For the "reasonable person," the "reasonable man," and "the reasonable woman" see Adler 1993; Arbery 1993; Ashraf 1992; Cahn 1992; Childers 1993; Collins 1977; Donovan and Wildman 1981; Ehrenreich 1990; Forell 1994; Glidden 1992; P. B. Johnson 1993; Reynolds 1970; R. A. Rosen 1993; Sanger 1992; Scheppele 1991; and Unikel 1992.
14. "If a married woman enjoyed no 'legal existence separate from her husband,' if women were not full 'persons,' and if their legal status in this country evolved from the English tradition that in common law 'a reasonable woman did not exist,' it was no accident that the legal model of rational behavior was personified in a male character" (Collins 1977, 319).

center of legal debate. We cannot even begin to argue about most issues without first asking what a reasonable person would do under the circumstances" (Fletcher 1987, 68–69).

Throughout more than a century of judicial decisions and legal scholarship, this hypothetical entity has been constructed as a neutral, objective, rational, cautious "person," who adheres to society's norms. He has been allowed no idiosyncrasies and only "reasonable" faults and weaknesses. He has been allowed no social affiliations: he is genderless, raceless, and classless. His physical features are flexible: in each particular case he takes on the features of the person whose behavior he helps estimate, "whether blind, crippled, or in excellent shape" (Reynolds 1970, 415). As Robert Adler notes, this creature actually incorporates into one fictional character two distinct models, "(1) an ideal, albeit not perfect, person whose behavior served as an objective measure against which to judge our actions, and (2) an average or typical person possessing all of the shortcomings and weaknesses tolerated by the community" (Adler 1993, 807). In short: he is the "ideal average man" (see also Collins 1977, 312 n. 2).

In criminal cases (as in tort common law, where the creature originated), this "reasonable person" is hypothetically introduced in the specific case before the court, and placed in the defendant's shoes.

> This person is placed in the position of the actor at the time and place of injury, and we are left to decide what he would have done. He is equipped for his job with, according to various definitions, ordinary care, sense, and skill, and is influenced by factors that usually affect human conduct. (Reynolds 1970, 415)

His hypothetical behavior determines whether the defendant before the court acted as this exemplary "reasonable person" would have. The "reasonable person" is therefore a hypothetical actor that functions as the *defendant*'s "reasonable" shadow, his literary double.

For well over a century, this character has played a central role in one court case after another. In his hypothetical, fictional state, he is neither quite alive nor really dead. He derives his life and existence in each legal story by taking on those of the defendant; in so doing he often deprives the defendant of his own freedom, and sometimes of his life. He transcends the distinction between civil law and criminal law (by appearing in cases of both categories), and he transgresses the boundaries between male and female, officially being, simultaneously, neither and both. Like Frankenstein's creature, he is a synthetic, man-made creature, artificially composed of bits and pieces of traits of people who have appeared before courts of law over the years. Since he appears in any and almost every story that comes before a court of law, he is, within the legal world, everywhere. In each legal story, he sees all, but is never seen himself; no gaze can objectify him. Like a spying Satan, he exposes people's weaknesses, facilitating their condemnation. He is the defendant's almost perfect shadow, his (superior) double, his threatening reflection in the mirror of social reasonableness. When the defendant's behavior is determined to differ from that of the "reasonable person," this character becomes a Dr. Jekyll and turns the defendant into his unreasonable Mr. Hyde. In other words, the "reasonable person," "the legend *par excellence* of the legal profession" (Collins 1977, 312), is the male stalker par excellence of the legal world's stories.

From a literary point of view, it is fitting that California law should have incorporated the legal discourse's fictional stalker into its story of stalking. Unfortunately, the particular manner in which the "reasonable person" test has been constructed in antistalking legislation is disconcerting.

Subjecting the Victim to Judicial Scrutiny

Interestingly, when introducing the "reasonable person" test into antistalking law, California's legislature dramatically departed from the traditional usage of this test within criminal law and attached the hypothetical actor to the *victim* rather than to the *defendant* (thus reversing the usual practice in Anglo-American criminal law). The California law defines harassment as a course of conduct that causes substantial emotional distress to the victim and would also cause a "reasonable person" to suffer substantial emotional distress *if he were in the victim's place.* This double test establishes that if the victim suffered substantial emotional distress under circumstances in which the "reasonable person" would not have done, then the *victim* is not a "reasonable person" and the defendant's behavior does not constitute criminal stalking.

The attachment of the "reasonable person" to the victim places her in the defendant's traditional place, blurring the distinction between victim and defendant; she is thus a semidefendant. Accordingly, the double test subjects the victim to a judicial process of determining his or her reasonableness. The argument in support of applying this test is that the reasonable person's perspective is necessary in order to set an objective standard of unacceptable behavior and to protect defendants from complaints filed by hypersensitive, hysterical victims (Gilligan 1992, 310). But if so, why add the additional, subjective test to the objective one? Once the defendant's behavior is determined (by the objective test) to be objectively acceptable or unacceptable, the victim's subjective feelings should make no difference and there seems to be no rational need to inspect them. (Consider, for example, theft: once the perpetrator's behavior is deemed objectively unacceptable, the victim's subjective emotional response is not considered relevant to the legal determination that a crime has occurred). In fact, the double test serves only to subject the victim to a comparison with the reasonable person and places the victim in the position of being considered legally unreasonable.

The reasonable person's declared neutrality and objectivity emphasize his superiority over the victim's merely subjective perspective, thus placing the victim in an innately apologetic starting position. The gender gap between the "reasonable person" and most victims of stalking renders the double test even more problematic.

> The vast majority of stalking victims are women. The male-biased reasonable person standard is inadequate for determining whether stalking a woman is likely to cause "reasonable fear of death or great bodily harm." For example, a woman's fear of rape should satisfy the requirement of great bodily harm because men and women simply do not have the same perspective on what is "reasonable fear" regarding rape. (Forell 1994, 778)

Despite his new, politically correct, alleged sex neutrality, the reasonable person "has always been identified with the male sex" (Donovan and Wildman 1981, 436) and, to a large extent, continues to be the "reasonable man."[15] Victims of stalking, on the other hand, seem to be mostly women.[16] The victim, then, is usually a woman, whereas her hypothetical, reasonable shadow, her "legal stalker," is a man who, within the legal story, spies on and judges her. In other words, Eve's legal stalker is a "male superego Mary" who stalks her much as the defendant did. This unusual construction has two significant implications. First, as with Christian theology, the legal discourse presents Eve in the worst possible light by comparing her to the unattainable "superego Mary." Being a "male Mary," the "reasonable person/man" is an even less attainable model and is more likely to expose the female victim of stalking as unreasonable. Second, the structural resemblance between the (stalking) defendant and the victim's (stalking) fictional shadow further associates the victim with the defendant. Much like Laura Mars, the victim becomes structurally guilty through association.

Some writers, referring to sexual harassment law, advocate the substitution of "reasonable woman" for "reasonable person."[17] This would solve some problems, replacing them with others. Of the many arguments raised against the "reasonable woman" standard, the most compelling is that it essentializes women, reinforcing stereotypes of women and of their "otherness," sensitivity, and vulnerability.[18]

15. See also Forell 1994. This is even more so since 1991, when the Ninth Circuit adopted the "reasonable woman" standard in hostile environment cases. Now that there is a "reasonable woman," her reasonable counterpart is clearly not a "reasonable woman." See *Ellison v. Brady*, 924 F. 2d 872 (9th Cir. 1991).

16. For supporting accurate data see chapter 9.

17. See in particular Ehrenreich 1990; Forell 1994; Glidden 1992; Sanger 1992; Scheppele 1991. Additionally, many writers on sexual harassment address this issue.

18. See Adler 1993; Arbery 1993; Ashraf 1992; Cahn 1992; Childers 1993; R. A. Johnson 1993; and Unikel 1992.

Determination of Damage

As I mentioned earlier, the "reasonable person" test establishes that under circumstances in which the "reasonable person" would not have suffered substantial emotional distress, the defendant's behavior does not constitute criminal stalking. In other words, in antistalking statutes, the "reasonable person" determines which behavior constitutes stalking and which does not. This construction is flawed in several ways.

In the past, when damage was done by one person to another, the "reasonable man" was used to determine whether the person causing the damage acted with the amount of caution and care expected and demanded of members of that society.[19] The "reasonable man" was the individual who embodied that amount of caution, and was therefore a convenient "ruler" by which the courts could measure specific behavior. What the "reasonable man" was *not* expected to do was to determine *whether* damage was done, nor to define it. These substantial elements were either explicitly determined by legislation or so fundamentally rooted in the community's social consensus that they simply went without saying. When a person deprived another of his or her cow or eye, society knew that there was damage and knew what the damage was. The function of the "reasonable man" was only to help determine whether the manner in which the damage was caused was excusable or not, and accordingly which of the two parties must endure the cost.[20]

But much like Frankenstein's creature, this judicial *golem* acquired its own personality, taking over more and more power and control. In (hostile environment) sexual harassment law, as in stalking laws, it is used not only to evaluate the amount of caution manifested in a behavior that caused damage, but also to determine both *whether* damage was done and the essence of that damage. In hostile environment sexual harassment cases, if a "reasonable person" or a "reasonable woman" would not have felt sexually harassed by the defendant's conduct, then, legally speaking, *that type of behavior is not sexual harassment.* The "reasonable person" or the "reasonable woman" has become responsible for deciding *the damage of sexual harassment.* In antistalking legislation the "reasonable person" plays the same role. Stalking as a criminal offense, and the social value this prohibition is meant to protect, are all defined by this hypothetical entity, not by the legislature, or the "people," or even the court, but by the "reasonable person," as he is envisioned by a particular judge or jury. This usage of the standard is flawed.

Caroline Forell rightly states that "because it applies existing commu-

19. For the "reasonable man" standard of care see in particular Reynolds 1970 and Collins 1977.
20. For criticism even of this narrow role see in particular Reynolds 1970 and Collins 1977.

nity norms, the reasonable man/person standard of care is deeply conservative and supports the status quo. Thus, the reasonable person standard is likely to be a barrier to those seeking to change the norms defining acceptable conduct" (Forell 1994, 772). In Nancy Ehrenreich's terms, the reasonable person is "a mechanism for importing a pre-existing societal consensus into the law" (1990, 1181). The reasonable person, says Ehrenreich, is a symbol of

> a neutral and impartial reflection of societal norms. By thus symbolizing societal consensus, *the image obscures the existence of diversity and conflict among groups* . . . rendering invisible those who differ from the "average" person it creates. . . . [It] reinforces the message that those who deviate from the norm are just that: deviants. (1212–13, emphasis added)

The concept of the reasonable person assumes a prelegal social consensus that it introduces into any given case. It is, therefore, inherently out of place in (1) areas where there is no clear social consensus and (2) cases where the legislature intends a law to prescribe a change in what it perceives as the social consensus. Sexual harassment and stalking are two examples of areas in which both these conditions apply. At least to the extent that both sexual harassment and stalking relate to women's social status, American society seems to be conflicted. If the traditional perception of women and their social status still amounts to social consensus, then clearly (or at least hopefully) sexual harassment and antistalking laws seek to challenge and change this consensus.

Both sexual harassment and stalking laws seem to prescribe that women be treated as independent and autonomous persons and not be objectified through traditional, patriarchal behavior. In this respect, these laws are practically revolutionary: they aim to liberate women from widespread, oppressive social norms. Since the fictional reasonable person allegedly symbolizes the social consensus, that is, these oppressive norms, he cannot and should not be the one to determine either the scope of women's rights, or any particular behavior's reflection on such rights. The legislature should bear sole authority for the determination of such fundamental value judgments; it should not pretend to assume social consensus where it does not exist.

The legal system's usage of the double reasonable-person standard in both stalking and hostile environment sexual harassment law suggests that the legal system, in both cases, is not sure how to classify the behavior, and that it does not take the objective harm caused by the behavior seriously. It needs to justify judicial interference by reassuring itself that real harm has occurred. Additionally, the system is haunted, it seems, by a fear of hysterical, hypersensitive women. There seems to be an undertone of suspicion in the system's behavior in both these areas of law. These doubts and fears lead to the demand that every complainant's reasonableness be evaluated and established.

Insertion of Cultural Images

The reasonable-person standard allows for an interesting integration, in the real-world setting of the courtroom, of the legal stalking story with fictional narratives of stalking. Let me illustrate this point using the case of "a young teacher in suburban Westchester County [who] was convicted in May of shooting to death . . . the wife of her lover . . . then meeting him for drinks and sex. . . . the case was likened to the movie *Fatal Attraction*" (Kiley Armstrong, *Chicago Tribune,* 23 November 1992). Suppose the defendant did not shoot the woman but left the man messages, killed his rabbit, and attacked his car; suppose she were charged with stalking. The jury then would have to determine whether the described course of conduct would cause a "reasonable person" to suffer substantial emotional distress. A "reasonable juror," and especially one who has not experienced stalking and has never personally encountered such a situation, might recall Michael Douglas's convincing portrayal of a victim in *Fatal Attraction* and base his or her decision on the fictional character's emotional response to his stalking. It does not take a juror with a fictive personality to resort to this solution, since the "reasonable person" is himself a fictional entity, and it seems perfectly consistent (and "reasonable") to model one fictional character on another. In addition, Michael Douglas' Dan would probably be the only stalking victim that the jurors (as well as the judge) had actually "seen" cope with this ordeal, and he would be a natural, convenient common ground for jury discussion. *Fatal Attraction* portrays Dan as a perfect candidate for "the reasonable person," and the media's insistence on associating the movie with the stalking laws only reinforces this linkage. The "reasonable person's" fictionality, then, facilitates the superimposition of film scenarios and victims onto the performances of the story in courts of law.

But just as the abstract "reasonable person" does not suitably define the social values protected by the criminal prohibition of stalking, neither does *Fatal Attraction*'s Dan. Film characters are created for a variety of different reasons; social justice and the creation of a socially desirable definition of protected values are not necessarily among them. In the hypothetical case described above, the defendant's "reasonableness" would be measured against Dan's character; Dan's cinematic response would also determine whether the behavior in question constituted legal stalking. Furthermore, film characters carry with them heavy, uncontrollable, baggage. In Dan's case, he is joined in the jury room by both Alex, the Lilit "bitch," and his perfect wife. If, in a given court case, the stalking woman does not resemble Alex, she may be unjustly acquitted for not fitting the stereotype. If she does resemble Alex—for example, if she is an assertive single career woman—this may influence jurors and judges, who may be more likely to find her guilty. It may also influence her public stigmatization, regardless of the legal outcome.

But Alex and the perfect wife are not the only uncontrollable ghosts accompanying Michael Douglas's Dan. A moviegoer may have seen Douglas in any number of his other popular films. In the 1992 *Basic Instinct*, he was a policeman stalked by a group of murderous blonde femmes fatales. In *Falling Down* (1994), he stalked his estranged wife and turned into a raging serial killer. That same year, in the scandalous *Disclosure*, he was victimized and sexually harassed by his boss (and previous girlfriend), who then took her revenge on him by filing a false sexual harassment complaint against him. Which of these images accompanies Michael Douglas's Dan into the jury room? How many of the fatal, hysterical, treacherous women are evoked in the courtroom by his "presence"? And how will they work for or against the defendant and the victim?

Determining the response of the "reasonable person" is even more difficult when the victim of a real stalking case is a woman: who should the jury envision as the reasonable person? *Fatal Attraction*'s Dan? Is he a proper model for the neutral, genderless legal standard? Or should jury members and judges think of a fictional female film character? Joseph Ruben's *Sleeping with the Enemy* (1990) comes to mind, reinforcing the association of stalking with spouse abuse. (Here a battered woman, played by Julia Roberts, breaks away from her violent, jealous husband, only to be stalked and terrorized by him wherever she goes. She is not free until she finally kills him in self-defense.) But if the victim does not resemble the perfect Julia Roberts character, or one of the other virtuous "final girls" of the stalker-film genre, juries and judges may have difficulty identifying her as a reasonable person in the context of a stalking story. (Accordingly, if the defendant does not resemble *Sleeping with the Enemy*'s crazed, abusive spouse, or any of the other stalking spouses that appear in film, literature or the media, juries and judges may choose not to convict, and vice versa).[21]

In stalking films, as in many others, women are still either fair or dark: the fair ones are unjustly victimized by monsters, while the dark ones do the victimizing, and/or are justly subjected to it. In her powerful *Virgin or Vamp: How the Press Cover Sex Crimes*, Helen Benedict details how press coverage of rape cases reinforces the traditional binary stereotyping of women as well as men. Rape victims are portrayed either as whores who "asked for it" and "had it coming," or as angelic virgins. Correspondingly, their rapists are either reasonable men who were "led on," or are "bloodthirsty beasts." For decades, the women's movement has been warning that such stereotypes

---

21. As in Michael Douglas's case, Julia Roberts's screen persona may have unexpected influences. Many "reasonable people" may associate her with the prostitute she played in *Pretty Woman*. It is hard to predict how that would influence jurors' views of stalking victims.

obstruct justice by leading police, judges and juries (1) to distrust—or even blame—rape victims who do not fit the virgin model; (2) to find defendants guilty more easily if they resemble the raging-beast image and if their victim resembles the virgin; and (3) to acquit defendants who seem "decent," especially when their victims are not the virgin types. Facilitated by the stalking law's "reasonable person" standard, such stereotypes find their way into jury rooms, the minds of judges, and court decisions. And these images, of course, find their way back to the media and to the screen, closing the vicious cycle.

Scholarly Legal Discourse

Buying into the Moral Panic

The antistalking legislative domino effect was soon followed by a complementary snowball effect in academic legal writing: since 1992 (and especially in the years 1992–96) dozens of law review articles have analyzed stalking laws (particularly California's).[22] I mentioned earlier that every one of these law review articles has cited Robert Bardo and the tragic murder of Rebecca Schaeffer as the primary motivation for the antistalking legislation. Similarly, many have offered ample data regarding stalking, stressing that the social phenomenon is severe and widespread. A common claim in these articles is that "in recent days, stalking has become a tremendous problem plaguing American society" (Faulkner and Hsiao 1993, 1). Frequently, such statements are supported by data such as the following:

> [T]he statistics are alarming. According to one major psychiatric study, there are an estimated 200,000 people in this country who are presently stalking someone. The Senate Judiciary Committee has further determined that twenty percent of all women will be victims of a stalker at some point in their lifetimes. (Montesino 1993, 546)

This alarming data may reassure the readers that the fear of stalking is not a moral panic, but a response to a very real social problem. Unfortunately, none of this data is sufficiently based on fact. Montesino refers to a "major psychiatric study" as the source for the number of stalkers in the United States. Montesino cites a CNN television broadcast and a *Washington Post* article, neither of which is quoted as indicating what the study in ques-

---

22. In 1997 and 1998 the interest in the topic seems to have relaxed. See the list of articles in note 11 above. Perez actually comments, "when I began researching the topic of stalking in early 1992, . . . I expected to find three or four magazine articles . . . I never expected the explosion of new law and numerous articles dealing with the problem of stalking" (1993, 264).

tion was. Richard Lingg's personal communication with Dr. Park Dietz (documented in Lingg's law review article) sheds light on this mystery:

> Dr. Dietz explained that the number of stalkers will vary widely according to the definition applied. Dr. Dietz stated that this estimate of 200,000 was based on a definition of stalking as an "unwanted pursuit of a person to whom one is not related. . . , extending over a period of time greater than six months, but not necessarily involving an approach and not necessarily involving malicious intent." (Lingg 1993, 350 n. 19)

Dietz's definition of stalking has nothing in common with the legal definition enacted by many antistalking laws and discussed in law review articles. It is far wider in that it does not demand a credible threat, and far narrower in that it refers only to stalkers who are unrelated to their victims and whose stalking continues for more than six months. Clearly, data referring to such stalking behavior is irrelevant to the discussion of legally prohibited stalking. Furthermore, it is not clear on what Dietz's estimate relies. In 1991, Dietz et al. published two articles, "Threatening and Otherwise Inappropriate Letters to Hollywood Celebrities," and "Threatening and Otherwise Inappropriate Letters to Members of the United States Congress" (Dietz et al. 1991a, 1991b). Neither contains any reference to two hundred thousand stalkers. If that figure was based in any way on either of these studies, then the estimate of two hundred thousand stalkers refers to a single analysis of letters written to Hollywood celebrities and to Washington politicians.

The next "fact" stated in Montesino's article is that "the Senate Judiciary Committee has further determined that twenty percent of all women will be victims of a stalker at some point in their lifetimes." A note mentions National Public Radio's broadcast of *All Things Considered* on 29 September 1992. However, a States News Service report from that same date, written by Louise Palmer and covering Senator Cohen's initiative to create a model antistalking state law, states, "Stalking is a crime that is insidious, frightening and on the rise, Cohen said, noting that 5 percent of all women will be victims of stalking at some time in their lives." Five percent, and not 20; one of every twenty women. Palmer's article does not mention whether Senator Cohen revealed the source of his estimate. Dietz may be the origin of this figure as well. According to a report by Maria Puente in *USA Today*,

> Park Dietz, a clinical psychiatrist who conducted the one major study of stalking and who is writing a book about it, estimates there are about 200,000 people in the country who are stalking someone: a movie star or the girl next door, an important person or an ordinary one. "About 5% of women in the general population will be harassed, the victim of unwanted pursuit, at some time in their lives," says Dietz. ("Legislators Tackling the Terror of Stalking," 21 July 1992)

Once again, the 5 percent estimate may refer to Dr. Dietz's own research, which dealt with a very narrow, specific type of fan stalking, and it is unclear how that estimate was arrived at.

Law review articles also supply alarming information regarding stalkers and their victims:

It is also estimated that 90 percent of all stalkers suffer from at least one kind of mental disorder, which can include different forms of obsession and delusion. (Montesino 1993, 546)

Forensic psychiatrists have examined profiles of stalkers, and at least one has identified that 9.5% of stalkers studied are obsessed with erotomania (i.e., the stalker "falsely believes that the target, usually someone famous or rich, is in love with the stalker"); 43% are love obsessed (i.e., the stalker "is a stranger to the target but is obsessed and mounts a campaign of harassment to make the target aware of the stalker's existence"); and 47% are suffering from simple obsession (i.e., the stalker, "usually male, knows the target as an ex-spouse, ex-lover or former boss, and begins a campaign of harassment"). (552)[23]

The estimate that "90% of all stalkers suffer from at least one kind of mental disorder" is attributed to Palmer's article of 29 September 1992. Palmer reports that this estimate was made by Senator Cohen before the Judicial Committee. She does not report whether the senator mentioned the source of his information. One likely source the senator may have relied on is Maria Puente's *USA Today* article (21 July 1992), which has been quoted frequently in discussions of stalking. Puente's article includes the following information: "Research on celebrity-stalking, the only kind studied in depth, suggests that more than 90% of stalkers suffer from mental disorders." If Puente refers here to the researches conducted by Dietz et al., then the figure of 90 percent is, once again, related to a population of letter-writers to Hollywood stars, and the psychiatric analysis is based mostly on the letters themselves. This hypothesis is supported by a much earlier *Los Angeles Times* article (Scott Hays, 17 October 1990), according to which "Dietz and his colleagues made broad psychiatric diagnoses based on their analysis of the letters. They found that 95% of the writers were mentally ill."

In an ABC News broadcast, January 10, 1992, Dietz himself said the following:

None of the people who engage in stalking behavior are normal individuals. There's something wrong with each of them. Most of them are after the goal of some union with the person that they stalk, but if they

23. For similar analysis of stalkers see Diacovo 1995, 614; Sloane 1994, 385; Goode 1995, 30; Perez 1993, 273; Tucker 1993, 613; Lingg 1993, 350–51.

can't have magical and perfect union, second best is this tormented relationship because it's better than no relationship at all. (Available on Lexis)

When speaking of "stalkers" Dietz seems to be referring to erotomaniacs, including borderline erotomaniacs. He must be referring to the letter-writing fans whom he researched. Once again, the very limited perspective of one research study focusing on Bardo-type behavior became the "scientific" basis for wide generalizations regarding all stalkers.

The report that "9.5% of stalkers studied are obsessed with erotomania . . . 43% are love obsessed . . . 47% are suffering from simple obsession" is not Dietz's. It seems to misleadingly refer to Zona, Sharma, and Lane's research, conducted in Los Angeles and published in 1993. The research's purpose was "to analyze existing data from the case files of the Threat Management Unit (UTM) of the Los Angeles Police Department (LAPD) to compare erotomaniacs to nonerotomaniacs in this group, assessing differences and similarities between the groups" (Zona, Sharma, and Lane 1993, 895). The majority of the cases studied "were referred by those within the entertainment industry, the mental health community"; *"none of the cases involved domestic violence situations"* (896; emphasis added). Of the seventy-four people sampled, seven (9.5 percent) were defined as erotomanic, thirty-two (43.2 percent) were found to be love obsessive, and thirty-five (47.3 percent) were simple obsessive.[24] An interesting conclusion was that 43 percent of erotomaniacs (three out of seven) engaged in stalking, compared with only 21 percent of love obsessionals and 28 percent of the simple obsessionals (900). Simple obsessionals were found to be potentially most violent. As for the subjects' mental illnesses, Zona, Sharma, and Lane reported that

> using the DSM-III-R manual, all erotomaniacs, by definition, have a major mental illness, such as delusional disorder. Similarly, 12/32, or 37% of all subjects in the love obsessional group, and 40%, 14/35, of the simple obsessional group had either specific mention or clear evidence of a major mental illness. (898)

Clearly, Zona, Sharma, and Lane's research had nothing to do with what antistalking legislation defined as stalking. It surveyed a very small and specific group of erotomaniacs and obsessionals, who were referred by the Threat Management Unit of the Los Angeles Police Department. Only a

24. The results showed that most erotomaniacs (86 percent) were women (and 71 percent of their victims were men), and that most love obsessionals (88 percent) were men targeting women (83 percent). Simple obsessionals were 57 percent men (targets being 71 percent women). Only 15 percent of the erotomaniacs engaged in face-to-face contact, compared with 12 percent of love obsessionals and 22 percent of simple obsessionals (Zona, Palarea, and Lane 1993, 898–900).

small group of these people engaged in any stalking at all. Moreover, only twenty-six of the sixty-seven obsessionals sampled "had either specific mention or clear evidence of a major mental illness." But the media and the legal discourse knew better. In her influential *USA Today* article of 21 July 1992, Maria Puente quoted Michael Zona as saying that 9.5 percent of all *stalkers* were erotomaniacs, that 43 percent of *stalkers* were love obsessionals, and that 47 percent of *stalkers* were simple obsessionals. It seems to be principally from this source (available on Lexis) that this data entered the law review articles. Once introduced into the legal discourse, these "psychiatric findings" regarding stalkers were soon synthesized with other bits of media-distorted, irrelevant, psychiatric estimates.

Responding to the moral panic regarding Travis-Bardo–*Fatal Attraction*, legislatures around the country enacted antistalking laws, prohibiting the behavior they defined as stalking. Their definitions, though confused and inaccurate, nevertheless seemed to be neutral and general. But scholarly legal writings connected these broad legal definitions of stalking with psychiatric profiles of erotomaniacs and obsessionals. Distorting a tiny body of psychiatric data, some of these analyses established that *(a)* legal stalking was the activity conducted by Travis-Bardo–*Fatal Attraction* types, *(b)* this stalking was a psychiatric behavior, and *(c)* it was a dangerous "plague" threatening the nation. In other words, academic legal discourse made sure the antistalking legislation played into the moral panic that had instigated it. The legal profession, together with the psychiatric community, and greatly aided by the popular media, determined that people who engaged in stalking belonged to the category of the erotomanic serial killers, that they were filling the streets of America, and that the antistalking legislation was designed to get them. It was almost inevitable that some legal scholarship would demand that the law be used to classify stalkers into exact, clinical categories and that it enforce psychiatric treatment to cure the stalkers' illnesses.

The "Learned" Diagnosis

"From Imprudence to Crime: Anti-stalking Laws," by Kathleen McAnaney, Laura A. Curliss, and Elizabeth Abeyta-Price, is a remarkably expansive article that was published in 1993 and has been extensively quoted since. It may be the most influential law review article on the subject to this day. The article's second chapter is entitled " 'Stalker': Personality Profiles, Correlates of Violence, Prospects for Treatment, and the Impact of Stalking on the Victim." It was written by C. E. Abeyta-Price, who was at the time "a doctoral student in the joint Developmental and Counseling Psychology program at the University of Notre Dame," and it contains the most cohesive and thorough discussion of a stalker's psychology. Abeyta-Price establishes four psychological categories of stalkers: delusional erotomaniacs, borderline erotomaniacs, former-intimate stalkers, and sociopathic stalkers.[25] Her second category relies, uncritically, on Meloy's definition of borderline erotomania (McAnaney, Curliss, and Abeyta-Price 1993, 835). There is no mention of the fact that within the psychiatric community there is fundamental, substantive criticism of Meloy's paradoxical invention. Regarding "former-intimate stalkers," Abeyta-Price claims that in many cases they "have a prior history of abusive relationships" and that "the Former Intimate stalker exhibits several of the same personality characteristics and defense mechanisms that domestically violent individuals exhibit" (856), thus associating this type of stalker with the battering, abusive husband. Analyzing abusive male spouses, she quotes a study finding that they are likely to manifest six typical features: "low self esteem, low income levels, low occupational status, more frequent abuse of alcohol, a history of physical abuse victimization as a child, and the witnessing of parental violence as a child" (841). This conveniently associates them with her fourth category, which is labeled "sociopathic stalker," that is, what I have been referring to as the serial-killing stalker.

> Two groups of criminals that are notably absent from the "stalking" literature are serial murderers and serial rapists, an absence that is all the more remarkable given that the behavioral activities proscribed by most stalking laws are familiar characteristics of such individuals. (841)

She thus constitutes these stalkers as the fourth category.

Abeyta-Price suggests that legally defined stalking is conducted by persons who are all clinically determinable: they are either serial-killer characters, erotomaniacs, borderline erotomaniacs, or former-intimate stalkers, that is, abusive husbands, who often feature psychological symptoms similar to those attributed to serial killers. Moreover, she explicitly suggests that all four categories of stalkers are related. She states, "The relationship between the various types of stalker is unclear" (843), but her discussion of Ted Bundy offers a pretty clear theory. According to her narration of Bundy's exploits (based on Faith Leibman's telling of his story), Bundy started his serial raping and murdering when the woman he loved terminated their relationship. Abeyta-Price notes, "This pattern of behavior is similar to those of Former Intimate stalkers, except that his victim was not the former intimate herself" (843). The implication quite clearly is that at least some serial-killing stalkers are former intimate stalkers who displace their violence, replacing their ex-lover with a series of strangers: "Ted Bundy's killings are an excellent example of the outcome of a Sociopathic stalker's displacement" (848). At the same time, referring to Leibman's 1989

---

25. In another extensive article published that same year, Faulkner and Hsiao present and seem to accept this approach (1993, 4–5).

analysis of serial killers, she concludes that "several of the features that Leibman identifies in serial murderers can be found in the life histories of many borderline erotomaniacs and Former Intimate stalkers" (843). Former intimate stalkers, serial-killing stalkers, and erotomanic/borderline erotomanic stalkers, therefore, share the same psychological/psychiatric makeup; the differences in their specific types of stalking and in their specific types of stalking profiles are mostly circumstantial. In other words, a person performing what the law defines as stalking is a stalker of one or more of these types.

In 1993, when this study was published, there was no data to support the determination that legally defined stalking is actually performed by these four types or by them alone, or, for that matter, that these types even existed.[26] Moreover, defining the criminal offense of stalking as the conduct of certain *types* of people establishes psychiatric soundness as the social value protected by the criminal law of stalking. Once an offense is determined by its doers rather than by its effect on a social value, law becomes psychiatry, labeling people for what they are rather than for what they did. But unlike psychiatry, the law should be designed to evaluate people's actions and not their personalities. Like psychiatry, the law is a judgmental discipline; but whereas the psychiatric concern is "whose constitution manifests mental illness," the legal one should rightly be "whose behavior offended a social value defined and protected by the law." The "psychologization" of law not only exposes it to the uncertainties of that social science; it also undermines the law's normative agenda.

The described professional theory is as learned an explanation of contemporary America's stalking moral panic as one could hope for (or dread). It is as impressive, useful, and unfounded as the learned explanation of sorceresses as Satan-worshipping witches. It harnesses the law to the dangerous carriage of moral panic. In medieval Europe, common people complained that neighboring women cast evil spells on them. The contemporary learned approach, which was soon adopted by the courts, translated these stories into the professional stories of Satan worship and orgiastic sabbats. In 1641, when Massachusetts enacted its antiwitchcraft legislation, it did not prohibit the casting of evil spells, or interference with a neighbor's safety and good health. The state of Massachusetts legislated that "if any man or woman be a witch they shall be put to death." Our contemporary learned approach replaces actual complaints of stalking with types and categories of erotomaniacs and sociopathic serial killers. The next logical step will therefore be to have antistalking laws prescribe that "if any man or woman be an erotomaniac and/or a sociopathic serial killer they shall receive psychiatric treatment."

Abeyta-Price does not stop at defining psychological categories of stalk-

26. For discussion of the first significant data on stalking (U.S. Department of Justice 1998), see chapter 9.

ers; she goes on to suggest legal practices that would enforce the implications of applying these psychological profiles:

> A person arrested for stalking may fit one of the stalking profiles described above. Before trial, a comprehensive neurological, psychiatric, medical, and psychological evaluation should be conducted by specialists in these fields. The goal of such an evaluation is fourfold: to determine the appropriate stalker "classification," to establish the stalker's motives, to determine his risk for violent behavior, and to decide the appropriate clinical treatment, sentence, or both. (McAnaney, Curliss, and Abeyta-Price 1993, 860–61)

A suggestion made by Nannette Diacovo, also in a law review article, resembles Abeyta-Price's line of thought in important respects:

> Once convicted, it should be mandatory that the stalker undergo a mental evaluation and be placed within one of the three categories of obsessive behavior. Once the stalker is categorized, it should then be mandatory that the stalker be placed in a treatment program specifically designed to treat the stalker's mental infirmities. Although there may be no cure for stalking behavior, providing the stalker with the most effective mental health treatment available is a step in the right direction. (1995, 416–17)

Diacovo differs from Abeyta-Price in suggesting that the evaluation be performed *after* the stalker's conviction. In her version, the psychiatric evaluation will not influence the determination of whether the accused committed stalking, but rather influence the mandatory treatment to which he will be subjected. Another difference is that Diacovo would have the stalker placed in one of a different set of categories from those suggested by Abeyta-Price. Diacovo's categories include erotomanic stalker, love obsessional stalker, and simple stalker. These categories seem as scientifically sound as Abeyta-Price's.

In 1993, when McAnaney, Curliss, and Abeyta-Price's article was published, California's antistalking statute had already been amended (in 1992) to determine that "if probation is granted, . . . it shall be a condition of probation that the person participate in counseling, as designed by the court."[27] In 1994, the State of California amended its antistalking law once again, ordering the court, in every case, to

> consider whether the defendant would benefit from treatment. . . . If it is determined to be appropriate, the court shall recommend that the

---

27. Upon a showing of good cause, the court may find that the counseling requirement shall not be imposed. See California Penal Code #646.9(h) (West Supp. 1993).

Department of Correction make a certification. . . . Upon the certification, the defendant shall be evaluated and transferred to the appropriate hospital for treatment.[28]

In a 1998 law review article, Jennifer L. Bradfield, explicitly relying on all the data and analysis mentioned above, demands further amendments:

California's anti-stalking statute merely requires the sentencing court to consider whether a convicted stalker would benefit from mental health treatment. Because mental health treatment during incarceration is essential to maximize the victim's safety upon her stalker's release from prison, such treatment should not be left up to the discretion of the court. Rather, all anti-stalking statutes should have provisions mandating mental health evaluation and treatment for convicted stalkers. Although to date there are no studies on the effectiveness of mental health treatment for stalkers, providing stalkers with such treatment might result in the long-term protection of their victims. (1998, 259)

It is hard to predict how such legislative trends may develop. It is hard to anticipate what events may cause enough anxiety and rage to fuel the gradually developing moral panic, to influence the enforcement of the anti-stalking legislation, and to effect judiciary policy. It is hard to determine in advance what particular unpopular groups of citizens may be identified as stalkers and subjected to psychiatric scrutiny: single businesswomen, serial killers' mothers, or reporters and photographers. Future history books will be the judges of that.

Popular Culture Integrates Legal Innovations

The media and the film industry were quick to respond to the new legal formulation of stalking. In the first years following the new legislation, news stories covering stalking were commonplace, and Hollywood released one stalking film after another, each featuring an erotomanic serial killer. *Pacific Heights* (1990), *The Bodyguard* (1992), *Unlawful Entry* (1992), and, especially, *Copycat* (1996) are only a few of the more celebrated of these films. Another, which provides a good example of how quickly Hollywood internalized the new conceptualization of the subject, is the release from Republic Pictures in 1994, *Stalked*, which claims to portray "one man's obsession; every woman's nightmare." The videotape's cover gives the following summary:

28. California Penal Code #646.9(j) (West Supp. 1994). "Prior to the new amendments, the Director of Corrections decided whether a convicted stalker was suitable for mental health rehabilitation. This did not always prove to be effective" (Diacovo 1995, 414).

When a stranger saves her young son from a tragic accident, Brooke Daniels is beside herself with gratitude. She invites the handsome, soft-spoken Daryl to dinner, and before long strikes up a friendship with him. But his warm smiles hide a desperate desire . . . and a much darker nature. He begins following Brooke, monitoring her phone calls, reading her mail and planning their future together. By the time she realizes his intentions, it's too late . . . his desire has become an obsession. Brooke is suddenly thrown into a nightmare world of deception, torment and inescapable fear. From now on, the only thing harder than returning his love . . . will be surviving.

Stalked features familiar motifs: Daryl is a shy Norman Bates, dominated by a powerful mother; clear evocations of the alarming soundtrack of *Psycho*'s shower scene make sure the analogy is not lost on forgetful viewers. Like Travis, he keeps a diary (recording it as he drives). Like Ted Bundy (and the Hyena in *Love Kills*) he collects underwear from his love object. But Daryl is also a product of contemporary trends. His erotomania (or is it borderline erotomania?) is explicit: it sets in all at once and is accompanied by a previous record of other psychiatric disorders. Daryl manufactures dangerous situations from which he saves his beloved; he views her other male friend as an opponent and casts him as a danger from which he must save her; he gets rid of whoever he perceives to stand between himself and his love object; he constantly misinterprets her rejecting signals, and experiences extreme, contradictory emotions. And, of course, his erotomania goes hand in hand with his serial-killer personality, which leads to a series of murders. Daryl's first victim is none other than his own guilty Mother; his psychiatrist is his fourth and last victim. The target of his stalking, Brooke, is a perfect Mary character: she is both devoted mother and completely asexual.

Stalked is a direct response to the highly publicized antistalking legislation and the professional literature surrounding it. It portrays stalking as the behavior of a *stalker*, that is, a mentally ill individual, an erotomanic serial-killer character. This message is already effectively conveyed in the film's opening scene. While childhood photos of Daryl (actor Jay Underwood) cover the screen, a grave, semidocumentary voiceover declares:

It's difficult to pinpoint at what age it begins; when the seeds of obsession are planted. But one day, from behind the smiles of an innocent young boy, the dark world of delusion begins to emerge. Suddenly, one day, for no apparent reason, the simple attraction to a woman becomes compulsive, and rapidly turns into a relentless pursuit. The young man has become a stalker.

The male stalker has become an outlawed erotomanic serial killer, and he is out there, lurking behind every bush in every neighborhood.

CHAPTER 9

Law and Culture: An Informed Dynamic

In the previous chapter, I demonstrated that the legal treatment of stalking derived from the sociocultural construction of the notion. The law responded to an ensuing stalking moral panic, fueled by cultural images and conceptions. The hasty, noncritical legal response produced inadequately drafted laws that accommodated the developing moral panic, facilitated it, enhanced it, and supplied it with "professional," theoretical grounds. In this chapter, I submit an alternative model, one that provides a more critical legal response to cultural and social trends. Rather than play into the hands of a moral panic, the legal response can, and should, be based on a critical analysis of both cultural imagery and the ensuing moral panic. Applying a critical perspective, positive law can address the real social problem while combating the panic surrounding it.

In modern legal thought, positive law determines norms relating to social behavior of individuals that affects the well-being of other members of society and common social values. Unlike literature, psychology, or sociology, positive law and criminal law, in particular, declare and constitute specific social norms, which are enforced through coercive, authoritative means. Law need not, and should not, speculatively explore human emotions, the psychological and psychiatric makeups of individuals, or the sometimes paradoxical logic of human behavior in emotional situations. It should not, uncritically, play into the hands of moral panics. In its treatment of a particular issue, positive law must define a social phenomenon, establish whether it involves any social values worthy of legal protection or regulation, and, if so, determine the relevant values and the most effective ways of accommodating them. Positive law must define social behaviors that have a clear, direct bearing on specified social values and that can, and should, be legally regulated.

As with any other case, authorities in charge of positive law must commence by examining the concrete, defined social phenomenon that is publicly identified as stalking and determine whether it constitutes a problem (i.e., whether it offends social values to the extent that necessitates and justifies authoritative, regulating intervention). The legislature must review accurate, reliable data and hear the public narrate its experience and perception of the issue. I suggest that, at this stage, a critical review of stalking stories, as they have been told by the relevant culture, can be enlightening and helpful in understanding the subtleties of the effects stalking may have on targeted victims; it may shed light on the damage, anxiety, and anguish they may suffer. It may elucidate the common, public understanding of the perpetrators' motivations, as well as the stereotypes and misconceptions that have become inseparable from the public view of the subject at large. This extended view might enable a legislature to determine whether social values are at stake, whether they must be regulated by legal intervention, and, if so, what would be the most effective and desirable type of legal intervention.

Data on Stalking

In April 1998 the National Institute of Justice published the first research supplying fundamental, reliable data regarding the social phenomenon that has, in recent years, been labeled stalking (U.S. Department of Justice 1998).[1] The research relied solely on a nationally representative telephone survey of eight thousand U.S. women and eight thousand U.S. men. It established that 8 percent of women and 2 percent of men in the United States have been stalked at some time in their life; accordingly, an estimate of 1,006,970 women and 370,990 men (1,377,960 people) are stalked annually; based on this estimate, 8.2 million women and 2 million men have been stalked at some time in their lives (U.S. Department of Justice 1998, exhibit 1).

It must be noted, and emphasized up front, that the survey defines stalking as "a course of conduct directed at a specific person that involves repeated physical or visual proximity, nonconsensual communication, or verbal, written or implied threats." This definition of stalking is significantly broader than the legal definitions used in U.S. antistalking laws. To mention only the most eminent differences, the NIJ's definition does not require a "credible threat," the stalker's malicious intent to induce serious fear, the victim's substantial fear, or that the "reasonable person" would experience such fear if in the victim's place. Actually, only less than 45 percent of the surveyed men and women who defined themselves as victims of stalking reported any kind of overt threat (U.S. Department of Justice 1998, exhibit 12), which means that on that score alone 55 percent of them would very likely not be defined by most laws as victims of "legal stalking."[2] Of the 1,377,960 estimated annual victims of stalking, only 758,000 would, perhaps, be implicitly threatened, whether "credibly" or otherwise. It is very hard to predict how many of their stalkers would intend to cause great fear and how many would experience the legally required reasonable fear. Furthermore, only 12 percent of the stalkers referred to by the surveyed population were

1. Partial findings from the research were first published in U. S. Department of Justice 1997.

2. Many laws settle for "implied" threats, but demand they be "credible." It is very difficult, if not impossible, to guess how many of the threats reported by the surveyed women and men would have been legally defined as "credible."

prosecuted, and of these, only 54 percent were convicted. In other words, it could be argued that, among those respondents who defined themselves as victims of stalking, the legal authorities only established that 6 percent were actually victims of "legal stalking." 6 percent of the estimated annual 1,377,960 is less than 83,000. Simply put, the legal definition and the survey's definition of stalking are different; this greatly confuses the issue.[3]

But whether a 1.4 million U.S. citizens or only 83,000 are annually stalked, the NIJ is correct in determining that, judging by the public's perception, "it is imperative that stalking be treated as a legitimate criminal justice problem and public health concern" (U.S. Department of Justice 1998, 14). Moreover, if we accept the researchers' plausible definition of stalking, many of their findings are fundamentally significant. Most notably, of the sixteen thousand men and women surveyed, 78 percent of stalking victims were women. At the same time, 87 percent of (identified) stalkers were men.[4]

30 percent of male victims were stalked by intimate partners, gay men being more likely to suffer from this type of stalking (U.S. Department of Justice 1998, 6). Men tend to be stalked by strangers and acquaintances, 90 percent of whom are men (6). On the other hand, 38 percent of the women victims were stalked by current or former spouses, 10 percent by current or former cohabiting partners, and 14 percent by current or former dates. Overall, 59 percent of women victims were stalked by some type of intimate partner (exhibit 7). 43 percent of these women were stalked after the relationship ended, 36 percent were stalked both before and after the relationship's termination, and 23 percent were stalked before the breakup. Eighty-one percent of women who were stalked by an intimate partner were also physically assaulted by him, and 31 percent were sexually assaulted by him; stalking intimate partners are four times as likely to physically assault women and six times as likely to sexually assault them as compared with nonstalking partners.

> The survey also provides compelling evidence of the link between stalking and controlling and emotionally abusive behavior. . . . The survey found that ex-husbands who stalked (either before or after the relationship ended) were significantly more likely than ex-husbands who did not stalk to engage in abusive and controlling behavior of their wife. (U.S. Department of Justice 1998, 8)

3. For a similar reason, the research's conclusion that there are five times as many U.S. women stalked than previously estimated by Dietz is misleading. Dietz's definition of stalking seems to have been totally different, and therefore any comparison is irrelevant.

4. Ninety-four percent of women victims (who identified their stalkers) were stalked by men; 60 percent of male victims (who identified their stalkers) were stalked by men.

Judging by their victims' telephone replies to the surveyors, stalking male spouses are often jealous or possessive, make their female spouses feel inadequate, shout and swear at them, and frighten them (9).[5]

Eighty-two percent of women victims (and 72 percent of men victims) were followed and spied on; 61 percent (and 42 for men) received unwanted phone calls; 33 percent (27 for men) received unwanted letters and items; 29 percent (30 for men) had their property vandalized; 9 percent (6 for men) had their pets killed or threatened.

When asked for their views of their stalkers' motives, 21 percent said their stalkers wanted to control them; 20 percent said they wanted to keep them in relationships; 16 percent said their stalkers wanted to scare them; 12 percent were not sure; 5 percent said stalkers liked the attention; and 1 percent said stalkers wanted to catch them doing something. Significantly, *only 7 percent estimated that their stalkers stalked them because they were either mentally ill or because they were abusing drugs or alcohol.* "The survey results dispel the myth that most stalkers are psychotic or delusional" (U.S. Department of Justice 1998, 8). This last statement is, of course, of limited value, as the survey can only offer the nonprofessional speculations of self-proclaimed victims regarding their stalkers' mental health. Nevertheless, the survey clearly does not, in any way, support the myth that stalkers are all serial-killer types and/or erotomaniacs.

Analysis

According to this initial research on stalking, it seems that the social phenomenon of stalking that is troubling contemporary U.S. society is, above all, an abusive behavior committed by men on women. This conduct, like rape, like domestic violence, like sexual harassment, is, to a large degree, a crime against women. In this respect, it is a form of patriarchal oppression, maintaining women's subjugation to men through violence, aggression, control, and surveillance and thus perpetuating discrimination against them and preventing social equality. Much like rape, domestic violence, and sexual harassment, stalking is often performed by men who know their women victims and wish to control, frighten, terrorize, and demean them. Judging by the surveyed women's responses, as well as by women's evidence before legislative committees,[6] stalking often reduces women, in their own minds, to entrapped, helpless animals. It undermines their autonomy, independence, self-determination, privacy, and dignity. It prevents and precludes

5. The survey clearly supports approaches that have been associating stalking with domestic violence and abuse. For a compelling analysis of stalking as a separation assault and the "fourth phase" in the cycle of domestic violence, see Bernstein 1993.

6. For several examples of such testimonies see chapter 1.

their self-fulfillment and frustrates the potential improvement of their personal and collective social standing.

Each type of crime against women oppresses them and discriminates against them in a particular fashion. So, for example, sexual harassment in the workplace makes it difficult for women to perceive themselves as professional persons. It undermines their self-confidence, identifies them as sexual objects, humiliates them, and discourages them from pursuing prestigious, "manly" jobs in which they are unwelcomed by some men (MacKinnon 1979, 1987).[7] A close reading of our culture's stories of stalking sheds light on stalking as a patriarchal social mechanism and on the specific manner in which male stalking is likely to oppress victimized women and women at large, perpetuating women's social inferiority. In previous chapters, presenting fictional stories of male stalking, I suggested that it often operates as a patriarchal disciplinary mechanism that differentiates "virtuous" from "fallen" women and subjugates them all to the male authority. In light of these narratives, it is not surprising that actual stalking should be performed by men as a means of dominating women. Specific elements of these stories illuminate the subtleties of this sociocultural phenomenon. They convey deep experiences shared by many victims of stalking, while simultaneously influencing victims', as well as society's, constructions and interpretations of stalking's damage and harm, and of the social value stalking endangers.

The cultural stalking narratives I surveyed suggest that male stalking of a woman objectifies her, posing her as "matter" for her stalker's subjecting, controlling gaze. It undermines her subjectivity, dehumanizing and humiliating her. It constitutes her as naked, vulnerable, helpless, and blind. These narratives reveal that stalking traps the victim in a sense of cyclic, repetitive time; it brings the past into her present, preventing her from moving into a self-determined future. The unwelcome entrapment may have a paralyzing effect, inducing despair and a sense of defeat. Depriving a woman victim of her sense of security, in both her time and her space, stalking leaves her uprooted and disoriented. Stalking stories, especially those using vampire terminology and imagery, describe the female victim as gradually losing her blood and life to her stalker. This cultural metaphor may capture the experience of real victims, as well as induce them to feel that stalking weakens them, draining their vitality. These narratives also show, especially through the vampire metaphor, that stalking is experienced as undermining the most fundamental categories of human experience, including those of life and death, existence and nonexistence. A victim of stalking may experience the loss of fundamental, reassuring convictions that are taken for granted by most people.

7. For an annotated bibliography on sexual harassment see Chamallas 1993. More recent publications (with detailed reference to literature) include Franke 1997; Bernstein 1997; and Schultz 1998.

Furthermore, male stalking is likely to be experienced by a woman as deadly, since it is culturally associated with the stalker's return from death and with living death. In this emotional respect it may reasonably be experienced as deeply threatening even if no threat is ever made. Additionally, male stalking carries traditional connotations of the stalked woman's guilty sexuality. A female victim of stalking is likely to be suspected, as well as to suspect herself, of being a "whore" (like Jack the Ripper's victims). She is also likely to be suspected, as well as to suspect herself, of "having asked for it," since a vampire (and, therefore, a stalker) is known to enter a home only if invited in. She may be humiliated by stalking's pornographic connotation in much of its narration. Manipulated by the romantic logic of stalking stories, a victim may feel that she and her stalker are eternally united in a supernatural bond and that her reluctance to submit to his terror is no less than betrayal. This perception may also induce a feeling that the stalking is inevitable and inescapable. The victim may feel that she shares in the responsibility for her own stalking (and maybe even of other women, similarly to Laura Mars). Influenced by the logic of Hollywood's "final girls," a woman subjected to stalking may feel that no social force can possibly save her and that she will survive only if she is pure enough to "do the right thing." (Only if she is "pure" will her action save herself and her community). As in many stalking stories, the stalker is apparent only to his victim, invisible to everyone else. Women may fear that if they discuss their experience, they will not be understood or believed.

Influenced by the image of Frankenstein's creature, a victim of stalking may feel guilty for having abandoned the tormented stalker and may feel responsible for generating the monster. In a book dedicated to his daughter Kristin, who was slain by her stalker, George Lardner summarizes a paper Kristin had once written about Shelley's creature. "'Just as Frankenstein hated the monster it brought to life, so society hates the monsters it creates' Kristin said" (1997, 72). After her death, Lardner reassures Kristin that her stalker's unhappy life was not her fault. "Kristin did not make the monster who killed her. She tried to help him," he implores—as if trying to convince the dead woman who, he suspects, might have felt responsible for "her monster." All these factors may deter a woman victim of stalking from reporting her plight to the authorities.[8]

Similarly, a close reading of stalking stories may also shed light on the experiences of male victims of stalking. Tales such as Shelley's *Frankenstein,*

8. Currently, only 54.6 percent of women who suffer from stalking report it to the police (only 47.7 percent of men report stalking to the police, but men seem to suffer from different types of stalking, and may have different reasons for not reporting). Victims of stalking who do not report their stalking explain that it is "not a police matter" (20 percent), that "police couldn't do anything" (17 percent), that they are "afraid of reprisal from stalker" (16 percent), that they "can handle it" themselves (12 percent), that the police would not believe them (7 percent), or that it is a "private, personal matter" (6 percent) (U.S. Department of Justice 1998, exhibit 16).

Hitchcock's *Strangers on a Train,* and both versions of *Cape Fear* illustrate the homosocial aspects of male-on-male stalking. They suggest a potentially strong identification between victim and perpetrator that causes deep confusion, fear, guilt, and shame. Stories of female stalking, from the ancient tale of Lilit to *Fatal Attraction*'s Alex, illustrate and construct men's longing for and fundamental anxiety about powerful women who can liberate them from their patriarchal roles but also rob them of the power and stability these roles provide.

Stalking stories may also provide explanations of what motivates actual stalkers. Tales of male stalking illustrate the male's need to control, his urge to spy, condemn, and punish, his desperate yearning for the victim and his desperate inability to let go. They portray male stalkers' perceptions of eternal, supernatural bonds with their victims, entwined with feelings of unjust abandonment and rejection by them. These confused, passionate emotions trigger the literary male stalker's grudge and vengeance. Stalking narratives manifest stalkers' total inability to view their victims as independent, separate individuals, or to respect their autonomy, privacy, and self-determination. These narratives suggest that stalkers may view themselves as victims, as weak and wronged, as evil, as avengers, saviors, romantic heroes, as fighting for their lives. These cultural portrayals of male stalkers may mirror and influence stalkers' self-perceptions, victims' perceptions of them, and general social attitudes.

A critical review of available data regarding actual stalking, read together with the stalking moral panic, may shed more light on the prevalent perception of stalkers. Judging by the data supplied by the *Stalking in America* survey (U.S. Department of Justice 1998), male stalkers seem to be ordinary men who are unable to internalize and accept women's full personhood and its implications for the men's own lives. Like men who rape, who commit domestic violence and sexual harassment, male stalkers seem to assert control over women who do not wish to participate in their traditional visions of femininity, masculinity, and the social order of things. They attempt to maintain oppression through coercive means. They rely on cultural images and perceptions regarding stalking to express frustration, anxiety, confusion, and weakness and to cause pain and damage to their female victims. Like rapists, abusive male spouses, and sexual harassers, most male stalkers are, therefore, probably not mentally ill.

An analysis of the present moral panic suggests one explanation of how these men were erroneously labeled erotomanic serial killers. As described in the previous chapters, the cultural image of the erotomanic serial killer developed as a mediating image that connected the ancient anxiety of stalking with contemporary discomfort in the face of disturbing social groups. It expresses a host of anxieties involving contemporary alienation, castration, and moral confusion, which these social elements seem to represent.

Through legislation and the legal literature, all stalkers were formally associated with the erotomanic serial-killer image. However, this Travis-Hinck-
ley-Bardo stalker at the heart of antistalking law has nothing to do with the
actual social phenomenon of stalking that, judging by *Stalking in America,*
seems to be disturbing many members of society.

In the previous chapter, I mentioned disadvantages of confusing actual
stalking with mythological imagery of stalkers. Some men resembling *Taxi
Driver*'s Travis may be wrongly accused and convicted of stalking, while
actual stalkers who do not resemble him may be wrongly acquitted. Some
stalkers may be justly convicted, but unjustly stigmatized as erotomanic serial killers. A further danger arises. If male stalking is committed by ordinary
men on women they attempt to dominate, then the moral panic focusing on
erotomanic serial killers diverts attention from the actual social problem.
The panic thus prevents public discussion of the real social phenomenon
and deflects serious attempts at developing effective solutions. If male stalking, like sexual harassment, is performed by ordinary men, then mental
diagnosis and treatment is not a relevant issue. Rather, male dominance,
oppression, and inequality are the issues to be addressed. Alienation and
castration anxieties need to be identified as such and treated critically, not
through mythological imagery.

Legislation

Based on the suggested analysis, I would propose that legislatures pause
and rethink the current legal treatment of stalking. I suggest that adequate
antistalking legislation must address both the data supplied by surveys such
as *Stalking in America* and insights derived from a critical, cultural analysis of
both stalking stories and the moral panic. Legal treatment of stalking must
accurately define the problematic social phenomenon and the relevant social
values. It should not be trapped in terminology that does not capture the
essence of stalking merely because it has been constitutionally approved in
other contexts. Antistalking laws must aim to define and prohibit stalking as
accurately as possible; courts will then be required, in each particular case,
to guarantee fundamental rights of both victim and defendant.

As this is not the place to offer a full legislative treatment of stalking, I
will merely sketch an outline of one possible approach. I suggest that an
antistalking law should begin by stating (in a preamble, perhaps) the social
significance of stalking, defining the prohibited behavior's social implications and declaring the legislation's protected values. The statute might state
that stalking is a crime of dominance and control, interfering with a person's
rights to dignity, liberty, personal security, self-determination, and privacy;
that since stalking is, to a large extent, a crime against women, it perpetuates

social discrimination against women, undermining their full social equality. Such a statute might include three components in its definition of the prohibited stalking.

1. *A specific intent.* This intent may be one to establish, reestablish, maintain, or reinforce a nonconsensual, personal relationship with the targeted person; or, with no lawful justification, to control the targeted person, or to punish him or her, or to prevent him or her from creating, pursuing, or continuing a relationship with another person, or to severely frighten or terrorize the targeted person, or to undermine her or his sense of personal security, or to severely harm him or her bodily or mentally.
2. *A course of conduct directed at the targeted person.* The course of conduct may involve repeated or continual unwelcome following, lying in wait, surveillance, trespassing, peeping, physical proximity, harassment, communication, vandalism, or threatening. It must be defined as excluding behaviors that are part of the stalker's legitimate lifestyle, or part of his or her professional and/or lawful practice.
3. *The stalker's actual or normative knowledge, that is, his or her awareness of the likely consequences of his or her behavior.* The law may require that the stalker knew, or should have known, that the ensuing course of conduct was sufficiently severe or pervasive to significantly alter the targeted person's conditions of life and to create for her or him a hostile, abusive or personally insecure environment.

Such a definition does not restrict stalking to cases where the stalker made a "credible threat" while intending to cause substantial fear. It does not subject the victim to judicial comparison with the "reasonable person." It further refrains from making the victim's actual emotional response, as well as its reasonableness, a central element of the crime. The unwarranted focus on the victim's response and its normative validity suggests legislative uncertainty regarding the objective, substantial social harm of stalking per se, inviting judicial scrutiny of both victims and the reliability of their emotional responses. (In most criminal offenses, such as theft, the victim's emotional response is irrelevant to the social and legal determination of the harm caused by the perpetrator's behavior.)[9]

The proposed statute's definition of stalking defines a course of con-

9. "[T]he inclusion of this element is both unnecessary and potentially dangerous to women who are victimized by men. First, it makes the woman and her perceptions part of the offense. This exposes victims to cross-examination on the nature of their fear and on its objective reasonableness. Experience with sexual assault has demonstrated that courts have great difficulty in both understanding and characterizing women's perceptions" Canadian Advisory Council on the Status of Women (Briefing Notes and Recommendations on Bill C-126, 26 May 1993, p. 4), in Way 1994, 396.

duct, specifies the stalker's intent, and requires that he or she knew or should have known that the stalking was sufficiently severe or pervasive as to significantly alter the targeted person's conditions of life and to make those conditions hostile or abusive. The prohibited course of conduct described includes many behavioral elements that appear in many anti-stalking laws, in stalking stories and, more importantly, in testimonies given by victims of stalking. The definition of the required criminal intent is derived mostly from victims' portrayal of their experiences; it is further supported by analysis of prevailing stalking narratives.

The requirement that the defendant know that his or her conduct creates a hostile environment for the victim is influenced by hostile environment sexual harassment law, as established by the U.S. Supreme Court. Sexual harassment is currently treated within U.S. law predominantly as a constitutional workplace issue. Stalking, on the other hand, is perceived as a criminal behavior. Nevertheless, the two share similar motivations and outcomes and offend similar social values. Scholarly legal arguments in the United States have already been made in support of prohibiting sexual harassment in every social context and of criminalizing at least some of its manifestations (see Browman 1993; Baker 1994). Other legal systems treat sexual harassment as a criminal behavior.[10] Comparison of the legal treatment of the two types of behavior is both logical and potentially fruitful and would stress the similar abusive, dominating, discriminatory aspects of both sexual harassment and stalking. This is why I suggest the usage, in this context, of definitions coined by the Supreme Court in the context of sexual harassment.[11] The formula "sufficiently severe or pervasive to alter conditions" was established by the Supreme Court in 1986[12] and has become widely familiar. Judges seem to have no difficulty applying it to the cases before them.[13] I believe it captures the essence of the harm enforced on victims of stalking, as well as on victims of sexual harassment.

The stalker's knowledge that his conduct is severe or pervasive enough to significantly alter the victim's life and to create for her a hostile or abusive environment may be conveyed by the victim herself, or by any third party. It is suggested that the law also be satisfied with the stalker's normative obligation to have known the consequences of his behavior even when not specifically given notice. Thus if courts should choose to use the "reasonable person" standard to determine whether a defendant "should have known"

10. Israel's new Law for the Prevention of Sexual Harassment, 1998, is the most prominent example. See Kamir, forthcoming.

11. The term *unwelcome*, which I propose as part of the definition of the prohibited course of conduct, is also used in the context of sexual harassment.

12. See *Meritor Savings Bank v. Vinson*, 477 U.S. 57 (1986).

13. My definition is a variation on the original wording, which requires that both victim and the "reasonable person" actually endure the described harm, thus emphasizing the victim's emotional response and its "reasonableness."

the likely consequences of his behavior, at least the reasonableness test would be applied to the defendant and not to the victim.

According to constitutional standards, legislation must not be vague or overly broad. Various terms and phrases included in the suggested legislative approach must, therefore, be carefully defined to prevent misunderstanding by the public and arbitrary enforcement by the authorities. As many of the suggested terms are already defined in states' antistalking laws, existing definitions offer ample variety to choose from. One significant point not fully addressed in the definitions offered by existing statutes is that stalkers often follow, harass, threaten, or intimidate other persons closely related to the targeted victims, and even the victims' pets. In their definitions many states have referred to close family members and even to persons who are not family members, but dwell with the stalker's targeted victim. Judging by victims' testimonies and stalking cases, stalkers sometimes address their targeted victims' coworkers, employers, friends, neighbors, and therapists.[14] A "course of conduct" must therefore be defined to include the stalker's behavior toward such categories of people, as well as pets, as long as the said behaviors are clearly part of a pattern targeting the stalker's intended victim.[15]

Many states' antistalking laws offer interesting and important legal avenues to be considered, such as civil remedies for victims of stalking. The *Antistalking Legislation* report offers a comprehensive, well-informed list of recommendations, aimed at assisting state legislatures in addressing the issue. The first three recommendations (U.S. Department of Justice 1996, C-1):

> Because stalking defendants' behavior often is characterized by a series of increasingly serious acts, states should consider establishing a continuum of charges that could be used by law enforcement officials to intervene at various stages of stalking cases.
> States should consider creating a stalking felony to address serious, persistent and obsessive behavior that causes a victim to fear bodily injury or death.
> States should consider establishing a sentencing scheme for stalking that permits incarceration as an option for all stalking convictions.

Findings published in *Stalking in America* may be useful for the legal treatment of stalking. For example, in light of the fact that "[o]f those who obtained restraining orders, 69 percent of women and 81 percent of the men said their stalker violated the order" (U.S. Department of Justice 1998, 11),

14. See, for example, *People v. Tauber*, 49 Cal. App.4th 518, 56 Cal.Rptr.2d 656, 96 Cal. Daily Op. (No. D022697).

15. "Communication" may be defined as including, but not limited to, telephone calls, faxes, email or other electronic messages, letters, or nonverbal messages conveyed through means such as flower deliveries.

restraining orders may not be an efficient legal measure in this context. On the other hand, the report recommends that instead of focusing on stalkers' mental illness, "The mental health community should receive comprehensive training on the appropriate treatment of stalking victims."

> The survey found that about a quarter of all stalking victims seek psychological counseling as a result of their victimization. In addition, stalking victims are significantly more likely than nonstalking victims to be very fearful for their personal safety, to carry something on their person to protect themselves, and to think personal safety for men and women has declined in recent years. To better meet the needs of stalking victims, mental health professionals need additional information about the characteristics of stalking, the mental health impact of stalking, and the mental health needs of stalking victims. (U.S. Department of Justice 1998, 14)

Finally, I suggest that stalking legislation refer, specifically, to stalking performed by serial killers as preludes to murders. Although such cases may be few and atypical, they constitute the most severe form of stalking. This is why the statute proposed here includes a specific paragraph determining that a person is guilty of stalking if he or she initiates a course of conduct involving repeated or continual following, lying in wait, surveillance, trespassing, peeping, physical proximity, harassment, communication, vandalism, or threatening, in preparation to cause the targeted person or anyone closely related to her or him death or bodily injury.

In this concluding chapter I have emphasized the importance of a critical, informed relationship between law and culture. Yet another conclusion is no less important. The social phenomenon of stalking, much like the stalking moral panic, indicates a deep social problem. According to victims of stalking, stalkers, somewhat like the legendary erotomanic serial killers, seem to express alienation, insecurity, immaturity, dependence, and frustration. Their torment becomes another person's predicament. The law can punish, and sometimes prevent, some of the prohibited behavior. It cannot solve the fundamental crisis that brings about the suffering that is eventually manifested in stalking. If the public and policymakers wish to address the problem thoroughly, they must recognize that legislation and law enforcement are merely a first step.

Bibliography

Abarbanell, Nitza. 1994. *Hava ve-Lilit* (in Hebrew). Jerusalem: Bar Ilan University Press.

Ackerman, Susan. 1992. *Under Every Green Tree: Popular Religion in Sixth-Century Judah.* Atlanta: Scholars Press.

Adler, Robert S. 1993. The Legal, Ethical, and Social Implications of the "Reasonable Woman." *Fordham Law Review* 61 (March): 773.

Albright, William Foxwell. 1968. *Yahweh and the Gods of Canaan: A Historical Analysis of Two Contrasting Faiths.* London: University of London, Athlone Press.

Allen, Virginia M. 1983. *The Femme Fatale: Erotic Icon.* Troy, N.Y.: Whitston.

Alster, Bendt. 1971. Ninurta and the Turtle. *Journal of Cuneiform Studies* 24:120.

Anderson, Susan Cullen. 1993. Anti-stalking Laws: Will They Curb the Erotomanic's Pursuit? *Law and Psychology Review* 17:171.

Andrew, J. Dudley. 1976. *The Major Film Theories: An Introduction.* New York: Oxford University Press.

Arbery, Walter Christopher. 1993. Symposium: Individual Rights and the Powers of Government: Note: A Step Backward for Equality Principles: The "Reasonable Woman" Standard in Title VII Hostile Work Environment Sexual Harassment Claims. *Georgia Law Review* 27 (winter): 503.

Aronson, Elliot. 1976. *The Social Animal.* San Francisco: W. H. Freeman.

Aschkenasy, Nehama. 1986. *Eve's Journey: Feminine Images in Hebraic Literary Tradition.* Philadelphia: University of Pennsylvania Press.

Ashraf, Saba. 1992. The Reasonableness of the "Reasonable Woman" Standard: An Evaluation of its Use in Hostile Environment Sexual Harassment Claims Under Title VII of the Civil Rights Act. *Hofstra Law Review* 21 (winter): 483.

Auerbach, Nina. 1995. *Our Vampires, Ourselves.* Chicago: University of Chicago Press.

Bachofen, J. J. 1967. *Myth, Religion, and Mother Right.* London: Routledge and Kegan Paul.

Bakan, David. 1979. *And They Took Themselves Wives: The Emergence of Patriarchy in Western Civilization.* San Francisco: Harper and Row.

Baker, Carrie N. 1994. Sexual Extortion: Criminalizing Quid Pro Quo Sexual Harassment. *Law and Inequality Journal* 13:213.

Bal, Mieke. 1987. *Lethal Love; Feminist Literary Readings of Biblical Love Stories.* Bloomington: Indiana University Press.

———. 1991a. The Bible as Literature: A Critical Escape. In *On Story-Telling: Essays in Narratology,* ed. David Jobling. Sonoma, Calif.: Polebridge Press.

———. 1991b. Narration and Focalization. In *On Story-Telling: Essays in Narratology,* ed. David Jobling. Sonoma, Calif.: Polebridge Press.

Ball, Nicholas. 1993. *The Diary of Jack the Ripper: The Discovery, the Investigation, the Debate.* Beverly Hills, Calif.: Dove Audio. Audiocassettes.

Baring, Anne, and Jules Cashford. 1991. *The Myth of the Goddess: Evolution of an Image.* London: Viking.

Baron, Frank. 1978. *Doctor Faustus: From History to Legend.* Munich: Wilhelm Fink Verlag.

Barton, Anne. 1992. *Byron: Don Juan.* Cambridge: Cambridge University Press.

Baudry, Jean-Louis. 1992a. The Apparatus: Metapsychological Approaches to the Impression of Reality in the Cinema. In *Film Theory and Criticism,* ed. Gerald Mast and Marshall Cohen. 4th ed. New York: Oxford University Press.

———. 1992b. Ideological Effects of the Basic Cinematographic Apparatus. In *Film Theory and Criticism,* ed. Gerald and Marshall Cohen. 4th ed. New York: Oxford University Press.

Beatty, Bernard, and Vincent Newey, eds. 1988. *Byron and the Limits of Fiction.* Liverpool: Liverpool University Press.

Beaver, Frank E. 1983. *Dictionary of Film Terms.* New York: McGraw-Hill.

Becker, Ernest. 1973. *The Denial of Death.* New York: Free Press.

Belein, Herman. 1991. Judicial Views on the Crime of Witchcraft. In *Witchcraft in the Netherlands from the Fourteenth Century to the Twentieth Century,* ed. Marijke Gijswijt-Hofstra and Willem Frijhoff. Rotterdam: Universitaire Pers Rotterdam.

Bell, Shannon. 1994. *Reading, Writing, and Rewriting the Prostitute Body.* Bloomington: Indiana University Press.

Ben-Yehuda, Nachman. 1988. The European Witchcraze. In *Social Deviance,* ed. Ronald A. Farrell and Victoria Lynn Swigert. 3d ed. Belmont, Calif.: Wadsworth.

Benedict, Helen. 1992. *Virgin or Vamp: How the Press Covers Sex Crimes.* New York: Oxford University Press.

Berger, John. 1974. *Ways of Seeing.* New York: Penguin.

Bernstein, Susan E. 1993. Living under Siege: Do Stalking Laws Protect Domestic Violence Victims? *Cardozo Law Review* 15:525.

Bettelheim, Bruno. 1977. *The Uses of Enchantment: The Meaning and Importance of Fairy Tales.* New York: Alfred A. Knopf.

Biggs, Robert D., ed. 1967. *Texts from Cuneiform Sources.* Vol. 2, *Sa.Zi.Ga Ancient Mesopotamian Potency Incarnations.* Locust Valley, N.Y.: J. J. Augustin.

Bingham, Dennis. 1994. *Acting Male: Masculinities in the Films of James Stewart, Jack Nicholson, and Clint Eastwood.* New Brunswick, N.J.: Rutgers University Press.

Birkhauser-Oeri, Sibylle. 1988. *The Mother: Archetypal Images in Fairy Tales.* Toronto: Inner City.

Blais, Joann. 1994. Negation and the Evil Eye: A Reading of *Camera Lucida.* In *Negation, Critical Theory, and Postmodern Textuality,* ed. Daniel Fischlin. Boston: Kluwer Academic Publishers.

Bloch, Robert. 1989. The Real Bad Friend. In *No, But I Saw It in the Movie,* ed. David Wheeler. New York: Penguin.

Bloom, Harold, ed. 1987. *Modern Critical Interpretations: Lord Byron's "Don Juan."* New York: Chelsea House.

———. 1992. *The American Religion: The Emergence of the Post-Christian Nation.* New York: Simon and Schuster.

Bly, Robert. 1992. *Iron John: A Book about Men.* New York: Vintage.

Bourget, Jean-Loup. 1992. Social Implications in the Hollywood Genres. In *Film*

Theory and Criticism, ed. Gerald Mast and Marshall Cohen. 4th ed. New York: Oxford University Press.

Boyarin, Daniel. 1993. *Carnal Israel: Reading Sex in Talmudic Culture.* Berkeley and Los Angeles: University of California Press.

Boychuk, M. Katherine. 1994. Anti-stalking Laws Unconstitutionally Vague or Overbroad? *Northwestern University Law Review* 88 (winter): 769.

Boyd, James, ed. 1949. *Notes to Goethe's Poems.* Oxford: Basil Blackwell.

Bradfield, Jennifer L. 1998. Anti-stalking Laws: Do They Adequately Protect Stalking Victims? *Harvard Women's Law Journal* 21:229.

Brakhage, Stan. 1992. Metaphors on Vision. In *Film Theory and Criticism,* ed. Gerald Mast and Marshall Cohen. 4th ed. New York: Oxford University Press.

Brantlinger, Patrick, and Richard Boyle. 1988. The Education of Edward Hyde: Stevenson's "Gothic Gnome" and the Mass Readership of Late-Victorian England. In *Dr. Jekyll and Mr. Hyde after One Hundred Years,* ed. William Veeder and Gordon Hirsch. Chicago: University of Chicago Press.

Breslin, Jimmy, and Dick Schaap. 1978. *.44.* New York: Viking Press.

Brooks, Peter. 1984. *Reading for the Plot: Design and Intention in Narrative.* New York: Alfred A. Knopf.

Browman, Cynthia Grant. 1993. Street Harassment and the Informal Ghettoization of Women. *Harvard Law Review* 106:517.

Buckley, Thomas, and Alma Gotlieb, eds. 1988. *Blood Magic: The Anthropology of Menstruation.* Berkeley and Los Angeles: University of California Press.

Bulfinch, Thomas. 1994. *The Golden Age of Myth and Legend.* London: Senate.

Byron, George Gordon, Lord. 1986. *Don Juan* and *Cain.* In *The Oxford Authors: Byron,* ed. Jerome J. McGann. Oxford: Oxford University Press.

Cahn, Naomi R. 1992. Symposium: The Looseness of Legal Language: The Reasonable Woman Standard in Theory and in Practice. *Cornell Law Review* 77 (September): 1398.

Cameron, Deborah, and Elizabeth Frazer. 1987. *The Lust to Kill: A Feminist Investigation of Sexual Murder.* Worcester: Polity Press.

Campbell, Joseph. 1968. *The Hero with a Thousand Faces.* Princeton, N.J.: Princeton University Press.

Campbell, Joseph, and Charles Muses. 1991. *In All Her Names: Explorations of the Feminine in Divinity.* San Francisco: Harper.

Carmichael, Calum M. 1985. *Law and Narrative in the Bible: The Evidence of the Deuteronomic Laws and the Decalogue.* Ithaca, N.Y.: Cornell University Press.

Carmody, Cristina. 1994. Deadly Mistakes. *ABA Journal* (September): 68.

Carmody, Denise Lardner. 1992. *Mythological Woman: Contemporary Reflections on Ancient Religious Stories.* New York: Crossroad.

Carr, David. 1991. *Time, Narrative, and History.* Bloomington: Indiana University Press.

Carter, Margaret L., ed. 1989. *The Vampire in Literature: A Critical Bibliography.* Ann Arbor, Mich.: UMI Research Press.

Cassuto, U. 1990. *The "Quaestio" of the Book of Genesis* (in Hebrew). Translated from the Italian by M. E. Arton. Jerusalem: Magnes Press, Hebrew University.

Cavell, Stanley. 1987. Psychoanalysis and Cinema: The Melodrama of the Unknown Woman. In *Images in Our Souls: Cavell, Psychoanalysis, and Cinema,* ed. Joseph H. Smith and William Kerrigan. Baltimore: John Hopkins University Press.

Cawley, A. C., ed. 1993. *Everyman and Medieval Miracle Plays.* Rutland, Vt.: Everyman.

Chatman, Seymour. 1992. What Novels Can Do That Films Can't (and Vice Versa). In *Film Theory and Criticism,* ed. Gerald Mast and Marshall Cohen. 4th ed. New York: Oxford University Press.

Childers, Jolynn. 1993. Is There a Place for a Reasonable Woman in the Law? A Discussion of Recent Developments in Hostile Environment Sexual Harassment. *Duke Law Journal* 42 (February): 854.

Clover, Carol J. 1992. *Men, Women, and Chainsaws: Gender in the Modern Horror Film.* Princeton, N.J.: Princeton University Press.

Cohan, Steven, and Ina Rae Hark. 1993. *Screening the Male: Exploring Masculinities in Hollywood Cinema.* New York: Routledge.

Cohen, Stanley. 1980. *Folk Devils and Moral Panics: The Creation of the Mods and Rockers.* Oxford: Martin Robertson.

Cohen, Tova. 1990. *Saints and Hypocrites; Goddesses and Lilliths: Studies in the Works of Abraham Mapu.* Tel-Aviv: Papyrus, Tel-Aviv University Publishing House.

Cohen-Montagu, Heftsiba. 1994. Maidens of the City and the Sacred Service. In *Local Goddesses: From Ancient Deities to Mythical Women of Today* (in Hebrew). Jerusalem: Museum of the History of Jerusalem.

Cohn, Norman. 1975. *Europe's Inner Demons: An Inquiry Inspired by the Great Witch-Hunt.* London: Sussex University Press.

Collins, Ronald K. L. 1977. Language, History, and the Legal Process: A Profile of the "Reasonable Man." *Rutgers-Camden Law Journal* 8:310.

Cooper, J. C. 1985. *Fairy Tales: Allegories of the Inner Life.* San Bernadino, Calif.: Borgo Press.

Coote, Robert B., and David Robert Ord. 1989. *The Bible's First History.* Philadelphia: Fortress Press.

Copelan, Dean. 1994. Is Georgia's Stalking Law Unconstitutionally Vague? *Mercer Law Review* 45:853.

Copper, Basil. 1975. *The Vampire in Legend, Fact, and Art.* London: Corgi.

Corwin, Miles. "When the Law Can't Protect." *Los Angeles Times,* 8 May 1993.

Crawford, O. G. S. 1957. *The Eye Goddess.* London: Phoenix House.

Creed, Barbara. 1993a. Dark Desires: Male Masochism in the Horror Film. In *Screening the Male: Exploring Masculinities in Hollywood Cinema,* ed. Steven Cohan and Ina Rae Hark. New York: Routledge.

———. 1993b. *The Monstrous-Feminine: Film, Feminism, Psychoanalysis.* London: Routledge.

Crook, Margaret Brackenbury. 1964. *Women and Religion.* Boston: Beacon Press.

Cross, Frank Moore. 1973. *Canaanite Myth and Hebrew Epic: Essays in the History of the Religion of Israel.* Cambridge: Harvard University Press.

Dalley, Stephanie. 1989. *Myths from Mesopotamia: Creation, the Flood, Gilgamesh, and Others.* Oxford: Oxford University Press.

Daly, Mary. 1985. *Beyond God the Father: Toward a Philosophy of Women's Liberation.* Boston: Beacon Press.

Dame, Enid. 1989. Lilith's Sestina. In *The Tribe of Dina: A Jewish Woman's Anthology,* ed. Melanie Kaye and Irena Klepfisz. Boston: Beacon Press.

Dame, Enid, Lilly Rivlin, and Henny Wenkart, eds. 1998. *Which Lilith? Feminist Writers Re-create the World's First Woman.* Northvale, N.J.: Jason Aronson.

Dan, Joseph. 1980. Samael, Lilith, and the Concept of Evil in Early Kabbalah. *Association for Jewish Studies Review,* vol. 5. Cambridge, Mass.: Association for Jewish Studies.

———. 1993. Something on the Conception of Myth in Contemporary Research (in Hebrew). *Alpaym* 8:145.

David, William J. 1994. Is Pennsylvania's Stalking Law Constitutional? *University of Pittsburgh Law Review* 56 (fall): 205.

Davis, Lebbard J. 1983. *Factual Fictions: The Origins of the English Novel.* New York: Columbia University Press.

Day, Peggy L., ed. 1989. *Gender and Difference in Ancient Israel.* Minneapolis: Fortress Press.

Deane, Hamilton, and John L. Balderston. 1971. *Dracula: The Vampire Play.* Garden City, N.Y.: Nelson Doubleday.

Dettman, Bruce, and Michael Bedford. 1976. *The Horror Factory: The Horror Films of Universal, 1931–1955.* New York: Gordon Press.

de Vries, Ad. 1974. *Dictionary of Symbols and Imagery.* Amsterdam: North-Holland.

Diacovo, Nannette. 1995. California's Anti-stalking Statutes: Deterrent or False Sense of Security? *Southwestern University Law Review* 24:389.

Dietz, Park Elliot. 1984. A Remedial Approach to Harassment. *Virginia Law Review* 70 (April): 507.

Dietz, Park Elliot, et al. 1991a. Threatening and Otherwise Inappropriate Letters to Hollywood Celebrities. *Journal of Forensic Sciences,* JFSCA, no. 1, 36:185.

———. 1991b. Threatening and Otherwise Inappropriate Letters to Members of the United States Congress. *Journal of Forensic Sciences,* JFSCA, no. 5, 36:1445.

Dika, Vera. 1990. *Games of Terror: "Halloween," "Friday the 13th," and the Films of the Stalker Cycle.* Cranbury, N.J.: Associated University Press.

Diner, Helen. 1965. *Mothers and Amazons: The First Feminine History of Culture.* New York: Julian Press.

Doane, Mary Ann. 1991. *Femmes Fatales: Feminism, Film Theory, Psychoanalysis.* New York: Routledge.

———. 1992. Film and the Masquerade: Theorising the Female Spectator. In *Film Theory and Criticism,* ed. Gerald Mast and Marshall Cohen. 4th ed. New York: Oxford University Press.

Donovan, Dolores A., and Stephanie M. Wildman. 1981. Is the Reasonable Man Obsolete? A Critical Perspective on Self-Defense and Provocation. *Loyola Los Angeles Law Review* 14:435.

Douglass, Jane Dempsey. 1974. Women and the Continental Reformation. In *Religion and Sexism: Images of Women in the Jewish and Christian Traditions,* ed. Rosemary Radford Ruether. New York: Simon and Schuster.

Driver, G. R. 1956. *Canaanite Myths and Legends.* Edinburgh: T.and T. Clark.

Driver, G. R., and John C. Miles. 1952. *The Babylonian Laws.* Oxford: Clarendon Press.

Dundes, Alan, ed. 1992. *The Evil Eye: A Casebook.* Madison: University of Wisconsin Press.

Edwards, Carolyn McVickar. 1991. *The Storyteller's Goddess: Tales of the Goddess and Her Wisdom from around the World.* San Francisco: Harper.

Ehrenreich, Nancy S. 1990. Pluralist Myths and Powerless Men: The Ideology of Reasonableness in Sexual Harassment Law. *Yale Law Journal* 99 (April): 1177.

Eisler, Raine. 1991. The Goddess of Nature and Spirituality: An Ecomanifesto. In *In All Her Names: Exploration of the Feminine Divinity*, ed. Joseph Campbell and Charles Muses. San Francisco: Harper.

Eliade, Mircea. 1959. *Cosmos and History: The Myth of the Eternal Return.* Trans. Willard R. Trask: New York: Harper.

———. 1963. *Myth and Reality.* Trans. Willard R Trask. New York: Harper and Row.

Estes, Clarissa Pinkola. 1992. *Women Who Run with the Wolves: Myths and Stories of the Wild Woman Archetype.* New York: Ballantine.

Everson, William K. 1974. *Classics of the Horror Film.* Secaucus, N.J.: Citadel Press.

Fairclough, Melvyn. 1991. *The Ripper and the Royals.* London: Duckworth.

Faludi, Susan. 1991. *Backlash.* New York: Doubleday.

Faulkner, Robert P., and Douglas H. Hsiao. 1993. And Where You Go I'll Follow: The Constitutionality of Antistalking Laws and Proposed Model Legislation. *Harvard Journal on Legislation* 31 (spring): 1.

Fein, Robert A., et al. 1998. Preventing Attacks on Public Officials and Public Figures: A Secret Service Perspective. In *The Psychology of Stalking: Clinical and Forensic Perspectives*, ed. J. Reid Meloy. San Diego: Academic Press.

Fewell, Danna Nolan, and David M. Gunn, eds. 1992. *Reading between Texts: Intertextuality and the Hebrew Bible.* Louisville, Ky.: Westminster/John Knox Press.

———. 1993. *Gender, Power, and Promise: The Subject of the Bible's First Story.* Nashville: Abingdon Press.

Fish, Stanley. 1980. *Is There a Text in This Class? The Authority of Interpretive Communities.* Cambridge: Harvard University Press.

Fletcher, George. P. 1987. The Right and the Reasonable. In *Justification and Excuse: Comparative Perspectives*, ed. Eser Albin and George P. Fletcher, vol. 1. Freiburg: Eigenverld Max-Plonck Institut fur Auslandisches und Internationales Strafrecht.

Florescu, Radu, and Raymond T. McNally. 1992. *The Complete Dracula: "Dracula," a Biography of Vlad the Impaler, and In Search of Dracula.* Acton, Mass.: Copley.

Forell, Caroline. 1994. Essentialism, Empathy, and the Reasonable Woman. *University of Illinois Law Review* 1994:769.

Forsyth, Neil. 1987. *The Old Enemy: Satan and the Combat Myth.* Princeton, N.J.: Princeton University Press.

Foucault, Michel. 1973. *The Order of Things: An Archaeology of the Human Sciences.* New York: Vintage.

———. 1978. The Dangerous Individual. In *Politics, Philosophy, Culture: Interviews and other Writings, 1977–1984.* New York: Routledge.

Fox, William Sherwood. 1916. *The Mythology of All Races.* Vol. 1, *Greek and Roman.* Boston: Marshall Jones.

Frankel, Ellen. 1989. *The Classic Tales: 4,000 Years of Jewish Lore.* Northvale, N.J.: Jason Aronson.

Frayling, Christopher, ed. 1978. *The Vampire: Lord Ruthven to Count Dracula.* London: Victor Gollancz.

Freud, Sigmund. 1919. The Uncanny. In *The Standard Edition*, ed. James Strachey, vol. 17. London: Hogarth Press and Institute of Psycho-Analysis.

————. 1920. Beyond the Pleasure Principle. In *The Standard Edition*, ed. James Strachey, vol. 18. London: Hogarth Press and Institute of Psycho-Analysis.

————. 1922. Medusa's Head. In *The Standard Edition*, ed. James Strachey, vol. 18. London: Hogarth Press and Institute of Psycho-Analysis.

Friedman, Richard Elliott. 1989. *Who Wrote the Bible?* New York: Harper and Row.

Fromm, Erich. 1967. *The Forgotten Language: An Introduction to the Understanding of Dreams, Fairy Tales, and Myths.* New York: Holt, Rinehart and Winston.

Frost, Brian J. 1989. *The Monster with a Thousand Faces: Guises of the Vampire in Myth and Literature.* Bowling Green, Ohio: Bowling Green State University Popular Press.

Frye, Roland Mushat. 1960. *God, Man, and Satan: Patterns of Christian Thought and Life in "Paradise Lost," "Pilgrim's Progress," and "The Great Theologians."* Princeton, N.J.: Princeton University Press.

Frymer-Kensky, Tikva. 1992. *In the Wake of the Goddesses: Women, Culture, and the Biblical Transformation of Pagan Myth.* New York: Free Press.

Gabler, Neal. 1988. *An Empire of Their Own: How the Jews Invented Hollywood.* New York: Anchor Books Doubleday.

Gaer, Joseph. 1961. *The Legend of the Wandering Jew.* New York: Mentor.

Gamman, Lorraine, and Margaret Marshment, eds. 1989. *The Female Gaze: Women as Viewers of Popular Culture.* Seattle: Real Comet Press.

Garnett, Richard, ed. 1897. *Poems of Samuel Taylor Coleridge.* London: George Routledge and Sons.

Geduld, Harry M. 1983. *The Definitive "Dr. Jekyll and Mr. Hyde" Companion.* New York: Garland.

Gelder, Peter Van. 1990. *That's Hollywood: A Behind the Scenes Look at Sixty of the Greatest Films of All Times.* New York: Harper Perennial.

Gennep, Arnold van. 1969. *The Rites of Passage.* Chicago: University of Chicago Press.

Gerrard, Nicci. "Possessed." *Observer,* 18 December 1994.

Giannetti, Louis. 1982. *Understanding Movies.* Englewood Cliffs, N.J.: Prentice-Hall.

Gijswijt-Hofstra, Marijke. 1991. Six Centuries of Witchcraft in the Netherlands: Themes, Outlines, and Interpretations. In *Witchcraft in the Netherlands from the Fourteenth Century to the Twentieth Century,* ed. Marijke Gijswijt-Hofstra and Willem Frijhoff. Rotterdam: Universitaire Pers Rotterdam.

Gilbert, Sandra M., and Susan Gubar. 1979. *The Madwoman in the Attic: The Woman Writer in the Nineteenth-Century Literary Imagination.* New Haven: Yale University Press.

Gilligan, Matthew J. 1992. Stalking the Stalkers: Developing New Laws to Thwart Those Who Terrorize Others. *Georgia Law Review* 27 (fall): 285.

Gimbutas, Marija. 1989. *The Language of the Goddess.* San Francisco: Harper and Row.

Ginzberg, Luis. 1912. *The Legends of the Jews.* Vol. 1, *Bible Times and Characters from the Creation to Jacob.* Philadelphia: Jewish Publication Society of America.

Ginzburg, Carlo. 1985. *The Night Battles: Witchcraft and Agrarian Cults in the Sixteenth and Seventeenth Centuries.* New York: Penguin.

————. 1990. *Ecstasies: Deciphering the Witches' Sabbath.* London: Hutchinson Radius.

Girard, René. 1965. *Deceit, Desire, and the Novel: Self and Other in Literary Structure*, trans. Yvonne Freccero. Baltimore: John Hopkins University Press.

Gledhill, Christine. 1992. Recent Developments in Feminist Criticism. In *Film Theory and Criticism*, ed. Gerald Mast and Marshall Cohen. 4th ed. New York: Oxford University Press.

Glidden, Elizabeth A. 1992. The Emergence of the Reasonable Woman in Combating Hostile Environment Sexual Harassment. *Iowa Law Review* 77 (July): 1825.

Glut, Donald F. 1973. *The Frankenstein Legend: A Tribute to Mary Shelley and Boris Karloff*. Metuchen, N.J.: Scarecrow Press.

Gold, Judith Taylor. 1988. *Monsters and Madonnas: The Roots of Christian Anti-Semitism*. New York: New Amsterdam.

Goldberg, Herb. 1976. *The Hazards of Being Male: Surviving the Myth of Masculine Privilege*. New York: Signet.

———. 1979. *The New Male: From Macho to Sensitive but Still All Male*. New York: Signet.

Goldenberg, Judith Plaskow. 1974. Epilogue: The Coming of Lilith. In *Religion and Sexism: Images of Women in the Jewish and Christian Traditions*, ed. Rosemary Radford Ruether. New York: Simon and Schuster.

Goldenberg, Naomi R. 1979. *Changing of the Gods: Feminism and the End of Traditional Religions*. Boston: Beacon Press.

Goldstein, Robert Lloyd, M.D., J.D. 1986. Erotomania in Men. *American Journal of Psychiatry* 143 (6): 802.

Goode, Erich, and Nachman Ben-Yehuda. 1996. *Moral Panics: The Social Construction of Deviance*. Cambridge, Mass.: Blackwell.

Goode, Matthew. 1995. Stalking: Crime of the Nineties? *Criminal Law Journal* 19:21.

Gordon, Cyrus H. 1961. Canaanite Mythology. In *Mythologies of the Ancient World*, ed. Samuel Noah Kramer. New York: Anchor.

Graham, Peter W. 1990. *Don Juan and Regency England*. Charlottesville: University Press of Virginia.

Greenberg, Harvey Roy. 1993. *Screen Memories: Hollywood Cinema on the Psychoanalytic Couch*. New York: Columbia University Press.

Greenburg, Dan. 1978. *Love Kills*. New York: Pocket.

Gruber, Mayer I. 1992. *The Motherhood of God and Other Studies*. Atlanta: Scholars Press.

Guy, Robert A. 1993. The Nature and Constitutionality of Stalking Laws. *Vanderbilt Law Review* 46 (May): 991.

Haberman, A. M., ed. 1975. *Hadashim Gam Jeshanim: Texts, Old and New*. Jerusalem: Rubin Mass.

Hall, Doris M. 1998. The Victims of Stalking. In *The Psychology of Stalking: Clinical and Forensic Perspectives*, ed. J. Reid Meloy. San Diego: Academic Press.

Hardison, O. B. 1965. *Christian Rite and Christian Drama in the Middle Ages*. Baltimore: Johns Hopkins University Press.

Hardy, Phil, Tom Milne, and Paul Willemen, eds. 1985. *The Aurum Film Encyclopedia: Horror*. London: Aurum Press.

Harmon, Ronnie B., Richard Rosner, and Howard Owens. 1995. Obsessional Harassment and Erotomania in a Criminal Court Population. *Journal of Forensic Sciences* 40:188.

Haskell, Molly. 1978. *From Reverence to Rape: The Treatment of Women in the Movies*. New York: Penguin.

Hauptman, Judith. 1974. Images of Women in the Talmud. In *Religion and Sexism: Images of Women in the Jewish and Christian Traditions*, ed. Rosemary Radford Ruether. New York: Simon and Schuster.

Henning, Clara Maria. 1974. Canon Law and the Battle of the Sexes. In *Religion and Sexism: Images of Women in the Jewish and Christian Traditions*, ed. Rosemary Radford Ruether. New York: Simon and Schuster.

Hershman, Debby. 1994. Local Goddesses. In *Local Goddesses: From Ancient Deities to Mythical Women of Today* (in Hebrew). Jerusalem: Museum of the History of Jerusalem.

Hickey, Eric W. 1991. *Serial Murderers and Their Victims*. Pacific Grove, Calif.: Brooks/Cole.

Hindle, Maurice, ed. 1992 *Frankenstein; or, The Modern Prometheus*, by Mary Shelley. London: Penguin.

Hirsch, Gordon. 1988. *Frankenstein*, Detective Fiction, and *Jekyll and Hyde*. In *"Dr. Jekyll and Mr. Hyde" after One Hundred Years*, ed. William Veeder and Gordon Hirsch. Chicago: University of Chicago Press.

Hoffmann, E. T. A. 1982. *Tales*. New York: Continuum.

Hogan, David J. 1986. *Dark Romance: Sexuality in the Horror Film*. Jefferson, N.C.: McFarland.

Hollander, Marc H., M.D., and Alfred S. Callahan III, M.D. 1975. Erotomania or de Clerambault Syndrome. *Archives General Psychiatry* 32:1574.

Hollinger, Veronica. 1994. Putting on the Feminine: Gender and Negativity in *Frankenstein* and *The Handmaid's Tale*. In *Negation, Critical Theory, and Postmodern Textuality*, ed. Daniel Fischlin. Boston: Kluwer Academic Publishers.

Horwitz, Margaret. 1986. *The Birds*: A Mother's Love. In *The Hitchcock Reader*, ed. Marshall Deutelbaum and Leland Poague. Ames: Iowa State University Press.

Hurwitz, Siegmund. 1992. *Lilith—the First Eve: Historical and Psychological Aspects of the Dark Feminine*. Einsiedeln, Switzerland: Daimon Verlag.

Huss, Roym, and T. J. Ross, eds. 1972. *Focus on the Horror Film*. Englewood Cliffs, N.J.: Prentice-Hall.

Hutchings, Peter. 1993. *Hammer and Beyond: The British Horror Film*. New York: Manchester University Press.

Idel, Moshe. 1994. The Bride of God. In *Local Goddesses: From Ancient Deities to Mythical Women of Today* (in Hebrew). Jerusalem: Museum of the History of Jerusalem.

Iverson, Jeffrey. 1992. *In Search of the Dead: A Scientific Investigation of Evidence for Life after Death*. New York: Harper San Francisco.

Jacobus, Mary. 1982. Is There a Woman in This Text? *New Literary History* 14:117.

James, E. O. 1959. *The Cult of the Mother-Goddess: An Archaeological and Documentary Study*. New York: Frederick A. Prager.

Johnson, Paul B. 1993. The Reasonable Woman in Sexual Harassment Law: Progress or Illusion? *Wake Forest Law Review* 28:619.

Johnson, Robert A. 1991. *Owning Your Own Shadow: Understanding the Dark Side of the Psyche*. San Francisco: Harper.

Jones, Ernest. 1972. On the Nightmare of Bloodsucking. In *Focus on the Horror Film*, ed. Roy Huss and T. J. Ross. Englewood Cliffs, N.J.: Prentice-Hall.

Jordan, Michael. 1993. *Encyclopedia of Gods: Over 2,500 Deities of the World*. New York: Facts on File.

Kamir, Orit. Forthcoming. Honor and Dignity Cultures: The Case of *Kavod* and *Kvod ha-adam* in Israeli Society and Law. In *Human Dignity*, ed. David Kretzmer and Francine Hazan. Dordrecht: Kluwer Academic.

Kastor, Frank S. 1974. *Milton and the Literary Satan*. Amsterdam: Rodopi N.V.

Katzanelenbugen, M. L., ed. 1986. *Torat Chaim Chumash*. Jerusalem: Mossad Harav Kook.

Keats, John. 1970. *Lamia, Isabella, The Eve of St. Agnes, and Other Poems, 1820*. Yorkshire, England: Scholar Press.

Kieckhefer, Richard. 1976. *European Witch Trials: Their Foundations in Popular and Learned Culture, 1300–1500*. London: Routledge and Kegan Paul.

Kienlen, Kristine K. 1998. Developmental and Social Antecedents of Stalking. In *The Psychology of Stalking: Clinical and Forensic Perspectives*, ed. J. Reid Meloy. San Diego: Academic Press.

Kinsley, David. 1989. *The Goddesses' Mirror: Visions of the Divine from East and West*. New York: State University of New York Press.

Knee, Adam. 1993. The Dialectic of Female Power and Male Hysteria in *Play Misty for Me*. In *Screening the Male: Exploring Masculinities in Hollywood Cinema*, ed. Steven Cohan and Ina Rae Hark. New York: Routledge.

Knoepflmacher, U. C. 1979. Thoughts on the Aggression of Daughters. In *The Endurance of "Frankenstein": Essays on Mary Shelley's Novel*, ed. George Levine and U. C. Knoepflmacher. Berkeley and Los Angeles: University of California Press.

Kofman, Sarah. 1991. *Freud and Fiction*. Boston: Northern University Press.

Kolb, Tracy Vigness. 1994. North Dakota's Stalking Law: Criminalizing the Crime before the Crime. *North Dakota Law Review* 70:159.

Kors, Alan C., and Edward Peters. 1989. In *Witchcraft in Europe, 1100–1700: A Documentary History: Malleus Maleficarum*, by Jacob Sprengler and Heinrich Kramer. Philadelphia: University of Pennsylvania Press.

Kosofsky, Eve Sedgwick. 1985. *Between Men: English Literature and Male Homosocial Desire*. New York: Columbia University Press.

Kracauer, Siegfried. 1966. *From Caligari to Hitler: A Psychological History of the German Film*. Princeton, N.J.: Princeton University Press.

Kramer, Samuel Noah. 1945. Enki and Ninhursag: A Sumerian "Paradise" Myth. *Bulletin of the American Schools of Oriental Research, Supplementary Studies* 1:1.

———. 1961. Mythology of Sumer and Akkad. In *Mythologies of the Ancient World*, ed. Samuel Noah Kramer. New York: Anchor.

———. 1963. *The Sumerians: Their History, Culture, and Character*. Chicago: University of Chicago Press.

———. 1969. *The Sacred Marriage Rite: Aspects of Faith, Myth, and Ritual in Ancient Sumer*. Bloomington: Indiana University Press.

Kruger, Kathleen. 1995. Panel Presentation on Stalking. *University of Toledo Law Review* 25:903.

Lake, Deborah Mann. 1995. "Empowering Yourself against Stalkers." *Houston Post*, 12 February.

Lamb, Lady Caroline. 1816. *Glenarvon*. London: Henry Colburn.

Lambert, W. G. 1960. *Babylonian Wisdom Literature*. Oxford: Clarendon Press.

Langdon, Stephen Herbert. 1964. *The Mythology of All Races in Thirteen Volumes.* Vol. 5, *Semitic.* New York: Cooper Square.

Laqueur, Thomas. 1990. *Making Sex: Body and Gender from the Greeks to Freud.* Cambridge: Harvard University Press.

Lardner, George, Jr. 1997. *The Stalking of Kristin: A Father Investigating the Murder of His Daughter.* New York: Penguin.

Lavalley, Albert J. 1979. The Stage and Film Children of *Frankenstein:* A Survey. In *The Endurance of "Frankenstein": Essays on Mary Shelley's Novel,* ed. George Levine and U. C. Knoepflmacher. Berkeley and Los Angeles: University of California Press.

Lawrence, D. H. 1953. *Studies in Classic American Literature.* New York: Doubleday.

Leach, Edmund R. 1967. Genesis as Myth. In *Myth and Cosmos: Readings in Mythology and Symbolism,* ed. John Middleton. Austin: University of Texas Press.

Leatherdale, Clive. 1987. *The Origins of Dracula: The Background to Bram Stoker's Gothic Masterpiece.* London: William Kimber.

———. 1993. *Dracula: The Novel and the Legend.* Brighton: Desert Island.

Lederer, Wolfgang. 1968. *The Fear of Women.* New York: Harcourt Brace Jovanovitch.

Lee, Rebecca K. 1998. Romantic and Electronic Stalking in a College Context. *William and Mary Journal of Women and the Law* 4:374.

Lehman, Peter. 1993. "Don't Blame It on a Girl": Female Rape-Revenge Films. In *Screening the Male: Exploring Masculinities in Hollywood Cinema,* ed. Steven Cohan and Ina Rae Hark. New York: Routledge.

Leland, Charles G. 1974. *Ardia: Gospel of the Witches.* New York: Samuel Weiser.

Lerner, Gerda. 1986. *The Creation of Patriarchy.* Oxford: Oxford University Press.

Lesser, Wendy. 1991. *His Other Half: Men Looking at Women Through Art.* Cambridge: Harvard University Press.

Levack, Brian P. 1989. *The Witch-Hunt in Early Modern Europe.* New York: Longman.

Levine, George. 1979. The Ambiguous Heritage of *Frankenstein.* In *The Endurance of "Frankenstein": Essays on Mary Shelley's Novel,* ed. George Levine and U. C. Knoepflmacher. Berkeley and Los Angeles: University of California Press.

Levine, Stewart, and Susan Levine. 1976. *Short Fiction of Edgar Allan Poe: An Annotated Edition.* Indianapolis: Bobbs-Merrill.

Ling, Trevor. 1961. *The Significance of Satan: New Testament Demonology and Its Contemporary Relevance.* London: S.P.C.K.

Lingg, Richard A. 1993. Stopping Stalkers: A Critical Examination of Anti-stalking Statutes. *St. John's Law Review* 67 (spring): 347.

Lion, John R., et al. 1998. The Stalking of Clinicians by Their Patients. In *The Psychology of Stalking: Clinical and Forensic Perspectives,* ed. J. Reid Meloy. San Diego: Academic Press.

Lipson, Glenn S. 1998. Stalking, Erotomania, and the Tarasoff Cases. In *The Psychology of Stalking: Clinical and Forensic Perspectives,* ed. J. Reid Meloy. San Diego: Academic Press.

Liptzin, Sol. 1976. Rehabilitation of Lilith (in Hebrew). *Dor Le Dor* 2:66. Jerusalem: World Jewish Bible Society.

Lloyd-Goldstein, Robert. 1998. De Clerambault On-Line: A Survey of Erotomania and Stalking from the Old World to the World Wide Web. In *The Psychology of Stalking: Clinical and Forensic Perspectives,* ed. J. Reid Meloy. San Diego: Academic Press.

Lorenz, Konrad. 1969. *On Aggression.* New York: Bantam.

Lubin, Orly. 1994. The Divine Echo and the Temporal Voice. In *Local Goddesses: From Ancient Deities to Mythical Women of Today* (in Hebrew). Jerusalem: Museum of the History of Jerusalem.

MacDonald, D. L. 1991. *Poor Polidori: A Critical Biography of the Author of "The Vampyre."* Toronto: University of Toronto Press.

MacKinnon, Catharine A. 1979. *Sexual Harassment of Working Women.* New Haven: Yale University Press.

———. 1987. *Feminism Unmodified: Discourses on Life and Law.* Cambridge: Harvard University Press.

Magnuson, Paul. 1974. *Coleridge's Nightmare Poetry.* Charlottesville: University Press of Virginia.

Mahoney, Martha. 1991. Legal Images of Battered Women: Separation. *Michigan Law Review* 90:1.

Malinowski, Bronislaw. 1926. *Myth in Primitive Psychology.* New York: Norton.

Maloney, Clarence, ed. 1976. *The Evil Eye.* New York: Columbia University Press.

Mann, Thomas, ed. 1948. *The Permanent Goethe.* New York: Dial Press.

Manning, Peter J. 1987. The Byronic Hero as a Little Boy. In *Modern Critical Interpretations: Lord Byron's "Don Juan,"* ed. Harold Bloom. New York: Chelsea House.

Martin, Jay. 1988. *Who Am I This Time? Uncovering the Fictive Personality.* New York: Norton.

McAnaney, Kathleen G., Laura A. Curliss, and Elizabeth Abeyta-Price. 1993. From Imprudence to Crime: Anti-stalking Laws. *Notre Dame Law Review* 68:819.

McLaughlin, Eleanor Commo. 1974. Equality of Souls, Inequality of Sexes: Woman in Medieval Theology. In *Religion and Sexism: Images of Women in the Jewish and Christian Traditions,* ed. Rosemary Radford Ruether. New York: Simon and Schuster.

Meier, Gerhard. 1937. *Die Assyrische Beschworungssammulung Maqlu: Neu bearbeitet* (in German). Berlin: Im Selbsfverlage des Herausgebers.

Meloy, J. Ried, Ph.D. 1989. Unrequited Love and the Wish to Kill. *Bulletin of the Menninger Clinic* 53:477.

———. 1990. Nondelusional or Borderline Erotomania. *American Journal of Psychiatry* 147 (6) (June): 820.

———. 1992. *Violent Attachments.* Northvale, N.J.: Jason Aronson.

———. 1998. The Psychology of Stalking. In *The Psychology of Stalking: Clinical and Forensic Perspectives,* ed. J. Reid Meloy. San Diego: Academic Press.

Metz, Christian. 1985. The Imaginary Signifier. In *Film Theory and Criticism,* ed. Gerald Mast and Marshall Cohen. 3d ed. New York: Oxford University Press.

Meyers, Judith. 1998. Cultural Factors in Erotomania and Obsessional Following. In *The Psychology of Stalking: Clinical and Forensic Perspectives,* ed. J. Reid Meloy. San Diego: Academic Press.

Midelfort, H. C. Erik. 1972. *Witch Hunting in Southwestern Germany, 1562–1684: The Social and Intellectual Foundations.* Stanford: Stanford University Press.

Migal, Gedalyah. 1983. *"Dybbuk" Tales in Jewish Literature.* Jerusalem: Rubin Mass.

Miller, Jane. 1990. The Seduction of Women. In *Don Giovanni: Myths of Seduction and Betrayal,* ed. Jonathan Miller. New York: Schocken.

Miller, Jonathan, ed. 1990. *Don Giovanni: Myths of Seduction and Betrayal.* New York: Schocken.

Miller, Robert N. 1993. "Stalk Talk": A First Look at Anti-stalking Legislation. *Washington and Lee Review* 50 (summer): 1303.

Miller, William Ian. 1993. *Humiliation and Other Essays on Honor, Social Discomfort, and Violence.* Ithaca, N.Y.: Cornell University Press.

———. 1995. "I Can Take a Hint": Social Ineptitude, Embarrassment, and the *King of Comedy, Michigan Quarterly Review* 33:322.

Modleski, Tania. 1989. *The Women Who Knew Too Much: Hitchcock and Feminist Theory.* New York: Routledge.

Moers, Ellen. 1979. Female Gothic. In *The Endurance of "Frankenstein": Essays on Mary Shelley's Novel,* ed. George Levine and U. C. Knoepflmacher. Berkeley and Los Angeles: University of California Press.

Mohandie, Kris, et al. 1998. False Victimization Syndrome in Stalking. In *The Psychology of Stalking: Clinical and Forensic Perspectives,* ed. J. Reid Meloy. San Diego: Academic Press.

Montesino, Braulio. 1993. "I'll Be Watching You": Strengthening the Effectiveness and Enforceability of State Anti-stalking Statutes. *Loyola of Los Angeles Entertainment Law Journal* 13:545.

Morville, Dawn A. 1993. Stalking Laws: Are They Solutions for More Problems? *Washington University Law Quarterly* 71:921.

Moss, Leonard O., and Stephen C. Cappannari. 1976. The Mediterranean: The Evil Eye Hovers Above. In *The Evil Eye,* ed. Clarence Maloney. New York: Columbia University Press.

Mulvey, Laura. 1992. Film and Visual Pleasures. In *Film Theory and Criticism,* ed. Gerald Mast and Marshall Cohen. 4th ed. New York: Oxford University Press.

Murray, Margaret Alice. 1921. *The Witch-Cult in Western Europe: A Study in Anthropology.* Oxford: Clarendon Press.

Nead, Lynda. 1988. *Myths of Sexuality: Representations of Women in Victorian Britain.* Cambridge, Mass.: Basil Blackwell.

Neale, Steve. 1993. Masculinity as Spectacle: Reflections on Men and Mainstream Cinema. In *Screening the Male: Exploring Masculinities in Hollywood Cinema,* ed. Steven Cohan and Ina Rae Hark. New York: Routledge.

Nestrick, William. 1979. Coming to Life: *Frankenstein* and the Nature of Film Narrative. In *The Endurance of "Frankenstein": Essays on Mary Shelley's Novel,* ed. George Levine and U. C. Knoepflmacher. Berkeley and Los Angeles: University of California Press.

Neumann, Erich. 1974. *The Great Mother: An Analysis of the Archetype.* Princeton, N.J.: Princeton University Press.

Nicholson, John. 1993. *Men and Women: How Different Are They?* New York: Oxford University Press.

Noll, Richard. 1992. *Vampires, Werewolves, and Demons: Twentieth Century Reports in the Psychiatric Literature.* New York: Brunner/Mazel.

Norris, Joel. 1988. *Serial Killers: The Growing Menace.* New York: Doubleday.

Notestein, Wallace. 1911. *A History of Witchcraft in England from 1558 to 1718.* Washington, D.C.: American Historical Society.

Ofek, Uriel. 1981. *The Glass-Slipper of Puss-in-Boots: Folktales and Their Versions.* Tel-Aviv: Reshafim.

Ong, Walter J. 1991. *Orality and Literacy: The Technologizing of the Word.* London: Routledge.

Orion, Doreen. 1997. *I Know You Really Love Me: A Psychiatrist's Journal of Erotomania, Stalking, and Obsessive Love.* New York: Macmillan.

Orlin, Louis L. 1969. *Ancient Near Eastern Literature: A Bibliography of One Thousand Items on the Cuneiform Literature of the Ancient World.* Ann Arbor, Mich.: Campus Publishers.

Osborne, Lawrence. 1994. *The Poisoned Embrace: A Brief History of Sexual Pessimism.* New York: Vintage.

Pagels, Elaine. 1988. *Adam, Eve, and the Serpent.* New York: Random House.

Panter, David. 1980. *The Literature of Terror.* New York: Longman.

Pardes, Ilana. 1992. *Countertraditions in the Bible: A Feminist Approach.* Cambridge: Harvard University Press.

Parvey, Constance F. 1974. The Theology and Leadership of Women in the New Testament. In *Religion and Sexism: Images of Women in the Jewish and Christian Traditions,* ed. Rosemary Radford Ruether. New York: Simon and Schuster.

Patai, Raphael. 1990. *The Hebrew Goddess.* Detroit: Wayne State University Press.

Pavel, Thomas G. 1986. *Fictional Worlds.* Cambridge: Harvard University Press.

Perez, Christina. 1993. Stalking: When Does Obsession Become a Crime? *American Journal of Criminal Law* 20:263.

Persaud, Rajendra D. 1990. Erotomania. *Contemporary Review* 258:148.

Peters, Edward. 1978. *The Magician, the Witch, and the Law.* Philadelphia: University of Pennsylvania Press.

Phillips, John A. 1984. *Eve: The History of an Idea.* Cambridge: Harper and Row.

Phipps, Melissa Perrell. 1993. North Carolina's New Anti-stalking Law: Constitutionally Sound, but Is It Really a Deterrent? *North Carolina Law Review* 71 (September): 1933.

Pitts, Michael R. 1981. *Horror Film Stars.* Jefferson, N.C.: McFarland.

Polidori, John. 1819. *The Vampyre.* London.

Potts, Albert M. 1982. *The World's Eye.* Lexington: University Press of Kentucky.

Prawer Siegbert S. 1980. *Caligari's Children: The Film as Tale of Terror.* New York: Oxford University Press.

Praz, Mario. 1951. *The Romantic Agony.* New York: Oxford University Press.

Price, Theodore. 1992. *Hitchcock and Homosexuality: His Fifty-Year Obsession with Jack the Ripper and the Superbitch Prostitute—a Psychoanalytic View.* Methuen, N.J.: Scarecrow Press.

Prusak, Bernard P. 1974. Woman: Seductive Siren and Source of Sin? In *Religion and Sexism: Images of Women in the Jewish and Christian Traditions,* ed. Rosemary Radford Ruether. New York: Simon and Schuster.

Quennell, Peter. 1957. *Byron in Italy.* New York: Viking Press.

Rank, Otto, 1971. *The Double.* Chapel Hill: University of North Carolina Press.

———. 1975. *The Don Juan Legend.* Trans. and ed. David G. Winter. Princeton, N.J.: Princeton University Press.

———. 1992. *The Incest Theme in Literature and Legend: Fundamentals of a Psychology of Literary Creation.* Baltimore: Johns Hopkins University Press.

Raphael, Ray. 1988. *The Men from the Boys: Rites of Passage in Male America.* Lincoln: University of Nebraska Press.

Rappoport, Angelo S. 1966. *Myth and Legend of Ancient Israel.* Vol. 1. New York: Ktav.

Rashkow, Ilona N. 1993. *The Phallacy of Genesis: A Feminist-Psychoanalytic Approach.* Louisville, Ky.: Westminster/John Knox Press.

Rebello, Stephan. 1990. *Alfred Hitchcock and the Making of "Psycho."* New York: Dembner Books.

Reiner, Erica. 1958. *Surpu: A Collection of Sumerian and Akkadian Incantations.* Graz: Im Selbstverlage des Herausgebers.

Reynolds, Kimberley, and Nicola Humble. 1993. *Victorian Heroines: Representations of Femininity in Nineteenth-Century Literature and Art.* New York: New York University Press.

Reynolds, Osborne M. 1970. The Reasonable Man of Negligence Law: A Health Report on the "Odious Creature." *Oklahoma Law Review* 23:410.

Riley, Philip J. 1990. *"Dracula": The Original 1931 Shooting Script.* Atlantic City: Magic Image Filmbooks.

Rimmon-Kenan, Shlomith. 1989. *Narrative Fiction: Contemporary Poetics.* London: Methuen.

Roberts, John M. 1976. Cross Cultural: Belief in the Evil Eye in World Perspective. In *The Evil Eye,* ed. Clarence Maloney. New York: Columbia University Press.

Romero, Joan Arnold. 1974. The Protestant Principle: A Woman's-Eye View of Barth and Tillich. In *Religion and Sexism: Images of Women in the Jewish and Christian Traditions,* ed. Rosemary Radford Ruether. New York: Simon and Schuster.

Rosebury, B. J. 1979. Fiction, Emotion, and "Belief": A Reply to Eva Schaper. *British Journal of Aesthetics* 19:12.

Rosen, Barbara. 1969. *Witchcraft.* London: Edward Arnold.

Rosen, Richard A. 1993. On Self-Defense, Imminence, and Women Who Kill Their Batterers. *North Carolina Law Review* 71 (January): 371.

Rossetti, William Michael, ed. 1911. *The Diary of Dr. John William Polidori: 1816.* London: Elkin Mathews.

Roth, Phyllis A. 1982. *Bram Stoker.* Boston: Twayne.

Rothman, William. 1982. *Hitchcock—the Murderous Gaze.* Cambridge: Harvard University Press.

Rudden, Marie, M.D., John Sweeney, Ph.D., and Allen Frances, M.D. 1990. Diagnosis and Clinical Course of Erotomaniac and Other Delusional Patients. *American Journal of Psychiatry* 147 (5): 625.

Ruether, Rosemary Radford. 1974. Misogynism and Virginal Feminism in the Fathers of the Church. In *Religion and Sexism: Images of Women in the Jewish and Christian Traditions,* ed. Rosemary Radford Ruether. New York: Simon and Schuster.

Ruff, D. James. 1972. Introduction to *Glenarvon,* by Lady Caroline Lamb. Delmar, N.Y.: Scholars' Facsimiles and Reprints.

Russell, Jeffrey Burton. 1986. *Mephistopheles: The Devil in the Modern World.* Ithaca, N.Y.: Cornell University Press.

Saberhagen, Fred, and James V. Hard, eds. 1992. *Bram Stoker's Dracula: A Novel of the Film Directed by Francis Ford Coppola.* New York: Signet.

Sadeh, Pinhas. 1983. *Sefer ha-dimeyonot shel ha-yehudim* (in Hebrew). Jerusalem: Schoken.

Salame, Laurie. 1993. A National Survey of Stalking Law: A Legislative Trend Comes to the Aid of Domestic Violence Victims and Others. *Suffolk University Law Review* 27 (spring): 67.

Samuels, Robert. 1998. *Hitchcock's Bi-Textuality: Lacan, Feminisms, and Queer Theory.* Albany: State University of New York Press.

Sanger, Carol. 1992. Gender, Race, and the Politics of Supreme Court Appointments: The Import of the Anita Hill/Clarence Thomas Hearings: The Reasonable Woman and the Ordinary Man. *South California Law Review* 65 (March): 1411.

Sankey, Benjamin T., Jr. 1967. Coleridge on Milton's Satan. In *Coleridge: A Collection of Critical Essays,* ed. Kathleen Coburn. Englewood Cliffs, N.J.: Prentice-Hall.

Sartre, Jean-Paul. 1966. *Being and Nothingness: A Phenomenological Essay on Ontology.* Trans. Hazel E. Barnes. New York: Pocket.

Saunders, Rhonda. 1998. The Legal Perspective on Stalking. In *The Psychology of Stalking: Clinical and Forensic Perspectives,* ed. J. Reid Meloy. San Diego: Academic Press.

Schaafsma, Karen. 1987. The Demon Lover: Lilith and the Hero in Modern Fantasy. *Extrapolation* 28:52.

Schaper, Eva. 1978. Fiction and the Suspension of Disbelief. *British Journal of Aesthetics* 18:3144.

Scheppele, Kim L. 1991. The Reasonable Woman. *Responsive Community* 1 (fall): 45.

Scholem, Gershom. 1948. New Chapters in the Story of Ashmedai and Lilith (in Hebrew). In *Tarbitz* 19:160. Ed. J. N. Epstein. Jerusalem: Hebrew University Press Association.

———. 1965. *On the Kabbalah and Its Symbolism.* New York: Schocken.

———. 1976a. *Elements of the Kabbalah and Its Symbolism* (in Hebrew). Jerusalem: Byalik Institute.

———. 1976b. The Jewish Mysticism and the Kabbalah (in Hebrew). In *Devarim be-go.* Tel Aviv: Am Oved.

Schwartz, Howard. 1988. *Lilith's Cave: Jewish Tales of the Supernatural.* Cambridge, Mass.: Harper and Row.

Sedgwick, Eve Kosofsky. 1985. *Between Men: English Literature and Male Homosocial Desire.* New York: Columbia University Press.

Segal, Jonathan H., M.D. 1989. Erotomania Revisited: From Kraepelin to DSM-III-R. *American Journal of Psychiatry* 146 (10): 1261.

———. 1990. Letter to the editor. *American Journal of Psychiatry* 147 (6): 820.

Senn, Harry A. 1982. *Were-Wolf and Vampire in Romania.* New York: East European Monographs, Boulder, Distributed by Columbia University Press.

Sevastakis, Michael. 1993. *Songs of Love and Death: The Classical American Horror Film of the 1930s.* London: Greenwood Press.

Shachar, Shulamit. 1994. The Virgin Mary: From Cult to Feminism. In *Local Goddesses: From Ancient Deities to Mythical Women of Today* (in Hebrew). Jerusalem: Museum of the History of Jerusalem.

Sharma, Arvind. 1987. Satan. In *The Encyclopedia of Religion,* ed. Mircea Eliade, 13:81. New York: Macmillan.

Shelley, Mary. 1992. *Frankenstein; or, The Modern Prometheus.* Ed. Maurice Hindle. London: Penguin.

Shenhar, Alizah. 1982. *Sipur ha-amami shel adot Yisrael* (in Hebrew). Tel-Aviv: Cherikover.

Shepard, Leslie, ed. 1991. *The Book of Dracula.* Avenel, N.J.: Wings.

Shuttle, Penelope, and Peter Redgrove. 1978. *The Wise Wound: Eve's Curse and Everywoman.* New York: Richard Marek.

Singer, Stephen F., M.D. 1991. Erotomania. *American Journal of Psychiatry* 148 (9): 1276.

Sklar, Robert. 1975. *Movie-Made America: A Cultural History of American Movies.* New York: Vintage.

Skoler, Glen. 1998. The Archetypes and the Psychodynamics of Stalking. In *The Psychology of Stalking: Clinical and Forensic Perspectives,* ed. J. Reid Meloy. San Diego: Academic Press.

Slater, Philip. 1990. *The Pursuit of Loneliness.* 3d ed. Boston: Beacon Press.

Sloan, Christine Olie. 1994. Standing Up to Stalkers: South Carolina's Antistalking Law Is a Good First Step. *South Carolina Law Review* 45 (winter): 383.

Smeed, J. W. 1990. *Don Juan: Variations on a Theme.* London: Routledge.

Snef, Carol A. 1988. *The Vampire in Nineteenth Century English Literature.* Bowling Green, Ohio: Bowling Green State University Popular Press.

Snider, Clifton. 1991. *The Stuff That Dreams Are Made Of: A Jungian Interpretation of Literature.* Wilmetter, Ill.: Chiron.

Speiser, E. A, ed. and trans. 1964. *The Anchor Bible: Genesis.* Garden City, N.Y.: Doubleday.

Spooner, Brian. 1976. Anthropology and the Evil Eye. In *The Evil Eye,* ed. Clarence Maloney. New York: Columbia University Press.

Steinberg, A. Z., ed. 1980. *Midrash Rabbah Ha-Mevo'ar* (in Hebrew). Jerusalem: Hamachon Hamevo'ar Institute.

Steinman, Lisa Ilene. 1993. Despite Anti-stalking Laws, Stalkers Continue to Stalk: Are These Laws Constitutional and Effective? *St. Thomas Law Review* 6:213.

Steinsaltz, Adin. 1984. *Biblical Images: Men and Women of the Book.* New York: Basic.

Stern, Dina. 1986. *Violence in an Enchanted World: Violence in the Feminine Fairytale.* Ramat-Gan, Israel: Bar-Ilan University.

Stoker, Bram. 1897. *Dracula.* In *The Annotated Dracula,* ed. Leonard Wolf. London: Archibald Constable.

———. 1910. *Famous Imposters.* New York: Sturgis and Walton.

Stone, Merlin. 1976. *When God Was a Woman.* New York: Harvest/HBJ.

———. 1984. *Ancient Mirrors of Womanhood: A Treasury of Goddess and Heroine Lore from around the World.* Boston: Beacon Press.

Storey, Mark. 1986. *Byron and the Eye of Appetite.* London: Macmillan.

Strikis, Silvija A. 1993. Stopping Stalking. *Georgetown Law Journal* 81:2771.

Strudlar, Gaylyn. 1992. Masochism and the Perverse Pleasures of the Cinema. In *Film Theory and Criticism,* ed. Gerald Mast and Marshall Cohen. 4th ed. New York: Oxford University Press.

Summers, Montague. 1928. *The Vampire: His Kith and Kin.* London: Kegan Paul.

———. 1961. *The Vampire in Europe.* New York: V. Books.

———. 1966. *The History of Witchcraft and Demonology.* New York: University Books.

Swirski, Barbara. 1984. *Daughters of Eve, Daughters of Lilith: On Women in Israel* (in Hebrew). Givatayim: Second Sex.

Sykes, Charles J. 1992. *A Nation of Victims: The Decay of the American Character.* New York: St. Martin's Press.

Tishby, Isaiah. 1991. *The Wisdom of the Zohar: An Anthology of Texts.* Vol. 2. Oxford: Oxford University Press.

Trachtenberg, Joshua. 1979. *Jewish Magic and Superstition: A Study in Folk Religion.* New York: Atheneum.

Trevor-Roper, H. R. 1970. The European Witch-Craze. In *Witchcraft and Sorcery,* ed. Max Marwick. Baltimore: Penguin.

Tripp, Edward. 1974. *The Meridian Handbook of Classical Mythology.* New York: Meridian.

Trombley, Stephen. 1985. Lilith or Inanna: What Difference Does It Make? *History Today* 35:3.

Tropp, Martin. 1990. *Images of Fear: How Horror Stories Helped Shape Modern Culture (1818–1918).* Jefferson, N.C.: McFarland.

Truffaut, Francois. 1985. *Hitchcock.* Rev. ed. New York: Touchstone.

Tucker, James Thomas. 1993. Stalking the Problems with Stalking Laws: The Effectiveness of Florida Statutes Section 784.048. *Florida Law Review* 45 (September): 609.

Tudor, Andrew. 1974. *Image and Influence: Studies in the Sociology of Film.* London: George Allen and Unwin.

Twitchell, James B. 1981. *The Living Dead: A Study of the Vampire in Romantic Literature.* Durham, N.C.: Duke University Press.

———. 1985. *Dreadful Pleasures: An Anatomy of Modern Horror.* New York: Oxford University Press.

———. 1987. *Forbidden Partners: The Incest Taboo in Modern Culture.* New York: Columbia University Press.

———. 1989. *Preposterous Violence: Fables of Aggression in Modern Culture.* New York: Oxford University Press.

Unikel, Robert. 1992. "Reasonable" Doubts: A Critique of the Reasonable Woman Standard in American Jurisprudence. *Northwestern University Law Review* 87 (fall): 326.

Ursini, James, and Alain Silver. 1975. *The Vampire Film.* New York: A. S. Barnes.

U.S. Department of Justice. National Institute of Justice. 1993. *Project to Develop a Model Anti-stalking Code for States.* Final summary report. Washington, D.C.

———. Office of Justice Programs. 1996. *Domestic Violence, Stalking, and Antistalking Legislation.* Annual report to Congress under the Violence against Women Act. Washington, D.C. Full text available at <http://www.ojp.usdoj.gov /nij/victdc96.htm>.

———. 1997. *The Crime of Stalking: How Big Is the Problem?* Washington, D.C.

———. Centers for Disease Control and Prevention. 1998. *Stalking in America: Findings from the National Violence against Women Survey,* by Patricia Tjaden and Nancy Thoennes. Washington, D.C.

Varney the Vampire, or the Feast of Blood. 1970. Ed. Devendra P. Varma. New York: Arno Press.

Waardt, de Hans. 1991. Prosecution or Defence: Procedural Possibilities following a Witchcraft Accusation in the Province of Holland before 1800. In *Witchcraft in the Netherlands from the Fourteenth Century to the Twentieth Century*, ed. Marijke Gijswijt-Hofstra and Willem Frijhoff. Rotterdam: Universitaire Pers Rotterdam.

Waldman, Diane. 1981. "Horror and Domesticity: The Modern Gothic Romance Film of the 1940's." Ph.D. diss., University of Wisconsin, Madison.

Walker, Julie Miles. 1993. Anti-stalking Legislation: Does It Protect the Victim without Violating the Rights of the Accused? *Denver University Law Review* 71:273.

Walker, Lenore E. 1979. *The Battered Woman*, New York: Harper and Row.

———. 1989. *Terrifying Love: Why Battered Women Kill and How Society Responds*. New York: Harper and Row.

———. 1998. Stalking and Domestic Violence. In *The Psychology of Stalking: Clinical and Forensic Perspectives*, ed. J. Reid Meloy. San Diego: Academic Press.

Walkowitz, Judith R. 1980. *Prostitution and Victorian Society: Women, Class, and the State*. Cambridge: Cambridge University Press.

———. 1982. Jack the Ripper and the Myth of Male Violence. *Feminist Studies* 8 (3): 542.

Waller, Gregory A. 1986. *The Living and the Undead*. Urbana: University of Illinois Press.

Walpole, Horace. 1963. *The Castle of Otranto*. New York: Macmillan.

Walsh, Keirsten L. 1996. Safe and Sound at Last? Federalized Anti-stalking Legislation in the United States and Canada. *Dickinson Journal of International Law* 14:373.

Walton, Kendall. 1980. Appreciating Fiction: Suspending Disbelief or Pretending Belief? *Dispositio* 5:1.

Warner, Marina. 1976. *Alone of All Her Sex: The Myth and the Cult of the Virgin Mary*. New York: Alfred A. Knopf.

Watson, Nicola J. 1994a. *Revolution and the Form of the British Novel, 1790–1825: Intercepted Letters, Interrupted Seductions*. Oxford: Clarendon.

———. 1994b. Trans-figuring Byronic Identity. In *At the Limits of Romanticism: Essays in Cultural, Feminist, and Materialist Criticism*, ed. Mary A. Favret and Nicola J. Watson. Bloomington: Indiana University Press.

Way, Rosemary Cairns. 1994. The Criminalization of Stalking: An Exercise in Media Manipulation and Political Opportunism. *McGill Law Journal* 39:379.

Wehr, Demariss S. 1989. *Jung and Feminism: Liberating Archetypes*. Boston: Beacon Press.

Weinberg, Judy. 1976. Lilith Sources. *Lilith* 1. New York: Lilith Publications.

Weissman, Judith. 1987. *Half Savage and Hardy and Free: Women and Rural Radicalism in the Nineteenth-Century Novel*. Middletown, Conn.: Wesleyan University Press.

Werblowsky, R. J. Zwi. 1952. *Lucifer and Prometheus: A Study of Milton's Satan*. London: Routledge and Kegan Paul.

West, Robin. 1996. *Narrative, Authority, and Law*. Ann Arbor: University of Michigan Press.

Wexman, Virginia Wright. 1988. Horrors of the Body: Hollywood's Discourse on Beauty and Rouben Mamoulian's *Dr. Jekyll and Mr. Hyde*. In *"Dr. Jekyll and*

Mr. Hyde": After One Hundred Years, ed. William Veeder and Gordon Hirsch. Chicago: University of Chicago Press.

White, James Boyd. 1984. *When Words Lose Their Meaning: Constitutions and Recon-stitutions of Language, Characters, and Community.* Chicago: University of Chicago Press.

Wickens, James C. 1994. Michigan's New Anti-stalking Laws: Good Intentions Gone Awry. *Detroit College of Law Review* 1994 (spring): 157.

Williams, Linda. 1992. When the Woman Looks. In *Film Theory and Criticism,* ed. Gerald Mast and Marshall Cohen. 4th ed. New York: Oxford University Press.

Williams, Selma R., and Pamela Williams Adelman. 1992. *Riding the Nightmare: Women and Witchcraft from the Old World to Colonial Salem.* New York: Harper Perennial.

Wilson, Colin, and Donald Seaman. 1990. *The Serial Killers: A Study in the Psychol-ogy of Violence.* London: W. H. Allen.

Wilson, Stan Le Roy. 1993. *Mass Media/Mass Culture: An Introduction.* New York: McGraw-Hill.

Wilt, Judith. 1979. *Frankenstein* as Mystery Play. In *The Endurance of "Frankenstein": Essays on Mary Shelley's Novel,* ed. George Levine and U. C. Knoepflmacher. Berkeley and Los Angeles: University of California Press.

Wolf, Leonard, ed. 1975. *The Annotated Dracula: Dracula, by Bram Stoker.* New York: Clarkson N. Potter.

———. 1997. *Dracula, the Connoisseur's Guide.* New York: Broadway.

Wolkstein, Diane, and Samuel Noah Kramer. 1983. *Inanna, Queen of Heaven and Earth: Her Stories and Hymns from Sumer.* New York: Harper and Row.

Wollstonecraft, Mary. 1992. *A Vindication of the Rights of Women.* London: Every-man's Library.

Wood, Brian E., D.O., and Richard O. Poe, M.D. 1990. Diagnosis and Classification of Erotomania. *American Journal of Psychiatry* 147 (10): 1388.

Wood, Michael. 1975. *America in the Movies, or: "Santa Maria, It Had Slipped My Mind."* New York: Delta.

Wood, Robin. 1989. *Hitchcock's Films Revisited.* New York: Columbia University Press.

———. 1992. Ideology, Genre, Auteur. In *Film Theory and Criticism,* ed. Gerald Mast and Marshall Cohen. 4th ed. New York: Oxford University Press.

Wordsworth, Jonathan. 1993. Introduction to *Glenarvon,* by Lady Caroline Lamb. Facsimile reprint. Oxford: Woodstock.

Wright, Elizabeth. 1987. *Psychoanalytic Criticism: Theory in Practice.* New York: Methuen.

Yassif, Eli. 1984. *The Tales of Ben Sira in the Middle-Ages: A Critical Text and Literary Studies* (in Hebrew). Jerusalem: Magnes Press.

Young, Martha M. 1989. The Salem Witch Trials Three Hundred Years Later: How Far Has the American Legal System Come? How Much Further Does It Need to Go? *Tulane Law Review* 64:235.

Žižek, Slavoj, ed. 1992. *Everything You Always Wanted to Know about Lacan (But Were Afraid to Ask Hitchcock).* New York: Verso.

Zona, Michael A., Russell E. Palarea, and John C. Lane, Jr. 1998. Psychiatric Diag-nosis and the Offender-Victim Typology of Stalking. In *The Psychology of*

Stalking: Clinical and Forensic Perspectives, ed. J. Reid Meloy. San Diego: Academic Press.

Zona, Michael A., K. K. Sharma, and J. Lane. 1993. A Comparative Study of Erotomaniac and Obsessional Subject in a Forensic Sample. *Journal of Forensic Sciences* 38 (4): 894.

Zuckoff, Aviva Cantor. 1976. The Lilith Question. *Lilith* 1. New York: Lilith Publications.

Filmography

Basic Instinct. 1992. Paul Verhoeven.
Birds, The. 1963. Alfred Hitchcock. (Universal).
Blair Witch Project. 1999. Daniel Myrick.
Bodyguard, The. 1992. Mick Jackson.
Bram Stoker's Dracula. 1992. Francis Ford Coppola.
Burning, The. 1981. Tony Maylam.
Cabinet of Dr. Caligari, The. 1919. Robert Wiene. (Germany).
Cape Fear. 1962. J. Lee-Thompson.
Cape Fear. 1991. Martin Scorsese. (Universal).
Cat People. 1942. Jacques Tourneur .
Clockwork Orange. 1971. Stanley Kubrick.
Conspiracy Theory. 1997. Richard Donner.
Copycat. 1996. Jon Amiel.
Day of the Jackal, The. 1973. Fred Zinnemann. (Universal).
Deer Hunter, The. 1978. Michael Cimino. (Universal).
Disclosure. 1994. Barry Levinson.
Dr. Jekyll and Mr. Hyde. 1921. John S. Robertson.
Dr. Jekyll and Mr. Hyde. 1931. Rouben Mamoulian.
Dr. Jekyll and Mr. Hyde. 1941. Victor Fleming.
Dracula. 1931. Tod Browning.
Dressed to Kill. 1980. Brian De Palma.
Eyes of Laura Mars, The. 1978. Irvin Kershner.
Falling Down. 1994. Joel Schumacher.
Fan, The. 1996. Tony Scott.
Fatal Attraction. 1987. Adrian Lyne.
Fatal Instinct. 1993. Carl Reiner.
Friday the 13th 1980. Sean S. Cunningham.
Friday the 13th Part 2. 1981. Steve Miner.
Golem, The. 1920. Paul Wegener. (Germany).
Gorgon, The. 1964. Terence Fisher.
Graduation Day. 1981. Herb Freed.
Halloween. 1978. John Carpenter.
Happy Birthday to Me. 1981. J. Lee Thompson. (Canada).
Invisible Man, The. 1933. James Whale. (Universal).
King of Comedy, The. 1982. Martin Scorsese.
Lodger, The. 1926. Alfred Hitchcock. (Great Britain).
M. 1931. Fritz Lang. (Germany).
Mary Shelley's Frankenstein. 1994. Kenneth Branagh.

Mummy, The. 1932. Karl Freund. (Universal).
Mystery of the Wax Museum. 1933. Michael Curtiz.
Night Stalker. 1979. Dan Curtis.
Nosferatu. 1921. F. W. Murnau. (Germany).
Pacific Heights. 1990. John Schlesinger.
Pandora's Box. 1928. G. W. Pabst. (Germany).
Phantom of the Opera, The. 1925. Rupert Julian. (Universal).
Play Misty for Me. 1971. Clint Eastwood. (Universal).
Pretty Woman. 1990. Garry Marshall.
Prince of Darkness. 1987. John Carpenter.
Prom Night. 1980. Paul Lynch.
Psychic, The. 1979. Lucio Fulci. (Italy).
Psycho. 1960. Alfred Hitchcock.
Raging Bull. 1980. Martin Scorsese.
Rear Window. 1954. Alfred Hitchcock.
Rebecca. 1940. Alfred Hitchcock.
Shadow of a Doubt. 1943. Alfred Hitchcock. (Universal).
Shining, The. 1980. Stanley Kubrick. (Great Britain).
Silence of the Lambs, The. 1990. Jonathan Demme.
Sleeping with the Enemy. 1990. Joseph Ruben.
Stalked. 1994. Douglas Jackson.
Strangers on a Train. 1951. Alfred Hitchcock.
Student of Prague, The. 1913. Paul Wegener. (Germany).
Taxi Driver. 1976. Martin Scorsese.
Terror Train. 1980. Roger Spottiswoode. (Canada).
To Catch a Thief. 1955. Alfred Hitchcock.
Truman Show, The. 1998. Peter Weir.
Unlawful Entry. 1992. Jonathan Kaplan.
Vampire in Brooklyn. 1995. Wes Craven.
Vertigo. 1958. Alfred Hitchcock.
Werewolf of London, The. 1935. Stuart Walker. (Universal).
When a Stranger Calls. 1979. Fred Walton.

Index

Adam, 4, 13, 20, 29, 36–42, 49, 68, 70–72, 74n. 11, 81, 84, 90–93, 104, 170, 171

Anat (Anath), 21, 27, 27nn. 11–12, 32, 45n. 6, 47–48. *See also* Ashera; Astarte; Great Goddess; Inanna; Ishtar

Ancient Mariner, 69, 86, 91, 102. *See also* Flying Dutchman; Wandering Jew

Antichrist, 69n. 2, 74, 83–84

antiquity, 13, 20, 27, 34, 43–48, 51, 68, 70, 79

antistalking legislation, 1, 3, 9, 14, 165, 175–203, 205, 211–15; in California, 1, 14, 175–79, 180–85, 186, 188, 201–2; vague and/or overly broad, 185, 214

Anzu-bird, 25, 27–28

archetypal stalkers. *See* stalkers, archetypal

Artemis, 35n. 25, 55–56, 136–38. *See also* Diana

Ashera, 27, 32, 45n. 6, 47–48. *See also* Anat; Astarte; Great Goddess; Inanna; Ishtar

Astarte, 27n. 12, 45n. 6, 48. *See also* Anat; Ashera; Great Goddess; Inanna; Ishtar

autovampirism, 178

Bardo, Robert, 175–79, 183, 194, 197, 198, 211

Basic Instinct, 193

Bates, Norman (*Psycho*), 134–35, 136, 138, 142, 154, 159, 167, 172, 181, 203. *See also* Hitchcock, Alfred

Ben-Yehuda, Nachman, 6–8, 11–12, 52–53, 58

Berkowitz, David Richard, 143–45. *See also* Son of Sam

Bible, 12, 13, 29n. 47, 30, 35, 36, 37, 83; Latin translation of, 35, 37, 74; Song of Songs, 22n. 3

Bickle, Travis (*Taxi Driver*), 141–45, 147, 152, 153, 159, 161, 162, 163, 164, 165, 167, 168, 175, 178, 182, 198, 203, 211

Blair Witch Project, 160n. 21

Bodyguard, The, 202

Bride of Corinth, 108

Bundy, Ted, 148–49, 153, 154, 157, 168, 182, 199, 203

Burning, The, 160

Byron, George Gordon, Lord, 87, 90, 102, 107–8

Cabinet of Dr. Caligari, The, 121–23, 124, 125, 127. *See also* horror films

Cain, 37n. 28, 69, 86, 90

Caleb Williams, 108

Cape Fear, 17, 92, 132–33, 159, 160, 165, 210

Cat People, 127

Chapman, Mark David, 162, 176, 177, 178

Christ, 74, 78, 83–84, 102n. 21, 124n. 28

Christabel, 108

Clerambault, Gaeetan Gatian de, 161–64, 172

Clockwork Orange, 142n

Close, Glenn, 4, 9, 171, 172, 173

Clover, Carol, 115n. 6, 155nn. 11–12, 156n, 158n. 17, 159n. 20, 168–69

Cohen, Stanley, 5–8

Cohn, Norman, 54, 55–57, 60, 62

Coleridge, Samuel, 69n. 3, 91, 108

collective unconscious, 19n, 38, 41

Conspiracy Theory, 176n. 3

Contagious Diseases Act, 65

Coppola, Francis Ford, 131, 176